THE
DARKENING
WEB

THE DARKENING WEB

The War for Cyberspace

ALEXANDER KLIMBURG

PENGUIN PRESS
NEW YORK
2017

PENGUIN PRESS
An imprint of Penguin Random House LLC
375 Hudson Street
New York, New York 10014
penguin.com

LIBRARY OF CONGRESS CATALOGING-IN-PUBLICATION DATA

Names: Klimburg, Alexander, 1976- author.
Title: The Darkening Web: The War for Cyberspace / Alexander Klimburg.
Other titles: War for Cyberspace
Description: New York: Penguin Press, [2017] | Includes
bibliographical references and index.
Identifiers: LCCN 2017008579 (print) | LCCN 2017016551 (ebook) |
ISBN 9780698402768 (ebook) | ISBN 9781594206665 (hardcover) |
ISBN 9780735223882 (international edition)
Subjects: LCSH: Internet and international relations. |
Information society—Political aspects. | Cyberspace—
Government policy. | Information
warfare—Risk assessment. | Internet—Political aspects. | Computer
crime—Prevention. | Security, International. | Power (Social sciences)
Classification: LCC JZ1254 (ebook) | LCC JZ1254 .K56 2017 (print) |
DDC 327.0285/4678—dc23

LC record available at https://lccn.loc.gov/2017008579

Printed in the United States of America
1   3   5   7   9   10   8   6   4   2

DESIGNED BY MEIGHAN CAVANAUGH

to my mother

CONTENTS

NOTE ON TERMS

Everything is ambiguous in cyberspace. We can't even agree on how to spell the very word itself, so it shouldn't be a surprise that we have difficulties in defining it. Spelling, as always, is a reflection of one's preferences: those who spell "cyber space" as two words are implying that the domain is not an entirely separate or unique entity, just as writing "cyber security" as two words implies that it is just another form of security, like "maritime security," and not special at all. Those, like myself, who believe that cyberspace has unique identifiers that make it like a physical domain (like airspace or the seas) spell it as one word, just as the contentious term "cybersecurity" written as a single noun implies something new, rather than an extension of the old. The term "cybersecurity" is given an in-depth treatment on account of its overall rejection among some parts of the civilian technical community.

Also, in some cases choosing the single-word noun form is a necessary delineation from other terms. For instance, I use the term "cyberattacks" throughout this book, which is an admittedly ungainly attempt to bring together two highly conflicting standards: the insistence of some professionals (and most of the media) on referring to any violation of data confidentiality, integrity, and availability as a cyber "attack," and the rigorous dismissal of the term "attack" by international lawyers, who insist that there must be widespread death and destruction for this term to be properly used. In this context, the prefix "cyber" is sometimes used as a standalone shorthand, as is common among government intelligence and security professionals, to indicate the general area of practice associated with national security affairs and cyberspace. As is also explained in the text, there is a difference between the Internet and an internet—the former being the worldwide Internet we know today, the latter simply any internetworked computer arrangement. Similarly, the terms "cyberspace" and "the Internet" are sometimes used interchangeably as is common practice, although the difference between the two is repeatedly made clear throughout the text.

The military and intelligence communities are big on capitalizations and abbreviations. While I follow some of these communities' naming conventions, I have abandoned others for the sake of readability—for example, the traditional practice of writing the code names of military and intelligence operations in all caps, including official cyber operations (like "OLYMPIC GAMES").

INTRODUCTION

As Hermes once took to his feathers light,
  When lulled Argus, baffled, swoon'd and slept,
So on a Delphic reed, my idle spright
  So play'd, so charm'd, so conquer'd, so bereft
The dragon-world of all its hundred eyes

—John Keats, *A Dream, After Reading Dante's Episode*
  of Paolo and Francesca

There is an ancient Indian parable, best reinterpreted in an old *New Yorker* cartoon, of what an elephant must feel like to a roomful of blind men trying to describe it. One man would feel the trunk and identify a snake, another would feel its sides and identify a wall, another would feel the legs and identify a tree, and still another would feel the ears and identify a fan, and so on. The image has always been popular with those who seek to describe the Internet, for the difficulty of grasping the entire cyberspace beast is tremendous, and the way you approach it inadvertently defines the way you see it. Some observers may concentrate on the economic impact of cyberspace, others on the socially transformative aspects, yet others on the technological development itself, or on the behavior of cyber criminals. This is a book about security, and in particular international security.

A very great number of people probably don't spend much time think-ing about security and cyberspace. When the word "cybersecurity" (itself a contentious term, as we shall see) comes up, most of us probably think of cyber crime—the danger that our credit card or banking data may be sto-len, or our devices infected with a virus, or our social network profiles hijacked. A slightly smaller section of the population may think about ram-pant cyber espionage pitting states against each other in a constant strug-gle, with governments and businesses hacked on an almost-daily basis. Others may be concerned with the prospect of catastrophic cyberattacks (another contentious term) on critical infrastructure, most notably the power grid. And some may also wonder how the Internet itself can be gov-erned, how human rights can be guaranteed while at the same time ensur-ing a basic level of data security for the average user. Although these seem like disparate issues, they are all connected.

Security in cyberspace is in itself a vast subject—a whole new elephant to analyze, with each attempt to grapple with the beast inherently bearing the risk of overemphasizing that particular component. This book is ori-ented toward one part of that body—the tusks, if you will—that represents the security interests of nation-states and their governments in cyberspace. It is rooted in the ongoing debate on cyberspace and international relations conducted today in both research organizations and governments world-wide. This book is therefore largely concerned with how governments per-ceive and address what are loosely referred to as international cybersecurity issues and how they are framing this new domain as a means to project power.

The aspirations of states in cyberspace, together with the technical real-ities of this new artificial world, are creating significant risks for human welfare writ large. These risks are associated with new means to not only inflict large-scale destruction in interstate conflict and war but also do catastrophic damage to liberal democratic societies through a subtle re-framing of information overall as a weapon. Ultimately, we face the small but real prospect that in the not-too-distant future the Internet, a fabulous artifice of human civilization largely perceived today as a domain for advancing freedoms and prosperity, could become instead a dark web of subjugation.

The goal of this book is to show how the activities of states are making cyberspace a domain of conflict, and therefore increasingly threatening the overall stability and security not only of the Internet but also of our very societies. Sketching out this vision is not a simple task, because cybersecurity is not one of the easiest subjects to understand—for a few reasons. First, the vast majority of significant cyberattacks on government and businesses are secret and not reported on in public, most often to avoid embarrassment or subsequent political or legal fallout. Second, each distinct aspect of cybersecurity (say, cyber crime, intelligence, military issues, Internet governance, or national crisis management) operates in its own silo, belonging, for instance, to a specific government department or ministry. Each of these silos has its own technical realities, policy solutions, and even basic philosophies. Even if you become proficient in one area, it is likely that you will not have the time to acquire more than a rudimentary knowledge of the others. Your part of the elephant will dominate, and inevitably distort, how you see this beast.

Accordingly, this book will function as an introduction to some topics for some and a more advanced reader for others. While each chapter could easily be expanded to be its own book, there remains a great volume of details to integrate. Hopefully, at least some of these details are helpful in tracing the individual footsteps in the sands of the history of the cyberspace domain, not only showing where we have come from, but also pointing toward our likely destination.

In August 1995, the cover of *Time* magazine blared two words in large block letters: "Cyber War." The accompanying article described in considerable detail the evolving American military thinking and capabilities of what was interchangeably called "information warfare" (IW) and "cyberwar." It included references not only to the power grid crashing and armies being immobilized by cyberattacks but also to the US military's and intelligence services' ability to bring down governments by vanishing their funds or toppling national leaders by waging comprehensive psychological operations. Despite being written in the Stone Age of the Internet, much of what was said then holds true today. Most pertinently, it seemed to instinctively grasp the two different shades of the debate. On the one hand, the kinetic-effect "cyberwar" discourse, which involved hacking and bringing down critical infrastructure and the like. On the other, the psychological-effect "information war" discourse, which raised covert influencing campaigns to a new and much larger scale, using propaganda and other means to subtly influence entire populations. The article also grasped many of the existential issues this development presented, unconsciously paraphrasing the philosopher Marshall McLuhan when it said that "infowar may only refine the way modern warfare has shifted toward civilian targets." And, most presciently, the author asserted that "an infowar arms race could be one the US would lose because it is already so vulnerable to such attacks. Indeed, the cyber enhancements that the military is banking on . . . may be chinks in America's armor."

This article has been effectively lost to history, as have others that have followed in irregular cycles, each drawing attention to the threat of framing cyberspace as a domain of war, and each soon drowned out by the next revelation of increased cyber hostilities between nations. But more than twenty years later, much of what was announced in 1995 has become reality. The United States, and with it much of the industrialized world, has become locked in something approaching the very cyber arms race that many warned against long ago. Further, the rapid expansion of cyberspace has meant that even activities such as cyber espionage now have significant effects, not only the theft of national secrets and economic records, but also the casual acquisition of the average citizen's data by governments and criminals alike. And, even more significantly, we have moved toward a reconceptualization of interstate conflict and "war" altogether, one where states routinely engage in hostile acts that skirt around and under the threshold of recognized war and increasingly manage to reposition "information," including everything from computer viruses to the workings of the media, as a weapon, with potentially existential implications for democratic societies. For while the term "information war" disappeared from public and government use in the West in the late 1990s, its precepts remained and are starting to reassert themselves, despite the warnings made twenty years ago. Especially in the West, we seem conceptually trapped in thinking of the new challenges of cyberspace as being purely technical, instead of being very much human.

In hindsight, this should not come as a surprise. We don't have to go very far back in time to explore systematic errors of judgment, and indeed the noted historian Barbara Tuchman wrote a powerful treatise, *The March of Folly,* on the recurring inability of governments to adequately assess risk and act according to their interests. Some of these failures to fully understand risk are technical and systematic and can endure for decades. Some are temporal and appear at the beginning of a transition. But other false estimations are purely human, significant political miscalculations that can have wide-ranging implications if the coin toss goes wrong. And when that coin toss doesn't go wrong, we assign false probability and move on to repeat the same mistakes again.

Unlike any other major technological invention since at least the introduction of the combustion engine or even the movable-type printing press, computing and its networking have transformed our world totally and will continue to do so. We may think that we control many aspects of this "information revolution" and its ramifications, but we do not. The late Harvard political scientist Karl Deutsch often implied that history sometimes amounts to nothing more than a litany of unintended consequences and unforeseen side effects. This is obviously true in cyberspace, where the development of the technology has outstripped government's ability to regulate and legislate around it. The speed of this development has had profound implications for national security, creating the essential bottom-up-driven policy process: it seems the technical ability leads the policy component, which in turn is ahead of the legal and wider political framework. The rapid development of the technology means that even governments that have decades of institutional experience in dealing with cyberspace operations are liable to make significant strategic mistakes or simply repeat the old ones in new ways. However, this is hardly unique to the advent of cyberspace. We don't need to go far back in history to see that government has struggled with managing disruptive new technological paradigms before—be they nuclear weapons or the increased computerization of capabilities. This became most obvious when during the Cold War these two developments were brought together without being well understood.

For instance, on September 27, 1983, a software bug nearly triggered a nuclear war. On this night, Lieutenant Colonel Stanislav Yevgrafovich Petrov of the Soviet Air Defense Forces started his graveyard shift as the senior watch officer at *Serpukhov-15,* a bunker complex south of Moscow. The complex was one of the command centers responsible for providing early warning of an incoming nuclear strike, this one based on information gathered by the Russian *Oko* satellites orbiting Earth. The *Oko* satellite system was connected with the most powerful supercomputer the Soviet Union had produced: the M-10. Specifically designed for image analysis, the M-10 could tell the difference between, say, a forest wildfire and a genuine missile launch, and it was no slouch. Today, we know that it actually outperformed its American counterpart—the Cray-1 supercomputer—in some tasks and at the time was probably one of the best of its kind worldwide.

This did not mean the system was foolproof—far from it. According to David Hoffman's excellent account in *The Dead Hand,* the system regularly showed about twenty objects of interest every day. These were not reported as launches, but required manual observations with the backup telescope array to discount. This was the day-to-day work of the watch center, whose job nearly exclusively dealt with managing potential sightings.

When therefore the sirens went off around 3:00 a.m. on September 27, it was a unique event indeed: the system had registered a launch at a US missile field. To make matters worse, the computer pronounced it a "high confidence" event, virtually excluding that an error had been committed. Petrov had very little time to confirm or discount the event. But how was he to proceed? It was a bad time for direct visual observation, so the fact that the backup telescopes could not see anything wasn't indicative. Also, it was too early for radar to be useful. Petrov, according to Hoffman's account, had only his gut feeling to go on, and Moscow was on the line, demanding to know whether this launch was real or not. Petrov remarked that the likelihood of a sole missile launch was so bizarre—and out of character for what he had been led to expect to see in the opening of a nuclear war—that he discounted the validity of the launch on this basis alone. It was, of course, not completely bizarre; there were plenty of scenarios that could potentially have exploited this exact uncertainty and would have started with a single missile launch. All of this was probably on Petrov's mind, but he nonetheless stuck to his conclusions and reported to the higher command that it had been a false alert.

Only minutes later, the system again went active—this time recording four launches, one after the other, from the same missile field. The extent of the alert triggered an automatic MISSILE ATTACK warning, flashed to higher command. Petrov was suddenly faced with the likelihood that the original alert had been correct after all. Instead, he doubled down and—again without any supporting evidence—announced that the alerts were false.

It was later determined that a rare optical illusion had led to the event, something the computers had not been programmed for. Petrov, a computer programmer for most of his career, knew how important debugging the software of the M-10 was. This was done largely through the laborious process of identifying so-called "false positives": alerts due to previously unconsidered natural phenomena, like a forest fire. Once captured, the new phenomena were then entered into the database as a parameter to discount in the future. Not all false positives generated the same type of alert. Some, after all, were expected, and besides generous fault-checking code there was an entire backup process, the telescopes, to help check things out. Nobody really wanted to risk a nuclear holocaust, and there were—so Petrov said in his interview—numerous fail-safes to prevent such a catastrophic false alarm. These fail-safes all failed on September 27, and it was only the human element that—contrary to orders and even conditioning—prevented a potentially world-ending outcome.

This incident was not just a case of careless Russian planning. Four years earlier, the United States had completed its first significant "digitization" of its nuclear command and control infrastructure and early-warning apparatus. According to documents declassified in 2010, between 1979 and 1980 the US Strategic Command suffered no fewer than four serious computer-related mishaps and false alarms. One of these alerts in November 1979 led to President Carter's national security adviser, Zbigniew Brzezinski, being woken to be told that there were signs of a nuclear attack under way. In another case in June 1980, according to The George Washington University's analysis of the affair, a failed forty-six-cent computer chip ended up producing a warning that two hundred ballistic missiles were about to strike the United States. The message triggered emergency survivability measures by the US military, including ordering bomber pilots and crews to their stations and alerting bombers and tankers to start their engines.

The Soviet and American incidents can partially be chalked up to teething troubles: the exact ramifications of the new computer technology, and its network effects, were still very new to everyone concerned. Both Western and Eastern designers had spent decades contemplating civilization-ending outcomes and had an inkling of the destruction that nuclear warfare could wreak. It would be natural to believe that they tried their best given the standards of the time to avoid accidents of all sorts with nuclear weapons.

Or so we thought. In hindsight, we can say that the risk assessments of many of those thousands of highly qualified scientists, engineers, and strategic planners were deeply flawed. According to the highly regarded book *Command and Control* by Eric Schlosser, the Cold War was full of lucky rolls of the dice on potentially catastrophic accidents, from disasters on nuclear submarines to accidentally dropped atomic weapons. The United States lost control of its nuclear weapons far more often than has been publicly disclosed, and the truth is that we have no idea how often something similar might have occurred in the Soviet Union. Further, some of the safeguards installed to prevent nuclear weapons from being misused were simply ignored. The most famous example involved the deployment of the permissive action links, a code lock mounted on all nuclear bombs after the Kennedy administration decided that the threat of a rogue general launching the force was too serious to ignore. However, the members of the Strategic Air Command (SAC)—whose power the code lock was directly set to constrain—decided that these codes were dangerously limiting to them and, according to the scholar (and former launch officer) Bruce Blair, set the code to eight zeros—"00000000"—and kept it like this for more than fifteen years. This was essentially the widely cited ultimate "launch code" considered in popular lore to be the most important of all government secrets, an absurdity that was seemingly widely known throughout the SAC until higher-ups finally rectified the issue in 1977. Nuclear mishaps and poor control procedures were so common that in the 1990s General George Butler, the new commander of the US Strategic Command, was quoted in a secret memo saying that after having reviewed the secret trove of decades of historical data, "I came to appreciate the truth . . . we escaped the Cold War without a nuclear holocaust through some combination of skill, luck, and divine intervention, and I suspect the latter in greatest proportion." If this analysis is true, it has serious implications for the cybersecurity arena today, because it shows us that mankind's track record in controlling highly destructive technology is poor. What is particularly striking is the idea that these accidents and mishaps weren't simple, one-off miscalculations but rather a hugely complex and pervasive and systematic failure, not just of the technology itself, but of its management. The mistakes were not limited to a single individual, but involved whole classes of scientists, engineers, policy makers, and strategic thinkers—across different societies and educational systems. In a nutshell, everyone—perhaps tens of thousands of individuals over decades and continents—simply did not grasp the true risks associated with the command and control of nuclear weapons, related both to the weapon handling itself and to the more complex interplay of various sensors, organizations, and technologies that effectively constituted the nuclear forces of both sides. Instead, they cross-referenced each other's policies, risk-management metrics, and technical specifications to create a perfect web of illusory safety, a closeted epistemic macro-community that in hindsight fed a mass single self-delusion: that our grasp of the complexities of the new technologies involved was anywhere near complete.

The fact that the massively complex socio-technical systems brought to bear in the Cold War did not malfunction with civilization-ending results was likely nothing more than dumb luck: as far as we can tell, the probability was very much against us. The fact that we had such a fortunate escape might, however, have provided us with a false sense of security; if, after all, the strategic control of nuclear weapons stood the test of time, won't a new era of game-changing cyber weapons be equally easy to control?

This, in my mind, is one of the great fallacies of the current deployment of cyber means by nation-states. Like the Cold War era's balance of mutual assured destruction, substantial trust is being put into warning, attribution, and weapon control abilities—all of which could well be of doubtful quality. The consequences of getting these issues wrong in the nuclear context were pretty much evident to everyone: the horror of the nuclear mushroom cloud was burned into the minds of a generation of decision makers. This is decidedly not the case when it comes to cybersecurity today, because governments and the public alike have not had a "Hiroshima moment": we have little to no idea what the consequences of getting it wrong in this domain would be. But at least as problematic is that during the Cold War the two sides shared one worst-case scenario, one ultimate single nightmare that they both wanted equally to avoid. That is simply not the case in the arena of cyber conflict.

There is no real wider awareness of what a state-directed all-out "cyber war" could mean. One would assume that the absolute worst case in a cyber conflict could not possibly come close to a nuclear exchange, and this assumption is probably right. A controversial 2008 US congressional inquiry into the effect of a large-scale electromagnetic pulse attack, however, concluded that if most of the civilian electronics and the US power grid were "destroyed" (meaning they were unable to reconstitute themselves), then such an attack could create conditions for widespread famine, because the food supply network would fail along with the refrigeration centers that store perishables. The reality is that we do know what a simple, reversible, short-term blackout can cost on its own: in 2003, a blackout affected some fifty-five million people in the northeastern United States and parts of Canada. In most cases, power was restored within a day, probably a much faster response than what would be possible with the deliberate destruction of transmission equipment via cyberattack. Nonetheless, this relatively contained event probably caused some $6 billion in economic damages.

A well-resourced cyber actor aiming at causing maximum destruction could cause far, far more damage than this—not only switching off power, but destroying parts of the power grid for prolonged periods of time, deleting financial information, significantly disrupting transportation, and shutting down the media and telecommunication network, just to name a few possible strategies. In reality, pretty much any form of destruction is achievable through cyber means; for those with the resources, the only limitation is their own creativity. While we do not know for sure how far the United States has gone in deploying such country-crashing capabilities, or how many nations are seeking to do the same to the United States, we know that the United States was planning on doing exactly that to Iran in case open hostilities had erupted over its nuclear enrichment program. A number of countries have also been shown to be engaging in what could be called preparations for cyber war against the United States, securing persistent access to the power grid, the banking system, and even the air traffic control and rail management systems. Many governments have facilitated the formation of a covert "dragon world" in cyberspace, a parallel dimension where the seemingly magical powers available are only dimly apparent to those who are not versed in these dark arts. This lack of transparency as to the extent and type of offensive cyber capabilities not only raises the chance of misunderstandings leading to all-out conflict. It also threatens to legitimize a completely new type of conflict, a world of information warfare in which the aim is to achieve not a physical effect but a much subtler psychological one. Indeed, the worst possible cyber event may not be that the lights go out but that they will never go out—that some of humanity, maybe most of humanity, will slip into a totally controlled environment of Orwellian proportions.

This disaster scenario comes without the death and destruction. It is driven by a slow, hardly measurable, and yet steady reinterpretation of information as a weapon. It is the conversion of something that many of my generation—the first natives of the World Wide Web—considered an unqualified good into a dark web that can be perceived only as a tool of domination, oppression, and control. It is the perversion of cyberspace from a vehicle that profoundly empowers humans to one that threatens to disempower us, maybe even just as drastically.

Imagine a world where literally all information consumed—from your news, your commercials, your entertainment, your access to a *Wikipedia*-type encyclopedia via your search engine of choice—is wholly built around you. And not necessarily your own perfectly controlled set of preferences, but instead your implied preferences—things you probably like. These implied preferences can help customize a marketing ad, determine the price of a product, or even steer the selection of news you receive to get you to vote, buy, and think in a particular way.

We are already halfway there. Google searches, for instance, have long been fully personalized in a filter bubble: everyone gets his own individual search results based on previous searches, the neighborhood he is in, the computer he is using, and many other factors. Even the prices you pay during online shopping can vary according to what your ever-growing market profile says about you: literally the same product can be priced higher or lower depending on who is viewing it—for example, airline tickets. And it is very easy to determine who you are online, even if your unique personal identity is less significant than the *type* of person you are. There is no way to escape this, other than perpetually using specialized software to cover your tracks in cyberspace, rigorously avoiding any type of commercial interaction, and of course doing without a conventional cell phone, let alone a smart phone. Our behavior online is already increasingly steered by special interests subtly manipulating our preferences, and an entire burgeoning industry exists that is finding new (new, that is, for the private sector) ways of extracting psychological personality profiles of unique users from big data, and finding out exactly how to best target them for commercial or political online messaging, while our online and off-line behaviors are increasingly inseparable.

As bad as this may seem, however, it can get much worse. At present, if you are living in a liberal democratic society, these efforts are largely if not wholly commercial: they want to better sell you something and, most important, many different things. At present, there is not a single overriding product that these various marketing tools (although that term hardly does it justice) try to get you to choose, and, most important, that product is not a political choice, like the support for your government—although, of course, these techniques are increasingly used to support electoral campaigns in democracies. But this could be just the beginning of something else, as may already be apparent in other parts of the world. In China, for instance, serious thought is being devoted to the idea of a mandatory social-scoring system for all its citizens. Citizens who do "good things"— praise the government, avoid foreign Web sites, pay their bills, and maybe even refrain from foul language—will have a higher credit score and derive benefits such as improved access to travel exit visas. And states are not restricted to trying to influence political life within their own countries. Information war, with fake news items and covert influencing directed at entire populations, is rapidly becoming the new normal in the West as well.

And these attacks are directed not just at the news media itself but also at all those who make and comment on the news—the political pundits, private corporations, academia, and even civil society members who participate in the wider political discourse.

This is a book about cyber dreams. The very rise of the Internet was due to one deceptively simple dream: the ability to test a new communications theory based on information packets. Then came other dreams: the idea of a decentralized command and control network for some, the ability to share computer resources for others. And then the dreams multiplied: of virtual business, of boundless entertainment, of a sea of globally accessible data, of a web of democratic ideals and equal participation. But these dreams, familiar as they all are, were not alone. There are other dreams. These are about the ability to defeat an enemy air-defense network, the pursuit of espionage on a historic scale, the control of all facets of information consumed by a population. And while these dreams all coexist, the dreams of states increasingly dominate them.

For those who have watched cyberspace evolve from the Internet in the 1990s to what it is today, this is a dreadful realization. Like many, I was marked by the cyber utopianism of the 1990s. Authors like John Barlow enchanted my generation of wannabe hackers with magical declarations of independence of cyberspace: "*Governments . . . I come from Cyberspace, the new home of Mind. On behalf of the future, I ask you of the past to leave us alone. You are not welcome among us. You have no sovereignty where we gather.*" Such words, spoken with something like Druidic fervor, were already looking a bit quaint in 1999, the year the first major cyber-espionage campaign became public. Now, in 2017, they look not like a naive solemn pronouncement but like a plea: *leave us alone.* Maybe Barlow should have added "*please.*"

Governments did not make the Internet. Even today, governments in some ways are the least critical entity in actually building and populating cyberspace. Civil society—the academics, individual volunteers, inspired programmers—to this day builds and maintains the Internet, developing the computer protocols and procedures that are essentially its nervous system. The private sector is no less important: it builds, owns, and operates nearly all physical aspects of the Internet besides being responsible for the bulk of the data residing on it. Government, in comparison, can really only watch—listen in on cyberspace, if you will. But, increasingly, it can manipulate and destroy it, both intentionally and inadvertently.

Not all states share the same aspirations, and as we will see, there are marked differences between the "hacking" and technical-attack-oriented cyber-war narratives of liberal democracies and the psychological-attack information-warfare narrative on which countries like Russia and China are fixated. Likewise, there are significant differences in how both sides see the actual governance of the Internet itself. In theory, the two factions are sharply oriented against each other, with the liberal democracies led by the United States fighting for a non-state and "free" Internet rather than the government-controlled model favored by authoritarian governments. Liberal democracies are supported in their mission by the rise of a whole new type of governance, called the multistakeholder model, which tries to balance out the new importance of the non-state actors with the right-to-rule claims of the old nation-states. But those same democracies whose universal political goal is to defend the free Internet that we know today are also sometimes inadvertently, and unconsciously, undermining it and furthering the ambitions of authoritarian states. In my mind, this is the true tragedy of cyberspace: free societies may be able to protect against one of the two threats for a short while—either resisting the "weaponization of information" and the routinization of information warfare (and therefore also propaganda and censorship), or resisting the takeover of the Internet by an intergovernmental body—but are unlikely to succeed at both tasks without a real awareness of the threat we face. At one point the pressure to sacrifice

one dream for the sake of the other will be too powerful. And if that occurs, the second dream will soon be lost as well.

This book is about how the dreams of states are shaping international
cybersecurity—the rising term to describe efforts to develop an international security architecture around state behavior in cyberspace. Within
this context, I have often talked about "cyber power" as the ability of states
to exert power through and via cyberspace.

There are two different approaches to state cyber power: viewing it as
simply another tool of traditional state conflict and espionage, on the one
hand, and viewing it as a full-blown enabler of information warfare with
overtones of propaganda and information control, on the other. There is no
doubt which side favors which issue. For nearly two decades, Russia, together with like-minded states such as China and Iran, has repeatedly
brought forward international resolutions attempting to support what is
today called "national cyber sovereignty." The Cyber-sovereignty faction
consistently tries to emphasize that information in all its forms is a weapon,
most often employed by "terrorists" but really extending to any information (read: Internet content) that is uncomfortable to the ruling elite.
Essentially, it is shorthand for enabling wide-reaching Internet censorship
and other types of activity to ensure the regime stability of these authoritarian states.

To date, liberal democracies, led by the United States and bound together in what I call the Free Internet coalition, have been engaged in what
amounts to a holding action on this issue. In fact, they have largely refused
to engage in it at all, instead emphasizing discussions on the more traditional use of cyber capabilities for both war and covert action. Discussions
have ranged on examining thresholds for war—the United States has
clearly stated that a serious cyberattack could be interpreted as a *casus
belli*—and the application of international humanitarian law in any kind of
cyber conflict. Some of these discussions have been conducted for many

years already—not too dissimilar to strategic arms control talks during the Cold War. But there is a major difference between these talks and those aimed at reducing and controlling nuclear weapons: there is no commonly desired end state, no shared nightmare that the two sides equally fear. And this means that it is difficult to see that the Cyber-sovereignty advocates may, in fact, be making headway with their core wish: the framing of information as a weapon. Over time, this could exert irresistible pressure to change the present Web to something much darker, where information is managed rather than free flowing and where instead of more freedom we will enjoy comprehensively less.

The litany of Cold War near-disasters involving nuclear weapons points to one factor: despite the considerable effect of a path dependency laid down by decades of practice—working across military standard operating procedures, political mores, and even the state of scientific knowledge—individuals have often made a decisive difference in preventing a cataclysm. Individuals such as Lieutenant Colonel Stanislav Petrov, who singularly acted against all training and received wisdom and instead decided on nothing else than gut instinct and, perhaps, an innate moral compass. Petrov would probably be the first to point out that he was not a particularly remarkable man. His actions the night of September 26, 1983 were not even completely unique—the history of the Cold War is full of remarkable decisions that were made by individuals who acted against conditioning and made the right choice at a crucial moment. There were anywhere between six and twelve (depending on how you count them) historically well-researched close calls that could have triggered a nuclear exchange. Some of the individuals involved in these close calls were military men in submarines or command bunkers who have had books and movies written about them, but others were spies, or politicians, or comparatively low-ranking scientists and officials whose feats are largely unknown. We don't know most of their stories, and many will never be revealed. Yet they have had a decisive effect on history.

It is evident that despite the most rigorous mental conditioning, humans can overcome even the deepest path dependency and act according to their own rational and moral sense. While the moral sense may be a function of culture, the rational sense is a function of knowledge—and this makes it so vital for all of us that there is a basic understanding of the complexities of these systems and the potential consequences of their use. Unlike the nuclear age, when the vast majority of the populace could only passively wait on the earth-shaping decisions made by a select few in bunkers and labs, in the cyber age we are all potentially in play. The essentially non-state aspect of cyberspace means that it is formed by everyday users and their decisions, rather than governments negotiating among themselves. The Web could one day darken due to interstate conflict, and that, in my mind, is a significantly underappreciated risk, as governments everywhere become increasingly comfortable with the notion of conflict in cyberspace and engage in the militarization of this new domain. But at least as great a danger is the threat of the slower, and less discernable, undermining of the entire purpose of the Web itself, recasting it into a singular tool for control and domination, rather than as the undeniable boon for human civilization it currently is.

This is an Armageddon that all of us in liberal democracies have the power to avert. It requires a wide-scale rejection of the increased aggression of states in cyberspace, not only against our economies or critical infrastructure, but against the media and sources of political information. The specter of full-scale information warfare, with deluges of fake news, propaganda, and wide-scale attempts at strategic influencing, is very real, and in 2016 was discernable even to the public at large. The intended efforts are aimed at devaluing the most important currency in democracies—trust—and thus upending the ability of governments to function. The best national resistance to this type of challenge is also trust—not a trust conjured up from crude propaganda and half-truths, but one that is based upon the individual and his or her innate ability to discern fact from fiction. It seems that liberal democracies, and in particular the government of the United States, need to recall the existential need to be trusted by their populace, and go many steps further than they currently have to engender that trust through transparency and openness on cyberspace and national security matters.

Only liberal democratic societies were able to give birth and nurture the Internet into its young adulthood, and, for me and many others, the ascent of cyberspace and the current governance of the Internet is one of the most perfect proofs that political freedoms really do exist, and that they make a meaningful difference in the most practical and measurable of ways. Given the intractable relationship between political freedoms and the Web, it is perhaps not surprising that the greatest threat to these freedoms can come from the Web as well—but only if liberal democracies forget who they are, or misunderstand the power of this magical new world they have created.

PART I

Chapter 1

THE BODY OF CYBER

Cyber is not what it used to be. The term used to mean sex. Today, it means war.

Ever since the mathematician Norbert Wiener coined the term "cybernetics" in 1948 to describe the communication and automated control of complex systems of both man and machine, the prefix "cyber" has had a life of its own in popular culture. In 2013, the tech site Gizmodo traced the development of the term since the 1950s and established that in 1989 the term "cybersecurity" was introduced at virtually the same time as "cyberporn." In the heyday of the late 1990s, the social aspects of "cyber"— cyber stalking, cyber crime, cyber community—outweighed any other interpretations. If someone on an Internet chat asked, "Do you cyber?" they were talking about cybersex.

It is not clear when exactly security issues took over, but in 1995 *Time* magazine ran a cover featuring the term "cyber war." In 1999, a high-ranking US defense official used the term "cyber war" in a briefing to Congress, and although the term stuck in the public imagination, until very recently it was never used in official documents. What did stick was the association of cyber with conflict, in particular with computer network hacking. What was forgotten was the original description of cyber as actually being about controlling both production and thought processes, putting it somewhere between management science and marketing. Today, if someone in the United States asks you if you are into cyber, it is more likely he means a form of information technology (IT) security. In other countries, however, it can also mean propaganda and censorship.

Cyberspace is virtual but not imaginary. Like finance, it is a purely artificial domain that largely exists in the abstract and that has no intrinsic value beyond that which we place on it. Unlike finance, it is still very new, and therefore often only barely understood by both the public and policy makers alike. Despite having only a very recent history, cyberspace already plays an increasingly concrete role in everyday life for billions of people. For many of us, life without cyberspace, or its most visible manifestation in the global Internet, is simply difficult to envision anymore. Not only do we as individuals share and communicate information—data—in ways only dimly imagined some decades ago, so do our institutions of daily life: our governments, our businesses, our universities, our centers of research and worship. And not only do these institutions communicate in cyberspace, but our very possessions—from heavy machinery to cars to fridges and even toasters—are increasingly online. They are all wrapped in an ever-increasing web that in its complexity and dimensions leaves it only dimly comprehensible. This exchange of data has become so integral to our daily life that some observers have gushed that "data is the new money." Others have even said that "data is even more important than money."

Just like the confusion that individuals in premodern societies might have felt with the introduction of paper currency, it can be difficult to conceptualize what this hugely significant development of cyberspace and the Internet actually is. Most of us are completely ignorant of the technology that makes up cyberspace, and many of us would struggle to define it. This isn't something to be embarrassed about, because in fact there is no single correct definition of what constitutes cyberspace. We cannot even agree on how to write it. Sometimes we may write "cyberspace" as one word, sometimes we write it as two separate words, and sometimes we even put a hyphen in between, if we are uncertain. As Eric Schmidt, the executive chairman of Alphabet (the owners of Google), once put it, "The Internet is the first thing that humanity has built that humanity does not understand." If the Internet is hard to understand, cyberspace is even more difficult to envision.

We often use the terms "cyberspace," "the Internet" (or "the net"), and "the World Wide Web" (or "the Web") interchangeably. Previously, they were considered unique entities and effectively subsets of each other: the Web is therefore a subcategory of the global Internet, which itself is only one component of what is increasingly called cyberspace. But although the specific differences still matter, in common usage these terms have begun to merge into a single domain: the information domain that is effectively synonymous with cyberspace.

And this domain is huge. During the summer of 2015, over three billion humans were considered regular Internet users, interacting with it daily for both personal pleasure and business. The world's leading economies have derived nearly a quarter of their overall annual growth from the Internet, and today the Internet economy itself accounts for 5–9 percent of the economy of the largest twenty nations worldwide. The size of the global Internet, including the Web, is difficult to estimate, but with over a billion Web pages (itself a content measure increasingly obsolete) in 2014 it was estimated to store information of around one million exabytes. A byte is a data unit comprising eight bits and is equal to a single character in one of the words you're reading now. An exabyte is one billion billion bytes. Another way to view this is that the presumed amount of information stored on the Internet is equivalent to around fifty *billion* copies of the entire US Library of Congress.

This is just what is referred to as the "indexed" Internet, reachable for most of us through our Web browsers. But the non-indexed Internet, that which is not captured by search engines or commonly accessible, like business and government repositories but also your private data at home, is much larger. Some conservative estimates have put the size of the non-indexed Internet, often called the "deep web," at around five hundred times larger than the World Wide Web. Other recent measures have estimated that it is now four thousand to five thousand times larger. The "deep web" itself is only one measurable component of cyberspace, which can be described as the domain of potentially interconnected data. While you may think you are able to take yourself off the Internet, in a modern industrial society it is virtually impossible to disappear from cyberspace: data about you that you did not necessarily intentionally create is stored somewhere and shared somewhere else. You may think you can escape the Internet, but you cannot escape cyberspace.

While the "Internet" is a technical term, the notion of "cyberspace" is rooted in the social sciences and science fiction. As such, it has historically been treated with disdain by some technical practitioners who consider the term bogus and effectively meaningless. Often viewed as the tool of overtly jocular industry salespeople, sensationalizing journalists, and sinister politicians, the term "cyberspace" (let alone "cybersecurity") has stayed the *bête noire* of much of the technical community for a remarkably long time, the concept that everyone is eager to hate. The mockery of the term "cyber" by many self-proclaimed hackers had a brief hiatus only when it became transparent, thanks to the former National Security Agency (NSA) contractor and mega-leaker Edward Snowden, that the über-hackers of the NSA and the GCHQ (its U.K. equivalent) happily used the prefix "cyber" in various forms—and had effectively always done so. Rejecting the term "cyber" looks more like a mark of ignorance than one of insight, but social mores have always been difficult to change—especially in the largely self-referencing geek culture that unites the technical community.

The importance of the term "cyber" in US national security wasn't a total secret before the massive leaks of intelligence documents in 2013 either. As far back as 1998 the White House published one of the earliest and most important documents on protecting critical infrastructure and used the prefix "cyber" around fourteen times, without defining it. In 2008, the US government defined cyberspace thus:

> Cyberspace means the interdependent network of IT infrastructures, and includes the Internet, telecom networks, computer systems, and embedded processors and controllers in critical industries. Common usage of the term also refers to the virtual environment of information and interactions between people.

Everything that depends on internet technology, even if it is not actively connected to the global Internet at all times, is part of cyberspace. Cyberspace includes the vast number of private internets, many of them separated ("air-gapped," in the lingo) from the Internet per se, but nonetheless reachable through the use of thumb drives or other portable media. Your supermodern kitchen fridge, if it is in any way connectable to the Internet, is a part of cyberspace, as is your car, your phone, the data stored on your USB stick, your bank records, or your gym membership account. Anything you do or say or try to affect through internet technology—ranging from declaring your love via Facebook to planning a trip to looking up the weather—is part of cyberspace. Simply put, cyberspace is the "world behind your screen." The U.K. government definition from June 2009 therefore puts it most succinctly: "Cyberspace includes all forms of networked, digital activities; this includes the content of and actions conducted through digital networks."

Cyberspace therefore includes not only technology but also human behaviors and arguably Internet technology-enabled social interactions. This therefore includes considerations of Internet censorship and online information control, but also freedom of speech and expression, respect for property, protection of individual privacy, and the protection from crime, espionage, terrorism, and acts of warfare. This means that cyberspace is defined not only in technical terms but also very much in human terms.

Despite considerable advances in recent years in academic and legal literature on the definition of cyberspace, what exactly it is will remain in flux. Governments, businesses, and citizens know intuitively that cyberspace is the sum of all existing and future uses of the Internet by humans and that therefore the definitions are constantly changing. William Gibson, author of the 1984 novel *Neuromancer* and widely considered the creator of the term "cyberspace," famously described it as a "consensual hallucination." He did not mean that cyberspace did not exist in some form. Rather, he meant that it was an artificial domain made real by our shared perception of it. And therefore when our perception of it changes, it will change as well.

Cyberspace is a fully functioning ecosystem. Imagine going to a museum and viewing a diorama featuring a slice of planet Earth—or better yet the ocean—with the different layers of this domain separated and explained individually. This type of representation can be attempted in cyberspace as well, with two notable caveats. First, it is an abstraction—much more than the two-dimensional representation of the layers of the ocean. Second, it is completely man-made: the only immutable physical laws, like gravity, in this domain are the ones we have set ourselves.

The model that best explains cyberspace is a four-layered pyramid, with, however, the pyramid standing on its head. Each of these individual layers, from the tip of the pyramid on which it stands to the largest layer on top, represents an essential and very different underlying structure of cyberspace. The first layer—the tip of the pyramid on which all else depends—is the physical or hardware layer. It represents the bones of cyberspace and everything tangible within it: the computers, the cables and communicating equipment, and the switching technology that connects them. The second layer is the logic layer. It represents the coded behavior of the domain: the various computer protocols and software programs that form the neurons and nervous system of cyberspace. The third is the data layer: unlike the code layer that precedes it, the data residing here is usually understandable by the average human being. It includes business documents and scientific inquiries but also simple e-mails, photographs, messages, and everything possibly categorized as personal identifiable information in the United States or personal data in the EU. It can also include the rapidly increasing array of machine-to-machine data, highly streamlined and efficient data streams that are totally automated. This data layer is analogous to the human muscle system, and even the difference between skeletal and cardiac muscle, because while some of the data is created intentionally and voluntary, other data seemingly works fully autonomously and can be difficult (or impossible) to consciously control.

All of these layers work together to support the ultimate layer: the social layer. This is the actual Internet of people, the total sum of human actions and aspirations that make the Internet and cyberspace what they are. If cyberspace can be said to have a soul or mind, this is where it is.

The White Mountain facility is a pretty good starting place for any kind of review of the hardware layer—the bones—of cyberspace. White Mountain—known by the Swedish name *Pionen*—is a data center and an Internet service provider (ISP). It also was the first physical home of the contentious WikiLeaks whistle-blower platform. Today, the old WikiLeaks server is used as a bar prop.

Pionen is a nuclear-hardened former Cold War bunker facility one hundred feet beneath the suburbs of Stockholm. It has been extensively converted by a local company—an Internet service provider called Bahnhof—into something more akin to a Batman cave, complete with caverns blasted out of bedrock and a two-story office structure sheltered within. The office arrangement includes a panoramic meeting room fit for an evil overlord's control center, and the bunker is decorated with copious tropical vegetation basking in its own sunlamps and even has a partially functioning waterfall—all buried thirty meters under granite and behind a two-foot-thick and twenty-ton blast-proof door. The waterfall actually has a practical function: it helps humidify the twenty thousand square feet of routers, switches, servers, and other specialized computers that occupy various rented jail-sized mesh cages running the length of Pionen's three caverns, with room for more than six thousand servers fully deployed. The whole system is completely self-contained, with backup submarine diesel generators that can power the facility for a long time after the lights have gone out outside. Pionen and its sister facilities together provide a decent chunk of local bandwidth, routing about 10–15 percent of Sweden's entire national Internet traffic, or about 100 gigabits per second. As a comparison, 1 gigabit per second equals 8,000 megabits per second, and the average US household in 2015 had a broadband speed of about 11 megabits per second, around 0.0014 gigabit per second.

Pionen represents only one of the four data centers of the ISP Bahnhof, and Bahnhof itself is not a particularly unusual small to medium-sized enterprise. Yes, it was one of the first ISPs to start in Sweden, and like many early participants in this field it has a strong ideological and cyber-libertarian streak. But as a company, it is not particularly large or powerful. In fact, with only around 120 employees and annual revenue of about $28 million in 2012, Bahnhof is not even one of the top five ISP companies in Sweden and certainly doesn't manage the largest facilities. While as an ISP it is an important gateway to the Internet for many people, it is not in any way important for the Internet overall. In fact, Pionen and its owner are far from unique, but actually somewhat average. It is simply that average in Internet terms can look pretty bizarre for everyone else.

In fact, many of Sweden's large Internet exchange points (IXPs, basically large ISPs that together form the Internet backbone)—each of which conducts a multiple of the traffic that Pionen does—are hosted in similar or even much larger bunkers, repurposed from the Cold War. The largest of these facilities is maintained by the Swedish company Netnod, which also hosts one of only three non-US Internet root name servers, which function as the basic telephone book of the Internet. Its four facilities together average a throughput of 773 gigabits per second, a respectable total that is still smaller than the greatest in the business. The two biggest IXPs in the world, located in Frankfurt and Amsterdam, average between 2,500 and 3,500 gigabits per second of traffic, and this number is steadily increasing. Together, these companies—and the facilities they maintain—are responsible for routing (that is, directing) much of the world's Internet traffic. Some of these facilities do look as secure as the layman thinks they should be, installed in former nuclear bunkers and in similar dramatic settings. Most, however, hide in plain sight—featureless cubes hulking away in business parks and protected by layers of unobtrusive security. Often the only way to spot them is by the large number of backup generators needed to keep the massive ventilation systems going to cool the machinery inside.

The power needs of data centers give an idea of how many there are and how large an industry they represent. By 2018, all those data centers should occupy a bit less than two billion square feet—a bit more than three times the size of Manhattan—and in the United States in 2010 the total use of electricity by data centers already amounted to roughly the annual electricity consumption of Belgium (in 2016, it is likely twice that). Official numbers for the Internet giants' data centers are hard to come by, because they are such a key part of their global strategy and good summaries are scarce. In 2016, Google ran dedicated data centers at nine locations in the United States, one in South America, four in Europe, and two in Asia, but it is quickly building new ones without disclosing the exact numbers. Microsoft has reported that it manages more than a hundred data centers. Amazon Web Services, the cloud computing branch of Amazon, runs, by one informed estimate, eighty-seven data centers. Facebook has three huge data centers, is building an additional one, and rents space in at least ten other locations in the United States. There are hundreds of other data centers of note across the world, and this number is steadily growing. Internet giants need their data to be secure, which means that the data needs to both remain in their own infrastructures and be readily available to their customers. This availability problem is one of the reasons why massive data centers are being built everywhere: the closer the nearest data center, the lower the time necessary to deliver the information (that time is called "latency," the unsung champion of Internet traffic).

The physical underpinning of the Internet bears resemblance to the old telephone systems from which it evolved in the 1970s. Indeed, the very backbone of the Internet is made of cables that run across continents and under the seas, with a smattering of satellite links as well. Instead of the electricity that telephone networks usually carry, Internet cables are typically fiber-optic trunk lines and carry flashes of light, strung together to increase their capacity: each of those cables can carry an average TV show episode every single second. But the Internet's most significant departure from the old phone system is its reliance on a totally different technology to communicate information: network packet switching.

Packet switching forms the core of Internet technology. It is the process by which communication is divided into a series of "network packets" that can be delivered to their intended destination along various routes, such as different telephone lines, and still make a coherent message at their destination. One useful way to think of it is to imagine the individual network packets as individual envelopes. Sending an Internet message is therefore like sending a book split up into different individual envelopes. Each one can carry only part of the book and may even take different routes depending on traffic conditions. Most important, the entire book has to come together intact at the final destination for the trip to be considered a success. The process of directing these individual envelopes—packets—along the fastest route, and reassembling the message at the end, is what packet network switching is all about.

While less efficient for normal telephone conversations than the alternative model (called circuit switching and in use since 1878), packet switching always had one major advantage: it was much less prone to interruption due, for instance, to physical destruction of the cables. In that case, these data envelopes—the network packets—would just take another route. Each packet is coded to include information like "to," "from," or "priority" on its "envelope," as well as the actual content. An average text-only e-mail will therefore make up something between three and eight packets. The journey an Internet Protocol (IP) packet takes from sender to receiver can be similar to that of a physical letter being sent from a rural home to a rural home. First, the packet proceeds down a country road, the last mile between the end node (that is, you) and your local ISP. Once at that local ISP, your IP packet hops to a two-lane feeder system that takes it to the nearest IXP—the gateway to the Internet backbone, the interstate superhighway of the packets. Once on this information *autobahn,* the packet will hop from IXP to IXP, the intersections of the backbone that use switches to route the packages effectively, until it is closest to its destination. Here the process reverses itself, until the packet finally trundles down to its receiver, potentially at the end of its own country road. Here it is mated with other IP packets that might have taken a totally different route and reassembled into the content it was before. Ideally, the whole process takes less than a second.

The bandwidth consumed by these end nodes—you the sender and your friend the receiver—is created at specific points of the network: the IXPs, where ISPs connect to each other and to the Internet and create the bandwidth that they sell to their customers. These IXPs are full of large wire and steel cages that other organizations can rent. This is where companies, including ISPs but also simply businesses that need a lot of bandwidth, put their servers. Sometimes these individual servers in their cages will directly connect with each other, amounting to no more than a cable being cast from one cage to the next. IXPs are the heart of the Internet, where you can see that the Internet is indeed a network of networks running on a set of interconnection agreements, physically embodied by hard cables running from one cage to the other in an often madly confusing jungle of multicolored plastic tubes.

IXPs therefore create bandwidth, a commodity that can be exported and traded on the market. Not all countries have their own IXPs and therefore have to import bandwidth; in 2015, around eighty-seven countries imported 100 percent of their bandwidth, a potential hindrance to their national development. The country with the largest number of IXPs is the United States (eighty-three IXPs), while the Netherlands, according to Bill Woodcock, the executive director of Packet Clearing House, is the world's largest net exporter of Internet bandwidth: IXPs in the Netherlands produce more broadband used in other countries than any other IXP in the world. IXPs and other bandwidth-delivering infrastructures are undoubtedly critical for the Internet. Even if the biggest fail, however, the Internet will continue—albeit at much-reduced capability. In an interview in Andrew Blum's *Tubes,* a great book dedicated to the physical layer of the Internet, heads of two of the largest IXPs said that they weren't really essential infrastructure; if they went down, the global Internet bandwidth would simply decrease, nothing more. Much more critical, Blum argues, is the existence and work of corporate data centers, such as those hosted by Google, Amazon, IBM, and others. For they actually host data—data that can be lost forever if they are destroyed.

That is only partly right. Corporate data centers are critical for the data they hold, and there is a remarkable lack of knowledge of what would happen if, for instance, Google lost a number of data centers due to any kind of calamity. IXPs certainly do matter, however, especially if the goal you are considering falls short of complete destruction of the data. For while you might not be able to destroy data directly at an IXP, you can intercept it— tapping the communications directly. This allows the information to be not only examined and collected but changed surreptitiously. IXPs have often been called the airports of the Internet, and like other airports they can pass on dangerous elements, either unknowingly, with passengers carrying illnesses, or knowingly, effectively fitting out the airplane with a hostile payload. They are therefore critical to international security and at the very core of the global Internet.

. . .

The physical layer of cyberspace is of course just the skeleton: the bare bones, the tangible part of the Internet. But the logical layer is akin to the nervous system, a sea of neurons: the universe of computer code that powers all the functions of the physical layer and enables information to travel over it. Just like the human nervous system, the logical layer is a slightly mysterious artifact that is rather at odds with the rest of the cyber body.

To begin with, software code defines our very experience and perception of everything related to cyberspace. As Lawrence Lessig, founder of the Stanford Center for Internet and Society, most famously put it, "Code is law." Computer code, intentionally or not, helps set not only our behavior but also our expectations in cyberspace: what is realistic, and what is not, how things are done, and how things *should* be done.

There are a great number of computer standards that are relevant to the Internet and Internet communication. The two most important for understanding the Internet are the transmission-control protocol/Internet protocol (TCP/IP) and the domain name system (DNS). One of the most essential functions of the TCP/IP was described previously: it effectively determines the shape and size and behavior of network packets, the most basic element of data in Internet communications. TCP in particular is responsible for assuring that IP packets arrive where they are supposed to.

Internet protocol numbers represent the most basic identifier on the Internet, which is why they are also referred to as IP addresses. An IP address is a string of values that identifies the physical location of a computer that is connected to the Internet (PCs, servers, smart phones, or, again, your fridge, if so enabled). It is the string of numbers that hides behind the uniform resource locator (URL) you type into your browser to get to a certain Web site; in other words, it is something like the telephone number of the Internet.

In the early 1980s, a total number of 4.3 billion IP addresses (referred to as IPv4) was considered enough for the foreseeable future. For a better overview, IPv4 addresses are usually displayed in four groups of decimal numbers, separated by dots and ranging from 0 to 255 (for example, 208.80.152.2). In theory, every device connected to the Internet has its own IP number; if it does not have an IP number, it is not connected to the Internet. The explosive demand for IP addresses over the last thirty years, however, has proven that the original quantity of IP addresses was inadequate.

The world ran out of IPv4 space in 2011, necessitating a shift to IP version 6. IPv6 addresses look quite different from IPv4 addresses: they are usually written in eight groups of four-digit, hexadecimal values (0–9 and A–F), separated by colons (for example, 21DA:00D3:0000:2F3B: 02AA:00FF:FE28:9C5A). IPv6 provides a massive increase in potential cyberspace, allowing for 340 undecillion (or a trillion trillion trillion— 3.4×10^{38}) Internet connection points. With an estimated world population of 6.8 billion living human beings, the potential number of IPv6 addresses would enable *each individual* to connect around 1.2 *billion* devices to the net. All of human possessions (now, and for the foreseeable future) could potentially be "tagged" and made accessible over the Internet. The new Internet is therefore just beginning. As of 2016, this shift is still in progress and will take some years yet.

The rollout of TCP/IP in 1983 is a prime example of Lessig's maxim that "code is law." TCP/IP fixed the distributed nature of the Internet for the future and, according to the Columbia Law School professor Tim Wu, directly represented the founding ideology of the Internet: not only because it was nonhierarchical, but because it was "tolerant"—intended to work across telephone networks owned by different companies using different standards. And most important, it was "trusting."

Not everything within the logic layer is decentralized. The introduction of the IP numbers as universal identifiers was always going to be a problem: navigating the Internet would effectively require the memorization of hundreds of "Internet telephone numbers"—not something most humans were likely to want or even be able to do. Therefore, the Internet needed two things: a directory or telephone book of all the world's IP numbers, and a way of changing these IP numbers into something more manageable—such as changing "170.149.168.130" into "http://www.nytimes.com." While some IP numbers will remain fixed, others—including perhaps that of your PC at home—will change dynamically. This need to account for changing IP numbers yet maintain a stable overall identity—the name of the Web site—required a basic authoritative directory of the Internet: thus the domain name system was born.

DNS is in some ways the nasty digestive tract of the Internet. Unlike the resolutely non-centralized Internet itself, DNS is by its very necessity a hierarchical system. When you type a Web address—www.nytimes.com—into your browser, the address is queried to a recursive domain name server (often simply called name server) for the correct address. In this case, it will query the domain name server responsible for all the addresses ending in .com that itself checks in with a more authoritative name server regularly. The authoritative name servers maintain the master document as to which URL maps to which IP address for the name servers' own respective domain, just like each US state maintains responsibility for the telephone book within its jurisdiction. Each authoritative name server is responsible for maintaining the records for its individual "top-level domains" (called TLDs, for example, .com, .net, but also .uk, .de, and increasingly new domains such as .wine and .money) and holding the entries for all the subdomains under its control, like the sub-groupings of every company registered to the British domain space ".uk." Depending on the size of the TLD in question, there may be only a couple of physical authoritative name servers, or hundreds; in any case, they will maintain the same file for their zone. In turn, these authoritative name servers get their status from the next level up, the so-called DNS root zone. There are thirteen DNS root servers that maintain the master list of all of the Internet's authorized TLDs, and updating them is indeed quite a ceremony with unbelievably tight security procedures.

The thirteen root name servers are labeled from *a* (maintained by Verisign) to *m* (maintained by WIDE, a Japanese company). The Swedish company Netnod described previously maintains the *i* root name server. Thirteen authorities maintain these servers: all but three are based in the United States, and three of them are directly US government. While originally there were physically only thirteen root servers that held the "telephone book" of the Internet, this was always considered a little risky; knocking out all of them (or even most of them) would have effectively grounded the Internet. Today, over five hundred actual physical root servers are distributed worldwide in dozens of locations, from Reykjavík to Dallas to Tahiti, all of them copies of the thirteen individual root name servers. This would, seemingly, guarantee that the root zones would be secure from all but the most world-ending physical attacks.

The root servers are not all equal, however. In fact, the root zone file itself is only a single file—until relatively recently, a tiny one of fewer than 278 kilobytes, smaller than an average PowerPoint file. The file is now a bit over 1 megabyte as the newest version of DNS, DNSSEC, takes hold. The single authoritative file is generated within *a*-root and is called the "hidden master root," because its specific location is a closely guarded secret. All other root zone files are simply copies of this one file. What are known are the administrative arrangements for making changes to the root zone file. These procedures—and the management of the domain name system itself—are at the core of the policy component of Internet governance. At this point, it is only important to highlight that all the "laws" that exist to work in the DNS space are very malleable; the fact that there are thirteen and not fifteen or a hundred root servers, for example, is simply an artifice of decision making, with plenty of scope for negotiation.

While code always came first, some choice principles emerged out of the most sensible traditions in code. If there is one set of laws or principles that governs the Internet above all others, it is the end-to-end principle (often abbreviated e2e). In its simplest form, the principle states that all innovation on the network should occur at the "ends" (the edges—in other words, the end customer, the average user) rather than at the center (in other words, where the telecommunication and infrastructure carriers are). In practical terms, this means that the carriers—the ISPs and telecommunication providers—are supposed to simply deliver traffic and not set policy. Policy is instead decided through consumer choice, at the "ends." The e2e principle is intended to encourage innovation and eschew centralized control.

The implementation of the e2e principle has always been subject to interpretation, even among Internet pioneers. But the principle has come under sustained fire from cyberspace intermediaries who wish to make more money from the Internet. The push by telecommunication companies (particularly in the United States, but also globally) to be able to extract higher fees from the Internet is a case in point.

In the United States, telecom companies like Comcast have tried to make the case that the rise of video-related traffic (especially Netflix) has meant that carriers should have the option to provide differentiated services to consumers. This would mean that customers wanting to access some types of content (such as video on demand) would pay different rates from those who did not. This seemingly innocuous shift would have significant consequences: in effect, the carrier would decide what content its consumers are allowed to receive—potentially extending then to services such as Facebook, Skype, Google, and anything else the carrier decides is of special interest.

As a result, the e2e principle has been recast in policy terms as net neutrality: the idea that the infrastructure should be as neutral as possible for the content it transports. In the beginning of those debates, there were reports that Verizon had been throttling Netflix traffic because it thought it was legally able to do so. Indeed, as many companies develop businesses that use increasing quantities of bandwidth (video services like YouTube and Netflix have been in the spotlight because streaming quality is so crucial to the service they provide), telecom providers have been arguing that those services that represent the lion's share of backbone usage should supply a proportionate contribution to backbone development. However, a public outcry to uphold the e2e principle helped inform the FCC's decision on February 26, 2015, toward net neutrality. Part of this decision was the groundbreaking change that from then on the FCC was going to regulate broadband Internet providers as a public utility (rather than as a luxury, as the telecom companies had insisted), and therefore have a strong say on any kind of discrimination policy such as "blocking, throttling, and paid prioritization." This was the final chapter in a process that actually made code real law: starting with code, moving to general principles to provide continuity when the individual code became obsolete or was updated, and finally formalizing these policies into traditional law.

If the physical layer equates with the bones of the Internet, and the logic layer with the human body's nervous system and neural networks, then the data layer—itself a contentious construct—could be described as the Internet's muscle fabric. It is both the muscles that we consciously control and those muscles that seemingly work of their own accord. It keeps the information company going the same way coal and oil fueled the Industrial Revolution. "Data is the new oil," gushed *Forbes* magazine in 2012. From a technical perspective, everything else—the physical layer, the logical layer—exists only to help deliver data.

The amount of data moving in cyberspace is astronomical. According to a 2016 report by Cisco, in 2016 the world's Internet traffic was expected to hit the magic number of one *zettabyte* of traffic and keep on increasing. This will mean nearly one hundred *exabytes* of traffic every single month. For perspective, one exabyte is equal to one billion *terabytes* (one terabyte is the size of the average home PC storage capacity) or one trillion *gigabytes*. Every gigabyte, if transmitted as text, would account for ten thousand thick books. Basically, the Internet is rapidly approaching the point where the equivalent of the entire world's domestically held data (as in the data you have saved on your PC or handheld devices) is exchanged *every single month* over the Internet.

Already today, videos—including everything from home movies to feature releases—account for 65 percent to 85 percent of all traffic, a figure that keeps on increasing. Still, this does mean a lot of non-video traffic is out there as well. Much of this data is highly personal: e-mails, blog posts, and the like. Increasingly, some of it is seemingly impersonal: data exchanged between machines like smart phones, home appliances, or networked industrial equipment. Moreover, the data exchanged is not in, for instance, complicated Office documents or bloated PowerPoint files but in machine-optimized and therefore much more efficient formats, much in the way that there is the same amount of information in a list of bullet points as in an elaborate PowerPoint presentation of this list. Machine-to-machine communication is much more efficient than human-to-human communication in terms of pure information transmitted.

The Internet of Things (IoT) may be tipping that balance even further. To define it briefly, according to one of its leading engineers the IoT is the "network of networks which enables the identification of digital identities and physical objects directly and without ambiguity." Beyond computers, new devices are in the process of being connected to the Internet to be able to retrieve, store, transfer, and process data relating to them—and metadata relating to this data. The increasing mass of data produced this way challenges the very concept of anonymity, blurring even further the line between metadata and personal identifiable information.

The Internet of Things is not coming; it is already here. Sometime in 2009, machines connected to the Internet started to outnumber the number of humans online. In January 2015, a US Federal Trade Commission report estimated that there were twenty-five *billion* connected devices already, around eight times as many humans as are considered online. This number will grow to fifty billion devices worldwide by 2020. These devices—our smart phones, our home appliances, even, in the future, our very clothes—collect vast amounts of information on industrial, organizational, and personal behavior and gather users' preferences to improve delivery of products and services, health, education, entertainment, and shopping. They also provide for a large number of different attack vectors on unsuspecting consumers—both from criminals and from government actors.

This data is far from impersonal, for in each case it provides information on a human or group of humans and their activities—be it in the number of phone calls a person places (and to whom, and for how long), the energy usage specifics of every household in a small city, or indeed who is always chronically late in buying milk for their fridge (there is a strange obsession by some appliance makers that often seek to justify the networked kitchen so as to help avoid the horror of running out of milk in one's fridge).

Much of this data will be metadata—data that provides only an indication of other, underlying data flows—in other words, data about data. The most famous examples of metadata include those that the US government has been shown to collect on US citizens regarding whom they talk to by telephone and for how long, rather than the actual contents of the phone calls. Other operators—specifically Web-based businesses and above all Google—collect reams of metadata, most specifically Web sites (that is, IP numbers) visited. These companies effectively mine personal data, provided freely and with various degrees of awareness by the average Internet user, to convert it to accurate marketing profiles that are used for targeted ads and recommended search results: this is what makes providing their service free of charge a financially sustainable business model. Sometimes the data they mine is very personal indeed: Google's Gmail service, for instance, scans your e-mails for keywords that then influence the advertisements you see. That's why when you are exchanging e-mails about your upcoming vacation, you may magically get some suggestions on last-minute flights or car rentals. Equally, small pieces of tracking information inserted into your Web browser—called cookies—have been a stable part of the Internet experience from the very early days. They were invented by a Netscape engineer named Lou Montulli to make sure an online retailer retained a record of your planned purchases—often called your online "shopping basket"—even when you changed Web pages. According to legend, their name derives from fortune cookies, and they are indeed little bites with a message crammed inside. Cookies can have a variety of functions, but the most common is to track your Internet whereabouts and behavior, such as the Web sites you visit, so as to better discern your interests and offer appropriate content—and this content is big business. Internet marketing already accounts for nearly one-quarter of the global spending on marketing (including TV, radio, and print) and was worth more than $160 billion in 2016. A huge chunk of this will go to Google, which in 2014 accounted for nearly half of the total marketing spend on the Web—all of which is derived, to various degrees, from the value of personal data.

As Michael Morell, a former CIA official and member of the US president's Review Group on Intelligence and Communications Technologies, said, "There's not a sharp distinction between metadata and content. It's more of a continuum." Spun together, different parts of metadata can deliver a very accurate picture. For instance, a very large number of phone calls last exactly, say, three minutes. That information alone would be next to useless. But if you know the day of the phone call, the city where the person called from, and the brand of the mobile phone used, you may be able to transform this metadata into personal identifiable information—in other words, to clearly narrow the amount of similar calls down to only one or two individuals. And that holds more generally: so-called re-identification of metadata can happen through the combination of several data sets of metadata. This is why the production and availability of more and more data sets make it easier for our metadata to be re-identified. In this context, it is becoming harder to know which of our data is successfully anonymized and which can be easily re-identified.

In January 2015, for instance, a group of researchers studied three months of credit card metadata and came to the troubling conclusion that four data points (such as amount purchased, location, time, and type of credit card) "are enough to uniquely re-identify 90% of individuals." Another example is the online tool provided by the Electronic Frontier Foundation, Panopticlick. It collects the information your browser routinely shares with Web sites you visit (the user agent, the http headers, the plug-in details, time zone, and other metadata about how you use your browser) and returns a corresponding score of uniqueness: one in X browsers has the same fingerprint as yours. It is not surprising that one of the biggest battles on the Internet is how to keep this information safe—meaning out of the hands of corporations and governments, as well as criminals. The technical battle is largely focused on making the collection of personal data by governments or businesses either impossible or very expensive. This protection is achieved primarily through encryption, for both the data at rest (for instance, on your home PC or smart phone, which, however, can also be local data of your movements on the Internet) and the data in motion (like your e-mail). The original discussions were conducted mostly by cyber libertarians, who focused on how to expand on personal cryptography and have shadowed the Internet since its earliest days.

Some of these discussion groups fit the definition of anarchistic or hyper-libertarian, but their concerns in the 1990s have proved at least somewhat prophetic. The Cypherpunks were one of the most well known and prolific of such groups, loosely based on an e-mail list that started in 1992. They shared a fervent wish to see the Internet as a tool that would pose the end of government control over individuals. According to them, on its own, the Internet would become subverted by both government and big business and would enslave people through a web of surveillance facilitated by the overtly trusting nature of the Internet's original design. As was stated in their manifesto,

> Privacy is necessary for an open society in the electronic age. . . . We cannot expect governments, corporations, or other large, faceless organizations to grant us privacy. . . . We must defend our own privacy if we expect to have any. . . . Cypherpunks write code. We know that someone has to write software to defend privacy, and . . . we're going to write it.

The Cypherpunks were true to their word. A number of key technical products were developed by members of that community and are still used today; indeed, many of their most powerful ideas became mainstream only in recent years. Most important among these are undoubtedly the PGP (Pretty Good Privacy) encryption standard still widely used today for e-mails and files (at least by people who know how to use it), as well as the Tor network and browser for anonymous Web surfing. Of course, while these tools are often used to protect civil society and human rights workers, they are even more often used to underpin a gray and black Internet economy of informal and often illicit marketplaces.

The development of hidden marketplaces has been greatly assisted by the rise of Bitcoin, the latest and to date by far most successful version of online currencies that has the power to circumvent traditional control mechanisms of the state. Unsurprisingly, the development of such crypto currencies was always a key goal of the Cypherpunks. Bitcoin, which was invented in 2008 by an unknown individual (or group) called Satoshi Nakamoto, has already entered the realm of respectability, and its use will continue to grow. While the price of an individual Bitcoin fluctuates widely, in May 2015 there were over fourteen million Bitcoins in circulation, with a total market value of $3.2 billion. While new Bitcoins are increasingly released to the market (in a fabulously complicated process called "mining" that, suffice it to say, guarantees a stable, albeit decreasing, increase in supply for some years yet), the price is free to fluctuate. No one can say what the price of Bitcoins will be by 2018, let alone 2020. While many speculators would like the price of a single Bitcoin to be $10,000, a total collapse of the market is nearly as likely.

The rise of Bitcoin, the Tor network, and the increased use of encryption on a personal level were massively accelerated by the revelations on the extent of NSA and allies' espionage activities in cyberspace. This is undoubtedly fitting, because the rise of the Cypherpunks and assorted likeminded individuals was triggered by the increasing attempt of the US government (but also other governments, such as in the U.K. and France) to tightly control the use and export of encryption by, among other strategies, continuing to classify encryption as a "munition" of war—a common practice throughout the Cold War. Caught between the demands of business (which increasingly needed encryption, especially in financial services) and those of the intelligence and law enforcement agencies, the government first tried introducing its own standard—DES—in 1975, but two decades later DES was shown to be much too weak and was probably therefore never secure against an organization such as the NSA. But another approach didn't even pretend to be secure against so-called lawful intercept attempts.

The ill-fated introduction in 1994 of the "clipper chip" (a special computer chip that would have been at the heart of the crypto products, such as phones) proved to be the last-gasp attempt of the government to meet both the demands of business and the wishes of the intelligence and law enforcement communities to have access to communications if necessary. It was intended to be installed in telephones (where requested) and famously included a "back door" to allow for "lawful intercept"—meaning that a specific password would allow the FBI or the NSA to gain access to the encrypted communication. This of course presumed that only the lawful entities were able to open these back doors (and, indeed, that they were acting according to the law), rather than cyber criminals or foreign powers—a dubious proposal from the start. The fight against the clipper chip became the rallying call for digital libertarians everywhere, among them the Cypherpunks. In a flurry of lawsuits and technical developments, they fought back: In 1996, the clipper chip was abandoned, and by 2000 the US government had dropped the last vestiges of attempts to control the export of computer code, including for cryptography. The Cypherpunks—whose fight was loudest and most evident—claimed victory, although that victory was to be a temporary one. Indeed, in light of the recent NSA revelations, that victory looks uncertain; what it did was increase the efforts of the NSA (and presumably others) to undermine commercial cryptographic efforts, as well as software per se, and it probably contributed to the existing practice of bulk collection of metadata. For if specific information was not available for targeted collection, the intelligence and law enforcement communities had no other recourse but to collect unspecific mass information and sort it out later.

Indeed, the clipper chip idea—in this case, the idea of government-mandated access to encrypted data—was put back on the agenda in 2014 and aired in the United States in 2015. In particular, the FBI has been adamant that it needed to ensure that it had access to encrypted devices and files if necessary. This time, however, business has taken the lead in turning down the request, and in the spring of 2015 it looked unlikely that the proposals would go through. "Strong encryption is the cornerstone of the modern information economy's security," said an open letter signed in May 2015 by more than 140 tech companies, prominent technologists, and civil society groups. Recent terrorist attacks in France and elsewhere, however, have rekindled a debate around encryption. The outcome of the debate seems much less obvious than before.

Law enforcement (in particular the FBI) has lobbied that Apple and Google not be allowed to create commercial products on smart phones that would effectively be unbreakable by law enforcement. A common example is the iMessage system on iPhones, which has often been claimed to be unbreakable, at least by law enforcement; so, for instance, drug dealers and terrorists would be able to communicate with impunity on this device without worrying that the messages can be intercepted and decrypted. In regular meetings between the Department of Justice and businesses, cases that would have been impossible to solve without this access are often discussed, and examples such as the case of a murdered boy cited by the FBI's director, James Comey, in October 2014 have repeatedly been floated to argue for law enforcement access—arguments that anticipated a 2016 standoff between Apple and the FBI. Others, however, are not so sure that such iMessage encryption is in fact that secure; there have been repeated claims that it can be broken, especially by an organization such as the NSA.

That remains the crux of the issue: the abilities of law enforcement and intelligence are dramatically different. While the police most likely cannot access this data with their own resources, intelligence actors probably can.

The rejection of government back doors will probably have one of perhaps two different results. On the one hand, it is possible that the police and the justice system will work more closely with the intelligence agencies, ask for their assistance, and copy their methods and resources. The limits of this were shown during the height of the powers of the US Patriot Act, which also enabled US law enforcement to be much more casual with tap and trace measures. These increasing spook capabilities, however, can sometimes be better replaced with simple good police work, like traditional personal covert observation. And the old ways still work very well: in a case in Europe involving a suspected online jihadist, the counterterrorism authorities, faced with the problem of cracking a presumably encrypted computer, resorted to the simple expedient of filming the suspect when he was typing in his password. One of the most high-profile takedowns of a cybercrime marketplace, the Silk Road bazaar hosted over Tor, was another such example. Despite all the encryption involved at various stages, the FBI was still able to trace and, in 2013, finally apprehend the suspect behind what was reported as being the greatest illegal marketplace in the history of the Internet, with maybe up to $1.2 billion in revenue for illicit goods ranging from drugs (most common) to contract killing (advertised, but never proved to have been delivered). Despite the proficiency of the founder, the self-named Dread Pirate Roberts, the FBI was able to track him down. And it bypassed the encryption problem by simply grabbing the computer in question while he was logged in.

Those advocating policy responses often concentrate on the laws and processes associated with data protection, which is taken more seriously in Europe than in the United States. Article 8 of the European Convention on Human Rights provides a fairly broad view of privacy and seems designed to prevent unlawful correspondence as well as protect private property. In contrast, the US Supreme Court, in its interpretation of the Fourth Amendment of the Constitution (which protects against unreasonable search and seizure), has expressly concentrated on the "household" (property) and may have even left out all other issues, such as communication. Data privacy (often called "data protection"—a revealing difference) advocates and their organizations in Europe have long histories and are often well-established parts of their civil societies. These social groups have been playing a decisive role in the rise of one of Europe's most interesting political groups—the technophile and quasi-libertarian Pirate Party. The party's position can be easily summarized. "All data leaks," says the founder of Europe's first Pirate Party, the Swede Rick Falkvinge. He argues that the historical experience of Europe, in particular the Holocaust, should provide adequate proof that because no data is ever discarded, eventually that data will be misused—"with mathematical certainty." The Pirates' solution is similar to that of other privacy advocates in Europe: the only way to prevent the misuse of data is to not collect that data.

This is a somewhat drastic solution. As was indicated above, much of the business-to-consumer economy of the Internet depends on this type of data to create a value proposition. Or to put it another way, the ostensibly free services of Google, Facebook, and others are in fact paid for by the data the users voluntarily provide, an idea captured in the rising academic field studying the concept of digital labor. A French report from 2013 even argued that the collection of personal data was equivalent to unpaid labor and therefore had to be taxed as such. Companies like Facebook have different options on how to collect this data: they can track what you do on their services, they can see where you go outside their services, and they can quite literally buy data from data brokers—companies such as Acxiom, whose mission statement boasts of being able to "accurately identify relevant audiences for all of your media campaigns." If they don't earn money by collecting your data, the only other option would be actually charging for the services, leading to a two-tiered data regime where only the rich would have some sort of privacy. According to the writer Evgeny Morozov, "Facebook isn't a charity. The poor will pay by surrendering their data."

Most users of Gmail accept Google's assertion that all matching is done by algorithms without any human intervention. In the words of a Google executive in the early days of Gmail, "Worrying about a computer reading your e-mail is like worrying about your dog seeing you naked." Of course, much of the same can be said about the work of intelligence agencies: it is very unlikely, for instance, that the US intelligence community actually has humans looking at more than 1 percent of the data it collects—including personal e-mails. However, when James Clapper, the director of national intelligence, tried to make this argument in public and was asked if the NSA collects any type of data on millions of Americans, he answered, "No, not knowingly." For him, the difference between the machine collecting the information and a human actually reading it was everything. His answer was widely derided.

The derision is partially understandable. For libertarians such as the Pirate Party, the principle remains that even though the data is currently not being looked at by humans, there is no guarantee that it will not fall into the wrong hands—be they the hands of criminals or spies hacking their way in, companies buying up the information for some shady purpose, or even a government taking a turn down a particularly dark path toward its own citizens.

We have talked about the bones, the nervous system, and the muscles of cyberspace. And indeed this is all that's needed for the body of cyber to operate technically; hence the common representation of cyberspace often talks of three layers, not four. But just as a body without a mind or even a soul would be inert and lifeless even if physically healthy, the Internet needs more than the technical layers if it is to actually exist. It needs human desires and interactions, without which the Internet has no function.

This is the fourth layer of cyberspace, the social layer, which encompasses all types of human interactions facilitated by cyberspace. The very notion of a fourth specific social layer is derived from how the US Cyber Command (USCYBERCOM) has characterized cyberspace. For operational (read: targeting) purposes, the US military describes "the physical network layer, the logical network layer, the cyber-persona layer, and . . . people." This approach is crucial for reminding us to not get too lost in the technical specifics of code and hardware, but rather concentrate on something all hackers know: in the end, all questions about cybersecurity are essentially ones about human beings and human decision making—for good and for ill.

Chapter 2

MIND OVER MATTER

Kevin Mitnick is a hacker of nearly legendary repute. The subject of a number of documentaries, books, and films, he shot to public fame through his 1995 arrest and subsequent five-year incarceration due to a host of computer-related crimes. Mitnick's sentencing was particularly controversial because despite his large-scale hacking of a number of targets, he never seemed to damage the systems he penetrated—for instance, by stealing or manipulating data. But as interesting as the controversy surrounding his sentencing and his subsequent media career following his release were, the most fascinating thing about Mitnick was that he wasn't much of a coder. His technical skills simply weren't that great.

But that didn't mean he wasn't a great hacker. For Mitnick understood what all hackers understand—that the shortest way to your target is through the social layer. Tapping cables on the hardware layer, exploiting vulnerabilities or bugs in the logical layer, or even getting access to files directly in the data layer—all that is just a detour. Because fundamentally

the best hack is to call someone up and get him to give you his password—
or better yet, simply do what you want him to do.

Mitnick was most famous for his so-called social-engineering skills.
This was his ability to call up employees on the phone, pretend to be a colleague or technician, and ask his victims outright to divulge key aspects of
their network, like the unit numbers on their PCs or even their passwords.
In his most recent post-jail iteration as a consultant, Mitnick continues to
do what hundreds of other legitimate security testers offer to do as well: test
a system, and gain access, purely through the power of social engineering.

Getting the basic information needed for social engineering can be a
dirty business; it can require actual Dumpster diving: rummaging through
trash to find tidbits of information that can facilitate the attack, like
hand-scribbled notes, addresses of employers, or even photographs—
anything that will help you get closer to getting or guessing a password. But
often such behavior is not even necessary anymore. At a talk at the DEF
CON 22 hacker meeting in Las Vegas in 2014, Mitnick explained how, in
his legitimate job as security contractor, he was able to exploit the built-in
vulnerability of modern pass cards to do his job of testing a company's
defenses. He might simply be hanging out at the smoking corner in the
parking lot outside his client's building, touting a hidden RFID scanner the
size of a laptop as he chatted with his supposed colleagues. This RFID
scanner was powerful enough to read the building access cards employees
would keep in their suit pockets. This allowed him and his team to copy
the cards and gain access to the supposedly secure building itself. Once
there, he was able to wander the cubicles of the unsuspecting employees
and, where possible, simply observe cubicle dwellers typing in their passwords, potentially assisted by miniature cameras implanted in fake eye-
glasses.

According to a friend, himself a legendary hacker of no less repute but
with ironclad technical abilities, Mitnick's coding skills during his original
hacking spree in the early 1990s were largely negligible. But his ability to
persuade people to hand over their passwords was unsurpassed. When in a

silly mood I mused that Mitnick and I were probably the same level of hacker, my friend retorted, "Yeah, the difference being Kevin has balls of steel." This was not as much a pronouncement on my supposed timidity as a statement of fact: Mitnick's pure obstinacy, his total lack of regard for his personal safety, and his limitless self-belief got him into a multitude of targets, including the bus network of the greater L.A. area, Pacific Bell's voice mail systems, and—allegedly—computers at Motorola, Nokia, Fujitsu, Novell, NEC, Sun Microsystems, the University of Southern California, and California's Department of Motor Vehicles. They also got him caught by the police and sentenced—three times.

Kevin Mitnick's story is emblematic of many key features about conflict in cyberspace. It shows that attacking the body of cyber (the technical layers) is often only a detour to attacking the mind (the human being). It also shows that "cybersecurity" is a wide-ranging term, one that goes beyond the technical and includes the psychological dimension. It illustrates that defense in cyberspace is a difficult proposition and often much harder to execute than offense. And finally, it tells us something about that elusive and highly distortable category: the hacker.

Today, social engineering, as Mitnick practiced it, is more likely to utilize e-mail than voice call. This is the nature of phishing, which is derived from an amalgamation of the terms "phreaker" (an early type of hacker who in the 1980s concentrated on fooling with the phone system) and "fishing." First employed by hackers trawling for AOL e-mail account details in 1996, it involved nothing else than a faked e-mail purporting to be from AOL maintenance, requesting that the e-mailed victims hand over their passwords for testing.

Phishing comes in many forms, the most dangerous of which is spear-phishing—a highly targeted form where it is very difficult to spot that the e-mail is in fact fake. The most dangerous of these attacks will try to get you to open a contaminated attachment (like a PDF) or route you to a compromised Web site where your browser will download the infection for you. The attacks can be quite crude, avoidable for those people who pay a little attention: often the e-mails will be poorly written (or in broken English) and refer to random topics. Also, cunningly hidden links can sometimes be obviously fake Web sites; even though, say, a Bank of America logo may be prominently displayed in the e-mail, if you hover your mouse over the link, you may see that it refers back to a different Web site altogether. Many phishing attacks are therefore neutralized with good cyber hygiene and a little paranoia.

Phishing Web sites are the bastard child of these two attacks: they are often full copies of actual Web sites, such as an e-banking site, and prompt users to give up their core access data. If the e-banking system is sufficiently primitive and lacks features such as two-factor authentication (where, for instance, an SMS on your phone will prompt you with a four-digit code to enter into the Web site for additional security), this is really all the attacker needs to empty your bank account. I was shocked to observe how many e-banking systems in the United States still lack the basic defense measures of two-factor authentication and are therefore easy to compromise.

In fact, phishing e-mails of this kind are often behind large-scale cyber crime, effectively specializing in stealing personal access to e-banking accounts, and other moneymaking schemes, like social-service fraud and identity theft. Of course, popular targets include companies from which to steal credit card records (as in the case of Target in 2013 and Home Depot in 2014) but also commercial cryptography companies. For instance, the large encryption company RSA was hacked around 2011, a breach that subsequently allowed hackers to gain access to US defense suppliers' networks. Such attacks also reveal the complex methods used by multinational gangs of hackers: one was discovered in December 2014 to have installed malicious software on ATMs as early as 2013, then slowly drained bank accounts, stealing over $300 million. Some crimes are a little more complicated. Another gang targeted fake news releases to organize an alleged "massive insider trading ring" based on the stock market, which netted them $100 million before they were apprehended.

By far the most likely result of the subversion of a computer (including the smart phones we carry in our pockets) is that it will be tied together with other computers, similarly compromised, and made into its own computer network. While such a network is most often referred to as a botnet, the second favorite term, "zombie army," is not wrong, either: a large botnet can have hundreds of thousands or even millions of bots, ready to obey the command of their master. The largest botnet to date, most agree, was created in 2008–2009 by the Conficker worm, which infected up to fifteen million computers and enrolled a subset of three million to four million computers in the actual botnet. As large as Conficker was, there have been others that are nearly as large, are of equally unknown provenance, and, like Conficker, have never been completely destroyed. To this day, Conficker's masters and the purpose of the botnet remain a mystery.

Botnets are highly useful for those seeking to perpetrate cyber crime or even engage in state-affiliated cyber espionage. Botnets can be used by hackers for a variety of tasks: they are truly the Swiss army knives of cyberattacks. The most common of these uses—outside spreading malware and setting up even more botnets—is to spread spam. Spam, which has been the vernacular for "unsolicited bulk e-mail" since nearly the beginning of e-mail and increasingly refers to unwanted marketing material, has been a major part of the cyber-crime income stream for over a decade. A noted journalist specializing in cybersecurity, Brian Krebs, dedicated a recent book to uncovering the links between spam operators and Russian organized crime. Spam remains remarkably profitable, generating as much as $1 billion a year, because it can cost as little as $10 to send a million e-mails.

The same botnet that is used for spam can, however, also be used for much more harmful purposes: for attack. The distributed denial of service (DDoS) is the most visible of all cyberattacks, and "loud" is certainly an apt description. Although there are many different subtypes of DDoS attacks (and new ones are being introduced every couple of months), they all have one similarity: the use of a large number of compromised computers to flood or overtax the resources of a single target computer or network, basically "yelling" at it, which can lead to the Web site or the entire network being forced off the global Internet. The consequences are felt not only at the target but in the entire network that it connects to, creating substantial collateral damage in the process or providing cover for more serious cyber intrusions, which then go unnoticed due to the confusion.

DDoS attacks have become a fixture in recent years. In many ways, they represent the ultimate asymmetric attack: a simple botnet-run DDoS can cost as little as $38 an hour to execute while generating a cost of as much as a whopping $40,000 per hour to the defender. Script-kiddies (the term for the least skilled hackers, barely able to use existing attack programs and often minors) are known to use simple tools from the legal penetration-testing world, like the cutely named "Low Orbit Ion Cannon," to join in voluntary botnets and attack political targets. Kids as young as twelve have created botnets and used them to attack their enemies in online gaming clans. Minors, increasingly based in the United States, have discovered DDoS as a great blackmail tool, and indeed blackmail produces a major income stream for DDoS attacks at all levels.

DDoS attacks are certainly political tools as well, much like real-world protests. As ubiquitous as DDoS attacks have become for simple criminal gain, the political DDoS attack has seen a renaissance in recent years. Sophisticated DDoS attacks were also waged against the US financial system at the beginning of 2013, transforming networks of data centers into powerful weapons against online banking sites. These attacks flooded the Web sites with encryption requests, which consume more resources than the simple queries often used in DDoS. The consensus among the cyber community and foreign policy officials alike was that the attacks were of Iranian origin, possibly part of the Iranian response to the US-Israeli "Stuxnet" cyberattack on the Iranian nuclear program. Indeed, the list of possible victims is seemingly endless, and most high-profile institutions (including virtually all major US federal government institutions with a

Web presence) have already been subject to at least one major DDoS attack. In the worst cases, these attacks could potentially rise to the level of a national crisis.

In 2007, the highly networked country of Estonia was effectively forced from the global Internet by a huge (relative to 2007 terms) DDoS attack. The attack was substantial enough that besides government Web sites being forced offline, the efficiency of the media and even the banks was affected as well, with some banks unable to provide ATM or even basic account services. The Estonian government at one point even considered what would need to be done to distribute food to the population if the banking and payment system suffered a total collapse. The perpetrators of the attack were almost certainly in Russia and working together with Russian cyber crime, and many consider it likely that the attack was directly ordered by the Russian intelligence service FSB.

It is difficult to overestimate the importance of the 2007 Estonia cyberattack, which has even been called the world's "Cyber War I." Although the exact direct consequences of the attack are still unknown, its indirect influence has been significant: it played a major role in pushing cybersecurity into the forefront for policy makers. Today, the botnets are different, but the threat is the same, or even larger. With the rise of mobile devices, there has been a corresponding rise in the role of mobile botnets (often based on the Google Android operating system) or those using the burgeoning Internet of Things. The fear of a difficult-to-block massive DDoS attack from such a botnet is real and often constitutes one of the scenarios in major US and European cyber exercises.

Phishing remains one of the most effective means to trick a user to execute a program or divulge information that could allow access, including enslaving a computer to make it part of a botnet. But phishing is far from the only method to initiate an attack. It is also possible to attack a Web site directly and, through it, get hold of user credentials to start the process of burrowing into a network. Once in it, an attacker can secure the "hash": a cryptographic stream, looking like a jumble of symbols, which is how a user password would be stored. After securing the hash, the hacker can utilize some publicly available tools to try to decrypt it with brute force. These methods are not enough for the hardest targets, however. These require true loopholes in logic, vulnerabilities in the code itself, to effect entry into a system.

Attacking through errors in computer code—often called vulnerabilities, or "vulns" in the vernacular—is one of the most advanced forms of cyberattacks, especially of so-called advanced persistent threats (APTs). Also known as "low and slow," APTs represent the acme of traditional hacking, long-access attacks that burrow into a network and move through it silently, potentially for years, before being discovered. All major US attacks reported have been versions of APT attacks, and more often than not these attacks exploit unpatched vulnerabilities in software to get access.

There are always errors in code, at least that code produced by humans. These errors can be as simple as a missing comma or a double space where there should be a single space. As a general rule of thumb, in higher-end commercial programs there is usually an error every 20,000 lines of code or so, although some companies like Apple and Microsoft tend to achieve much higher (more secure) numbers, and others much lower. Still, with the old Windows 7 having 40 million lines of code, there is plenty of room for error. And just to provide a level of comparison, an average car has about 400 million lines of code, while the syphilis bacteria has only 1.2 million lines of code. Software code is therefore already much more complex than some forms of life.

Many advanced cyber campaigns depend on exploiting previously unknown vulns (known as zerodays, meaning that they have been known in the community for zero days when they are first used). The most advanced attacks use several: the Stuxnet attack on Iran included four Microsoft Windows zerodays, two of which remain undisclosed to this day. Zerodays have been called, variously, the "guidance system of a cyberweapon" and, more accurately, the "keys" for sophisticated cyberattacks, allowing as they do the possibility of bypassing traditional safety measures such as access controls and antivirus software. Most advanced cyberattacks will employ at least one or even several of these keys to help penetrate a system, making zerodays "the bullets of cyberwar," as the activist Chris Soghoian once put it.

Unsurprisingly, these zerodays can be bought and sold on a rather juicy market. A groundbreaking article in *Forbes* magazine in 2012 named prices for various zerodays: zerodays in Microsoft Word, Windows, and Firefox were each available for around $100,000. Another criterion influencing the importance of vulnerabilities is whether the bug is deep or shallow: a deep bug is one so ingrained in the code that addressing it will require significant rewriting of a section of code, while a shallow bug is more of a typo that can be easily fixed.

Two major characteristics of this zeroday market are its life expectancy and the presence of non-state actors. For the longevity, one could expect that zerodays once disclosed have a very short life expectancy. Even after being disclosed, however, those vulnerabilities often remain unpatched: a late 2013 report mentioned that the average zeroday remained unpatched for 151 days. This means that most attacks, even most advanced ones, don't actually need "real" zerodays, because even a 151-day vulnerability is often good enough for many targets. Also, as previously mentioned, finding zerodays is rather hard and expensive, and is largely unnecessary for the vast majority of cyber crime–related attacks. That is why non-state actors do not regularly employ them. However, they do find them, as numerous reports have named private companies and individuals who regularly trade on zeroday markets. Some of the companies, such as the French company Vupen but also the US defense contractor Endgame (which says it has long since stopped the practice), function as go-betweens, dealing with the shady underground world that actually sells these zerodays to the highest bidder—state or non-state.

The *Forbes* article unleashed a storm of further inquiry, directed mostly at discovering this supposedly hidden marketplace, which *The Economist* called "the digital arms trade" in 2013. Unsurprisingly, it was only a matter of time before the political space attempted to catch up with this burgeoning reality, and following more heavy media reporting, in 2014, a push started in favor of integrating the zeroday trade into an existing international arms control agreement, the Wassenaar Arrangement. That effort culminated in May 2015 with the first proposal by the United States to restrict the sale and disclosure of zerodays to non-US actors, and to this day there has been a robust discussion between the US government and its industry partners on that topic.

Dan Geer, the former chief information security officer of In-Q-Tel, has suggested one way to destabilize the zeroday market. He proposes that the US government drain the market for zerodays by first buying every single one, then making vulnerability reporting mandatory among companies. While it is not clear how much such a policy would cost, it could arguably be less expensive than continuous efforts to enhance security on the defense side.

Other solutions have to do with the stockpiling of zerodays by governments, and the NSA is widely considered to have the largest arsenal. Indeed, the government introduced a broad exception "for clear national security or law enforcement need" in its general rule of disclosing any major vulnerabilities that it finds. In December 2014, the US government disclosed parts of its VEP (Vulnerability Equities Process), a process by which the intelligence community decides whether it will keep a zeroday or disclose it. Unsurprisingly, there is little trust that the system functions very well.

As harmful as attacking a computer through a code error can be, this is not the only "logic loophole" to exploit. Other options are available as well, including targeting Internet traffic. Two of the most infamous examples of attacking a computer directly through the Internet traffic are the NSA Quantum program and the Chinese Great Cannon, both discussed later. But there are many more. Because few of the Internet's early architects imagined just how important it would become, security was not among their first preoccupations. "It's not that we didn't think about security. We knew that there were untrustworthy people out there, and we thought we could exclude them," said the Internet pioneer David Clark. And yet decades later, no amount of money seems likely to fix the original design shortcomings. It is hard to solve security problems if they have not been addressed at least partly at the design level.

As crucial as the logical layer is for attacks in cyberspace, the physical layer—the hardware—also offers its own avenues of attack. One of the most simplistic ways to overcome security features, such as a firewall, is simply to jump in behind them. The most widely used version of such an attack is the remote media attack, which involves nothing more than enticing unsuspecting users to connect a bit of hardware, usually a USB flash memory stick, but really anything that requires a USB connection or even removable media per se, from a CD-ROM to a computer mouse, to their computers. Unfortunately, humans often need little enticing to insert devices where they do not belong: simple curiosity does the trick.

An attack launched via USB stick in 2008 was, at the time, considered the worst breach in US government systems history. Though it is unclear whether the USB was picked up at a parking lot or bought commercially (and whether this occurred in Afghanistan or, less likely, in Qatar), someone plugged a contaminated USB into a US DoD network, widely presumed to have been the classified SIPRNet. Rapidly, a highly virulent worm known as Agent.btz (nearly certainly Russian) burrowed through the Pentagon networks, requiring a full shutdown of many DoD systems in an attempt to find and remove it. The effort to contain it was called Buckshot Yankee, and it took more than nine months to deal with the worst parts of the infection, an initiative that was formative in getting USCYBERCOM established. However, I also have personal knowledge that at a NATO conference in 2009, the government attendees walked home with a CD-ROM containing mostly unclassified presentations but including a version of Agent.btz hidden in the file structure. The nature of the attack indicated that possibly the worm had copied itself onto an eastern European host's network and then installed itself on the CD-ROM, just in time to be distributed to NATO's friends and allies. It is even possible, however, that the CD-ROMs used by the host to burn the data were already compromised when they were purchased—intercepted and infected someplace between the manufacturer and the consumer. The spread of Agent.btz to European government systems also helped concentrate minds in these countries and played an important role in getting these countries' governments to take government cybersecurity more seriously.

The supply chain is rife with opportunities for exploitation. Obviously enough, if USB sticks and CD-ROMs can be contaminated with malicious code and smuggled past the Internet defenses, then the same applies for actual hardware components themselves, including routers and telecommunications equipment as well as keyboards and even mice. Virtually every part of a computer or the hardware installed in a network can theoretically be tampered with, with drastic results.

The idea itself is far from new. In 1984, the US embassy in Moscow discovered that at least sixteen of its IBM Selectric typewriters had been tampered with such that they sent—in live communication over radio to a listening post down the road—every single keystroke performed on them, giving the KGB real-time access to every letter written on these machines. According to the legend, the United States had indications for years that something like this was happening, but it took the intervention of a European spy agency for the US to actually believe it. As is true today, no one likes to believe that they are completely exposed.

Since then, things have of course become much worse. In 2015, an attack that was known to be possible but had never been demonstrated affected Cisco routers; the attack, dubbed SYNful Knock, has hit almost twenty countries. The Cisco routers received an implant that was then activated remotely by an unusual pattern of network packets. In this case, the attackers did not even need a vulnerability: the back door was introduced by "taking advantage of routers that use passwords that are factory default or are somehow otherwise known" and could thereafter be activated at will. But often enough, attackers—nearly all government in this case—will physically tamper with hardware, even down to the level of chips. Such supply chain attacks have prompted countries to create programs to develop trust in certain lines of hardware.

The attacks described above range through the layers of cyberspace, from the social layer, to the data layer, to the logic layer, and to the physical layer. Sometimes they are the reserve only of the most sophisticated actor, but in the majority of cases the attacks can be accomplished with a minimum of skill, drawing on the many legitimate (and often free) pieces of software repurposed from security testing. And as the very example of Kevin Mitnick shows, all of these technical tricks can effectively be overcome with specific activities at the social layer. A common technical view is to confuse the technical hacking with cyberspace operations overall, but this presupposes that violating the confidentiality, integrity, or availability of data is the only goal of an attacker. What civilians often fail to appreciate, however, is that militaries and intelligence bodies do not necessarily want only to steal or manipulate data; they want to influence information and change opinions and perceptions. Viewed through this sinister lens, electronic or digital hacking is, in itself, simply a means to an end. While understanding how a technical hack is undertaken is an important step, it does not on its own answer the most fundamental question: why this is done in the first place. The difficulty in understanding this crucial difference is the difference between technical information security and government cybersecurity.

PART II

Chapter 3

EVERYONE CAN BE A GOD

The very term "cybersecurity" is nothing if not controversial. Much like the word "cyberspace," until recently it was not widely accepted as a technical term. Unlike the term "cyberspace," however, it still manages to inflame some from the technical community who think it is essentially meaningless: a vacuous term for the Internet and information and communications technology (ICT) system environments and a malicious sales pitch for government and security industry actors trying to advance an agenda. Even today, hardly a technical conference goes by without one ingratiating crowd-pleasing dig at the word "cybersecurity." The preferred term that most nongovernmental cybersecurity professionals work under is "information security" (often abridged to "InfoSec"), a heavily defined technical term of art specified by the international standards body ISO—a lodestone for engineers of all stripes.

Originally, the term "InfoSec" covered the protection of data regardless of the medium—be it paper or computer. In particular, InfoSec professionals concentrate on three primary attributes necessary in protection, captured in the so-called C-I-A principles first defined by ISO, the most important qualities that need to be protected of any information: the *confidentiality*, the *integrity*, and the *availability* of it. All tasks related to Info-Sec, ranging from the patching of software to the installing of physical locks on doors and providing firefighting equipment, are subordinate to these three protection principles.

Cybersecurity, no matter how hated, does exist, even if it continues to resist a single definition. Countries including the U.K., Germany, and the Netherlands have provided specific definitions that do not completely overlap; in a manual I edited for NATO, we identified no fewer than a dozen definitions across different governments. The US government in particular has proved remarkably reluctant to define the term "cybersecurity," despite using it for well over a decade in a number of high-level documents and appropriating billions of dollars in its name.

One reason for the reluctance to spell out what cybersecurity is, and where it diverges from information security, can be found in a recent statement by Gartner, a leading consultancy on information technology that is heavily staffed by former government employees:

> Use of the term "cybersecurity" as a synonym for information security or IT security confuses customers and security practitioners, and obscures critical differences between these disciplines. . . . Cybersecurity encompasses a broad range of practices, tools and concepts related closely to those of information and operational technology security. *Cybersecurity is distinctive in its inclusion of the offensive use of information technology to attack adversaries* [emphasis added].

The key here is that cybersecurity practitioners focus on not only defensive measures but also offensive ones. InfoSec professionals (who are nearly always non-state) may all be defenders, but cybersecurity professionals (who are often government affiliated) are expected to be proficient on both the attack and the defense. Indeed, one of the intractable challenges of cybersecurity is the tension between offense and defense, especially given that the reality of what exactly we are defending and attacking—not only code, but also human behavior—is often murky.

The question of balance between offense and defense is a ubiquitous one in conversations about cybersecurity today. Defense looks at patching systems, tracking down strange behavior on the network, analyzing unusual bits of code found in the system, and sharing those bits of code with other defenders. Offense looks to overcome all of these measures and have an impact on information—either violate the confidentiality, integrity, or availability of data, or even attempt to change human behavior by controlling information.

There is little doubt which side scores the most points. Chris Inglis, the former deputy director of the NSA, said that if we were to score cyber the way we score soccer, the tally would be 462–456 twenty minutes into the game— that is to say, all offense, with practically no one defending the goal. What's more, nearly anyone can be proficient on the offensive. Defending data in cyberspace can be extremely hard—it is first and foremost an organizational challenge—whereas attacking is often quite literally child's play. "In some hacking circles, 15 would be considered middle-aged," writes Misha Glenny in the *New York Times.* Hackers as young as thirteen years old have been arrested; the average age of most defenders is at least twice that. Similarly, that a semi-sophisticated distributed denial-of-service attack can cost the attacker as little as $40 (or even much less) and cost the defender $40,000 or even more to address reveals the asymmetry of offense versus defense. Unsurprisingly, this ratio is never replicated in governmental budgets, not even close. While all larger national cyber powers spend much more on defense than on offense, the ratios are much, much smaller than the 1:1,000 ratio stated previously, nearly certainly a factor of ten or even a hundred times smaller. For all its cost, cybersecurity (in particular its defensive-only InfoSec component) is heavily underfunded everywhere.

The total pilfering of the US government's Office of Personnel Management (OPM), discovered in June 2015, is a case in point. OPM not only held basic data on 21.5 million individuals; it also held most of the documents associated with the over 5 million individuals requesting a government secret or top secret clearance. These documents, which included very detailed biographical information as well as information on friends and associates, were undoubtedly a gold mine for the likely Chinese hackers, and it was apparently laughably easy to achieve root access within OPM. The Federal Information Security Management Act Audit reports dating back to 2007 revealed "a material weakness in controls over the development and maintenance of OPM's IT security policies," and those concerns only grew in subsequent reports from 2008 to 2014, which were probably very interesting reads for the attackers. OPM did little to address these concerns.

OPM is not the only famous target taken down as a result of seemingly poor security. In fact, almost every serious cyberattack that makes the news invites a nearly universal response from expert observers that an improved security apparatus could have prevented the breach. There are two problems with this statement as it stands: first, it implies that any given security failure is primarily technical in nature and that security could easily be addressed with installation of the right hardware and software; second, it implies that there are many targets that haven't been breached. Both assumptions are largely wrong.

While there exists a wide array of technical security products to improve cybersecurity, most commentators point out that the failure is nearly always organizational. An organization may buy the best packaged cybersecurity solution money can provide, but if the individual users of the institution do not engage in the most basic best security practices—such as not opening every e-mail attachment, not following every dubious Web link, and not using the most basic of default passwords for their accounts and e-mail—then many of the most basic attacks will work. This may not be enough, though, because some of the most dramatic breaches confirmed in public have occurred even among companies or organizations with good—or even great—security.

The key phrase here is "confirmed in public." The vast majority of cyberattacks never become public knowledge. They are kept secret, both by corporations and by governments: the former because of the economic consequences of reputational damage and legal ramifications, the latter because of the political costs of reputational damage and political escalation following finger-pointing. Even worse, in most cases you simply won't know that you have been breached—and those that may know, like intelligence agencies, can't tell you. "How many of the Fortune 500 are hacked right now?" an interviewer asked the famed cyber defender Mikko Hypponen. "The answer: 500." An informal poll among friends and colleagues within the InfoSec community (mostly non-state and technical) indicated a belief that only about one-quarter of the major breaches actually make it to the public domain and are reported on in the media. But this was beaten by another straw poll I did among government cybersecurity people: they presumed that maybe only one-tenth of the serious cyberattacks have been reported on in the public domain. I tend to agree more with the second assessment.

If the first truism of cybersecurity is that the majority of attacks could be avoided by taking basic defense measures, the second truism is that a dedicated attacker will always get in, no matter what—this also applies to hacks such as OPM, as described previously. This is actually not a contradiction: while there is no such thing as absolute security, there is such a thing as minimum security; the time wasted responding to avoidable incidents prevents organizations from anticipating and dealing with serious threats. If police detective efforts are tied up pursuing domestic burglary effectively encouraged by open windows, then the more serious cases—in which the safe was cracked and the crown jewels stolen—will not get the attention they need. Also, discovering a breach early will usually help limit the damage—in most cases, getting the "crown jewels" of data requires the thief to cart off a lot of junk as well, thus offering the opportunity to stop one in his tracks.

The defense side is far from powerless. At an institutional level, on the front line of the defenders are the actual "first responders," the cyber fire-fighters. Organized in small teams commonly called computer emergency response teams (CERTs or CSIRTs), they are the basis for defending against cyber threats in all types of organizations, from a small company to a government. CERTs are an omnipresent feature that is replicated throughout virtually all larger modern institutions and can range from a single individual working a normal workweek to dozens or even hundreds of specialists working 24/7 within secure facilities. While the number of information security professionals working on the front lines of cybersecurity is unknown, it probably is minuscule given the amount of people otherwise employed in IT-related security tasks.

These CERTs and similar defenders are supported by two groups of actors. The private sector plays an obvious key role: CERTs and day-to-day institutional defenders employ a large range of security products and solutions, from specific hardware to secure communications to prevent illegitimate access, to hardware designed to inspect packets in their networks. Corporations also provide large security teams to help shore up their clients' online defenses; for instance, a subsidiary of the Cisco hardware producer Talos has over six hundred specialists hidden away in undisclosed locations—unknown to even Cisco's senior management. Cybersecurity is truly big business: according to Gartner research, the total worldwide spending on cybersecurity amounted to $77 billion in 2015. Many or most of these products undoubtedly help, but their success depends on the level of security the company in question seeks to achieve. While they may be useful in dealing with most cyberattacks, at the very top level of threat they are only marginally useful, because a committed and well-resourced attacker will just continue trying until he is successful. An acquaintance at the NSA responsible for purchasing security solutions once said, "If you have a security product, I'll buy it. I buy all of them. But it won't work. None of them do."

As significant as the commercial sector is to the defense, there is a larger group that plays at least as important a role for the defenders. This is the InfoSec community itself, or just "the community." For outsiders, it is difficult to imagine that a system based on the voluntary investment of time and resources to help sometimes completely unknown recipients can be anything but a short-term fix. While this in fact may have a little bit of truth in it, these outsiders usually struggle to understand how much the entire Internet relies on moral actors, and how much those moral actors have already contributed to saving the Internet. The legendary story of how Dan Kaminsky did exactly that is an example of the power of that community.

In 2008, Kaminsky, then a perfectly average thirty-year-old security researcher, was sitting in his bed, remembering a trick he pulled off successfully to get free Wi-Fi at a Starbucks by using an apparent flaw in the DNS protocol. He wondered if there were more to this flaw than simply allowing him to slip by the Starbucks pay page. What he then unearthed was a truly fatal flaw in that fundamental protocol of the Internet.

What Kaminsky discovered was that under certain conditions, if you provided the DNS server with the location of a fake page in someone else's domain, the DNS server would start trusting you about other pages in that same domain, regardless of who you were and whether you were affiliated with the owner of the domain at all. He could basically send all the traffic from any Web site anywhere in the world to himself. And, even worse, his realization wasn't merely theoretical; it actually worked when he tried it. This meant he could effectively impersonate any Web site in the world—from Bank of America to the Department of Defense—and therefore steal the log-in data of those trying to access their networks through the Web site. Instead of stealing money from all the bank accounts in the world, reading the e-mail of anyone he wanted, or getting information about almost anything he was curious about, Kaminsky decided to e-mail Paul Vixie, one of the fathers of the DNS, who stepped out of a conference in San Jose to call him. Three minutes later, Vixie told Kaminsky to "never, ever repeat what [he] just told [him] over a cell phone." From that point, they talked either on landlines, in person, or via heavily encrypted e-mail, and set out to find a solution before the problem became public.

A few days later, on March 31, 2008, sixteen of the world's DNS experts were sitting in Building Nine of the Microsoft Campus at 10:00 a.m. without any idea of the purpose of the meeting when Kaminsky walked in and started talking about the fatal flaw he had discovered in the DNS. He announced that he would disclose it at Black Hat in Las Vegas on August 6— so they had better find a fix by then. The response from the assembly of sixteen experts is best captured by this quotation from the Internet entrepreneur and DNS expert David Ulevitch: "This is an amazingly catastrophic attack." A plan was designed: the sixteen experts were to go back to their companies and rely on a small team of trusted engineers sworn to secrecy to change the basic functioning of their DNS servers to eliminate that vulnerability without any usual testing or feedback outside the group. Then they were all to release the patches at the same time on July 8 and try to persuade all their clients to apply the patches before hackers could understand them and exploit the vulnerability that Kaminsky had discovered. Once patched, a system would stand a 1-in-4-billion risk of getting hacked— an unpatched one would have a 1-in-65,536 risk. The crux was that they couldn't even disclose why they had to apply the patches, because this would immediately expose the flaw to a wider audience and risk breaking the Internet. Finally, on August 6, Kaminsky arrived in Las Vegas and exposed the DNS flaw to the world, and everyone realized that he and the sixteen others had been right all along. In the meantime, the wide-ranging patching of the systems initiated a month earlier had largely closed this avenue of attack before its widespread publicity.

Today, Kaminsky's role in the community has been officially honored with some of its highest accolades. It is, however, a valid question to ask whether the next Kaminsky will act in the same spirit of altruism or auction off his discovery to the highest bidder—or even use it for nefarious purposes himself. There is no doubt that whereas previously many stunning discoveries in cybersecurity would have been shared within the community for little more than accolades and backslapping, in recent years money has become a much larger issue. There is simply too much money to be made selling your discovery, rather than engaging in philanthropy.

While the InfoSec community does have strong links to the private sector, the exchanges are truly community based, even if they are sometimes packaged and resold by the private sector as part of their products. Membership in this community is awarded on a personal basis, even for individuals working in large companies, such as Dell and IBM, and this means that in some cases a single engineer leaving a company may mean the loss of a very valuable intelligence feed.

There are many different ways to describe what the InfoSec community actually does. Some, like the nonprofit Team Cymru, concentrate on collating qualitative analysis on incidents and reports. Others, like the (equally nonprofit) Shadowserver Foundation, provide real data on varying degrees of "cyber badness," such as indications of which networks or IP addresses are being used by criminals. Some, such as the Spamhaus Project, go even further and actively blacklist parts of the Internet where there is "badness" (which can be criminal or state, it doesn't matter) where malicious behavior, such as spam, is coming from, which in turn is then blocked by many of the upstream Internet providers and thus isolated from the average Internet user. Without this amount of community activity, the everyday Internet would be a much, much more dangerous place; indeed it would probably be unlivable. And none of these organizations are affiliated with any government.

Obviously, this type of activity can greatly irritate cyber criminals and other types of attackers. When, in 2011, Spamhaus blacklisted the IP ranges of CyberBunker, a notorious hoster of dodgy content, its Dutch owner (who, among other things, supposedly boasted his very own Ecstasy laboratory) orchestrated a huge DDoS cyberattack on Spamhaus in revenge. At one point, this attack generated so much traffic that it constituted most of the Internet traffic in western Europe.

Organizations such as Spamhaus, Shadowserver, and Team Cymru are but one aspect of the InfoSec community. Much less visible but in many ways at least as influential are the informal exchanges among security professionals: highly vetted groups using encrypted communications. Some of these groups are visible, like NANOG (the North American Network Operators Group), whose membership is responsible for much of the routing of Internet traffic in the United States and who can basically reroute, and therefore block, Internet traffic at will.

Other groups are considered so secret that to talk about them can constitute a violation and grounds for expulsion. While this is slowly changing, many of these groups resolutely sail under the radar. If a member of a group becomes privy to restricted information, then he cannot share it with his employer, either; violations of this rule have led to the expulsion of entire companies, including noted hardware manufacturers, from these coveted communities.

The information on these lists is usually intelligence in its simplest form: what kind of suspect IP is being used for what purpose and how to counter it and, more often, requests for assistance in dealing with particularly mysterious incidents. These groups are therefore largely enablers, ones that by necessity sail in the shadows. Not only does the intelligence exchanged need to be kept from evildoers (cyber criminals, spies, or affiliates), but from nearly every organization's own legal department: some of the defenders' (and therefore employees') behavior is potentially legally actionable. However, those informal and secret networks are crucial even to the multibillion-dollar companies seeking to protect themselves, as it provides a venue for the defenders to engage in time-critical information sharing without the very arduous processes of clearing these exchanges through legal channels—and can protect them from facing indictment over liability and data protection issues if things go wrong.

Some of these informal groups of cyber defenders are highly paid consultants working for free, sometimes university researchers or experts in IT security companies, but also individuals in many of the world's largest corporations whose efforts to safeguard their companies are critical but remain unknown to their own boards. Unsurprisingly, the telecom and financial industries have some of the most proficient defenders on the payroll. An informal group of experts known as NSP-SEC was one of the very few organizations to send technical individuals to assist Estonia in 2007 when government assistance from other NATO members was, in comparison, late and ineffective. This lack of government efficiency wasn't a total surprise. When the mysterious Conficker botnet made a stunning international debut in November 2008, professionals all over the world formed the Conficker Working Group (CWG). CWG, assisted by industry leaders such as Microsoft, led the fight against the botnet, crippling it if not totally removing it from existence. Government contribution was minimal and described by a member of the CWG as "zero involvement, zero activity and zero knowledge."

These types of secure lists and informal groups are the bedrock of information security. There is a large debate occurring over how much of this effort can be aligned with, supported by, or even subordinated to government efforts. In the United States, for instance, there have been no fewer than four attempts by the White House to provide some kind of legal context for this kind of information sharing. Most failed due to resistance in Congress (most likely due to its poor relationship with the Obama White House), and President Obama responded by introducing aspects of these bills as presidential executive orders (EOs). One of these, the 2015 EO 13691, defined a new body called Information Sharing and Analysis Organizations (ISAOs). These ISAOs effectively include many of the informal and ad hoc networks described earlier, whose work was considered essential and who were thus to be brought into a more structured dialogue with government officials. While the details of the EO left this a somewhat unworkable proposition, the general notion was smart. It was a clear indication that government had accepted that some of the strongest defensive networks were going to remain in the shadows, and therefore decided to support and not hinder their work. This was a very big conceptual step for any government to take, but many of the networks did not respond with the same enthusiasm. For most of these informal networks are ideologically committed to the defense of the Web, which largely means defending against *all* attacks. Some of their members believed that the government writ large (both civilian and especially military) simply could not be trusted to be an impartial pursuer of "badness" on the Internet. The only "badness" any state is likely to pursue is by definition not its own.

This is the core issue for most true-blue members of the InfoSec community. For them, all offensive action, no matter what the intent and no matter who is behind it, is essentially bad, especially if it goes against the Internet itself—the "road" of the information highway that needs to be protected at all costs. One of those dedicated defenders, the Finn Mikko Hypponen, put the view most succinctly at a 2011 presentation at the NATO Cooperative Cyber Defence Centre: "In the end, it's all just about good versus evil." And, for this community, every government is inherently capable of doing evil.

The line between offense and defense can be a fuzzy one: Some of the best defenders are those who have developed the best attack skills, often working as so-called penetration testers of legal hackers to test their own systems, and maybe others' as well. Likewise, some of the best attackers (if not the very best, who are above such things) often depend on inside information on defense practices, especially being able to study cyber "weapons" and adversary attack infrastructures, to better improve their own operations. At a lower level of national cyber capability, it can amount to the ability to "throw back" a cyber weapon that was thrown at you, like a spear. Iran, for example, is suspected to be behind a massive 2012 cyber-attack on Saudi Arabia entitled "Shamoon," where tens of thousands of workstations were wiped using a direct copy of an alleged US attack module that was itself part of the "Flame" malware attack on Iranian actors discovered in 2011 (more of which will be discussed later).

The benefits of offensive capabilities come at a cost to your defensive ability—Iran's connections to the world's InfoSec community is fairly limited, to name one example. Western governments are more circumspect in putting both defensive and offensive capabilities together. While, for instance, a dedicated military cyber unit may find it useful to have both attack and defense jobs under one roof, it would be disastrous if an actual computer emergency response team (CERT) were perceived to have an attack role besides its defensive role. Customers and partners of the CERT would have to take into consideration the possibility that the CERT was not only interested in helping them but may have an interest in attacking—and maybe even attacking its own customer. This is not too different from a doctor actually being a killer (or executioner) on the side; the two missions are so antithetical to each other that you probably would not be comfortable with the same person having both jobs. Especially when the doctor treating you is also learning how to most effectively cause you harm.

In 2012, General Keith Alexander, then double-hatted head of the NSA and US Cyber Command, spoke at DEF CON, the legendary Las Vegas hacker convention. The audience was more friendly than expected; after all, this was a group that from its inception had hosted a SPOT THE FED T-shirt competition to root out suspected "spies." Alexander's speech, titled "Shared Values, Shared Response," was billed as an appeal to the InfoSec hacker community to cooperate on defense—more precisely, cybersecurity. On the surface of it, and in the pre-Snowden disclosure world in which it was delivered, this made sense, because the hacker community is certainly not all about the offensive. Indeed, the hacker—an individual who features prominently in every discussion of cybersecurity—is one of the few points of overlap between defensive and offensive cyber. Often used and misused, the term "hacker" is probably ripe for a closer examination.

The dominant definition—hackers are people who penetrate computer systems—is certainly not wrong. But it does fall short of an understanding of hackers' motivations: Why would anyone be so fanatically keen on penetrating a network that he would forgo sleep and food for days without the promise of financial gain? It is indeed difficult for the wider public to understand that the term "hacker" is value-free and can include all kinds of motivations, as well as different kinds of skill sets and skill levels. Similarly, it's easy to divide hackers into the good guys and the bad guys. On this basis, hackers are occasionally still classified by how law abiding they are— from nefarious "black hat" operators to upright "white hat" stalwarts to somewhat shifty "gray hats" lurking somewhere in the middle.

While such labels have their utility, more often than not they are misleading. In particular, it is important to account for perspective—for example, a Russian government–tolerated cyber criminal may well be a "white hat" in his own country and a "black hat" abroad. In short, it would be incorrect to narrow hacking down to one single gradient of activity, marked by an adherence to national legal codes. It is more helpful to segment hackers along behavioral types, regardless of political motivation. One of the least controversial segmentations would be to give those hackers three possible guises: the "pranksters," the "explorers," and the "builders." In the most extreme cases, literal sociopaths, spies, and saviors.

For some, hacking is nothing more than the wish to understand—and often enough build or fix or improve—a system. These hackers are most often simply intrigued by a system with which they have an innate wish to "play" (and their definition of "system" can extend well beyond that of a computer network to include sociopolitical systems as well). But some hackers really are just looking to have some fun—looking for the "lolz," in common expression. The definition of the hacker as a prankster has been considered useful outside the world of computer security as well. For instance, one of the most legendary "hacks" occurred during a 1982 Harvard-Yale football game. At one point, when the Harvard team seemed to be on the verge of winning, a large plastic ball started to inflate on the Harvard forty-yard line—with the letters "MIT" emblazoned on it. It reached a diameter of six feet or so before exploding. To this day, MIT, from the president on down, takes a lot of pride in this and similar pranks—pranks that are essentially harmless and sophomoric. Many of the original computer hackers were individuals who in the 1970s liked to play with the US telephone system. Those "phreakers" (the word is a combination of the words "phone" and "freak") explored the vulnerabilities of the phone system with automatic switches and especially its system of tone dialing, eventually moving to build and sell their discoveries as what was called "blue boxes"—in some ways the first hacking kits, but made physical. Many young engineers monetized this hobby among their friends; building and selling blue boxes was one of the first entrepreneurial activities of the future founders of Apple Computer, Steve Wozniak and Steve Jobs. It was also the start point for Kevin Mitnick and his original hacking spree.

In computer terms, pranksters are, in their most harmless variety, tied to expressions of skill, and they often do nothing more than boast. One of the very first PC viruses, Brain, was created in 1986 by two Pakistani brothers who probably wanted only to draw attention to themselves and their programming skills (which might be why they helpfully left their names and phone numbers in the code). There are, however, many more dramatic examples of this urge to show off. One example was the worm (a virus that concentrates on spreading) ILOVEYOU. On a single day—May 4, 2000—ILOVEYOU spread to millions of computers worldwide, eventually reaching over fifty million infections, something like 10 percent of all PCs connected to the Internet at the time. Unlike Brain, ILOVEYOU was not harmless, because it overwrote some files in its desire to spread more quickly. In the end, the "love bug" caused anywhere between $5 billion and $15 billion worth of damage. The Philippine programmer responsible was said to have done it largely to show that it could be done—and potentially impress recruiters for a software job. ILOVEYOU is not alone in functioning like some sort of deranged art portfolio for sociopathic hackers. Many of the world's most impressive early worms—BLASTER, CODE RED, NIMDA—were written by hobbyists, often trying out new concepts, sometimes costing the world economy hundreds of millions of dollars along the way.

The "explorers" are another variant of hacker: they work for themselves or, if paid, on behalf of others to infiltrate systems and discover something. The term "explorer" is certainly evocative, with positive connotations. It would, however, be more accurate to call them "exploiters" or, in marketing terms, "actualizers": they want to get things done. Unlike the pranksters, explorers are hacking for curiosity or, more common these days, for profit or political gains. They want one thing above all else: get in where they do not belong and not be seen in the process. They want to acquire information: credit card numbers, e-mail correspondence, intellectual property, or the truth behind government UFO programs. One of the more publicized attacks on the US Department of Defense was committed by the Scottish hacker Gary McKinnon, who in 2001 and 2002 allegedly penetrated numerous DoD computers in his search for evidence of "a UFO cover-up." At one point, he posted a helpful note on the DoD systems: "Your security is crap." Many other hackers have spent most of their time testing and exploiting systems for no other reason than to see if they could get in and sometimes even tried to fix the system once they were there. When he breaks the law when illegally accessing a system, this type of hacker is the one most likely to plausibly state, "But I was helping you!" On the other hand, many other hackers seeking to "explore" a system will have mischief on their minds, either for political purposes (as a spy) or for criminal gain.

The most sophisticated and capable hackers are usually not very interested in hacking, but rather like to build the code to support this type of activity—often for beneficial (that is, testing) purposes. These builders are the closest to the original engineers who constructed the Internet and very much reflect the basic engineering mind-set of "build, and be helpful." Often highly trained researchers, they have the strongest technical skills and are usually specialized only in one specific programming language or area. This is not to say that all of these hackers will work in regular, network-defense jobs; they are equally likely to be found within intelligence agencies, cyber-crime syndicates, or universities and small companies. They are not even necessarily more on the offensive or the defensive side of cyber. These individuals are responsible for the design of the most highly advanced hacker tools. In fact, there is often very little difference between security testing tools and so-called cyber weapons; like a hammer, it depends purely on what you want to do with it.

Take, as an example, the Metasploit tool, developed in 2003 by the researcher H. D. Moore to provide an easy way to combine the exploitation of a vulnerability in code (for instance, in an operating system, which is often needed to get into a system or network) with an actual payload (the piece of software that actually does something, like track all your keystrokes). It allows a less skilled attacker to plug known vulnerabilities into a helpful user interface and then simply run a program (like a virus) in the breach it creates. Metasploit was always intended for non-malicious purposes, like simply testing a system, but it has also had an unbeatable history as the go-to tool for cyber-crime authors, as well as less sophisticated government cyber spies. Indeed, even the FBI used a version of Metasploit to uncloak child pornography traders using the anonymization software Tor. There are many more hacking tools like Metasploit, often provided for free by these "builders," used for either beneficial or nefarious purposes.

This admittedly somewhat futile segmentation of the term "hackers" has one point: to illustrate that in all cases the term itself is value-free. It encompasses both malicious and non-malicious behavior, as well as many different types and levels of skill. Above all, it is about skill, which can range from true mathematical brilliance to breathtaking interpersonal charm to something most people would consider either pure stubbornness or obstinacy. The common element is simply that all these types of hackers see computers as a tool of transformational capability, able to empower those who can use them to seemingly godlike effect. In the best case, these capabilities also connect to concepts of ethics and personal responsibility.

Steven Levy, whose 1984 book, *Hackers: Heroes of the Computer Revolution,* has been credited as being the single greatest inspiration to legendary hackers like Jeff Moss and many others, tried to define the hacker ethic in concrete detail. For him, this included commitments to sharing, openness, decentralization, free access to information, and overall world improvement. It was a worthy attempt, but there remains too much variance among the pranksters, the explorers, and the builders to make a single definition useful. The only true sentiment all hackers would likely share was expressed by the onetime editor of *Popular Electronics* Les Solomon: "The computer is a magic box. It's a tool. It's an art form. . . . It's where everyone can be a god."

Chapter 4

RULING THE DOMAIN

f the Net does have a god," wrote *The Economist* in 1997, "then he is probably Jon Postel." In 1999, this god seemed to have second thoughts.

A resplendently bearded workaholic, Jon Postel was the director of computer network research at the University of Southern California. He was also one of a few true fathers of the Internet: along with Vint Cerf and Steve Crocker and a handful of others, he had played a decisive role in designing the Internet as it is today by helping to define its core protocols. In January 1998, the Internet was about to embark on a new age. The core of the domain name system, the critical naming and addressing function that is the foundation of the Internet, was about to get a new institutional home, courtesy of the US government. All changes to the root zone file—the file that stood at the very top of the DNS hierarchy—would flow from this new institution, in consultation with the US government. The file would then be replicated by the twelve root server organizations (which run the thirteen root servers).

For reasons that are not completely clear, on January 28, 1998, Postel sent an e-mail to eight of the twelve operators of root servers, asking them to recognize his own server as the master root server. Any changes he would make would be replicated across the network, including, for instance, deleting the .com domain or any domain he wished. Effectively, he was asking the others to accept him as the center of the Internet. All of the eight operators, including those in the U.K., Sweden, and Japan, immediately agreed, and just like that Postel had managed to hijack the Internet. With Postel in control of the root, there were effectively two Internets that day: the one managed by the eight root servers recognizing Postel's as the authoritative one, and the second managed by the remaining servers—mostly US government military and run out of the old master server managed by the US government in Virginia. Computers in the two networks would have asked two different roots to find their way on the Internet, and in theory those two roots could have yielded different results. Postel, however, was not interested in breaking the Internet, and when the White House called, pointing out to Postel and his supervisor at USC that they would be liable if this went on, Postel ended what he described as a "test" and gave the authority back to the government's root server within one week.

No one knows for sure why Postel did what he did that day, because he passed away suddenly some months later. He was due to become the head of the new organization, the artfully named Internet Corporation for Assigned Names and Numbers (ICANN), that was to help manage that very same root zone file, and was certainly not in danger of losing his influence. Instead, according to some who knew him, Postel was simply making a point to the US government: Though the government had played a crucial role in helping the Internet be born, it now belonged to the Internet community. And what the community gave, it could also take away.

The Internet is not merely a technical marvel. It is also a marvel of policy making and management: the institutions and processes developed to govern it are as novel as the Internet itself.

No one person or organization owns or runs the Internet. Rather, a miniature galaxy of different organizations and individuals—ranging from staid governmental bureaucracies to sharp-elbowed corporate warriors and sandal-wearing civil society researchers and advocates—all play various roles, often coexisting more than cooperating in an uneasy symbiotic community that maintains and builds the Internet. The roles that they fill are as different as the organizations themselves, and indeed some of the roles are obvious and well acknowledged (like the writing of computer protocols), while others are at best contentious (like the roles of some governments in trying to regulate certain aspects of the Internet).

When considering the question "who runs the Internet?" everyone sees something slightly different. Old-style engineers may point to the giant data centers and millions of miles of fiber-optic cables that connect them and see the commercial agreements that manage their use and interconnection as core to the running of the Internet. Technologists may list the importance of the computer protocols like DNS and BGP (used to route traffic) and emphasize the processes—most of them civil society and virtually all of them non-state—that give rise to the nervous system of the Internet. Others may actually concentrate on the naming and numbering functions of the Internet, without which most Internet traffic would not be possible. All these viewpoints have various institutions associated with them—ranging from brick-and-mortar legal entities with hundreds of employees to informal but decades-old meeting traditions aimed at getting business done. Together, these institutions constitute what is known as Internet governance.

The term "Internet governance" is generally used to describe the management of the world's Internet resources—the resources that effectively power cyberspace. Unlike, for instance, the oceans or outer space, cyberspace is a completely man-made domain; therefore, the resources—and even the physical laws—of cyberspace are man-made as well. While the oceans may have resources, such as fish stocks, that can be the object of human actions, their laws—like the trade winds or the actions of oceanic tides—are beyond the control of humans and at best can be only passively exploited, as the winds are exploited by sailing vessels. In cyberspace, resources like Internet protocol numbers may be finite, but if they are, it is only because we decided so. The laws of cyberspace may seem immutable, but this is an illusion. These resources, and the laws, can and do change, depending on developments in the larger domain and the needs and influence of various actors. Unlike on the sea or in space, it is we who decide what cyberspace is and how it functions.

The early Internet was funded by government money but conceived of and designed by individual researchers and engineers who followed their own agenda. Today, the part of the Internet that the vast majority of users see and interact with is the World Wide Web. It was given its name (and effectively invented) by the British software engineer Tim Berners-Lee, who between 1989 and 1990 developed one of the key protocols for navigating the Internet when he was working at the European Organization for Nuclear Research (CERN). What initially started as a simple project to help CERN physicists navigate through a wealth of information and various data sets was eventually released to the wider public in 1993 in an act of global philanthropy. This included not only protocols for finding Web sites (http) but also the language to design Web pages (HTML). Like the invention of e-mail, this proved to be yet another killer app of the Internet. Suddenly there were colors and pictures on the Internet and an easy way to navigate a world that had previously been visually featureless.

From this moment, the growth of the Internet has been nothing short of phenomenal. In September 1995, there were 19,705 host names (which roughly correspond to unique devices connected to the Internet). One year later, that number was already over 400,000. By September 2000, there were 21 million hosts. And by the end of 2015, that number was at over 900 million hosts. There has never been a piece of social technology that has spread so far, so fast.

Today, the World Wide Web remains the gateway for billions to access the Internet, but the two are not, strictly speaking, the same. The Internet underlies the World Wide Web and is much older. The concept of an *inter-network,* or simply *internet* (with a lowercase *i*), evolved from the notion of interconnecting computer networks. The key to this notion of inter-networking was the research into packet switching (described in chapter 1), to which many countries started to dedicate research resources from the 1960s onward.

The original American research done on packet switching was often sponsored by the military, which was obviously interested in resilient communication networks that could withstand attack. This has given rise to the notion that the Internet was conceived (or even built) primarily by the military as a means of developing communications that could survive a nuclear war. This is almost certainly an overstatement, for while the various research projects that eventually led to the Internet were often sponsored by military grants (as was a great deal of research during the height of the Cold War, especially after the so-called "Sputnik Shock"), the prime motivations of those academics that conceived and built the early Internet had little to do with anything other than the desire to prove to petrified AT&T engineers that the hypothesis of packet switching could work and consequently doom the POTS—the plain old telephone system, as it is called today.

ARPANET, the first true wide-area computer network, was born in 1969, with the first four nodes at UCLA, the Stanford Research Institute, the University of Santa Barbara, and the University of Utah. And it all started with a crash: according to the legend, the first message sent was "LO," instead of "LOGIN"; the Stanford computer crashed before the end of the message.

Although ARPANET was associated directly with the US Department of Defense Advanced Research Projects Agency (later DARPA), the then head of ARPANET, Bob Taylor, clearly dismissed the motivations for creating ARPANET as related to concerns over war, rather stating that it was simply a test bed for packet-switching technology—and later a handy tool for sharing costly computer resources (in the 1960s and early 1970s, computers easily cost the same as an average home).

In the 1970s and 1980s, a number of developments moved the Internet closer to the form we recognize today. In 1971, Ray Tomlinson invented e-mail (and the use of the "@" symbol) to provide a more formalized means of personal communication. Until this invention, the growth of the ARPANET had been relatively slow. Still, only two years later it was claimed that 75 percent of ARPANET traffic was e-mail: clearly, there was something else to do with a computer network than share computer time. Queen Elizabeth of Great Britain is said to have sent her first e-mail in 1976—long before the Internet as we know it today really existed.

The introduction of e-mail also necessitated a new way to route communication, because by 1982 it had become clear that the old system was not built to sustain the volume of messages that would follow. The new system, adopted in 1983, was the domain name system. The same year, ARPANET formally adopted the groundbreaking Internet protocol developed nearly ten years before by Vint Cerf, Bob Kahn, Bob Braden, Jon Postel, and other members of the Network Working Group headed by Steve Crocker at Stanford University. The Internet protocol also allowed different internets to talk to each other and brought them together. In 1983, therefore, the Internet that we know today was said to be born through the interconnection of ARPANET with other networks, a process that, however, took a number of years. Around the same time, the Department of Defense split from ARPANET to create its own dedicated network, MILNET, and ARPANET moved out of the funding of the Department of Defense into the National Science Foundation (NSF).

Each of these forms an "internet," with a lowercase *i*. The *Internet* (with an uppercase *I*), however, is the unique "global network of computer networks." The Internet today is essentially a collection of around forty-two thousand individual internets that agree to communicate with each other. Bound together via TCP/IP, the previously independent networks—such as

USENET and CSNET—were later described as "autonomous systems" (ASs) within the newly created global Internet. Each AS is a set of routers under a single technical administration, able to communicate externally with other autonomous systems or internally with the computers included in the AS. Some companies can own hundreds, or even thousands, of ASs. Today, the collection of these forty-two thousand or so ASs is the actual, global Internet itself.

From the start, the Internet was pushed by its community but funded by government; in fact, it at least partially belonged to the US government. The exact role of government was at times difficult to grasp, but at least in its early decades ARPANET was considered government property, and MIT even forbade private communication on it. Following ARPANET's ascendancy with the adoption of TCP/IP, the US National Science Foundation Network (NSFNET) would fuel ARPANET—now increasingly just called the Internet—from the mid- to late 1980s onward. The NSFNET represented a huge commitment of public money—hundreds of millions of dollars—to expand what is now the Internet backbone while at the same time funding a new collection of supercomputer research centers that were to profit from the increased ability to share computer resources over the net. It also set in stone the first step toward privatizing the network away from its large government research project component.

In 1988, the NSF initiated a number of meetings at Harvard's Kennedy School of Government on "com-priv," or the best method to achieve "commercialization and privatization of the Internet." This idea of loosening the Internet from government control does not seem to have been ever seriously questioned; with the departure of the Department of Defense in 1983, the most obvious security implications were thought to have been addressed. While at the time ARPANET and NSFNET were designed only for the academic and research communities, it was clear that there would be strong commercial interest as well; indeed, large companies (such as Xerox) were already setting up their own private internets. One of the outcomes of the Harvard discussions was a policy tool to force this development:

the controversial Acceptable Use Policy of the NSFNET, which effectively forbade any kind of commercial or private use and therefore purposely put the onus on the private sector to develop these services for itself.

By the late 1980s and early 1990s, there were a great number of commercial Internet providers that, however, routed through the NSFNET, which was costing increasing sums to keep up with growing demand. The 1991 High Performance Computing Act, commonly known as the Gore Bill after its sponsor, Senator Al Gore, contributed to the urgently needed expansion of the NSFNET. Gore didn't quite "invent the Internet" with this bill, but he certainly did a lot to build it up, funding the strengthening of the creaking NSFNET infrastructure as well as related research and development. Mosaic, the first Web browser, is often attributed to the Gore Bill. The bill might also have been directly responsible for helping to overcome the last difficulties in forcing the transition to a commercially led model for Internet access. This was finally accomplished in 1995, when the NSFNET backbone was decommissioned and the field left completely open to commercial services that had arisen in the wake of the NSFNET's success.

The era of government-funded Internet was over. From now on, the Internet would be left in the hands of the "community"—the commercial businesses laying the cables and installing the routers, and later setting up the Internet businesses, and the academic researchers and volunteers who basically wrote the code for cyberspace. When Jon Postel decided to temporarily make himself the center of the Internet in 1998, he might have been trying to make the point that no matter how much the US government had invested in it, the Internet belonged to that community.

One common view on how present-day Internet governance works is to split it in two overall categories: the "technical governance" and the "policy governance" components. It is important to reinforce that while normally a policy level would imply some sort of superior position in a decision-making hierarchy, the opposite is true in Internet governance.

In accordance with the bottom-up heritage of the Internet, the technical governance components create components that are then—reactively— managed in a policy context, not vice versa. This subdivision also fits into the only agreed-upon definition of Internet governance, the 2005 Tunis Agenda for the Information Society, in which governance issues are split between the "use" (policy) and "evolution" (technical) of the Internet.

"Technical Internet governance" is a fairly weak phrase that seeks to combine all of the basic technical research and development work at the heart of the Internet into some kind of manageable whole. The challenge is that the institutions that build the Internet, line of code by line of code, often don't exist as brick-and-mortar organizations. More often than not, the institution lies in the human processes and the relationships established by the thousands of volunteers who have built and continue to build the Internet.

Take, for instance, one of the most important organizations working on Internet protocols: the Internet Engineering Task Force (IETF). The IETF usually meets three times a year, in groups ranging from a few hundred to a few thousand researchers, and effectively decides much of what constitutes the Internet's nervous system; most protocols, such as DNS and BGP, are decided in these meetings, and the IETF is the only organization that can be said to have actually "built" the Internet. Except that it does not even formally exist: legally speaking, it is a subchapter of another organization, the nonprofit Internet Society (ISOC). ISOC was in fact started by the IETF in an attempt to find a financial and logistic home after the US government indicated that it would retreat from financing and supporting the Internet, and was therefore always seen as something like an administrative cover. The IETF never wanted to be bothered with such formalities as legal incorporation and remains so minded until this day.

The IETF was born out of the need to coordinate many different independent research initiatives, each with its own respective funding. One of its prime functions still is to maintain the capacity to present basic Internet research (organized in yet another group, the Internet Research Task Force) to the Internet community at large. While it also develops core computer protocols and similar instruments itself, it is more than anything else a clearinghouse of all different types of basic research being conducted that may be relevant for the functioning of the Internet. These disparate working groups, and the IETF itself, have three things in common in terms of the way they are organized.

First, the engineers are never paid by the IETF or similar groups. They are often not funded at all, but volunteer their vacation time pro bono. The term "hobbyists" is certainly accurate to describe much of this involvement, which is why it is accurate to characterize the IETF and similar groups as civil society organizations. Government employees, when they are present, are more often than not there on their own time, as interested citizens.

The second is the Request for Comments (RFC) process, which was invented (serendipitously) in 1969 by Steve Crocker when he started compiling notes of the first discussions around early Internet technologies because "everyone understood there was a practical value in choosing to do the same task in the same way." Because writing a memo could be seen as an assertion of authority, he labeled his first note a "Request for Comments." This quickly became the style in which Internet protocol standards were introduced, allowing ideas to be shared and adopted or rejected according to their merits. Unlike research or consensus decision by committees, RFCs are ex post facto: researchers come up with an idea, test it in the most basic form, and publish an RFC to invite input from the wider community. An RFC is never withdrawn; rather, if it is substantially changed, it is replaced by a new RFC and declared obsolete. If a group wants to start something new, they can start a "birds of a feather" process—a sub-working group of like-minded interested researchers. Whether someone or a group decides to endorse an RFC is therefore secondary because everyone is free to decide whether specific RFCs are relevant or not for their own purposes.

Third, endorsement is articulated through the process of rough consensus. IETF is not a strict membership organization: its members do not abide by a one-man-one-vote principle. Majority voting was simply seen as needlessly cumbersome, and the IETF solution is to hum—quite literally. This indicates rough consensus, which the legally minded insist on calling a supermajority—anywhere above 80 percent agreement or so. When a working group discusses its results and asks for an endorsement or a decision from attendees, the chair invites them to hum. If the hum in favor is loud enough (and the hum against much less so), then the RFC is endorsed or the resolution accepted. If not, either the solution is sent back to the drawing board, or those in agreement implement it while the others do not.

There are numerous stories associated with the origin of the hum as a tool to indicate preferences. Some like to point out that humming is not really that variable: unlike with shouting, you really can only hum at a roughly similar noise level. Others like to highlight the anonymity of the hum: it's not immediately obvious whether you are doing it or not. An RFC in the year 2014 (yes, they can be used for this purpose as well) reminds participants that the point of the hum is not to vote but rather to indicate a lack of support or indeed strong opposition to an idea. The intention is not to override opposition but to accommodate it—as far as it is practical to do so.

The confidence of the technical community in its own capacity to deal with any foreseeable threat to the free Internet is understandable. One little-known story illustrates how a significant potential threat to individual liberties was quietly addressed by the same community.

As discussed previously, IPv6 is a new version of the present Internet protocol number (IPv4) that is slowly being introduced. IPv6 has a number of advantages over IPv4, the most important of which is that it is effectively inexhaustible: while IPv4 addresses were always centrally assigned, it was not clear whether this was necessary or desirable for IPv6. For the sake of tidiness, the original technical document (RFC) therefore proposed a seemingly innocuous and efficient hack: the IPv6 address would be automatically generated from the computers' MAC addresses.

Because virtually every single piece of networked equipment has a unique MAC address assigned to it, this innovation seemed to have disastrous implications for those worried about privacy: it would mean that every single piece of networked equipment would have a fixed identity in cyberspace and could relatively easily be associated with an individual. Under IPv4, most address allocations—especially for individuals—are dynamic, not fixed. This means that it is not easily possible to identify someone in cyberspace, especially in real time. Generating IPv6 addresses out of a MAC address would change all this and make every piece of equipment instantly identifiable in cyberspace—forever. Today, most of us will have about half a dozen MAC addresses (on our phones, computers, smart cards, or even car key chains), which, however, often do not broadcast their user's identity, certainly not automatically. In the near future, with the advent of microchipped clothing and smart appliances—the burgeoning Internet of Things—this number will explode to many dozen MAC addresses per individual. Each of these will be sending different information—the famous networked fridge communicating that it needs milk—all of which under this scheme would instantly be attributable to a single person. Whereas previously your IP number could easily change and was therefore not always a secure identifier, now each piece of equipment would have a permanent identifier, one that could easily be compared with purchase records and the like, and therefore clearly establish your identity as a user. While this was a "neat hack" (that is, cool fix) for the technical problem of how to generate an IP address, from a policy or a civil rights point of view it was a total catastrophe. Indeed, some IETF engineers anticipated this problem and, through the reiterative RFC process, effectively disabled this feature in IPv6. It was never removed, however. It could be reactivated again if the technical community decided that it was necessary or, more to the point, if a government decided to mandate that all equipment sold within its jurisdiction have the feature enabled. And, for example, if a country like China decided to enforce this for all iPhones, what would Apple do? These are questions we rather hope don't become pertinent, but they may—which is why the IETF functions the way it does: keeping policy and politics as far away from itself as possible.

The IETF (as well as similar bodies) represents one of the most innovative parts of the Internet, and it is not technical but very much human. From its start, this group of hyper-smart individuals has been obsessed with leaving the old world of politicking aside and building a new one on the basis of nothing more than the joy of creation. This dream was best captured by one of its founders, David Clark, in 1991:

We reject: kings, presidents and voting.
We believe in: rough consensus and running code.

In the minds of many old Internet hands, technical Internet governance is the "pure" part of running the Internet: a bunch of no-nonsense rolled-up-sleeves engineers who just want the damn thing to work. By rejecting "kings, presidents and voting" and embracing the rough consensus standard, they are able to find quick, dirty solutions that enable them to manage the loose consortium of organizations and individuals engaged in the perpetual construction of the Internet. But the rough consensus approach is not easily adopted by non-engineers, let alone members of government. Involving them in the Internet grew more critical every year as questions beyond mere technical problems arose: political questions related to use, implementation, and, perhaps most important, resource allocation, such as who gets how many IP numbers. These "management" issues were not technical problems but policy challenges.

It is a remarkable quirk that, while technical Internet governance can claim not a single overriding father or hero but rather a dozen or more, the policy Internet governance field can be said to have had a wonderfully bearded patriarch who ruled over Internet policy for decades: Jon Postel. Although Postel was a true-blue engineer with hundreds of RFCs to his name, his final years were consumed with policy.

For well over a decade, Postel single-handedly managed what is known as the "Internet name space," the two categories that effectively enable navigation on the global Internet: the allocation of Internet protocol numbers (and associated autonomous system numbers) and the management of the domain name system. The management of these crucial resources was incorporated in the Internet Assigned Numbers Authority (IANA), but for the first ten years the IANA was basically just one man: Postel, working under contract to the US Department of Commerce, which had inherited the US government's supervisory function over parts of the Internet and, until 2016, retained a final say over the root of the Internet. Under Postel's rule, the Internet grew from a US-based research project to a truly worldwide network. He had tremendous power, and if he had power, he also had an innate sense of responsibility.

In some of the areas he managed, he had some help from the community. The management of the pool of IP numbers was accomplished by setting up geographic entities, known as Regional Internet Registries, that did some of Postel's IP allocation work at the regional level. From 1984 onward, Postel oversaw the expansion of the domain name system to cover the country-code top-level domains (ccTLDs), the system that covered everyone outside the United States. Who, for instance, would be responsible for granting a ".uk" address (for Great Britain) or a ".de" address (for Germany)? For all .uk domains the British company Nominet is the registry. If you want to register a Web site with a .uk address, ultimately Nominet decides on the application. Postel appointed a "registry" for each country to a trusted manager on a "handshake" basis—whoever was smart enough to know about this process would get in touch, and Postel, if he decided that the person was a responsible actor, gave him or her the job. By 1993, this ad hoc system had managed to distribute nearly all of the world's country codes to specific actors (virtually all of whom were members of the wider technical community) without much in the way of a dispute under Postel.

Today, the management of top-level domains like .com and .org as well as country-code top-level domains like .uk or .fr is big business, although it has somewhat bizarre overtones due to the history of Internet development. For instance, a large share of those are being run by a single company, Verisign, that may also be responsible for hosting some of the most critical components of Internet routing, such as the master DNS root zone file—the key reference document at the center of the Internet's address system. Other weird and wonderful quirks of DNS will most likely change with market preferences: in 2014–15, the world's most popular country-code top-level domain was not that of China (.cn, with about 12 million domains) or Germany (.de, with about 16 million domains, the second-most-sought-after country-code domain), but the semiautonomous South Pacific microstate of Tokelau (ccTLD.tk, population fourteen hundred) with a whopping 28.6 million domains. The .tk domains are particularly popular because they are mostly free—only a few special domains require payment. They also have very lax registration requirements, a charge that has meant that .tk is persistently mentioned in reports on spam and phishing as a consistent offender. While Tokelau derives comparatively little money from the .tk domain, other countries were luckier. The islands of Tuvalu, for instance, sold the rights to their domain to a Canadian entrepreneur, and today nearly 50 percent of the tiny government's revenue is derived from the sales of .tv domains.

I n the early 1990s, the socioeconomic potential of the Internet was starting to become obvious. In a decision whose significance is hard to overstate, the Clinton administration announced its intention to continue the process of cutting government strings to the Internet, enabling the transition of the management of Internet resources to a fully community-based structure. The new nonprofit charged with this oversight, ICANN, would be headed by Jon Postel, and would take on responsibility for core Internet maintenance functions (to be managed on behalf of the US Department of Commerce). ICANN got off the ground in earnest in 1998, and just as the IETF can claim a foremost role in technical Internet governance, ICANN is at the center of policy Internet governance.

ICANN is incorporated as a "nonprofit public-benefit corporation," according to the laws of California, and for a long time was physically based at the University of Southern California. Its purpose is to "coordinate, at the overall level, the global Internet's systems of unique identifiers." Entrusted with the IANA contract by the Department of Commerce, ICANN aimed to "manage Internet names and addresses" much in the way Postel managed them before. This relatively innocuous-sounding mission encompasses three of the most vital functions of the Internet: the allocation of IP number resources for individual computers or machines, the DNS "names" associated with these numbers, and the allocation of the so-called top-level domains to registries that actually assign these identifiers to individual users and organizations across the globe. Taken together, these three functions represent a considerable segment of Internet functionality.

ICANN has grown with the Internet—from a marginal budget of less than $1 million in 1999 to $60 million in 2010 and around $160 million in 2015. It has been challenged virtually from its inception by three different macrogroups of users—private businesses, governments, and civil society—and has fallen afoul of all of them at one time or another. Despite persistent challenges by all three groups, however, ICANN has survived and prospered—if that is indeed the right term for a nonprofit organization. It has not only increased its budget and manpower but also—at least for the moment—fought off extremely well-resourced attempts to question its legitimacy and core mission.

Even if it was fathered by government, ICANN was born within the Internet community and as such took over much of that community's habit of forming various working groups and committees. This has meant that ICANN's structure is awash with various boards, groups, committees, and similar organizations that together form an alphabet soup nearly impenetrable to outsiders: indeed, in 2015, the organizational chart of ICANN included the ASO (Address Supporting Organization), the ALAC (At-Large Advisory Committee), the ccNSO (Country Code Names Supporting Organization), the GNSO (Generic Names Supporting Organization), the

GAC (Governmental Advisory Committee), the RSSAC (Root Server System Advisory Committee), and the SSAC (Security and Stability Advisory Committee).

Ultimately, though, the ICANN structure is fairly simple: ultimate decision making resides largely within the board, with fifteen directors (plus four nonvoting liaisons), which also appoints the chief executive officer. This board is also the result of a bottom-up process by which prospective members are nominated from a host of various organizations, many of which are totally unknown to anyone but specialists in the field. In many cases, these organizations themselves are relatively open: anyone who is interested can apply to join and start contributing and, if his or her contributions are considered helpful by that community, be put forward for the board. Others are trade-industry or special technical interest groups.

Crucially, however, there are also nonvoting members of the board, who can observe and partake in discussions. Most prominently, this includes the only official government representation within ICANN: the Governmental Advisory Committee. Although the GAC was long accused of being largely unrepresentative of the global population due to the fact that only a couple dozen states bothered to send delegates to the meetings, this largely changed in recent years, and ICANN now boasts over 169 countries as GAC members as well as pretty high attendance rates, according to its minutes available online.

The lack of government voice, let alone a veto, in ICANN has long been a singular point of concern for some governments, many of which have consistently strived to elevate the position of the GAC. A counterargument to the importance of individual votes has long been that the idea of a consensus-driven approach largely changes what votes, and even what a veto, could mean; voting within the board is largely a formal act that is only undertaken when—true to the technical idea of a rough consensus—there has already been a large amount of agreement reached. Indeed, few of the ICANN board decisions have been by simple majority, and none have been razor-thin.

In March 2014, the Department of Commerce dropped a bombshell: the US government would entertain proposals to transit the IANA function away from its contractual relationship with the government. Put plainly, the United States was going to give up its last contractual means to influence the root of the Internet. For this, the Internet community was challenged to deliver an appropriate concept.

This triggered the greatest reform process in Internet governance history. In 2014, ICANN initiated a process not only to present a working plan to completely take over the IANA function but also to improve its own accountability toward the community. This even included a minor strengthening of government influence over the process by means of the GAC, although no veto over decisions. At the end of 2015, both of these processes resulted in some significant structural reforms, and with the wider consensus of the community these proposals were put forward both to the board of ICANN and to the Department of Commerce. The Department of Commerce is expected to approve of the reforms; however, the final act in the IANA transition may lie with the US Congress, many members of which have angrily indicated that they would not "let the US give up control over the Internet," as Senator Ted Cruz has often incorrectly opined.

The reason for the US government's cutting the final strings to its influence over ICANN and handing over IANA can be seen from two angles. On the one hand, it already did so—twice. Following the original 1998 memorandum of understanding with which the US government legitimized ICANN, it steadily started to devolve more and more responsibility to this organization. A first step was the Joint Project Agreement (2006), which was soon superseded by a new agreement, the 2009 Affirmation of Commitments, in which the Department of Commerce expressed that the so-called multistakeholder model of Internet governance was best suited to achieve ICANN's mission. It also eliminated ICANN's final requirement to report directly to the US government, leaving the IANA function as its last links to governmental oversight. This slow but steady process of releasing the core functionality of the Internet from government control was, remarkably, a consistently bipartisan feature in US policy, one that reached back to the Reagan administration and was always set at ensuring that the Internet remains a non-state endeavor. This process was endowed with a new urgency after the June 2013 Snowden leaks and the persistent backlash at US dominance in all things cyber following. Though the revelations produced by Snowden had little or nothing to do with Internet governance, they are without a doubt one of the factors that has most shaped and influenced the debate around how, and by whom, the Internet should be managed. For as much as the old guard technical community may dislike it, the Internet has long been a subject of intense interest to governments, and that interest is only increasing.

One thing all actors who claim some kind of stake in the management of the Internet would agree on is that Internet governance is composed of many different stakeholders, but that would probably be the extent of their agreement. Indeed, serious differences arise when normative preferences— that is, the "should be," rather than the "are"—are brought to the forefront. Although there are many factions and sub-factions in play, the battle lines among states in Internet governance can be drawn between two single viewpoints in particular.

On the one side stand those who consider the relatively weak position of governments within Internet governance a historical accident at best and a sinister US government plot at worst; Vladimir Putin famously declared that the Internet was a "CIA project." They have launched persistent and multipronged attacks on the present system of Internet governance and strive to create an international governmental agreement, most likely connected to the United Nations but also potentially to international law enforcement measures. This faction is variously known as the intergovernmental supporters, the multilateralists, or the Cyber-sovereignty adherents due to a similar line of argument that seeks to put government's control over "its own" portion of cyberspace above all other considerations. The strongest advocate of this position is Russia, with close support from China and occasional sympathy votes from much of the developing world, in particular India and Brazil (which both appeared to be slowly moving away from this view in 2016). Some international governmental organizations seeking to expand their mandate, in particular the International Telecommunication Union (ITU), have provided strong flanking support.

Aligned against the Cyber-sovereignty nations are those who believe that the present, unique system of governance on and of the Internet—in which a host of different actors operate more or less independently of each other and with minimal government involvement—is not a historical accident but rather an evolutionary development in the globalization of Internet resources. They point to the reality of the Internet as a largely non-state domain and the importance of all stakeholders working together, rather than trying to promote the role of one group (in particular government) over the others. The strongest advocate of this position is the United States, supported by the bulk of liberal democratic countries, as well as the (non-state) Internet governance institutions, foremost among them ICANN and the IETF/ISOC. I refer to this group of actors as the Free Internet advocates. These are the supporters of the so-called multistakeholder approach.

There is no single term that is more important to describe the policy side of Internet governance than the notion of the multistakeholder management of Internet resources. While, like the term "cyberspace," it does not have a single overriding definition, it does have an implicit definition. The core idea of the multistakeholder approach is that some issues are too complex and have too many independent operational stakeholders to be decided by one inevitably self-interested group (such as governments) and therefore require the participation of all stakeholders: the civil society, the private sector, and governments. For the Internet, this is seemingly grounded in reality: it is members of civil society (which includes state-funded university researchers, as well as corporate engineers working on their own time) who write the code of the Internet. It is business that builds and owns most aspects of the Internet, ranging from the cables to the Web sites to the software products that run on and in it. Government's role is relatively limited—it can spy on the Internet, and it can destroy it piece by piece—but it cannot manage it. It certainly cannot build it.

While multistakeholderism is the prevailing way of thinking about Internet governance, at least at face value (Russia is nearly alone in its total refusal), the different implicit definitions of what the term "multistakeholder" actually means are where the battle lines between the supporters of an intergovernmental model and what I will call the true multistakeholder model are drawn. The segmentation of the multistakeholder approach into three actor groups is a simplification: the most authoritative definition of the multistakeholder categories (included in the so-called 2005 Tunis Agenda) includes "States, the private sector, the civil society, the Intergovernmental Organizations, the International Organizations, the technical community and the academics." This definition has the advantage of being much more accurate and covering the shades of grey well, at the same time these shades of grey have been exploited by those who wish to use the complexity of the Internet governance processes against it.

As a Chinese official once said in an exchange that I helped chair, "It is not politically correct to oppose the multistakeholder term," which is why even its opponents are careful to claim to battle against its interpretation rather than the term itself. Because the term has never been explicitly defined, this interpretation is becoming one of the key features of Internet governance and therefore of the future of the Internet itself. It will help decide whether the Internet will continue to be a largely non-state affair or if it will become directly subject to strong governmental intervention.

The history of Internet governance until today features a number of shifts in power and influence of different actors. According to one rather reductive version of events, the government (in this case the US government) created the Internet and its precursors and has slowly retreated from this role, leaving the Internet community (largely understood to be civil society actors and industry players) to take over more responsibility. At the same time, other governments are demanding an increased say, and these actors have repeatedly tried to replace this multistakeholder model with something more akin to an intergovernmental model. Following a huge international meeting in December 2012 hosted by the International Telecommunication Union in Dubai called WCIT (which I called an "Internet Yalta"), I (re)used the term "cyber sovereignty" to describe the bloc of countries that made overt efforts to push Internet governance issues into the ITU. The move was not a total surprise because there had already been many subtle and less subtle attempts by Russia and its less vocal cyber-policy allies to position the ITU as the obvious intergovernmental candidate to pick up the DNS management role from ICANN. A direct confrontation ensued on the voting floor, where the Cyber-sovereignty bloc—led by Russia, China, and Iran—pushed for a confrontation with the Free Internet countries, led by the United States. In a stunning move, the Cyber-sovereignty nations managed to pick up a great number of nonaligned national votes, and the final tally was damning: eighty-nine countries signed the new telecom regulations document, which indirectly attacked the current practice of Internet governance, while fifty-five countries—the Free Internet faction, plus some supporters—abstained. In its 150-plus-year history (the ITU is the world's oldest international organization), there had never been such a contentious vote, and the ITU might have become permanently weakened as a result. But for the Cyber-sovereignty states, the chance to conjure up a "West against the rest" confrontation, win it, and secure for the ITU a mandate in Internet governance issues could only have been considered a stunning success.

This view of seeing two monolithic power blocs aligned against each other in Cold War poise has been criticized by others. According to Milton Mueller, a leading academic on Internet governance, this approach is indirectly contributing to "the militarization of the Internet" and leading to "an Internet policy landscape dominated by national security concerns and great power conflicts," leaving little prospect of common ground between the two antagonistic positions. Other experts, such as Wolfgang Kleinwaechter, have less problem casting the confrontation as a bipolar issue, given the evident activity and attempts to mobilize support. However,

Kleinwaechter says it would be more appropriate to consider the "Internet Yalta" as having occurred not in 2014 but at the important World Summit on the Information Society (WSIS) meeting in 2005, where the Chinese and the United States agreed to accept that the national domains (country codes like .cn) would remain completely under national sovereignty while the root of the Internet remained under US stewardship. According to this view, the 2014 clash occurred when one side (driven primarily by Russia) tried to reopen this Yalta-like division of the digital world—very much a traditional "great power" confrontation.

While I think the bipolar analysis is (sadly) correct, in many ways it is helpful to understand the shades of gray that lie between these seemingly absolute positions. It is true that upon closer examination these two political dreams of the Internet do not seem completely contradictory: many of the liberal multistakeholder-favoring governments do in fact also seek to exploit the Internet in a national security context, just as the Cyber-sovereigntists do in China and particularly Russia. But the devil is in the details—although from a radical Free Internet perspective all governments may indeed be evil, they certainly have very different views even on how state power in cyberspace should be cast. Simply put, the ideological differences between the Free Internet nations and the Cyber-sovereignty advocates is not too far away from the ideological confrontation that defined the Cold War. And as in the Cold War ideologies, some of the views expressed by both sides seem to be the essence of reasonability—until you give them a closer look.

The core notion of cyber sovereignty is on its surface beguilingly simple: a state should be totally sovereign within its borders, meaning that it should be free from the possibility of a foreign state's interfering with or threatening its essential national interest at will. This seemingly commonsense approach has two serious implications and is furthermore built on a legal fallacy. The first implication is that a state should be able to completely control the information that is consumed by its citizens so as to protect that population from the undue influence of other actors, which of course is

everyone but the ruling regime. The second is that a state should have control over the logical and physical infrastructure of the local Internet segment (a contentious term referring to the part of the global Internet that is
subject to national legislation, such as on content) to better protect not only
its citizens from bad content but also the critical infrastructure and government systems from hostile outside forces. The underlying legal fallacy
that underpins this assessment is that sovereignty of states is, in practice,
immutable and absolute. This is simply wrong.

As one of the heads of the ICANN Governmental Advisory Committee
once pointed out, all nations that participate in the Internet already accept
a certain loss of sovereignty that may even be illegal under some jurisdictions. ICANN, for instance, has more official control over some of the
registries, and therefore potentially a nation's critical infrastructures, than
that country's own government does. As unappealing as it may be, this violation of sovereignty is universal—that is, it applies to all nations equally—
and therefore does not actually constitute a relative loss of sovereignty. All
states lose some power in cyberspace, although they all do their very best to
make up for it otherwise.

There is little doubt that US stewardship of Internet resources came under
enormous pressure in 2013 and 2014 due to the mega-leaks on US intelligence gathering. Experts in the field have written that "the information
released by Snowden had huge repercussions in Internet governance," and
The Economist opined that "the big consequence of Edward Snowden's NSA
leaks will be that countries and companies will erect borders of sorts in
cyberspace." These disclosures therefore seemed to at least momentarily
strengthen the momentum of the Cyber-sovereignty powers, and their
focus was clearly on one thing: the root zone file of the Internet, often cast
as the actual heart of the Web. The process for managing the root is known
as the IANA function, and the IANA function was the very last component
that was connected, albeit indirectly, to the US government, which con-

tracted ICANN to manage the IANA function until finally releasing it in 2016. As discussed already, the US government announced in 2014 that it was prepared to transfer the IANA function to a multistakeholder body— in a politically brilliant move that conveniently undercut international voices that thought the United States would never do such a thing and planned to use this as a point of diplomatic attack. The notion that a US body—let alone a US government department—could even theoretically decide on Russia's or China's Internet was always given as an impossible loss of sovereignty for these countries. Paired with the ignominy of "not even having a root zone server," this was often treated as a sore point by these two countries, a humiliating aspect that no self-respecting major power should accept.

There are at least three levels of interpretation of how important the root zone file really is. On the most superficial level, there is no doubt that the IANA contract does represent a core functionality of the Internet per se: managing the root zone file is absolutely key to DNS and navigation on the Web. It is theoretically true that whoever controls entries into the root zone file is able to connect or disconnect the top-level domains from the Web at will. That is also why Postel caused something like panic when he made himself, in effect, the sole overseer of the root zone file in 1998— albeit temporarily. Theoretically, so the argument goes, the US government could, through the IANA contract, order that Russia or Iran be dropped from the global Internet telephone book, and there is nothing these countries could do to prevent it. Although these concerns were never realistic, the 2014 announcement to hand over absolute control of the root zone file to some kind of global body was designed to counter these concerns.

At the same time, for some observers handing over the keys to the Internet would effectively allow governments to install a worldwide censorship system; as Newt Gingrich tweeted, *What is the global internet community that Obama wants to turn the internet over to? This risks foreign dictatorships defining the internet.* Instead of nations being dropped, the root zone file could be used as a tool for "counterterrorism" (an abiding Russian obsession, as we will see later), which could specifically be aimed at those spreading "harmful information," which could mean dissident propaganda, radical recruitment sites, botnets, or child pornography, depending on one's mood. In the name of international law enforcement cooperation, the managers of the IANA function could be compelled in the worst cases to blacklist providers of bad content and force the managers of the zone files above them in the hierarchy to either automatically delist the offending content when it appears or be delisted in entirety themselves. If you wanted to host a Falun Gong Web site, for example, you would have to hunt for a domain (like .net) that would risk the threat of being delisted "at root" of the Internet in its entirety, or so the argument would go. At this basic interpretation, the root zone file provides a potentially unlimited amount of power, the ability to direct the entire global Internet at will and make unwanted information disappear. Similarly, if the US, as the former steward of the IANA function, was in open hostilities with a nation, it could potentially order that country to be disconnected from the global Internet by the simple, expedient action of disappearing its top-level domain. At least in theory.

At the second level of interpretation, however, US control of the root was simply never what it was perceived to be. The exclusion of an entire country or domain from the global Internet would require that all the thirteen root zone operators accept the zone file changes. While many of them are based in the United States, only three are under direct US government control, and three of them aren't in the United States at all. Under the current, soon-to-be-replaced IANA contract, the United States could mandate that, for instance, Iran be disconnected from the global Internet. Should the Swedish, British, Japanese, or indeed US-based civil society operators refuse to accept them, however, the changes would simply fail; the global Internet would fragment, as it did briefly when Postel hijacked it in 1998. This always made it very unlikely that such a deletion would occur, even in a case of open warfare. Further, ICANN policies are binding only on the so-called generic top-level domains (like .org and .com): country-code top-level domains (like .uk and .de) have no obligation whatsoever to conform to such decisions. This means that even an ICANN that has subsumed the IANA root control function, and has somehow turned into a worldwide law enforcer, would therefore automatically stumble and not have much power. Even if ICANN decided to, say, be responsible for enforcing Russian and Chinese censorship laws at the .org or .net level, it would not be able to control what individual countries (like .uk or .fr) could host.

A third level of interpretation is less sanguine. While it is true that there are a number of technical reasons why the IANA function currently does not lend itself well to the idea that authoritarian governments could establish a global "notice and takedown" (the official legal term for this type of content-control activity) regime, that does not mean that things could not change in the future. In fact, delisting content using the root zone file as the highest enforcement authority could be seen as the ultimate form of notice and takedown, an obligation that ISPs have in the United States since the Digital Millennium Copyright Act to make illegal content unavailable upon notice from the copyright holder. In Europe, the notice-and-takedown regime is based on the Electronic Commerce Directive adopted in 2000 that treats ISPs as "mere conduits" and ensures that ISPs are "not liable for the information stored at the request of" users if they did not have knowledge of illegal activity and act promptly when they are notified. There are few immutable elements of the Internet that could not foreseeably be changed through a simple act of will, and the notice-and-takedown regime is surely one of them, as governments who are investing resources to change it know very well. The notion may be that once the top-level domains are made to cooperate on such law enforcement issues, addressing the country-level domains would be simply a small further step.

The struggle to understand the ramifications of control over the root is a case study in how two cultures can view the same issue completely differently. The government of Russia, supported by a number of like-minded governments including especially China, seems to harbor the hope for a global Internet notice-and-takedown regime to deal with hostile content, perhaps based on the IANA function and therefore the root zone file, an intent that the Russians and others have been making increasingly clear in public documents such as those related to the Code of Conduct for Information Security, a document that represents the core of the Cyber-sovereignty movement. For technically minded experts within the Internet governance community, this is doubly puzzling. First, as was just explained, the IANA function at present simply does not seem to offer these kinds of possibilities. Second, the focus on a notice-and-takedown regime seems somewhat antiquated: while it is true that for many years this method was by far the most effective in removing "bad" content, in recent years Internet blocking and filtering technology (especially as employed by China) has advanced greatly and now seems to be quite effective in "shielding" a population from "harmful content."

So why do countries such as China bother with the legal approach, if technical censorship is working better than expected? The reason for this continued strategy was made clear to me in a conversation with a senior Chinese official. "Things change," the official said cryptically in response to some of the points above. The implication for me was clear: for China and Russia, the legal notice-and-takedown framework was simply a future-proof and safer bet than hoping to constantly build bigger and better Internet walls, walls that may suddenly be made obsolete through yet another Internet innovation. Likewise, the IANA function and even the ICANN contract could be reinterpreted or rewritten, if the political reality required it. And, of course, political reality can change even faster than technology. But the political reality today is that civil society—the Internet community—is largely responsible for maintaining the root zone file.

One of the most bizarre and, I believe, illustrative functions that the civil society performs is the process currently managed by ICANN to "sign" the root zone key, a crucial operation that enables the root zone file to be shared with other trusted parties securely. Much of the discussion on the policy level has been about the content of the root zone file, but a more interesting component is how the root is authenticated—that is, secured—using cryptography and information security. It says a great deal about how seriously the community takes its role as guardians of the Web.

A normal part of DNSSEC (a new version of DNS, with updated security) is the recurring renewal of the cryptographic keys that help prove that when someone connects to the root zone operators and gets a copy of the root zone file, it is indeed the right file and has not been tampered with. The entire DNSSEC principle works on a strict hierarchy, with the parent verifying to the child the validity of the code that it is passing on. This chain of trust is the entire basis of the new DNS-powered Internet, with successive layers of trust being verified by higher layers of trust. So who verifies the very top, the root zone, which has no parent? That is the role of the key-signing ceremony, conducted under a security regime that would put some intelligence agencies to shame.

The keys to the Internet are kept at two separate locations in the United States: El Segundo, California, and Culpeper, Virginia, where the root-signing ceremonies also take place. These are both maximally secure data centers, which require passing a battery of access controls (palm scanners and the like) before one enters what, in effect, is a safe within a cage within a vault within a bunker-like facility. The core of the ceremony is a small card reader, the hardware security model (HSM), a specially designed piece of cryptographic kit that has its own power source that cannot be replaced and whose only job is to generate those ultra-important keys. Those keys are then replicated onto USBs, carried by hand to their destinations, and distributed throughout the Internet.

The highlight is the actual authorization of the HSM, which is carried out by three crypto officers, who are trusted individuals of the community, each with his own credential key that he uses to authenticate the process. All three of these crypto officers must therefore verify that all is in order before the keys can be generated. While all seven individuals in the room and part of the ceremony are significant, the crypto officers are absolutely critical. They are so-called trusted community representatives, of which there are only fourteen in the world, and they effectively have the role of witnessing and endorsing the process of creating the keys of the Internet. The ceremony is repeated around four times a year, and each time a backup key is created as well. According to an excellent report on the process, "Each of these participants can only perform certain parts of the ceremony. Their roles are divided in a way that ensures less than a 1:1,000,000 chance that a group of conspirators could compromise the root-signing key, assuming a 5% dishonesty rate [yes, that's formally in the specification] amongst these individuals."

If some disaster strikes—if all four available HSMs are destroyed or considered unsafe—then the highest trust level is called upon. These are the seven recovery key shareholders. These select seven people physically carry with them a part of the digital key used to decrypt the backup key, itself held on a secret smart card. Five of these seven ultra-high-trust individuals have to come together and be mated with a secret backup key to restart the process with a new HSM. Without them, the Internet, which would rapidly decay in the absence of a confirmed root at its center, cannot be reset.

Who are these individuals, let alone the select seven who like characters in a fantasy novel have been given parts of the key to the modern world? They are certainly not government employees. Indeed, they do not represent any of the states of the world, although there is geographic diversity among them. They do not represent companies or other commercial entities. They are simply of the Internet community—like Dan Kaminsky, one of those key holders whose actions were recounted previously. The trust of the community in Kaminsky and individuals like him is emblematic of the trust that underpins the entire Internet and has made it what it is today.

Chapter 5

PIN-STRIPED CYBER

n May 2015, the Dutch government hosted the fourth Global Conference on Cyberspace, a large government-oriented international cybersecurity conference that had in earlier years taken place in Seoul, Budapest, and London. It featured fifteen hundred attendees, including around thirty governmental ministers from a number of countries, as well as assorted others as speakers. As one of the "others," I rode in a bus from the conference location to the dinner, trundling down the streets of The Hague as part of a motorcade with police outriders on motorbikes preceding the convoy. The motorbikes were slightly superfluous, for the entire route between the conference and the dinner location had been closed, with barricades manned with hundreds of police officers. "This is crazy," I said to the then CEO of ICANN, Fadi Chehadé, who sat next to me while I snapped pictures. "Yes, and all this for us," said Fadi quietly, "even though we are just Internet people." "Oh, it's not for us," I said, pointing to the stream of limos with dozens of state ministers following our bus. "It's for them."

Internet governance is only one side of the cyberspace security coin. The other side is often called international cybersecurity, part of the wider sub-ject of international peace and security, that element of international diplo-macy that deals with armed state conflict as well as related processes, such as arms control. Unlike Internet governance, which Western governments most often approach tentatively through their economics or infrastructure ministries, international cybersecurity is the realm of pure diplomacy, with issues of war and peace firmly on the table. And unlike in Internet gover-nance, government interest is certainly welcome. There is real and urgent need to address the growing possibility—and consequences—of state con-flict in and through cyberspace. The common goals are mostly defined in the attendant documents as trying to avoid "inadvertent escalation" (that is, accidental war) and a "loss of escalation control" (that is, the ability to manage a conflict or crisis once it has started).

The Cyber-sovereignty nations—foremost among them Russia and China—have a significant advantage in the political chess game for cyber-space: as those criticizing the status quo, they are continually on the offen-sive, and by challenging established orthodoxy, they are able to keep the initiative and political momentum compared with those forces trying to preserve the current arrangement. The front line is not only the definition of the multistakeholder approach, which remains nebulous. Parts of the battle are also for much more hallowed precepts, including basic under-standings of international law that are relevant to cyber, especially with regard to how information is treated as a subject of national security. Ulti-mately, the goal for the Cyber-sovereignty stalwarts Russia and China is simply a reconceptualization of the entire Western-defined global order.

Since 1998, Russia has been the undisputed leader of attempts to lobby the UN to take a stronger stance on international cybersecurity issues. This includes rejecting the terms "cybersecurity" and sometimes even "cyber-space," which Russia maintains are simply false terms at best and evidence of a Western plot at worst. Instead, Russia advocates the use of the term "information security," a cunning ploy because its connotation from the Russian perspective has nothing to do with the technical term favored by non-state professionals everywhere (those of the InfoSec community) and has an entirely different meaning. The Russian and Chinese definition of information security reflects those nations' attempts to legitimize state control over all aspects of information, in particular toward hostile content. While Russia has not managed to get the term accepted in the UN (the accepted compromise is ICT security, which is actually even further away from cybersecurity), it does not stop Russia from submitting the same UN resolution, again and again, in a persistent attempt to advance the term "information security."

The UN has long been a source of slightly tepid fascination for Russia and the Soviet Union. On the one hand, it represents much that is completely anathema to Russia: a Western-defined world order, based on a rule of law and human rights, and a de facto limitation of the sovereignty of nations, including the right to effectively interpret any hostile act as a *casus belli*. On the other hand, it seems to offer an irresistible opportunity to beat the West at its own game, by leading the majority of the 192 nations in the UN General Assembly (UNGA) who are not Western and not rich into a showdown—the dream of leading the poorer and more numerous "rest" against the heavily outnumbered West. Russia has long seen its ultimate global role as the natural leader of the antiliberal world order, an order that it thinks has the majority of the world's nations on its side. That it hasn't quite worked out that way (at least not yet) has been one of the more vexing issues for Russian diplomats.

At the UN, draft resolutions on different aspects of cybersecurity have been forwarded to the General Assembly by three of the six main committees: the Disarmament and International Security Committee (known as the First Committee); the Economic and Financial Committee (known as the Second Committee); and the Social, Humanitarian, and Cultural Committee (known as the Third Committee). The most relevant developments have taken place in the First Committee, which can be regarded as the most senior of all UN committees due to its emphasis on international peace and security. It addresses much of the work of the more senior UN Security

Council but has the benefit of being rooted in the UNGA and therefore open to all member states. Cyber-sovereignty nations, especially Russia, have consistently advanced cyber-related topics in this forum. Since 1998, the Russian government has annually introduced a draft resolution on "developments in the field of information and telecommunication in the context of security." With gradual changes, the resolution has been adopted by the UNGA every year. Because UNGA resolutions are not binding (unlike UN Security Council resolutions), they have largely had only a symbolic meaning but also help establish precedent and acceptance.

In the 2001 version of the resolution, Russia proposed the establishment of a group of governmental experts (GGE) to study existing and potential threats in the "sphere of information security and possible cooperation measures." The first GGE, convened in 2004, failed to adopt a consensus report due to the significant differences on terms, in particular what constituted an attack in cyberspace. Nonetheless, the involved nations including the United States—agreed that further discussions were sensible.

The second GGE agreed on a report in 2010 that specifically outlined the importance of developing "norms for state responsibilities in cyberspace": so-called rules of the road on what could and should be done by states in cyberspace. Gathering momentum, the third GGE report in 2013 emphasized the view that specific norms and their associated confidence-building measures (CBMs) should be developed also in the context of the regional security organizations. A CBM is a technical term for a policy device or instrument intended to reduce conflict or the consequences of conflict; the quintessential Cold War CBM, for instance, was the Washington-Moscow "Hot Line" for emergency communication. Based on the third GGE report, the Organization for Security and Co-operation in Europe (OSCE), and later the ASEAN Regional Forum (ARF), started separate but distinct processes to develop CBMs. The OSCE was in 2013 the first organization to develop a concrete list of cyber CBMs, including hotline communications and exchange of information, and similar measures.

The third GGE report was also notable for first managing to achieve consensus that international law applied in its entirety to all aspects of cyber conflict. This implicitly, therefore, included international humanitarian law (that is, the law of armed conflict, which regulated states' behavior in wartime). It also meant that the UN Charter applied fully—meaning that states had an inherent right to self-defense, including from cyberattack. China later distanced itself from these conclusions, however, as Russia later did in part as well. The fourth GGE report (2015) stood in the shadow of this retraction, which the US delegation was not able to reverse; in particular, Russia and China were concerned about the application of Article 51 of the UN Charter (self-defense) to cyberspace, wary that the United States was going to invoke this to respond to significant cyber espionage. Instead, however, the United States managed to get consensus to adopt three specific norms on state behavior: that states should not interfere with CERTs' ability to respond to incidents, or use them to attack; that states should support each other in investigations of serious incidents; and that states should refrain from interfering with each other's critical infrastructure. A fourth norm—a pledge to abstain from economic espionage—was not adopted. Nonetheless, the new norms represented a significant victory for the Free Internet bloc, despite the Cyber-sovereignty nations' refusal to agree to a statement that the entire UN Charter applies. In 2016, Russia requested that a fifth GGE be convened, with an expanded member base. There are indications that Russian as well as US support for the process is declining, and it is likely that there will not be a sixth GGE but that the process for norm development will instead continue in other forums.

The series of GGEs was not the only UN process dealing with the issue of international cybersecurity, but it was probably the most important. On balance, the GGE might have been more a loss for the Russian initiators than a win—which explained why they redoubled the effort to influence the international cybersecurity agenda in other areas. One axis of attack is the international acceptance of the so-called Code of Conduct, the principal document for the core Cyber-sovereignty states. The Shanghai Cooperation Organization, the quasi-security alliance between Russia, China, and a clutch of central Asian countries in between them, attempted to require states to provide law enforcement cooperation in pursuit of the "Three Evils" of terrorism, separatism, and extremism—terms that could obviously be extended to ban virtually any content. The ability to define information as a weapon is the ultimate goal for these nations, the one cyberattack that they fear above all others.

Throughout this book, I have used the term "cyberattack" often. This conforms with widespread public perception of the nature of these activities, as well as the InfoSec definition, which sees any violation of any of the principles of confidentiality, integrity, and availability as constituting an attack. This, however, is not a legal definition, for the term "attack" in international law is very tightly circumscribed to mean significant death and/or destruction. According to one of the government representatives on the UN GGE, "We have not yet seen an attack in cyberspace." This is certainly the opinion of most international lawyers as well.

The political scientist Thomas Rid once asserted that an attack in cyberspace could include a wide range of effects, including inflicting simple "mental harm" on its intended target. This is completely the opposite view of not only most non-state experts on the subject but also virtually all Western governments. But it perfectly suits the position of the Cyber-sovereignty advocates, as for them mental harm includes information that may undermine their governments' standing—such as public criticism. Countries like Russia, China, and Iran, but also many Arab states and others, have long since made the analysis that for them such inflictions of "mental harm" would be one of the worst possible outcomes, perhaps on par with kinetic-equivalent hacks on power grids and the like. This type of interpretation is directly connected to the general implicit political goal of being able to categorize all information as a potential "weapon" that needs control.

Luckily, one barrier to this simple interpretation is international law, which at least provides some clear guidance on what is considered force and violence in international affairs. As a result of this, the original US definition of "attacks" in cyberspace derives from clearly established thresholds of violence. As welcome as that may be for reinforcing the primacy of international law, it doesn't really map to all relevant expectations. For some national definitions of informational attack do certainly include definitions of "mental harm" at their core.

As we will see in the next chapters, the Western definition of what constitutes a so-called computer network attack (to use the original US military term) is not necessarily congruent with what most people would recognize as a cyberattack. To understand the shades of gray between the different definitions, we must first undertake a basic segmentation of the types of offensive government cyber activities that exist in today's cyber landscape.

The oldest and most basic approach can be called "battlefield cyber." This amounts to little more than a continuation of traditional military missions, such as electronic warfare, used largely to support other traditional military missions with their own kinetic effect—shutting down a radar system to allow bombers to penetrate, for instance. In what we can call "strategic cyber," the physical bombers are not necessary: the cyberattack itself has a kinetic effect and does not require additional support. Examples of strategic cyber range from surgical strikes on nuclear enrichment facilities without anyone's noticing, up to country-crashing cyber war with multiple overt attacks on critical infrastructure and military command links and supply chains. The third type of cyberattack is often circumscribed simply as "covert action." Leaving cyber intelligence aside (which, as we will see, requires special treatment), the ability to conduct the whole gamut of traditional spy games—including not only intelligence gathering but also persuasion, conversion, and covert influencing—has opened the door to seemingly unlimited opportunities in cyberspace. One of the more humorous of such operations was the British Operation Cupcake, whose perpetrators changed an online jihadi magazine's instructions for "making a bomb in your mother's kitchen" to recipes for cupcakes. But there are far less humorous examples as well. While all aspects of traditional covert action—including espionage, sabotage, and covert influencing—have been greatly transformed by cyberspace, covert influencing and propaganda efforts have entered a new dimension entirely. Leaked 2012 documents from the U.K.'s online covert action unit, the Joint Threat Research Intelligence Group (JTRIG), provide an inkling of what these operations can look like, with social media presences hijacked, rumors and fake news distributed, and incriminating evidence planted—a gamut of psychological effects directed at individuals best summarized by the presentation itself, which boasted that it could "take paranoia to a new level."

The difference between the first two types of cyber operations and the last one is obvious: the first two are more traditionally military, and the third is closer to traditional intelligence. The military activities are, at least in theory, closely regulated by international law.

The basic separation is between *jus ad bellum* (legal justifications for the right to go to war) and *jus in bello* (lawful conduct during an armed conflict). The UN Charter is very specific on the former, while the latter is covered by a body of law commonly associated with The Hague and Geneva Conventions and normally referred to as the "law of armed conflict" or international humanitarian law (IHL).

The UN Charter is designed to make war a rather difficult proposition. Article 2(4) of the charter generally outlaws the use, or the threat of use, of force as an element of international relations. The exemptions are limited and covered in chapter 7 of the charter, in particular Article 42, which explicitly allows the use of force at the direction of the Security Council, and Article 51, which covers the right to "individual and collective self-defense."

Article 51, the right of self-defense, explicitly refers to the right of states to respond to an "armed attack." The legal term of "armed attack" (which justifies an armed response, for example, war) is arguably a more serious case than a mere "use of force" (which does not justify an armed response). Unsurprisingly, this gap has provided the potential for endless discussion for lawyers.

For simplicity's sake, it should be noted that an "armed attack" is widely considered to require a significant kinetic effect, such as large-scale death and destruction. This could also include the disruption of critical infrastructure without immediate loss of life, if that disruption extended beyond a mere inconvenience to the population. It does not include the theft of data, or even the destruction of data, unless it results in one of the situations described above. In other words, a cyberattack that turns off the power for an hour across the United States may not be an act of war (unless there are significant casualties), but the total destruction of the US financial system through the large-scale and irrecoverable deletion of data would be. This focus on destruction thresholds has spawned a great deal of discussion on how to respond to accumulations of attacks that are just beneath the level of war—a discussion to which the Russian occupation of the Crimea and engagement in "hybrid warfare" in eastern Ukraine have lent a new level of immediacy.

Interestingly enough, the definition of an "attack" under international humanitarian law (that is, the law of armed conflict) is much wider. According to the International Committee of the Red Cross, under IHL it is possible to say that any action that disables the functioning of a system constitutes an "attack." This maps completely with information security's standard technical definition of an "attack" and is used by the majority of European states but not by the United States.

The United States, for instance, may consider any serious infringement of the integrity as well as availability of data to potentially count as an attack but, despite news reporting on, for example, Chinese cyberattacks, does not consider violations of confidentiality (that is, espionage) "attacks," at least in the legal sense. Most European nations, by contrast, consider any serious violation of data confidentiality to constitute a "cyberattack," alongside violations of data availability or integrity. For these countries, the US definition of a cyberattack is often called a "serious cyberattack" and maps well with the difference implied in the "use of force" and "armed attack" definitions employed in *jus ad bellum*. They are therefore not that far apart in practice. And by using the term "cyberattack" in a non-international-law context (that is, not insisting that "cyberattack" equals an "attack" under international law and therefore a potential *casus belli*), Western nations are free to use the term in a fashion more appropriate to the technical and public perception of the word without undermining the hallowed status of international law to alone determine what constitutes offensive action.

The adherence to the bedrock of international law as related to conflict is considered absolutely vital for the Free Internet countries. With these countries insisting on the applicability of the UN Charter in its entirety, governments are to be discouraged from engaging in particularly violent forms of cyber sabotage, for fear of crossing the border into all-out war. Governments are forced to evaluate all cyber operations as to their legality, distinction, proportionality, humanity, and military necessity, significantly limiting the targets that can be hit. Indeed, concerns over IHL are supposedly so marked in the US defense establishment that the vast majority of planned or suggested "cyberattacks" were canceled out of concerns that they may violate IHL. This careful attention to the law has produced a saying in USCYBERCOM: "It is easier to shoot someone than send an e-mail."

Unfortunately, not all states are this circumspect. Many—in particular China, and sometimes Russia—do not agree that international humanitarian law applies completely, or even partially, to the cyber domain. This is simply because of how they view the term "attack." For them, the prime component of cyber power is not the ability to blow up civilian infrastructure and the like but rather the ability to influence and direct the overall political discourse within the civilian space. Essentially, these nations consider cyber a means to control and influence populations, rather than simply an expansion of the conventional tool kit of war and espionage. The most important "cyberattack" skill may therefore not be measured in the sophistication of your hackers, but rather in the cunning and reach of your propagandists.

Western nations have tried resolutely to ignore this implication, commonly encapsulated in the notion of information warfare. Despite the mandate of intelligence organizations engaged in covert activity to strategically influence communication, there are some fairly stringent rules on how these strategic influencing operations can be deployed. In many Western nations, including the US, there is an implicit principle against the mass covert influencing of civilian populations through the spreading of untruthful and dishonest statements. A government is not supposed to try to unduly influence the debate in this space through covert means or by hiding its identity behind a proxy. This of course does not include so-called strategic communication or other public relations exercises, which by their very nature need to be both open (that is, self-identified) and, in the most direct sense of the term, honest in their analysis. Essentially, this means that government support for human rights NGOs, press releases, government briefings, and even paid-for advertising is permissible. However, covert influencing of a very restricted target set—like the military leadership of a dictatorship, for instance—can utilize the whole array of deception, as long as there is no collateral damage among the population at large.

What is not permissible, according to this Western view, are broad-media propaganda campaigns that clearly deal with falsehoods, or maintain "fake" bloggers and their so-called "troll army" associates, large-scale smear campaigns, fake news, or covert attacks against critical journalists and authors, or even attempts to subvert the democratic processes wholesale. Though the history of the West saw all of this (and more) exercised throughout the Cold War, an unspoken democratic consensus has existed for a number of decades that such measures are to be considered only in extremis, if at all, and should certainly not be the norm. With the advent of the Internet, the ability to conduct these types of operations is incomparably more effective and wide-ranging today than during the Cold War. The strategic environments are as incomparable as the nuclear environment of the 1980s compared with, say, the situation in the mid-1960s.

The notion that there is no clear link between technical and psychological cyberattacks is openly derided by Russian and Chinese officials and experts, both in print and within diplomatic contexts. In a Russian narrative—which has provided the basis for the Chinese narrative as well—there is a continuous link between the 1999 pro-democracy revolts in Belgrade, the so-called color revolutions of the early years of the twenty-first century, the Arab Spring, and finally the 2014 Ukrainian revolution: all are seen as having been directly plotted by Western intelligence—often enough the CIA—using NGOs as proxies. Some American NGOs did play a direct role in facilitating many of these revolts, and indeed there is US government financing for many of them. But for me, and for anyone else vaguely familiar with how Western civil society functions, this does not mean that these organizations are being controlled by the security apparatus, let alone the CIA. If anything, it is the opposite: these civil society organizations have fantastic political influence, in particular one NGO in the US probably has more access to lawmakers in Congress than most offices of the executive branch do—they are simply higher up the political hierarchy. Interfering with notable think tanks and NGOs could come at a serious political cost. For me, these organizations are more comparable with militant Christian missionaries, who are able to count on senior elected officials' support and are not easily dissuaded from their mission to convert others.

While I cannot completely discount the possibility that Western intelligence might have played a stronger role in triggering these uprisings than is commonly known, it would to me be so obviously foolish (the Arab Spring, for instance, did not seem particularly coordinated) that if and when the details were leaked of such a colossal blunder, the consequences would be dramatic. Unlike, perhaps, bulk collection and other intelligence programs, manipulating an entire democratic discourse is clearly not an ethical gray area; it is not something liberal democracies should be doing on any scale.

Opening the Pandora's box of information warfare is something that Western governments have largely avoided—until now. Russia's return to full-fledged propaganda war in recent years has prompted some Western governments to reopen discussions on elements that are essentially part of information warfare. The situation is further imperiled by the reality that though the United States in particular put thoughts of all-out information warfare to rest in 1999 (and instead backed information operations, or IO, and expanded signals intelligence gathering), some aspects of information warfare have proven harder to kill and continue to lurk in the shadows of standard operating procedures and concepts of operations. The threat of the information warfare narrative, with the overtones of "all information is a weapon," is one of the most dangerous challenges facing democratic society as a whole, for it threatens to make everything, including free speech and basic human rights, the battleground. As bad as the vision of kinetic cyber conflict is, with the lights going off and perhaps staying off for weeks or months, the idea of a full-blown information warfare defeat is even more disturbing. For at worst it would mean not simply a loss of national prestige or a shattering of alliances but even a fundamental weakening of democracy itself.

PART III

Chapter 6

NO ONE BUT US

The first cyberattack might have predated the Internet itself. In his 2004 book, *At the Abyss: An Insider's History of the Cold War,* Thomas Reed, a former member of Reagan's National Security Council, tells a remarkable story. Around 1981–82, the CIA received a flood of intelligence data on the ambitions of the KGB to steal Western technology to help shore up the Soviet Union's own creaking industrial base and lagging military and space capabilities. This program came to be known as the Farewell Dossier, and Western countries moved to counter it. The CIA received indication that the KGB was trying to steal a particular type of hardware-embedded software (an industrial control system, or ICS) from a Canadian company. This ICS was highly advanced for its time and promised to significantly reduce maintenance costs within an area of special Soviet interest: the delivery of natural gas via pipelines.

According to Reed, the CIA manipulated the software product in question and then allowed the KGB to steal it. When the Soviets installed it, they unknowingly installed along with it a program that included a "logic bomb": a piece of code that had been programmed to turn malicious at a certain point, without any outside intervention. It is worth quoting Reed at length:

> The pipeline software that was to run the pumps, turbines, and valves was programmed to go haywire, after a decent interval, to reset pump speeds and valve settings to produce pressures far beyond those acceptable to the pipeline joints and welds. . . . The result was the most monumental non-nuclear explosion and fire ever seen from space. At the White House, we received warning from our infrared satellites of some bizarre event out in the middle of Soviet nowhere. NORAD feared a missile liftoff from a place where no rockets were known to be based. Or perhaps it was the detonation of a small nuclear device. The Air Force chief of intelligence rated it at three kilotons, but he was puzzled by the silence of the Vela satellites. They had detected no electromagnetic pulse, characteristic of nuclear detonations. Before these conflicting indicators could turn into an international crisis, Gus Weiss came down the hall to tell his fellow NSC staffers not to worry. It took him another twenty years to tell me why.

Reed's story was picked up by the wider media but was quickly challenged and remains so today. A former KGB officer said that there had indeed been a pipeline explosion around that time, but in a different location, and that it was certainly not cyber related. The blogger and researcher Jeffrey Carr reported that "according to an informed source from one of the three-letter agencies, that explosion had nothing to do with CIA sabotage and everything to do with a Russian engineer who, when discovering a leak in the pipeline, simply kept increasing pressure to maintain the flow of natural gas." Numerous other reports have questioned the account as well.

The story was remarkable, however, not only because of the person who wrote it—who would have had to submit the script for review to the CIA as a matter of course before publication—nor even because the CIA evidently decided to let this bit of information go through. It was interesting because it quoted as a direct source the former senior NSC staffer Gus Weiss, who published his own book in 1996 on the wider Farewell Dossier. Besides the fact that his publication was also subject to approval by the CIA, the CIA has reprinted a large swath of it on its own Center for the Study of Intelligence Web site, in a version that validates much of Reed's account.

Independent of whether that attack happened or not (I am inclined to think something like it did occur), it seems that for whatever reason the CIA wanted the story out there. It could have just been a somewhat careless attempt on the part of the CIA to mark ownership over the general topic in a bureaucratic turf fight, given the rise of the NSA as the paramount cyber actor in the United States. But it could also have been a finely crafted strategic communication, timed nearly simultaneously with the launch of US covert cyber operations against Iran, intended to show that even kinetic cyberattacks already had a long history and that nobody executed them better than the US. It was the national security version of the hacker practice of declaring "pwnage" over your adversary—an indication of total domination over your foe, the digital equivalent of putting your foot on a prostrate body and pounding your chest while the defeated can only submit and hope for mercy. As questionable as this tactic is in the hacker world, applied to international peace and security, it does seem needlessly aggressive; forcefully demanding acceptance of one's dominance is not a winning medium- or long-term strategy in international relations. Ultimately, it was most likely a strategic message of deterrence: if we could do this twenty-five years ago, imagine what we can do now.

The Soviet pipeline attack, as it is known, perfectly captures two powerful tensions in US cyber: between the offensive and the defensive missions in cyberspace, on the one hand, and between the logical (that is, code) and the psychological aspects of cyber conflict (the information ops versus information warfare split), on the other. In the US case, offensive cyber activity has often been presented as a defensive measure: after all, in the account described previously the CIA did not plant the bad code, but let it be stolen.

But at least as significant as the blurring of offense and defense is that of pure hacking and kinetic-equivalent cyberattacks and the much wider information and propaganda war. Although the United States has supposedly forsworn the latter, the publication of the story was, at the very least, an act of propaganda. While the offensive/defensive dichotomy has long created conceptual difficulties for policy makers and the public wishing to follow the arc of US government cyber capability (just consider for a second whether you would put intelligence gathering in the offensive or defensive category, for starters), the tension between cyber operations and information warfare is even more acute. It is the difference between perceiving cyber as just another tool of warfare and seeing warfare completely transformed into a "guerrilla information war with no division between military and civilian participation," as the noted media thinker Marshall McLuhan said as far back as 1970.

The United States has traveled the longest of any nation on the road of cyberspace, and thus has an inherently dominant position that accompanies its status as the de facto birthplace of the Internet. The vast majority of cyber-relevant industry actors (hardware, software, and services) are American or based in the United States. The US government also likely spends more money on cybersecurity-related tasks, including espionage and offensive and defensive capabilities, than the rest of the world put together.

These sums are significant. The dedicated military cyber budget alone is $7 billion a year between 2017 and 2022, but it is only part of an overall DoD IT budget worth $37 billion a year, making it difficult to compare with other countries that are likely to count this spending as well. Furthermore, the $7 billion is only part of the federal cyber effort. For the fiscal year 2017 federal budget, $19 billion was earmarked for "cybersecurity." Besides not including general IT, however, it does not include large chunks of the "black budget" intelligence programs—like the $16 billion counterterrorism programs—that are nearly certainly also used in cyber contexts unrelated to counterterrorism. Finally, this is just the federal government and does not include the state and local budgets dedicated to cybersecurity, or the industry-alliance investment programs (such as that of the energy industry) that can be counted toward national cybersecurity expenditure. Together, the true extent of US cyber spending is probably $26 billion–$30 billion per year (taking 2016 as a measuring point), although these sums can be even larger if some other cost items are included. This is just about the entire defense budget of Germany.

Given the natural advantage of being the birthplace of most of cyberspace and the bonus of being able to boast the largest defense budget on Earth, the United States—like Great Britain and the world oceans in the late nineteenth century—sees itself as the natural hegemon of this domain and develops capabilities and strategies to fit this role. A flood of leaks from the intelligence community has provided an inkling of just how advanced those capabilities are, and it is safe to presume that for all practical purposes the United States is without peer in its capacity to exert hard power in cyberspace. These leaks, however, also provide an object lesson of how an excess of hard power can damage a nation's ability to exercise soft power—the ability to lead and influence without coercion.

In his 2012 book, *The Future of Power,* the international relations scholar Joseph Nye identifies "three faces" of how states can project power, effectively through "commanding change, controlling agendas, and establishing preferences." The first face aligns most closely with coercion, with the traditional notion of power as the ability to bend others to our will, for instance with overt force or even the hint of such—like deploying carrier battle groups as a show of force. The second face—agenda setting—is more cooption than coercion. It is effectively determining what issues are either on or off the table, and part of the wider discussion, like the ability to leverage international legal concepts in your favor. The third face of power—preference setting—is the least apparent. It is the ability to shape an individual's or group's beliefs and outlooks without any apparent outside pressure or direction at all. In its most benign form this has become known as quintessential soft power, the ability to lead and influence through positive attraction. But there is also a hard side to this third face of power—preferences that are not set through attraction, but through concrete manipulation and distortion. The US military can be said to primarily frame cyber as a "first face of power" tool, a classic military coercion instrument, with the threat or actuality of kinetic effect. However, the notion of information warfare and its psychological preference setting—the hard "third face of power"—was always there as well. After having been largely buried in the late 1990s it may be making a return in US cyber policy.

According to leaked NSA documents, the United States has pursued a strategy of achieving "global network dominance." According to the documents in question, dominance in this case is not defined as simply being resident (that is, having an intelligence presence) on virtually all networks it wants access to; this is simply Phase 0. Phase 3, the final goal, was the ability to achieve "real time controlled escalation"—in other words, to be able to do whatever you want to the adversary, whenever you want.

The goal of achieving dominance is not unique to cyber, nor is it necessarily nefarious in its own right; the US Navy and Air Force and Space Command also aim to achieve dominance in their own particular domains. But the US tradition of viewing cyber as just another domain obfuscates significant differences between cyber and air, land, sea, or space. For instance, the other domains work under implicit and explicit rules—both international laws and commonly accepted norms of behavior—that constrain not only the most dominant actor but also all others. Most important, they introduce measures of predictability and trust in international relations. Although in recent years the US State Department has pushed for a wider understanding of international law in cyber operations as well as the development of norms of behavior, there is nothing really comparable in the cyber domain to the rules and practices in force everywhere else; even space is more regulated than cyberspace. The reasons for this are fairly clear: until relatively recently, the US government was effectively encouraging a practice of pure cyber anarchy, with the right of the strongest reigning supreme. In the cyber domain, "dominance" meant not only setting the dial between offensive and defensive all the way to offensive and leaving it there; it also meant a casual blurring of the difference between civilian and military. Emphasizing offense, however, also affects the second great tension for Western democracies: the desire to limit cyber operations from spilling over into extreme psychological warfare, where the uninhibited spread of propaganda operations can contaminate not only foreign populations but also your own—and subvert democracy as a result.

This desire to achieve total dominance can be safely said to have totally backfired. It has at least partially contributed to escalating tensions in cyberspace and, even more seriously, weakened the strongest defense the United States had: the implicit trust that many other governments, but also vital civilian actors, had in US leadership. This has significantly limited the US government's freedom of action on a multitude of issues, domestically and internationally, of which cyberspace concerns are only part. The United States was clearly comfortable with the perceived lawlessness of cyberspace. Until recently.

The general preference for cyber anarchy has clearly failed, even for the most hawkish advocates of US hard power. Until very recently, cyberattacks against the private sector were skyrocketing year on year, in terms of both direct costs and sheer volume. A survey of top business and security leaders in 2015 indicated that three-quarters of them were more concerned with cybersecurity than in previous years. The defense industrial base, the powerful consortium of highly sophisticated contractors such as Lockheed Martin, has had its systems repeatedly breached, and losses include terabytes of data on multibillion-dollar weapon systems. Critical infrastructure is seemingly under constant cyberattack, from the energy sector and the power grid to the financial sector, the nuclear sector, and even the health sector—and most of these intrusions are most likely simple attempts at positioning for "real" attacks, including as part of an actual war. The US government itself has seemingly not fared much better, with repeated successful attempts against virtually every large federal government institution: just between August 2014 and June 2016, the Department of Health and Human Services, the US Postal Service, the White House, the State Department, the US Central Command, and the Internal Revenue Service have all been the victims of attacks varying in complexity and magnitude. Chief among them was a data breach of fantastic proportions, the repeated hacking of the Office of Personnel Management between 2013 and 2015.

The OPM breach is probably the most serious case of cyber espionage publicly disclosed. The data stolen includes not only 5.6 million fingerprints but the personal details of nearly 21.5 *million* individuals. The US government is likely to spend at least $130 million on enhanced identity-theft services for those whose data was compromised, and the real costs are likely to be many times that amount. Worse, OPM was also responsible for keeping the 127-page forms that those applying for security clearances (outside the CIA) have to fill out—extremely detailed information on family, acquaintances, hobbies, sexual proclivities, and more. The government has not said how many of these were lost, but a high-ranking Pentagon official put it succinctly in an interview in a military journal: "They got everyone's." The "they" in this case were nearly certainly China, and the Chinese government later claimed to have arrested "criminals" who were responsible. Overall, however, the Chinese hackers are considerably less capable than the Russians; indeed, they are probably also less capable than many more "friendly" nations that routinely attack US systems, making it unlikely that this kind of leak has been unique.

The OPM catastrophe was particularly stinging because, according to a few principles that the US government has lately advanced to bring some order to the anarchy of the cyber world, it was actually a valid target for state espionage. The United States has repeatedly stated that stealing secrets is a completely legitimate activity. As the former NSA and CIA director General Michael Hayden said during an Atlantic Council panel, "Adult nations steal information from one another, and steal my secrets, shame on me, not shame on you." General Hayden has been one of the driving forces behind early American cyber capabilities, and the significance of his statement cannot be overvalued. In recent years, the US government has tried to establish a difference between "legitimate" and "illegitimate" spying: regular government national security targets, on the one hand, and the private sector and in particular IP theft, on the other hand. But the OPM hack falls into the former and is therefore, in Hayden's words, a case of "shame on me."

Hayden was partly right in using the word "shame": the OPM case showed a dismal level of InfoSec at a key facility, a single point of failure that should have very obviously required the highest levels of cybersecurity protection. In a world where the threats from cyberspace were not grossly and collectively underestimated, this hack would not have been possible in the first place. It shows how poor some aspects of governmental cyber defense are, in stark contrast to the leaked information on the offensive might of the US. Unfortunately, the benefits of being "shamed" for poor security seem to inevitably strengthen the US's more offensive components, rather than increase the pressure to find better defensive solutions.

It is the essential chicken-or-egg question: Is US cyber defense so poor because the overemphasis of offense has bled defense of necessary funding? Or is the offense so strong because the impossibility of doing defense well makes it necessary to defend through deterrence? What is clear is that the United States overall just does not do national cybersecurity very well. A 2012 McAfee-paid poll of government InfoSec professionals put the United States only in the third tier of countries with good overall national cybersecurity, ranking it behind Israel and a number of European countries. This is despite the fact that the United States easily outspends the rest of the world in government-led national cybersecurity, and undoubtedly has some of the best technical expertise to boot.

The difference in sums is staggering. The United States probably spends

somewhere between three and ten times more than what all twenty-eight
EU member states and Switzerland manage to invest, and that is just in
government. Private-sector cybersecurity spending is similarly unbal-
anced, with European cybersecurity expenditure estimated at around
€27 billion and the US market estimated to be around $75 billion in 2015
(these numbers include sales to the government). But all this additional
spending is not doing the United States much good. According to a study
by Grant Thornton, in 2015 the private sector in North America suffered
lost revenue of around $61.3 billion compared with the $62.3 billion for the
entire EU (note that this is lost revenue, not total damage, for which there
are much higher estimates). Both economies are roughly the same size, and
the losses nearly identical, but that fails to account for the damage to government systems and defense contractors, which is doubtlessly more significant in the United States than in the EU. It does therefore seem that the
EU overall spends much less money on the problem for an apparently similar (or similarly poor) result. So what is the problem?

There are two principal and differing narratives as to why the United
States is seemingly so poor at national cybersecurity. The first narrative is
the one most common among the advocates of the US government course
of the last twenty-odd years and implicitly makes the case for General
Hayden's "everyone spies" assertion, as well as the overall offensive-first
strategy aimed at total dominance. The second narrative is diametrically
opposed to the first and speculates that, in effect, US governmental cyber
has a path dependency drift. This drift directly toward the military and
national security offensive has made defense more difficult not only in the
civilian parts of the government (such as under the Department of Homeland Security), but across the public as well. Although causality is difficult
to determine, it may have even have contributed to something akin to an
international arms race in cyber, something that most likely weakens US
security.

The first and most common narrative among US national security commentators is that the United States is uniquely vulnerable to cyberattacks

because it is simply unique, period. The world's largest national economy with the greatest high-tech capabilities would always attract maximum attention from cyber criminals. The world's only hyper-power would always be in an adversarial relationship with other aspiring great powers, such as Russia and China. The dominant global cultural force would always invite enemies, fighting for religious or other reasons against what they believe the United States represents. In other words, the United States is simply that great shiny object drawing the maximum of attention—because of greed, grievances, or geopolitics. The very size of the United States gives it an incomparably larger attack surface than the much smaller countries in Europe and elsewhere, with many more options for malicious actors to wreak havoc that many more bad actors are willing to exploit.

The asymmetric nature of cyber operations has long made them attractive to a number of less endowed foreign powers, and these countries have had an early interest in cyber as a tool to address the overwhelming conventional dominance of the United States. China, for instance, may have become interested in cyber operations in the late 1990s, and today its forces vastly outnumber the "cyber warriors" of the United States—if only in manpower terms, certainly not in technical ability. The US therefore needs to contend with a number of rising powers; it is no longer the only "god of the wires" with unchallenged cyber powers.

This two-pronged vulnerability of increased visibility and larger attack surface is further complicated by a third challenge: the legal environment. As a uniquely endangered and vulnerable nation, the United States needs a unique set of defensive institutions and tools, and developing these institutions and tools, under the current framework of the US Constitution and laws, is no easy task. National cybersecurity always profits from a coordinated exchange of information between government and the non-state sector, as well as a generally centralized approach to managing government systems, both federal and state. This is uniquely difficult in the United States.

In much of Europe and Asia, these efforts are connected to critical infrastructure protection (CIP) programs. These types of programs definitely exist in the United States: indeed, they were, in effect, invented there in the late 1990s. Today, the Department of Homeland Security (DHS) has the lead in protecting the .gov domain (which amounts to all of the federal government's cyber presence except the Department of Defense) and includes a basic cyber budget of at least $1.25 billion plus various associated programs. Despite this funding, however, the ability of the DHS to actually protect the US critical infrastructure is highly limited. The National Infrastructure Protection Plan (of 2013) identified sixteen critical infrastructure sectors, from chemical to water. The exact list of which assets are considered critical is confidential, however, and indeed the process to determine which assets are included is somewhat nebulous. More important, the US government has very little power to directly help any of the private sectors, or even state entities, on the list; they are primarily responsible for protecting themselves. There is wide disagreement as to how far US legislation goes in forcing private-sector companies to enact good cybersecurity systems: some voices consider there to be very little, while others consider there to already be a lot of legislation in this direction. What is certain is that many key aspects, such as the reporting of breaches and even the exchange of information, are largely (if not completely) voluntary, at least compared with Europe, Japan, and South Korea. Overall, the US government has much less influence over its critical infrastructure assets than other large Organization for Economic Cooperation and Development (OECD) countries and is largely reliant on voluntary cooperation. These basic legal challenges are accompanied by strong political opposition to most attempts at cyber legislation, which, although often imperfect, would at least raise the overall bar of national cybersecurity.

It so follows that if defense is so difficult, the only realistic option is to basically leave the private sector to fend for itself against lower-level cybercrime threats and try to deter serious state-directed cyberattacks through the threat of punishment and investment in offensive capabilities. As we will see later, while the United States did not have an explicit public deterrence strategy until 2016, over the last decade it certainly managed to build up a level of offensive capability (meaning both espionage and attack) that knows no equal, which therefore helped to inform an implicit deterrence posture, a policy that was referenced as far back as 1998. At the same time, the US government has covertly managed to signal to (or threaten, depending on your view) adversaries the extent of these capabilities, a vital step if deterrence is to be achieved. According to a common (but in my mind questionable) narrative, these capabilities have also sufficiently rolled back the overriding attribution problem to the extent that the US government thinks it can usually identify the assailant, eliminating the prospect of foreign governments claiming plausible deniability on some of the attacks originating in their territories.

The flip side of the narrative of America's inherent vulnerability is the argument that the attempt to strive for military and intelligence dominance has probably weakened US national cybersecurity more than strengthened it.

The previous viewpoints encapsulate a present-day truism—namely, that offense is simply much easier than defense in cyberspace—and do not question it. But could not some of the resources of the NSA and the US government be directed toward shoring up the Internet for everyone, rather than trying to secure advantages that may simply not be worth the cost? As we will discuss later, the NSA and the US government overall could do much to advance global cybersecurity. Would such a "defense-first" rather than "offense-first" strategy really be so much more expensive to support for the US government, and would it really offer less tangible foreign relations returns? After all, the situation today—with US businesses hemorrhaging intellectual property, cyber criminals and spies hoovering up personal data, and hair-trigger threats to critical infrastructure taking place on what seems like a weekly basis—does not indicate that the previous approach has been successful. Not only has defense failed, but the offense-first strategy might have encouraged more governments to become active in cyberspace than otherwise would have been the case.

According to this narrative, the United States, in its urge to defend itself from foes that might not have even existed, has played a decisive role in making cyber into a domain of conflict, perhaps even more than it needed to become. Causality is of course difficult to pin down here, and the efforts of China and Russia in cyber espionage also go back to the late 1990s and early years of the twenty-first century. But as will be discussed later, it is far from clear whether these actors were realistic existential threats, or even close to establishing capabilities comparable to those of the United States.

Furthermore, the war on terror turbocharged an already highly advanced US focus on offense and provided a political and psychological cover for the wish of the military and intelligence communities to achieve "dominance." This doubling down on an offensive strategy complicated even more the already difficult task of defense. Beyond the simple question of allocation of budgetary resources, it jeopardized the intangible resource most essential to national cybersecurity: trust.

Cooperation outside the federal government—among the state governments and, most important, the private sector—has always been difficult in the United States. But the reasons for this are not simply to be found in US law. There have been repeated attempts, especially since 2010, to provide enhanced frameworks for a whole-of-nation cybersecurity cooperation. Under President Obama, many of these failed bills have had aspects of them enacted as executive orders, including components of the ill-fated Cyber Intelligence Sharing and Protection Act and indeed the expansion of the technical cyber-defense program EINSTEIN, maintained by DHS. But the resistance of Congress toward legislation cannot be explained by the acrimonious relationship with the Obama administration alone. Especially after 2012, there has been substantial opposition by those outside government as well: civil rights groups, to be sure, but also the very companies that are supposed to be protected by such oversight. And this resistance all boils down to a fundamental loss of trust. "Silicon Valley simply does not

trust the US government," said a noted expert at a Washington, D.C., meeting I attended in 2015, adding, "anymore."

The reasons for this lack of trust cannot be traced back to a single event,
though one recent development does stand out. This was what Ashton Carter, in a 2014 meeting at Harvard before his tenure as secretary of state,
called the "Cyber 9/11" of the US government: the revelation of the extent
of American cyber capabilities in the Snowden disclosures. It is important
to note that the trust of many key companies and parts of the InfoSec
community at large was probably fraying before the public became aware
of the extent of US intelligence gathering, with the effects of the Patriot Act
still very much on many people's minds. There is no doubt that since 2013
and the resulting discussion of US cyber spying, however, the trust of key
companies and individuals in the ability of the US government to do the
right thing has been significantly damaged.

It is obvious that some new thinking is necessary. Indeed, under President Obama there have been significant attempts to turn around the present cyber discourse. A groundbreaking speech by Obama in January 2014
on new limits on intelligence gathering was clearly the start of a new effort
to address this animosity both at home and abroad and win back trust with
a policy of increasing openness. Since this speech, a number of others have
followed by numerous members of the cabinet in what was doubtlessly a
concerted campaign to win back the trust of the wider public in general
and the tech industry in particular. To date, this effort has proved only
marginally successful: public and international distrust in the US national
security establishment is still probably at its highest ever, especially as
far as intelligence collection activities are concerned. The Obama White
House sometimes seemed to be waging two battles: one to convince the
world that the United States will mend its ways, and one to persuade the US
national security establishment to actually do so.

The reasons why this turnaround in sentiment is so difficult can be
summarized in a term: "path dependency." This is a recognized factor in
international relations thought, and the Harvard scholar Graham Allison,

in his early 1970s treatise, effectively described path dependency as being one of the main contributors to outcomes of government decision making, using the Cuban Missile Crisis as a case study. In her book *Borderless Wars*, Antonia Chayes describes Allison's "Type II" model as amounting to an early rebuke to other thinkers like Samuel Huntington, who described government conduct in international security to be fundamentally rational, rather than heavily influenced by internal decision-making loops. This can be taken further, in that the fundamental challenge in national security decision making is that new challenges often need to use old concepts and doctrine, even when they are not the most appropriate solutions.

Change in established processes can happen suddenly—like in times of war, or after a catastrophic high-impact kinetic event, such as 9/11. Or less strongly after a high-impact informational event, such as the leaks on the US intelligence activities in 2013. The latter became the catalyst for a fundamental rethink of cyber operations at the highest levels of government, first announced in President Obama's wide-ranging speech on intelligence operations in 2014. But turning around established policy is no easy task, and when working across a polity involving tens of thousands of officials in dozens of different government organizations, it is easy to run afoul of a number of ingrained cultures and standard operating procedures.

The White House's obvious intentions after Obama's key January 2014 NSA speech may often have been challenged by the status quo in both thought and practice, leading to mixed results. When, for example, the White House announced that the Department of Defense would in the future be much more willing to hand over zerodays it had acquired to the public and the private sector and so help defense, many took this as a sign that the White House had subscribed to a wider "stability of cyberspace" narrative than the previous Hobbesian view of conflict in this domain. President Obama's coordinator for cybersecurity, Michael Daniel, even stated that for the US government "building up a huge stockpile of undisclosed vulnerabilities while leaving the Internet vulnerable and the American people unprotected would not be in our national security interest."

This announcement has unleashed a fierce controversy as to how far the US government should release these vulnerabilities, with both sides having vocal and knowledgeable adherents. In August 2016, it became clear that while some researchers calculated that the NSA at best kept a couple of zerodays a year and in total may have only around fifty zerodays in its arsenal, many zerodays from before 2012 have in fact not been released to the public. In early 2016, a clear discussion emerged regarding how trustworthy this VEP process was, and how many exemptions could be applied to prevent the full enactment of this policy. In an interview, General Hayden raised the "no one but US" issue as a potential factor that he said played a role in early deliberations on releasing individual (or perhaps classes of) vulnerabilities. This meant that when considering whether to disclose a vulnerability, the officials might have also considered whether this was a vulnerability that only the United States could exploit technically due to its advanced prowess. Morally, it was a highly interesting dilemma: releasing this vuln would perhaps draw attention to an attack vector that many did not know existed and could arguably be even more dangerous. Hayden seemed to imply that there might be whole classes of vulns that the US government has not released due to the fact that they were simply not exploitable, at least in its mind, by anyone but the US— a somewhat radical but probably authentic statement of dominance.

It is unclear whether something like the "no one but US" criterion actually existed or exists as a policy in the VEP process today, but it is a good example of how cyber officials can often make reasonable arguments against supposedly "radical" transparency measures. This encapsulates the most significant path dependency challenge that the White House faced in fully implementing a new line from 2014 on—namely, that many of the arguments are essentially technical, and require a substantial understanding of the nuances involved. Given this complexity, a natural trend toward favoring the "operator" (and in this case the supposedly technically knowledgeable) could have been expected to significantly influence political decision making. As will be discussed, there often seems to be a rigorously bottom-up culture of putting technical feasibility before political desirability, which is hardwired into the NSA and US cyber at large, and is perhaps representative of the post-9/11 national security climate. An underlying path dependency challenge may be that when a political leadership tries to de-emphasize one major component, it inadvertently strengthens the other. While President Obama's administration has repeatedly attempted since 2014 to address (at least the perception of) the dominance of offensive over defensive capabilities in US cyber operations, it might actually have accelerated America's drift from more conventional, technical cyber programs toward psychological information warfare.

The term "information warfare" (IW) is older than any other description of cyber operations, but its meaning has significantly changed over time. The US Air Force established the Air Force Information Warfare Center in 1993. At that time, the concept of information warfare in a military context was technical, built on established practices of electronic warfare (EW)—for example, the jamming and misdirection of enemy signals, including radar. Thus, IW in its early days was more likely to involve enabling an aircraft to penetrate an air-defense system than, say, persuading a government to take a course of action through propaganda and misdirection. However, that is exactly what happened in one of the first major uses of IW tools in 1994, when deployed in the form of psychological information against the Aristide government in Haiti. As one might expect, the mission was less to hack the Haitian Internet than to engage in large-scale covert influencing operations in order to convince Haitian security to surrender to US forces without a fight. At that time, no formal doctrine of information warfare seems to have existed, but draft documents circulated within the Department of Defense between 1996 and 1999 rapidly expanded the implicit definition of IW, partially based on the Haiti experience, and differentiated it from information operations: IO was described as more kinetic, while IW was clearly more psychological. At one point around 1998, it seemed that the IW discussion was getting ahead of itself, with virtual fantasies of dominating all aspects of the enemy's decision-making processes and using all assets, including manipulating the media further to do so. The Rand researcher Martin Libicki helped to put a stop to this, arguing that "most of what US forces can usefully do in information warfare will be defensive, rather than offensive. Much that is labelled information warfare is simply not doable further at least under rules of engagement the United States will likely observe for the foreseeable future."

The result of the discussion was the political banishment of the term "information warfare" in favor of the term "information operations." IO reduced the role of problematic information attacks, such as misdirection, propaganda, and other psychological operations, to a lower level of conflict, a localized military campaign rather than a national campaign. IO was effectively made a tool of brigades and divisions and air wings fighting in an individual theater of war but not a strategic weapon—one that was directly targeted at the critical infrastructure or the political leadership of a major nation. It therefore attempted to fix psychological operations to where they have been for most of the Cold War in Western militaries: focused on the operational and tactical battlefield, rather than the strategic and political capitals. But psychological operations themselves remained important.

The doctrine of information operations was first published in 1998 in the document JP 3-13, and for many years this paper was the keystone document in understanding at least the US military's overall approach to the topic. Although it has recently been superseded by a new document (JP 3-12), it has remained highly influential in directing the thought processes of generations of cyber operations and policy specialists—everyone entering military cyber, either operator or policy specialist, is indoctrinated with the basics of JP 3-13. I consider it also to be "Patient Zero" for understanding why US cyber has developed the way it has and what dangers it has produced. This policy is not only responsible for continuing to harbor the seeds of information warfare, but it has also played a key role in obscuring the roles of defense and offense. According to a former senior army officer who was responsible for the JP 3-13 drafting process back in the

1990s, this wasn't totally unintentional: many of the military officials involved simply chose information operations over information warfare for political reasons, "to make it sound more harmless."

JP 3-13 defines information operations as having five specific components or dimensions: computer network operations (CNO), psychological operations (PSYOPS), signals (maintaining communication), military deception (MILDEC), and intelligence/counterintelligence. The only true technical cyber function is CNO, which itself includes three main tasks: computer network defense, computer network exploitation (CNE—that is, espionage), and computer network attack (CNA). This definition of IO clearly and troublingly puts equal emphasis on the CNO task and the psychological warfare components, PSYOPS and MILDEC.

Equally problematic is that this definition of CNO, which has become standard across the Western world both inside and outside the military, has defined cyber operations in a way that may seem legally logical but is technically nonsensical and even politically misleading. Differentiating between CNE (espionage) and CNA (attack) was a handy way to express the obvious legal differences between looking at data and blocking, manipulating, or destroying it. It obscures the fact that in nearly all cases CNA requires CNE to be effective—and what is CNE can be switched to CNA with the ease it takes a uniformed soldier and a civilian spy to switch chairs. Further, espionage as a whole has often been cast as a neutral, in-between task, neither defensive nor offensive. As mentioned in the previous chapter, this does not conform to the more standard and non-legalistic interpretation of what constitutes a "cyberattack," which certainly does include violations of confidentiality. This misrepresentation has allowed espionage to be framed in high-policy-level documents as actually being defensive, despite the ability to instantaneously switch many espionage networks to attack. From a defender's point of view, it is nearly impossible to separate an act of espionage from preparation for war, which creates a highly risky situation ripe for potential misunderstanding and so-called inadvertent escalation, diplomatic speak for accidental war. The notion that CNE is a defensive task is not one that many cyber operators would agree with. But claiming that CNE is a defensive task has proved handy in presenting government cyber activity to the public.

The 2008 Comprehensive National Cybersecurity Initiative (CNCI) was a detailed White House strategy drafted in the closing period of the Bush administration. In its outward-facing components, it seemed largely oriented toward purely defensive measures. While much of the CNCI and some of the document it replaced remain classified, enough was made public to support the contention that these documents did not address anything that would be considered offensive.

This assertion was called into question as early as 2008, when the newly appointed cybersecurity chief of the Department of Homeland Security quit after only one year, objecting to the expanded role of the NSA in the then-draft CNCI. In 2012, it was confirmed that a massive NSA data center being built in Utah was connected to the CNCI in an effort to support "better intelligence cooperation." And in 2015, leaked NSA documents illustrated that in 2012 the CNCI was the direct justification for a $650 million per year expansion of NSA operations directed at securing presence on "endpoints" (that is, individual target computers and networks). The document is clear that this project, called the GENIE project, also supported "DoD Information Operation activities"—a category that includes defensive but also offensive cyber operations like the disruption of enemy communications or civilian critical infrastructure. Clearly, what was being sold under the term "defensive" would scream "offensive" to most observers. While this may make plenty of sense from a purely military or intelligence standpoint, the downside is that once shown to be misleading, such strategies lower the trust in the agencies charged with carrying out these tasks.

This tradition continues today. Despite calls for openness and transparency from high up in the Obama administration, the old ways simply seem hard to change. Attempts at transparency serve as additional examples of mixed messaging. In 2015, the US military for the first time gave details on its operational cyber forces and announced that it was in the process of setting up a 6,200-strong dedicated Cyber Mission Force within the Department of Defense, to be fully manned by 2018. Two of the three components of this new mission force, the Combat Mission Teams (CMTs) and Combat Protection Teams, seem to be exactly what they claim to be, with both attack and defense roles readily apparent. The old practice of blurring the line between defense and offense seemed to return in force, however, for the third and most interesting of the new cyber bodies being set up: the National Mission Force (NMF). As the only body directly under the direction of USCYBERCOM, the NMF is a unit co-located with the NSA that previously played a crucial role in operational cyber, but which seems to have been heavily pared back under the current strategy. The NMF is composed of eight "National Support Teams" and, most important, the thirteen "National Mission Teams." The assignment of the NMF is to "defend the United States and its interests against cyberattacks of significant consequence" or even "to help defend the nation's critical infrastructure," according to a defense industry publication, which seems to give it a previously nonexistent mandate to directly support critical infrastructure providers (which are all of course privately owned) in case of a serious cyberattack. A closer look seems to indicate that this mission cannot, strictly speaking, be limited to the "defensive" space, because the US legal environment makes this largely impossible even in a state of war. As the head of USCYBERCOM, Admiral Michael S. Rogers, said in testimony in the spring of 2016, the NMF is charged with waging "full-spectrum cyberspace operations to deter, disrupt and defeat adversary cyber actors." This clearly indicates that the force is intended to counterthreaten the adversary with offensive operations. The National Mission Teams therefore seem to be the true carriers of "strategic cyber" operations, able to strike back not only at the adversary's cyber or conventional forces but also at its government and civilian infrastructure. This most likely means the option of causing countrywide havoc on major nation-states in a situation of declared war, not too dissimilar to the purpose of strategic bombers. But it could also mean the option to effect an attack without the defender even knowing that an attack had been committed, left to think that the collapse of his stock market or the repeated derailment of his trains was instead due to his own internal issues.

The bizarre truth is that there is absolutely no public indication of what these teams could do, theoretically or legally speaking. The current widening of the definition of the previous "computer network attack" to the new concept of "Offensive Cyber Effects Operations" (OCEO) in the newest US doctrine has simply expanded the level of ambiguity of what these forces are intended to do. It is not simply a technical issue—as in how capable these teams are or what tools they have. It is also a "Concept of Operations" problem—from the outside, it is impossible to judge what, for instance, OCEO, or other classified terms known only due to leaks, actually mean. With the introduction of JP 3-12 and OCEO, as well as the flood of related terms, the US is entering its third generation of visualizing conflict in this domain. But these three generations of thought have developed in an epistemic bubble, one that is nearly impenetrable for outsiders and virtually separate from any kind of "external" input—more so than even classic intelligence operations. Equally troubling, in my experience, many of the men and women who have grown up in this silicon tower are also uninterested in how cyberspace operations are perceived abroad, even among their most capable adversaries. This seems to fit the essence of the path-dependency challenge outlined by Allison many decades ago—not only are internal decision-making processes significantly dominated by adherence to hallowed concepts, such as CNE, but the very "sensors" with which external stimuli are recorded and assessed are compromised, making them potentially "color blind" to the realities of others. One of these realities is that while strong secrecy and ambiguity on force capability and intent are helpful on the tactical and operational level, they can be potentially escalatory on the strategic and political level.

The wide-scale unknowns in cyber operations means that we probably now have a level of strategic uncertainty never before experienced in the history of post-Westphalian state conflict. When a new weapon such as the tank or poison gas was introduced in World War I, there was fundamentally no question as to what its purpose was. When the Soviet Union and the United States started to deploy various weapons of mass destruction, including nuclear and biological weapons, there was little question as to their actual intent, even when particulars such as the yield of the warhead or the accuracy of the missiles in question were not communicated. In fact, throughout the entire history of the Cold War (and with the notable exclusion of the "Star Wars" Strategic Defense Initiative), the adversaries had much more knowledge about the atomic, biological, and chemical weapons aimed at each other than we do about the "digital" weapons currently being deployed. As a thought experiment, if we score the ABCD weapon complex on a transparency scale, with 100 being maximum transparency and 0 completely unknown, I would guess that by the early 1980s the opposing sides had transparency levels of about 70 for atomic, 40 for biological, and 80 for chemical weapons. The mutual transparency levels on today's digital weapons could be as low as the single digits, that is, lower than 10. Of course, for the US cyber operators assessing adversaries, the situation is likely to be quite different, with perceived knowledge of the main actors probably being quite high and with detailed inside views of their cyber forces and structures. However, time and time again it has become clear that explaining the fundamentally different outlook of countries like Russia or China to, for instance, the US national security community at large, is a difficult proposition. They simply see things differently, and that is very difficult to compute when you have three generations of thought that clearly supported a singular view of operations in cyberspace.

Part of the problem is that cyber operations are certainly not only about blowing things up, or putting fires on target, to use another military term. Beyond the kinetic-equivalent attacks that we are sure can be delivered in cyberspace, there are many options for activities that are much less kinetic and more psychological. And while the kinetic cyberattack is framed by the law of armed conflict, the psychological information warfare component is essentially lawless. The United States has never unleashed those kinetic-equivalent strategic cyber forces with full effect, but it has come close. In February 2016, the creators of the documentary *Zero Days* revealed details of the US cyber-war plan against Iran, drafted between 2008 and 2010. Their reporting indicated that the NSA Tailored Access Operations (TAO) unit had prepared a massive cyber campaign, code-named Nitro Zeus, which was "devised to disable Iran's air defenses, communications systems and crucial parts of its power grid. . . . At its height, officials say, the planning for Nitro Zeus involved thousands of American military and intelligence personnel, spending tens of millions of dollars and placing electronic implants in Iranian computer networks to 'prepare the battlefield,' in the parlance of the Pentagon."

This report is crucial in understanding not only what cyber can do but also the importance of "preparing the battlefield," also known as operational preparation of the environment (OPE). It is unclear whether the OPE described in the reports meant that there were actual cyber weapons pre-deployed to Iranian networks or whether simple implants were signaling that "the door [to the enemy networks] remained open" and that the weapons could be dropped in as needed. This may seem a minor point, but the difference between two such scenarios is tantamount to having a skeleton key to a door that one can walk through at will or to having an already planted bomb inside the room, waiting to be triggered. The key point here is that when defenders see something truly menacing, they may get their own offensive components ready without a full understanding of the threat. Depending on how far-reaching OPE and similar authorities are, we should be extremely worried about the precedent that they may set. If, for instance, Russia or China were discovered to not only have planted back doors in US systems but have effectively deposited semiautonomous cyber weapons as well, would that not be of immense concern to the political leadership? The first public indications that presumably Russian cyber weapons were predeployed in the US power grid (DarkEnergy, which we will discuss later) were met largely with shrugs from some American cyber-operators I talked to—indicating that the inevitability of predeployment of cyber weapons has seemingly been accepted by at least part of the US establishment. However, that view may not be shared by the political class, and is most likely also not the view overseas, even among America's closest allies. In an event I attended in 2010 in the U.K., a high-level British official stated that planting a "primed" cyber weapon in the adversary's sensitive networks was the same as deploying sea mines in each other's harbors—arguably an act of war. If we do not want this type of activity to occur, would it be sensible for the United States to engage in it? Because we do not know exactly how OPE or implants work, let alone how they are intended to be used, we can't answer that question—which allows the adversaries of the United States to take the worst interpretations as their point of departure and act accordingly. This is the result of a commitment to support the offensive mission over the defensive mission, and we shouldn't be surprised if countries besides the United States start to emulate it.

Chapter 7

ATTACK TO EXCESS

On the eve of the breakout of World War I, militaries across Europe became entranced by the popular philosophy of the *attaque à outrance*, or "attack to excess." France officially discarded the entire concept of the defensive, directing its entire military doctrine to put great emphasis only on the attack, which was carried out with "audacity." Germany and Russia, too, reoriented their militaries purely with offensive considerations in mind. This led to disastrous miscalculations at every level, from the tactical battlefield bloodbaths when human wave attacks were met with machine guns and trenches, to the strategic error of France seeking to advance into Germany during the opening shots of the war while the French flanks crumbled, to the foolishly aggressive political considerations that all the major powers entertained when they so haphazardly triggered the confrontation.

In a January 2014 article in *Foreign Policy*, P. W. Singer and Allan Friedman pointed out the eerie similarity of much of present-day US cyber thought to the "attack to excess" mentality in the early days of World War I.

While there are a great deal of similarities between the two eras, the most concrete is probably how poorly the prevailing military thought in both eras was equipped to handle the new technological developments. For instance, until the breakout of the war many militaries continued to insist that the function of the new airplane was to act purely as a vehicle for artillery observation, rather than as a fully fledged military arm with its own strategic use. The early history of US cyber is little different, with military arms keen to integrate it into their own capabilities, rather than accept that cyber may have a stand-alone function.

It needs to be pointed out that the contention that US cyber operations are especially permissive or even excessively offense oriented is not one that many active and former US cyber operators share. In fact, many of these professionals will complain in conversation that the great amount of approval necessary for cyber operations puts it on a totally different plane than normal "kinetic" operations. As recounted earlier, the saying in the NSA that it was "easier to shoot someone than send an e-mail" is clearly indicative of these norms. However, it is also possible that this comparison—and therefore the sentiment itself—is wrong. For it is also much easier for the US military to shoot someone than to use nonlethal chemical weapons, and likewise it is easier to order a military operation with scores of casualties than a targeted assassination of an individual, let alone a political leader. Using the level of lethality as a yardstick by which to measure how much approval a mission should require may seem to intuitively make sense, but only at first glance. For while the law of armed conflict is very clear in conventional conflict, in cyber conflict there is much more room for interpretation, and therefore for potential missteps.

Before the first major strategies were published in the United States in the late 1990s, the government had already been dealing with cyber issues for over a decade, and without much public policy to speak of. An episode with a freelancing German hacker working for the KGB in 1988—quite possibly the first freelance cyber contractor for hire—certainly had an important role in getting operational information security, basic cyber defense, into the wider narrative. This German computer hacker had acquired root privileges on the system of the Lawrence Berkeley National Laboratory in California but was also responsible for many other attacks on the ARPANET and the MILNET, its military counterpart. An account of the hunt for the hacker was published in 1989: *The Cuckoo's Egg* went on to become a bestseller, maybe the very first one featuring IT security. This book helped create the policy momentum for the US government to start taking cybersecurity seriously. The first defensive US operational units akin to computer emergency response teams already existed in the early 1980s. The MILNET, the DoD's own network, was completely disentangled from what immediately after became the global Internet (with the introduction of DNS in 1983). When the Morris worm, the first significant case of a global Internet virus, hit American defense networks in 1988, the Department of Defense activated further defensive measures. During this early period of US cyber, there was mostly only defense; as no other nation had significant exposure to the (or an) Internet, no one could be attacked through this medium. Consequently, the lack of an offensive role made it relatively uninteresting for the military.

This changed with the explosive growth of the World Wide Web from the mid-1990s, and very soon defenders started to be able to carve out a much more glorious offensive role for themselves. An in-depth study by Jason Healey on the development of US cyber thought provides some insight into how much the military commanders of the earliest information operations units saw offense and defense as two sides of the same coin. In an interview, the commander of the US Air Force 609th Information Warfare Squadron—probably the world's first declared military cyber unit, founded in 1995—talked of how they saw offensive and defensive operations as being bound together in the same unit. He said that although "the split between defensive and offensive . . . was approximately 70/30, offensive being 30 percent . . . , during mission time it was probably reversed."

There is not much public history of what these units did in the early years of their lives, especially on the offensive side. Besides (probably) limited support of US operations against Haiti in 1994, it would seem that nearly all of these units' activities were training exercises and not directed against foreign foes. This helped formulate higher-level policy on the matter, which, however, might have been more of a result of what the United States could simply do to itself if it had the mind to, rather than what any likely adversary was at the moment (or near future) able to do.

The first national-level policy document was the Presidential Decision Directive-63 (PDD-63), signed by President Clinton in 1998. The opening of the document reads, "The United States possesses both the world's strongest military and its largest national economy. Those two aspects of our power are mutually reinforcing and dependent. They are also increasingly reliant upon certain critical infrastructures and upon cyber-based information systems." It focused on the need to defend the United States' critical infrastructures, including but not limited to telecommunications, energy, banking and finance, transportation, water systems, emergency services, and the cyber-based systems, from a host of possible adversaries, both state and non-state. PDD-63 was a massively important document that initiated the first series of attempts toward national cybersecurity, creating the concept of critical infrastructure protection within a "public-private partnership" context. Today, public-private partnerships are the bedrock of much cooperation between state and non-state actors within a formal environment, especially for the large CIP programs. These programs are huge: today, the US Department of Homeland Security maintains contact with thousands of critical infrastructure operators and is involved in a never-ending ballet (or mud-wrestling match) to encourage cooperation that involves coercion (laws to force compliance) and co-option (money), but sadly little in the way of the pure soft power of conviction.

PDD-63 defined a number of key factors for cybersecurity, including information exchanges and response teams. It showed a very high level of sophistication and in both its analysis and its recommendations could very well have been written in recent years. The language used is striking and shows that away from the public eye considerable thought and concern had already been put into the wider subject of the destructive potential of strategic cyberattacks. No evidence is cited, but it is clear that these concerns existed—even if they were not made public. The American intelligence community had apparently seen the havoc that cyberattacks could wreak, but for some time it was unclear whether these US nightmares of cybergeddon were based on the action of foreign adversaries, or whether the panic was simply based on the United States holding up its own capabilities to a mirror and taking fright.

That mirror might have been a 1997 senior-level military exercise called Eligible Receiver 97 (ER 97) and sponsored by the Pentagon's Joint Chiefs of Staff. NSA and DoD hackers were given free rein to wage unrestricted cyber war against the United States, posing as a hostile nation but operating largely from within the United States. The exercise involved the FBI, Department of Justice, Department of Transportation, and many others. What exactly occurred in the exercise is classified, although it conveniently generated a great amount of public media coverage in the late 1990s. The reports included quotations that the US power grid had been frighteningly easy to take over and that the deployability of US Pacific forces had been seriously curtailed. The key term here is "frighteningly"; one cyberlibertarian newsletter snarled that the entire exercise amounted to "a Pentagon ghost story repeated ad nauseam to journalists and the easily frightened in which ludicrous or totally unsubstantiated claims about menaces from cyberspace are passed off as astonishing deeds of techno-heroism performed by cybersoldiers working within a highly classified wargame." Though the article has a clear antigovernment bias, the author has a point: the sheer wealth of public and media statements on ER 97 certainly indicate its broader messaging purpose for the US government. It undoubtedly had a key importance for the formulation of PDD-63 just a year later.

Some of the implied claims of ER 97 were somewhat undermined by one of the few actual cyber incidents that are known to have occurred just a few years later. A series of attacks on the DoD networks, code-named Solar Sunrise, originally seemed to back the visions of state directed doom conjured up in ER 97. A number of wild theories were leaked to the press, with some even speculating that Saddam Hussein was getting into cyber warfare. It was therefore more than anticlimactic when it was discovered that the attackers were neither from Iraq, terrorists, foreign intelligence services, or even nation states but two teenagers from California coached by a student in Israel.

This nonevent, which should have been an embarrassment, turned out to be a media boon. The fact that they were seemingly harmless kids was used as an argument to support the contention that better-resourced attackers would doubtlessly be much worse: the ringleader was, at the time of the incident, nineteen years old. The event was not only a gift for the already nascent multibillion-dollar industry selling cybersecurity products and services to the government but also a true gift to military cyber seeking to expand its remit. And just in time too, for another attack made public in February 1998 turned out to be much worse.

First revealed to the public in a *Newsweek* article later that year, Moonlight Maze ranks as one of the most well-published cyber-espionage campaigns to take place prior to the Stuxnet campaign. Although remarkably little information of the specifics of the attack was ever released, the attack reached the public through a flood of innuendos, half leaks, and statements by senior policy makers.

Newsweek would reveal what little was known about "one of the most potentially damaging breaches of American computer security ever," allegedly conducted by "crack cyberspooks from the Russian Academy of Sciences" (another outlet reported that the Defense Department traced the trail back to a mainframe computer in the former Soviet Union) and targeting computer systems at the Departments of Defense and Energy as well as military contractors and leading civilian universities; the account made clear that it was serious enough for the Department of Defense to order all of its civilian and military employees to change their computer passwords.

While what exactly was stolen is not publicly known (initial reports by *Newsweek* that this could "include classified naval codes and information on missile-guidance systems" were later denied), one of the most captivating media quotations was from the then deputy secretary of defense, John Hamre: "We're in the middle of a cyberwar." This was the first time the term "cyberwar" was used by a senior official, and it stuck.

Despite additional tidbits of information that became public in later years, the attribution to the Russian government remained fuzzy to those without special briefings on the subject. For as advanced as Moonlight Maze may have seemed to the media and wider public, seasoned professionals were less impressed. The targeting was not only somewhat haphazard and—at least in its initial stages—marked by poor operational security, it was also unnecessarily "loud" and used more assets than were strictly necessary. Some commentators doubted that Russian intelligence would be so careless as to willingly sacrifice many of its best cyber assets; key logistic components (such as persistent access to a US research network that enabled the attacker to access unclassified Pentagon systems) were "burned" in the attack, and lost to future operations. The possible motivations for this first significant cyber-espionage attempt range from the personal enrichment of some Russian spooks (some of the targets seemed to have more commercial than political value), to an internal power play of the rising FSB (my favorite), to a much more nefarious distraction mission that simply was a cover for a much more serious (and publicly unreported) intrusion. The little we know of previous attempts by the Russians to exploit the Internet, however, indicates that they were far behind the United States, and these attacks confirmed that view: their much trumpeted success in stealing data was much more a feature of the poor cyber defenses than of advanced attack techniques. I have spent years interviewing various members of the intelligence community on this first major cyberattack, and on balance I think it is most plausible that the campaign was simply as good as Russian intelligence was able to do at that point in time—and that was not terribly good.

This would mean that the Russian capabilities of the time might have been overblown, and the claim that there was an actual "cyberwar" was, intentionally or not, significantly overstated. As a senior USCYBERCOM official confirmed to me in 2015, the Russians largely "went dark" for a bit less than a decade after Moonlight Maze, with little comparable activity until 2007, when a number of similar espionage networks, reusing parts of the same Moonlight Maze codebase and even some logistic support, became active again (one of these networks is now called Turla or Snake). The official backed my assumption that Moonlight Maze was in fact the best the Russians had to offer at the time—and, it needed to be said, that was simply generations behind the US capabilities. The Russian cyber bear was at best a cyber cub.

At the time of reporting, however, Moonlight Maze was still being presented as a case of the Russian cyber bear growling fiercely. This had a significant impact on releasing more funds for cyber within the US military, which might have been intended to address the obvious shortcoming in US defenses and in the DoD in particular. The military had other ideas, however, and playing defense was just not very sexy.

The US military seems to have had an inherent philosophical need to combine the offensive and defensive side that went beyond the obvious practical benefits and ranged into the emotional. The Joint Task Force–Computer Network Operations (JTF–CNO) was the result: set up in 2000 on the basis of a previous defensive organization, it was dedicated to both protecting US networks and launching cyberattacks on state adversaries. The reasons for this insistence on combining the offensive and the defensive mission are probably multifaceted and partially certainly sensible, but that insistence also led to a continued subordination of the defensive mission to the offensive that was to have a decisive effect in later years. The emphasis of the offensive mission might also have represented the desire by the Joint Chiefs to put down a bureaucratic marker claim to keep the offensive cyber mission in the military, instead of leaving it purely in the intelligence community.

There are indications that the CIA in particular was interested in the Internet from the very beginning. In his book *Tubes,* Andrew Blum repeats the rumor that one of the three earliest Internet exchange points in the mid-1980s, MAE-East, was located in Virginia to facilitate the CIA's snooping on Internet traffic. This is probably also partially the origin of the Russian president Vladimir Putin's oft-stated claim that the Internet was in fact a "CIA project." The CIA reportedly first set up its dedicated cyber division, the Information Operations Center (IOC), in October 2000. But the IOC, as we shall see later, had a different focus on cyber from the more kinetically minded NSA.

What was publicly reported is that in 1998 the NSA housed the Information Operations Technology Center (IOTC), a joint intelligence-military unit that had strong support from the NSA's P42 information warfare cell and the CIA's Critical Defense Technologies division. The IOTC appears to have provided the NSA with the back doors necessary for getting into actual attacks, which nearly always required previous "exploitation"—that is to say, espionage. It drew on the NSA's substantial technical expertise in two of the core areas of cyber operations: understanding how to protect information systems, and the ability to conduct signals intelligence (SIGINT). SIGINT is an old art that already played a war-defining role in World War II—the ability of the Allies to read Japanese and German communication codes is largely considered by many historians to have been decisive in the outcome of that conflict.

The best way to make your encryption secure is to continuously try to find ways to crack it. For this reason, the NSA and many other agencies like it worldwide often have a code-maker and code-breaker function under one roof. This code-maker/code-breaker duo was illustrated in some of the earliest public examples of cyber activities, and this duality seemed to perfectly align with the military narrative of the need to have defense and offense in the same team. The only problem was that the NSA mandate was clearly defined as being US Code Title 50 espionage (properly "national defense"), not Title 10 "armed forces," even if the NSA did belong to the

Department of Defense. This did not seem to stop the IOTC, and because the discrepancy was not called out, this turned out to be the cornerstone for the NSA's progress in taking over not only much of cyber intelligence but also other cyber operations as well. In the year 1999, it might have been obvious that "cyber" was the future, but national defense in the late 1990s was still in the process of downsizing after the Cold War. Information operations had been placed on a tight leash for the previous ten years, and besides limited operations against Haiti and Serbia there was not that much call for their full destructive power. That need dramatically changed two years later.

The impact of the September 11 terror attacks, and the resulting Global War on Terror, upended the existing national security landscape in the United States. Of course, this change was not instantaneous, but it seemed irresistible, especially in the early years after the attacks. It connected a massive increase in defense spending with an equally dramatic change in sentiment: the nation was at war, and many of the old rules and ways went out the window. The ability of cyberspace to accelerate preexisting trends was born out here to the fullest. While cyberspace, on its own, has a remarkable ability to reinforce general trends and accentuate specific developments, the changes that 9/11 had on the overall conduct of cyber operations cannot be overstated.

The dramatic change in the legislative environment was far-reaching. The Patriot Act of October 2001 created the largest signals intelligence apparatus ever designed. Revised in 2006 and finally allowed to expire (at least in parts) in 2015, the Patriot Act included legal measures to expand both domestic and foreign intelligence gathering and set the stage for billions of dollars of additional spending, primarily by the NSA, to that end. It also involved non-state actors to a much wider degree than was previously practiced, something that was later to play a key role in undermining the willingness of the private sector to continue cooperation some ten years later.

The two most visible components were within the Foreign Intelligence

Surveillance Act (FISA): the Section 215 domestic metadata bulk collection program and the Section 702 targeting of non-US persons overseas. The Section 215 metadata collection program was often given the most attention in the US media, because the collection of telephone records supposedly affected millions of Americans (no exact number is known). Government officials have taken great pains to assert that "no one was listening to your phone calls," because metadata in this context only meant the number dialed and the length of the call. Remarkably absent from the public debate was that Section 215 metadata also includes e-mails (to/from and subject headings) and, even more important, all IP addresses. Given that your average home PC or smart phone is probably in contact with dozens of IP addresses at any one time (even if you think you are just looking at one Web page), this program was much more significant in gathering intimate information on US persons than the phone metadata program, which consumed most of the public discussion. Section 215 also allowed for the collection of "tangible things" useful to a government investigation. According to the Electronic Frontier Foundation, "The list of possible 'tangible things' the government can obtain was seemingly limitless and could include everything from driver's license records to Internet-browsing patterns."

The expiry of the metadata collection program in the United States in 2015 did not, however, mean that the American intelligence community had lost its best tools—far from it. At least as intrusive domestically as the metadata program was the expansion of the practice of issuing national security letters (NSLs), effectively secret court orders forcing companies to comply with investigations. From 2005 to 2015, more than 300,000 NSLs were issued, mostly to Internet and telecom companies and banks. These NSLs did not have to apply to a specific person, but could involve any category of words deemed necessary to further the investigation. These words are called "selectors" and can be used to automatically scan and retrieve communications, such as e-mails, that comply. Sometimes a single NSL could have a number of selectors; a single NSL filed in 2013 included thirty-six thousand selectors. It is unknown whether each selector was regarding a specific individual, or whether it included general terms more likely to ensnare thousands on its own, such as the simple term "bomb." The use of NSLs was not discontinued with the end of the Patriot Act, although legislators have made repeated attempts to expand oversight of the program.

Much more powerful are the means included in Section 702 of the Foreign Intelligence Surveillance Act, as well as the little-known Reagan-era Executive Order 12333. In this case, the opposite is effectively the case: with some notable exceptions in FISA, the surveillance of US persons (a legal term meaning US citizens and resident foreigners) was effectively forbidden. Non-US persons, on the other hand, had virtually no protection whatsoever; all of their data was effectively fair game. The complications arose with regard to the application of so-called minimization procedures: methods to ensure that no US person was inadvertently surveilled. It was nearly always going to be impossible to ensure that US person information was not inadvertently collected (which in the NSA terminology is not the same as surveilled), and then only later minimized to reduce the chance that an analyst would see it. The Section 702 and EO 12333 programs, as we shall see, were able to collect most of the world's Internet traffic, including much more intimate data on US persons than was ever possible with Section 215 metadata collection. The Section 702 programs are due to expire in December 2017, but their importance is such that it is virtually unthinkable that, if this occurs, they will not be replaced with something similarly capable. For most of the NSA activities would be impossible without them.

The NSA is not the only home of US cyber operators, but it is one of the best understood organizations due to the flood of leaked documents. These documents show that the US intelligence-gathering capabilities, which are intertwined with cyberattack capabilities, are even more advanced than the most generous assessment. In the post-9/11 era, they were also being deployed in ways even the most pessimistic of civil rights advocates would not have expected.

A cyber operator working in the first dedicated NSA cyber unit, the TAO Remote Operations Center (ROC), raves about his job in an internal NSA newsletter from 2006: "What if your job was to exploit a target's computer, collect voice cuts from an adversary's phone system, use a terrorist's Web-based email account to infect them with a Trojan horse, and assist the military in locating a high value terrorist target for capture—all in a day's work? Then you would be working in the Remote Operations Center!"

The Fort Meade Remote Operations Center is the operational heart of an NSA organization previously known as the Tailored Access Operations group, which has now been upgraded to its own building at the Fort Meade NSA complex. TAO's predecessor had been around most likely since the late 1990s, a time when national cyber military structures were much less organized—until the Global War on Terror changed all that. TAO played and continues to play a key role in the US military's ability to "find-fix-finish" terrorist adversaries; for instance, a 2013 *Washington Post* article implied that TAO played a crucial part in tracking down Osama bin Laden's hiding location in northern Pakistan. Despite the obvious emphasis on counterterrorism, much of the focus of NSA cyber operations was probably rather more counterstate, given the overall low-tech nature of their adversary. The Patriot Act provided the boon, however, in that it also covered state-directed counterespionage operations. The overriding mission and philosophy of the ROC can be summarized by its unofficial motto: "Your data is our data, by any legal means." Given the relative ineffectiveness of much of the Patriot Act for counterterrorism purposes, as discussed later, it is probably safe to assume that most of this data belonged not to terrorist actors, as the Patriot Act intended, but instead to nation-state adversaries and their affiliates.

In 2015, the *Washington Times* reported that the FBI was not able to point to a single terrorist case that had been resolved with the help of Section 215 Patriot Act powers, but a White House review panel found that the

Section 702 powers exercised by the NSA had been "much more efficient" and had had a real effect in disrupting terrorist activity. The director of the NSA went on the record to say that more than "50 terrorist plots" had been foiled using Sections 215 and 702 authorities, so it would appear all of these successes, if accurate, were part of the 702 programs, many of which would have been executed by the TAO. I would advance the speculation, however, that these fifty foiled terrorist plots over a period of fifteen years could probably be compared with the many hundreds of significant cyberattacks and espionage activities that the 702 programs were also able to discover, if not always prevent. While it may be impossible to prove, even with access to confidential information, it is quite possible that the biggest beneficiaries of the counterterrorism legislation were cyber operations writ large— most of which would have inevitably applied to nonterrorist adversaries.

TAO probably amounted to no more than a thousand actual operators at its peak, and it represented a fundamental shift in the NSA's mission away from intelligence gathering toward covert action and sabotage. Previously, the NSA's overall SIGINT mission was applicable only if information was being transmitted from point A to point B. With TAO, SIGINT was suddenly being redefined in terms of "breaking and entering," much more the CIA remit, and the term "SIGINT at rest" (as opposed to "SIGINT in motion") was coined to allow this type of activity, which included both hacking a computer and the physical planting of a listening device. The NSA already had some experience in supporting physical covert action through its engagement in the joint CIA-NSA Special Collection Service (a special paramilitary organization maintained by the two agencies), but only at arm's length. The TAO represented an in-house commitment to covert action with physical effects, and even the potential fighting of a real war. It is not clear whether the NSA as a whole, let alone the TAO, had the right culture for this kind of mission, and it certainly did not have the experience that the CIA did. Suddenly the NSA was entrusting technical operators to make the kinds of geopolitical-critical decisions—evaluating sensitive trade-off such as value of intelligence versus the political repercussion of discovery—that previously only seasoned CIA case officers had to ponder. At the same time, the NSA was struggling to make the transition to the modern bulk Internet collection activity that the Patriot Act envisioned.

The first program, called Trailblazer, was largely outsourced to the private sector in 2002. Although the program managed to collect a large amount of data, the casual violation of privacy prompted a number of leaks and a highly critical DoD investigation in 2004. The program was shut down in 2007 due to massive cost overruns and dubious success and replaced with Turbulence. Turbulence later split into a host of other programs that were leaked primarily in the Snowden disclosures and that had a definitive impact on the view of US intelligence gathering. Taken together, these programs show that the United States has already accomplished much of its stated mission of "global network dominance," which, in its details, still remains classified.

These programs—which change their names every few years and are therefore less significant than the technology they represent—can be broken down into three broad categories: upstream collection, or targeting the major cables and routers called the Internet backbone; downstream collection, or targeting large content intermediaries and processors of data like Yahoo and Facebook; and end-point collection, or the prosecution of individual targets, be they individual terrorists or foreign governments, via their own devices, such as home computers or smart phones. While all of it could be described as "hacking," only endpoint collection really comes close to the traditional image of what hacking entails.

The NSA's role in upstream collection developed seamlessly from its preexisting global SIGINT mission, with one critical difference. While more traditional intercept programs such as Echelon (largely targeted at satellite communication) required a global presence, much of the collection carried out on the Internet could, at least initially, be executed from the continental United States. Indeed, until the turn of the millennium, nearly 80 percent of the world's traffic passed through US territory. Upstream collection therefore primarily involved setting up secure facilities within tele-com operators and large Internet exchange points. The system functions by first asking the telecom operator to segment traffic most likely to be of in-terest for "foreign intelligence" purposes—an important distinction, be-cause the NSA is not supposed to gather information on US persons. This segmented information is then filtered again using "selectors"—keywords or numbers relevant to national security—but also encryption, which was previously thought to indicate criminal activity and thus automatically at-tracted attention. This selected information is then shipped to an NSA data center for storage and possible later analysis and decryption if necessary. Using over a dozen locations in the United States as a physical point of ac-cess, upstream collection can cover around 75 percent of the entire Internet traffic transiting the United States. The NSA has similar commercial agree-ments with a number of telecom companies outside the United States, facil-itated mostly by local partners in the intelligence community.

Further, the NSA does not always ask for permission. Besides critical cables and IXPs overseas, the NSA has directly tapped into the networks of large content aggregators, in particular Google. Although forbidden to hack Google's data centers directly due to its US incorporation, the NSA sidestepped this restriction and simply tapped the cables connecting these data centers—another example of a violation of the spirit, if not the letter, of the law.

It was also largely unnecessary. The downstream collection method ac-complishes the same function. A prime example, the Prism program, has over a number of years compelled virtually all of the major American IT and content companies, including Yahoo, Facebook, Apple, and Google, to agree to an automated access of some of their data by the NSA. A leaked NSA PowerPoint presentation from 2013 shows that this data included e-mail, voice, chat, and video—anything really that occurred within that company's systems relevant to the target. It was falsely reported in the media analysis of the Snowden documents that Prism meant that all data was being collected: only information that conformed to the selectors was transmitted. Because, however, some of the selectors are probably very wide, this confirms that millions of US persons had their data collected—even if inadvertently.

End-point collection techniques have created nearly as much stir, partially due to their technical ingenuity but also their seemingly casual violation of privacy and property ownership. The most interesting—although a bit technical—is the Foxacid and Quantum family of programs, which execute what is known as a type of "man-on-the-side" attack. These had the ability to impersonate packets going in and out of a target's computer connecting to a legitimate Web site—say, for instance, Facebook—and inject malware directly into the target's computer. This made conventional security measures useless; if properly implemented, this kind of attack would frame any malware as traffic coming from Facebook, passing through virtually all but the most advanced and intrusive defense mechanisms. To accomplish this, the NSA needed to be closer—physically closer—to the targeted computer than Facebook's own computers and quite literally beat the speed of light (of communication). This meant having so-called monitors, computers in the geographic vicinity of every Facebook server that would observe the target, and so-called shooters, which would immediately intervene when one of the targeted computers reached out to Facebook and redirect it to one of the NSA's computers. What is really troubling is that instead of the NSA using its own computers for this monitoring and shooting, it used compromised private routers, sometimes civilian home computers whose only relevance was their physical approximation to the target, their high availability, and the quality of their bandwidth. Your Internet router at home could be used by the NSA as part of the Quantum network, making you part of this espionage campaign without even knowing it.

It's worth clarifying that all of these collection procedures are separate from actual analyses of the data. Some of these analysis frameworks, such as XKeyscore and Boundless Informant, have featured prominently in the media due to the photogenic appearance of their user interfaces. They are tools for use by a human analyst that draw upon data that is stored or instantly available. Surveillance begins when a human analyst views the data, and prior to that an automated "minimization" process is run to ascertain the likelihood that the communication involves a US person. The details of the process are unknown, but some information publicly disclosed provides glimpses of the NSA's big data muscle: minimization probably involves a hugely complex array of indicators, from language use to content indicators to location data, to provide a final probability score if in fact the data in question was from a US person. If the score is high enough, it was to be discounted for human analysis—read: surveillance—purposes.

Indeed, a major component in advanced intelligence gathering is the ability to crunch huge amounts of thinly related data—ranging from IP numbers to credit card transactions to fluctuations in the power grid—to draw conclusions about an actor's attributes, activities, or even identity. Akin to the way Facebook or LinkedIn can provide hints on the people that you may know—and how accurate these suggestions are—the NSA uses the same techniques to extract interesting information on a selected target out of a massive pool of information available. In some cases, these systems cheat: in the case of social networks, they register that, for instance, someone has looked at your profile and thus contend that you may know the person as well. In other cases, however, the systems conduct a variant of something called "contact chaining" to calculate the people you may know from the activity of your contacts. The US Patriot Act metadata program came under a lot of criticism because the NSA habitually did contact chaining out to three "hops": looking not only at whom you might have called but at whom that person might have called and whom those people might have called. So, if, for instance, one takes the 27,090 numbers that were used as selectors in 2009 and if one presumes only 10 contacts per person, then three hops represented approximately 27 million people. As part of the NSA's intelligence-gathering reform announced in January 2014, President Obama said that the United States would use only two hops in the future.

But the reason why this was abandoned might have also been simply technical, for old-style contact chaining on its own is very much obsolete. Instead, access to huge data "haystacks" collected in bulk (in the words of Keith Alexander, a former director of the NSA and USCYBERCOM) and massive processing power can truly unlock big data analysis beyond anything that can be imagined in the private sector. It allows you to know, for instance, that ten persons of interest in, say, Pudong just switched off their phones and then that a credit card receipt is generated two hours later by one of them for ten meals. Or that one of the ten then decided to unplug his home router, but that a Wi-Fi network close to his home has started to show signs of Tor communication. And that around the same time someone using a Tor network accessed Microsoft's Bing and searched for "Sony US Pictures." Taken together, that would indicate that some Chinese cyber spies had just been briefed on the Sony hack, but from the point of view of a spectator, not an active participant.

As it turned out, the US intelligence community used another source of intelligence to back its claim that North Korea was behind the Sony hack. This depended not on big data analysis but on something much more tangible: its ability to monitor the adversary's network and watch, in real time, how these attacks are coded and executed. The United States conducted this surveillance with the help of what the NSA calls "implants" that constitute a direct presence in a network without the network owner knowing about it. This is called "being resident on a network"—tantamount to breaking into a house and watching everything that was going on there without the residents detecting your presence. In 2013, it was reported that the NSA was resident on some fifty thousand networks worldwide. This is an astonishing number, because the global Internet (which does not include private networks) itself is composed only of around forty-two thousand networks.

A January 2016 article by the *New York Times* correspondent David Sanger was replete with juicy details on how the US government had conducted, since 2010, a surge program to penetrate North Korea, in particular the networks of its offensive cyber unit, Bureau 121. It explained the process of "implanting sensors" into key nodes of the enemy, and even into the very code of its offensive malware, so it would signal whenever an attack was launched—coincidentally called an "early warning" device.

A more in-depth analysis in another article drew upon documents supposedly released in the Snowden trove to show that this early-warning network was even more complex. It indicates that the information for the North Korea Sony network came from a South Korean cyber-spy network that the NSA had sneaked into—presumably without asking first—and that had extensively mapped the North Koreans. This is apparently standard practice and is called fifth-party collection; in other words, "the NSA spied on a foreign intelligence agency that was spying on a different foreign intelligence agency that had interesting data of its own." The only real surprise here is that the spy network that was penetrated belonged to South Korea, an American ally. While most outsiders may be bewildered about this casual indication of one's spying on one's friends, this is perfectly normal in the world of cyber. "Friendly nations spy on each other," Keith Alexander has said in closed gatherings, sometimes adding, "Get over it." He was publicly echoed by the researcher Max Boot: "I have a word of advice for American allies outraged by alleged NSA spying on their leaders: Grow up. . . . You just don't have the resources or capability to spy as effectively as the NSA does. But if you did, you would."

This episode encapsulates two challenges of how cyberspace can both accentuate path dependency issues, and bring them into sharp relief compared with other practices. On the one hand, Boot and Alexander were evidently reflecting common US practice that predated the Internet. On the other hand, it shows that this practice, no matter how long-standing, can mutate into something else entirely, even more evident in the world of cyber espionage. First, there are quite clearly various levels of violation of trust of friends and allies that remain undifferentiated in the blanket statement of "everyone spies." For me, it is obvious that passive SIGINT—collecting signals without actually having to tap a cable, even directed against a head of state (for instance, Chancellor Angela Merkel's mobile phone)—is one thing. Actively breaking and entering into a friendly property and planting bugs (as apparently happened in the European Commission) is quite another. And for most nonspooks it would seem obvious that any attempts to corrupt a member of a friendly intelligence agency to betray his or her oath of office and divulge secrets is nearly always a really risky proposition. This also occurred in Germany, where the German intelligence services discovered this only after the corrupted agent in question, a member of the foreign intelligence BND, was arrested trying to sell the same data to the Russians. Besides the very real and noticeable damage that this has done to the Western alliance as a whole on a political level, at a strategic level it can't be a logical objective to corrupt your allies to the point where they try to sell themselves to your common adversaries. As illogical as it may seem, however, I have been led to believe that this does indeed correspond with long-standing practice, as least as far as the CIA is concerned. Recruiting among friendly services is, bizarre as it may seem, part of the job description—and furthermore, during the episode described above, Germany was "on the verge of being considered a hostile service" due to its lack of intelligence cooperation. If one takes the view of Max Boot, then other countries do not engage in sophisticated espionage against the United States only because they lack the capabilities. I would think that virtually every nation on the planet has the fiscal capability to potentially bribe and corrupt a US official, and Americans should be very concerned with this precedent. Furthermore, governments are developing those technical capabilities at a rapid clip, and most of the advanced capabilities are with countries that are generally friendly toward the US. No matter what previous practice may have been, it seems to be pure folly to invite allies, some of whom have been directly trained and equipped by the US, into a culture of "everyone spies"—and thus inadvertently encourage them to try their hand at subverting US targets.

There is the obvious political challenge of carelessly endangering major allies over possibly minor intelligence collection issues. The blowback when they are discovered can have severe ramifications on all types of public policies, and insisting that Germany "get over it" from abroad does not help address the reflexive increase in anti-Americanism it helped engender. The ramification went so far as Germany and Brazil teaming up in the UN General Assembly to sponsor a resolution that effectively indirectly criticized the US practice—something probably unthinkable only a couple of years earlier. There is no doubt that the political ramifications of having these campaigns revealed have been a major body blow to a number of bilateral relationships with the United States. It also has very clearly weakened American soft power across Europe, creating a fertile ground for the virulent anti-American (and antiliberal) narratives that have been strewn, largely by Russia, as part of a clear attempt to further weaken the Western alliance.

There are also quite clear practical ramifications of the NSA narrative "trust no one." For if you are likely to conduct yourself in that manner with your friends, you can hardly complain when they do the same—as the US experience with Stuxnet, the first modern kinetic-equivalent cyberattack, amply showed.

The Stuxnet campaign is another candidate for being the "world's first major cyberattack": a joint US-Israeli cyber campaign against Iranian nuclear enrichment facilities spread across the country, but in particular at the facility at Natanz. It most likely started in 2008, and after making its way from network to network it finally managed to reach the heart of the Iranian enrichment process: the industrial control systems responsible for controlling the thousands of centrifuges that enriched uranium. This crucial step is necessary both for civilian uses and for building nuclear weapons. Stuxnet subtly manipulated the control software so that the roughly child-sized centrifuges would spin faster than their designed operating speed of sixty-three thousand revolutions per minute—up to one-third faster—than the instrumentation would show. This caused progressive decay on the centrifuges, wearing them out much faster than expected. Figures later published by the International Atomic Energy Agency (IAEA) indicate that the number of known Iranian centrifuges decreased in 2009–10 by around one-fifth, at a time when the Iranians had been more than doubling their centrifuge capacity every year since 2007. Seen from a purely tactical point of view, the operation was a clear success, impeding if not outright destroying the Iranians' nuclear program, while leaving them none the wiser as to the actual cause.

None the wiser, that is, until 2010, when Stuxnet "broke out" of its defined battlefield and went global. Stuxnet was so viral that before long it was found not only on Siemens ICS products (which the Iranians had pirated for use in their systems) but everywhere. At its height, in the summer of 2010, over 100,000 computers in dozens of countries worldwide were infected by a piece of malware that didn't seem to do anything and that no one understood. But it was only a matter of time before the initial erroneous reports were superseded by better technical analysis and investigative journalism, including Kim Zetter's *Countdown to Zero Day* and David Sanger's *Confront and Conceal*. The key chapter of Sanger's book is entitled "Olympic Games," which refers to the overall US code name for the covert operations against Iran. The book also has a wealth of insider source reporting that shows that while the policy side could be well thought out, the intelligence tradition of "trusting no one" could really haunt US spies as well.

According to Sanger, Stuxnet only "broke out" due to an update executed around March 2010 by the Israeli partners without informing or consulting the United States. "We think there was a modification done by the Israelis," an unidentified US source reportedly told the president, "and we don't know if we were part of that activity." Vice President Joe Biden then accused the Israelis of going "too far," a source told Sanger. But President Obama was persuaded by the NSA to keep the operation alive, because it had already achieved such good results.

It is unclear whether the president was truly made aware of the political ramifications of the attack becoming public, or indeed of the danger of the possibility of such a cyber weapon becoming available to third parties to replicate and use themselves. For while the Stuxnet "warhead" was specific to the Iranian enrichment program, the "worm" that made it so virulent could be copied and repurposed by America's enemies as well.

From the American point of view, the episode marked a case of "inadvertent release." This was the phrase that a number of senior US policy makers, both active and retired, used in 2010 when the topic of Stuxnet came up in informal discussions with my colleagues and myself. It was also the term used in a senior-level US meeting I attended in the summer of 2011 (which included two well-known journalists), when it was repeated so often that even those of us without secret clearance could not fail to get the message. The problem was, given the stated core notion to "trust no one," the US intelligence community should probably not have trusted anyone outside its Five Eyes intelligence family (which does not include Israel) with the critical task of maintaining and controlling the cyber weapon. Given the NSA logic, it was hardly surprising that the Israelis decided to take matters into their own hands and, unbeknownst to their US partners, update the code that made Stuxnet much more virulent. The Israelis might have, quite reasonably, expected that their US partners would do something contrary to their interests (such as canceling the program if diplomatic negotiations with Iran were successful) and simply acted first.

The case of Stuxnet shows that despite the best of policy intentions, the reality of the covert cyber world has its own rules that can invalidate the most elaborate policy safeguards. According to Sanger's book as well as some of my own conversations, the White House deliberations on Stuxnet were intense, including a demonstration of how the centrifuges would be damaged and extensive analysis of how the operation conformed with international law. Stuxnet could have been designed to be much more violent—to destroy the centrifuges with catastrophic effect, contaminating the work space and maybe even causing human casualties. The White House clearly wanted to avoid something that could be construed as "armed attack" under international law and therefore opted for a relatively soft option—one that would also fulfill the objective of remaining undiscovered. But these deliberations were superseded by partners who were evidently working on their own variant of "trust no one" and conducted their own unsanctioned update of the code, leading Stuxnet out of obscurity and into the history books—as well as doubtlessly the code repositories of hostile actors.

Stuxnet was not the only case of the culture of the intelligence community trumping what should have been common sense. The Flame cyber weapon, first revealed by Kaspersky in 2012, was concentrated on Middle Eastern targets, and in particular seemed to focus on countries and groups with strong connections to Iran. From a code perspective, it was a monster; the largest single piece of malware found by far, it incorporated a number of modules and functions and tied them together using different programming languages, a fairly unusual occurrence. It was far from elegant and more reminiscent of military brute force than the soft touch of signals intelligence professionals. It also had one highly controversial feature: it used the heavily encrypted Microsoft update feature to surreptitiously access the malware and update it and control it as necessary.

The use of a hijacked Microsoft certificate, which tricked the computer into thinking the malware was a legitimate Microsoft update, was a significant technical accomplishment. "Forging a Microsoft code signing certificate is the holy grail of malware writers," Mikko Hypponen, the chief research officer of F-Secure, wrote. He later speculated that this type of encryption cracking was possible only with very high-end computing support, verging on that of supercomputer capability. For him and for others, it was clear that the attack could probably have been instigated only by an American agency.

I and others found this very hard to believe. What US civil servant, I wrote, would think that the operational intelligence gathering on a paltry thousand machines, mostly in Iran, was worth the potential compromise of one of the biggest US companies, a national security asset of the first order? Weakening the trust in the Windows update function is akin to attacking the very core of the trust agreement between company and customer. What kind of intelligence-gathering operation would justify this kind of risk? I refused to believe that Flame was American, speculating that the attack instead was due to a stolen certificate, something that had also been known to occur. The US government would surely think twice before risking potentially massive damage to one of the United States' greatest economic assets.

I was wrong. Subsequent reporting and leaks have indicated that Flame was most likely American, or possibly US-Israeli, and potentially part of the Olympic Games campaign against Iran. I still have a hard time believing that experienced cyber operators (rather than, say, special-operations types outside the NSA) would be so single-minded in their pursuit of intelligence that they would take such a political risk. Even for the ROC and its motto "by any legal means," this was surely a stretch. It might have been legal, but it was definitely not smart and could hardly align well with the stated foreign policy objectives of the US government. But while the management of cyber operations (including intelligence) might have sometimes been questionable, the current process of messaging around these operations is outright dangerous and increasingly smacks of information warfare of the kind engaged in by countries such as Russia and China. While some cyber operations might have put the worldwide standing and reputation of the United States at risk, the process of leaking and subtly communicating information about these operations is potentially a threat to democracy itself.

Chapter 8

STRATEGIC INNUENDO

Both Flame and Stuxnet are symptomatic of a variety of decisions that have been made within US cyber that, although doubtlessly approved at the highest levels of government, appear to contradict many of the stated goals of the United States. While I have often been told to what extent the cyber operations are subject to extensive internal oversight and approval, this is often difficult to believe, as the operations seem to inevitably follow a "bottom up" approach that often seems to risk the strategic and operational objectives for the sake of achieving a tactical mission. It is otherwise difficult to ascertain why, for instance, missions such as Flame, with its seemingly casual imperilment of a major American economic asset, were approved to begin with. While some of these decisions, being in the nature of espionage, might have been made at the lower end of the command chain, others must have involved senior political leadership. Also, some of the communication of US cyber operations and capabilities has been undertaken by senior acting or former officials. While sometimes this communication (or messaging or signaling) has been through public briefings, or back-channel communication with senior reporters, other communication relies more on feeding information to journalists and civil society experts through hints and innuendo and instrumentalizing them for purposes of government in a manner that should give us pause. Half-transparency is exactly the same as half-truth; it is fundamentally misleading and is more an operational tool of information warfare than one of good public diplomacy. Unfortunately, the battle to keep information warfare outside the US cyber thinking was never really completely won, and twenty years later it seems to have reentered US strategic thought through stealth.

If we remember, the original conceptualization of computer network operations in JP 3-13 provided for a boundless opportunity to muddy the waters between offensive and defensive mission, giving rise to large-scale deployment of cyber espionage and covert action. But it also allows for information warfare, albeit in a limited form and kept to the battlefield. The danger is that this expanded concept of psychological warfare will leave the confines of the battlefield and infect the wider paradigm of security and therefore justify the Russian and Chinese assertion that information—all information—is indeed a weapon.

Just how information operations would be deployed in a military campaign was explained in an exercise scenario in 2003. Here, the US military deploys information operations to support a corps-sized ground invasion of a less sophisticated rogue state. The document details how the IO unit would engage in computer network operations. What is clear in the document is that the majority of tasks are in what can be loosely called psychological operations—a rightfully nebulous term that includes counterpropaganda but also simply propaganda. If one is interested in examples, one just has to think back to the first Gulf War, when image after image on TV news portrayed the accuracy of US smart bombs in all their glory, or even the use of loud rock music to "encourage" the Vatican embassy in Panama to hand over Manuel Noriega after he took refuge there following the US invasion in 1989.

This type of media and public relations management is very much part of traditional military efforts, and the military takes great care to prevent it from being considered "propaganda." For instance, lying and intentional falsehood are expressly forbidden. The pairing with tasks related to computer network operations, however, raises the question of how blurred that boundary was becoming. Throughout the 2003 exercise scenario, there is an uneasy coexistence between the propaganda and communication part, on the one hand, and the electronic warfare CNO part, on the other. The latter was concentrated on destroying the enemy's command and control links and preventing similar attacks on friendly forces. The former was tasked with refuting the adversary's media narrative, such as claiming battlefield successes where there had been defeats or referring to civilian casualties where none had occurred.

There is some indication that early cyber operations were conceived as strategic influencing tools. The CIA's cyber-operations department, the Information Operations Center, was established in the aftermath of the CIA's covert influencing programs aimed at removing Serbia's president Slobodan Milošević. What exactly the program did was unknown, although the former CIA director Michael Hayden said that the psychological operations component managed only to make "Milosevic's phone ring incessantly, but there is no evidence that it shortened any aspect of the Balkan conflict."

Theoretically, there is a legal safeguard to unfettered propaganda being directed at US citizens. The Smith-Mundt Act expressly forbids the US government from engaging in disinformation campaigns against its own citizens, and this also means inadvertently: if there is a good chance that propaganda meant for overseas could be consumed by Americans, and therefore influence their political behavior, it is expressly forbidden.

Or was. I have become increasingly doubtful that the Smith-Mundt Act—which has been amended a number of times since the 1950s—was really a bulwark against propaganda that could also inadvertently be consumed by US persons. According to General Hayden, during his tenure at the CIA, a repeated challenge in conducting "covert influence" campaigns was preventing the information from being accidentally consumed by US persons—even if, as he insisted, that information was always based on the truth. Today, this would probably be less of a legal challenge. In 2012, the Smith-Mundt Act was modernized, ostensibly to enable Voice of America and other government media outlets to compete with Russia Today (as RT was called then) and Al Jazeera in propagating a message of counter-extremism. One academic article noted that while the act's modernization was partially misreported in the media, it did go too far in that it effectively lifted all kinds of safeguards American citizens had previously enjoyed against being subjected to propaganda of their own government. The debate on the exact legal shift of repercussions is far from over, but to my knowledge it has not yet touched on issues of signaling or deterrence, let alone on covert influencing operations This is a pity, because there is potentially a lot of US cyber-related activity that benefits from the modernization (and effective repeal) of the Smith-Mundt Act.

Prior to the landmark speech by President Obama in January 2014 on US intelligence gathering, there were a number of attempts by senior US officials to influence the debate on cyber through different variants of strategic communication. Like the general issue of spying on one's friends and allies recounted previously, from a liberal democratic viewpoint there are clear moral gradients as to what should be acceptable in strategic communication—a term that, by the way, has become much too large for its intended usage and is in urgent need of renewal. The danger is that left on its own, strategic communication will mutate into full-blown Russian- and Chinese-style information warfare: a consistent and willful distortion of narrative aimed at influencing the adversary's decision making, where the adversary includes one's own citizens and the conflict is permanent. The fine line between information warfare and strategic communication should boil down to one word: "honesty." There must be a clear line of attribution, even if the information is confidential and off the record, that leaves no doubt to the recipient that the messenger is acting in some kind of official capacity and can be held to account if caught being dishonest. Regardless of the medium or messenger, deceitful statements, which include attempts at significant misdirection and obfuscation, cannot be a matter of cybersecurity practice. Covert influencing as a tactic is one thing if it is clearly targeted against a specific foreign individual as part of a sanctioned government operation with limited outcome; it is quite another thing if it is on a national scale and en masse, open ended, and inadvertently capable of influencing one's own electorate.

The CIA support of the story of 1983's Soviet pipeline sabotage may be an example of strategic communication: it corresponds to the clear intent of individuals to broadcast the historic capability of an American organization to engage in cyber operations for consideration in today's context. Its ethical value is entirely correlated with truthfulness: if this is a truthful account, then it has evident value as a historic point of reference. If it is untruthful, however, it is taking the widespread deception of the American public and politicians into account as a necessary sacrifice to communicate, quite simply, that the ends justify the means. While both options could function well for the sake of deterring potential nation-state adversaries, the latter approach simply comes with much too high a price attached.

While I am at least somewhat confident that the CIA pipeline attack example is in essence correct (and therefore not willfully distorted), other examples I am familiar with are manifestly not.

For instance, from around 2010 to 2012, there was a lively discussion among advisers, scholars, and government officials on the desirability of pursuing "deterrence in cyberspace." One recurring theme in the deterrence debate was the difficulty of doing attribution for cyber operations, which was essential for a good deterrence policy: if you didn't have a good idea of who was behind an attack, promises of retribution were pointless. In a seeming effort to counter this "attribution narrative," a number of former senior officials, top defense contractors, and others suddenly started to make exactly the same statement within these off-the-record, high-level meetings. The statement here was invariably the same sentence, namely a cryptic "I wouldn't worry about attribution." Sometimes this would be followed with some detail implying that the NSA intelligence collection had made such advances that attribution was nearly solved as an issue. One specific policy maker from the intelligence community went as far as giving specific numbers on "how often we could provide high confidence attribution" to a specific cyber event. Although these statements were nearly always given verbally, in at least one case it was uttered in a public statement at a think-tank conference and thus became a matter for the public record. The problem with this is not the quotation itself but the overall message, communicated to policy makers advising Congress as well as reporters and civil society researchers, namely, that attribution was "solved" as an issue. By 2014, this story line was making significant inroads into the policy-making communities as well as media. And it was manifestly untrue. This was addressed later by senior State Department officials and even the director of national intelligence, who from 2014 repeatedly tried to restore a more nuanced vision of attribution. But the damage was largely done: the public and many legislators had started to assume that the large-scale intelligence apparatus of the NSA was able to "solve" the attribution problem altogether.

The point here was again the nuance. While it is very likely that there had been significant advances in the intelligence community's ability to identify attackers in cyberspace, the level of attribution, the difference in confidence, is key: in my discussions, it seems clear that for many in the media and in the senior levels of government the idea of "knowing" who was behind a cyberattack implies something like "knowing" that a missile had been launched by an enemy at your country. But attribution by radar and overhead satellite imagery is unlike attribution in cyber. In the worst case, you can look only at hints in the code—how it was crafted, at what time, using what language setting. In the moderate case, you have abundant secondary data, like social network activity and general chatter from the attackers. In the best case, you actually see the attacks being planned and executed because you are sitting in the networks and watching them in real time, as was said to be the case for Sony Pictures. But even in this best-case scenario, where you think you are actually watching the attackers hit the keys on their computers, there is still a theoretical possibility that a hyper-proficient third party gained access to the system, pretended to be someone he wasn't, and spoofed (that is, misdirected) your collection capabilities, conducting a so-called false-flag attack while posing as another actor. As unlikely as this seems, it is certainly possible for the most sophisticated actors, especially when faced with a comparatively low-tech adversary whom they wish to imitate and thus incriminate. For this reason, even a "high confidence" cyber attribution will probably never be higher than, say, 70–80 percent. This may seem adequate, but consider that the so-called dual-phenomenology approach for detecting an incoming missile attack on the United States can probably produce ratios of above 98 percent certainty. "Sure" in cyber terms often communicates a similar level of confidence as "sure" in detecting an incoming ballistic missile, but this is manifestly incorrect. Regardless of how good the NSA attribution is, it will always be subject to some small chance of being "spoofed," of being tricked. But the attempted strategic messaging of a number of cyber policy makers and opinion formers has created this distorted picture that the attribution problem has been solved.

Beyond these attempts at strategic communication through innuendo, there are other communications that are only marginally more legitimate. The planted story is another. One example is the first deployment of a purported copy of a US battlefield cyber weapon, the Suter series of electronic warfare tools designed to hack enemy air-defense networks. This weapon (or its copy) was first reported used in the 2007 Israeli Operation Orchard, the bombing of a suspected Syrian nuclear enrichment facility. The only reported statement that the Suter system was employed was an article by *Aviation Week & Space Technology*, written by a veteran journalist long known as being a reliable conveyor of secret knowledge. In this case, the journalist in question was probably the first person ever to break the existence of a full-fledged cyber-weapon suite, one that was good enough to copy by other powers. I have no notion of who planted the story or even why, but it certainly helped to draw attention to a type of cyber capability that the public had largely ignored.

Besides the planted story, there is the old favorite of the background briefer, some of which involves "inadvertently releasing" significant information as a seeming sideline to a totally different query, but also the unofficial briefing to very specific queries. Some of these are classic leaks to seasoned journalists, such as during the overall assessment of Stuxnet attacks (such as the "inadvertent release" message that some in the policy world tried to convey in 2011) or when discussing the North Korea attribution following the attack on Sony Pictures. Others are probably intended as indirect warnings for adversaries and are part of a wider deterrence strategy. For instance, the noted journalist Bob Woodward was the first person to disclose some of the mammoth intelligence-gathering programs maintained by the NSA in his book *Obama's Wars,* in which he described the program Real Time Regional Gateway (RTRG), a direct predecessor of some of the global cyber data collection programs later captured in the leaked NSA documents. Despite the clear references of what Woodward described RTRG to be, there was no major echo, let alone outrage. Instead, in an ABC interview with Woodward, the journalist Diane Sawyer dwells on that only for a minute, actually puzzled as to why that would be something one would want to share with Woodward: "Isn't that one of the things you don't want your enemy to know?" She had inadvertently put her finger on the issue—it was exactly the opposite. In order to produce deterrence, which means to prevent actors from conducting activities that you deem adverse to your own interests, you need to be able to communicate what your cyber capabilities are to your enemy. It is revealing how few government officials were investigated (let alone indicted) for the leak of sensitive information that found its way to the media, especially given that the Obama White House has otherwise been one of the most zealous administrations in prosecuting such leaks. This alone is a powerful indicator that many, if not all, of these leaks were directly sanctioned as part of a wider communication strategy that depends on weak and strong signals being carried by the media and key opinion formers.

Signaling is an especially powerful weapon when there is ambiguity, and cyberspace is nothing if not ambiguous. It is, however, important to note the differences in the nongovernment signaling types described here. The background briefing is a tried-and-tested approach, where senior journalists are more likely to question motives and retaliate if it has been discovered that the leaks are untruthful or misleading. Planted stories are riskier, for they cast the reporter or researcher as nothing more than a mouthpiece for government messaging and could potentially end up discrediting both the messenger and the subject itself. But strategic communication through innuendo—at least when directed at civil society—is truly problematic. This can amount to a copy of the "inadvertent release" of the Stuxnet (or any other) cyber weapon, where a meme can go wild beyond its mission and proliferate uncontrollably, even infecting one's own citizens. When the medium for these messages (that is, those who are being depended on to carry the message further) is relatively unknown researchers, civil society advocates, or even businessmen, they have limited recourse if, in fact, they have been misled. They do not always have the resources or reputations of senior journalists, and the messages themselves can easily be interpreted, rightly or wrongly, as private statements. Those who support such activity should remember Marshall McLuhan's most famous statement: the medium is the message. Effectively, signaling this way turns the messenger into a proxy actor, one who is recounting hearsay as part of a purported strategic communication campaign or even part of a personal mission (there is no way to know which is which) and who can easily end up spreading completely misleading statements—in other words, propaganda—to the American public.

For those doubtful that such an event is likely to occur, think back to the end of the Cold War. The most famous and poignant example of this strategic communication through innuendo breeding a wild rumor was the so-called Bulgarian Connection theory. This was the overall focus of the early 1980s bestselling book *The Terror Network,* which falsely purported that virtually all of the major European terror groups were under direct control of the KGB. The book was so influential in the early 1980s in the United States that it is said to have played a strong role in influencing the first Reagan administration, which needed to be told that in fact much of the book was the result of a specific CIA disinformation operation. The book therefore had a significant (and misleading) impact on the public political discussion in the United States—something that the Smith-Mundt Act was expressly set up to prevent.

Before the first strategies were publicly discussed in 2015, deterrence already had a long history in US cyber, despite never having been concretely formulated in a top policy document. Some of the policy discussions around 2010–12 (partially framed by a seminal work, *Cyberpower and National Security,* by the National Defense University) had already concluded that deterrence responses to cyberattack did not have to be limited to cyber options, but could use the whole gamut of diplomatic, informational, economic, and military levers available to the United States. This also neatly sidestepped some of the attribution issues, because for everything but the most severe cyberattacks the responses could be time delayed (to allow for better attribution) and reversible (in case that attribution was wrong). The logical conclusion was therefore that economic levers—in particular sanctions—were the best tools to use for some of the medium-intensity cyberattacks, such as the ones being encouraged or sanctioned by China. In a previously unheard-of act, the Obama administration started to move strongly against the Chinese theft of intellectual property by first indicting Chinese military hackers for engaging in economic cyber espionage and finally dangling the threat of economic sanctions. When Xi Jinping therefore met Obama in September 2015, the executive order initiating those sanctions against China was ready to go, something the Chinese were certainly aware of. The result was the most massive reversal in the history of cyber conflict, with Chinese attacks on the nondefense private sector decreasing greatly in 2016, although at the time of writing it is unclear whether this drop-off is permanent or just a blip. Clearly, the Obama administration had discovered a useful foil with which to deter Chinese economic espionage. But for many lawmakers this practical policy was not enough; they demanded a concrete strategy of deterrence, one that publicly spelled out exactly what the United States would do in cases of catastrophic cyberattack, not only "slow-bleed" economic cyber espionage.

In December 2015, the White House followed up on repeated calls by Congress to draft a cyber-deterrence strategy. The document, which has been leaked only in draft form, expands on some public notions of deterrence that were made in the 2015 Department of Defense document but goes further into detail and at first glance seemed to be a welcome sign for those seeking to de-escalate tensions in cyberspace through greater transparency. But despite many promising phrases that indicate an incremental shift in thinking, the path dependency can be hard to overcome.

A disappointing thread in the document was the reinforcement of the offensive-defensive duality. Unlike the nearly simultaneously drafted National Security Space Strategy (NSSS), which provides a modern updating of the standard deterrence ladder (norms, entanglement, denial, punishment), the cyber-deterrence strategy is reduced only to denial and punishment components. This emphasizes the "hard" aspects of deterrence and relegates the "soft" aspects of deterrence, such as norms and entanglement, to a supporting role. The widest category in the document is titled "activities that support deterrence," which are presumably intended to work across both offense and defense. This includes the critical notion of norms of behavior in cyberspace as subcomponents of "international engagement," while in the NSSS the issue of "norms" seems to be given a higher ranking, even though in cybersecurity it is probably a much more pertinent issue. Beyond the document's reinforcing of the offensive-defensive narrative in US cyber, the truly troubling notion is that it inadvertently helps contribute to the information warfare narrative. While national security thrives on ambiguity, cyberspace already has an abundance of ambiguity built into it, and adding to the mix is likely to lead to unforeseeable reactions. The insinuation by the DoD in 2015, for instance, that the new National Mission Force would be a more defensive-oriented organization, rather than a more likely offensive one, is difficult to understand as a communications objective. Other US military cyber units have their offensive roles announced relatively clearly, so why should the NMF be any different? While it is possible that the NMF was not officially branded an offensive unit as part of a wider and unknown diplomatic strategy, it is likely that it was simply a habit of trying to obfuscate purpose—and to prologue the confusion as to what exactly is included in US cyber operations.

This was exactly the opposite of what the lawmakers, including a bipartisan group of senators, wanted; instead, they believed that deterrence was about making it clear what could be done in cyberspace, especially the how and the why. The point was not only to seek deterrence by "other means" (such as economic measures), but to explore in particular what deterrence by cyber means actually entailed. They therefore seemed to reject the draft of the White House strategy out of hand for its lack of openness on capabilities and the lack of clarity on what offensive measures were available. "Dr. Strangelove taught us that if you have a doomsday machine and no one knows about it, it's useless," Senator Angus King of Maine said during a September 2015 Senate Intelligence Committee hearing reported on Federal News Radio. "Having a secret plan as to how we will respond . . . [is pointless]. . . . The deal is they have to know how we will respond and therefore not attack in the first place."

The lawmakers were certainly right on some points. While it is important to underline that a good deterrence policy would also involve noncyber means as part of its retaliatory options, the offensive cyber missions still need to be spelled out to some extent. It remains unclear in the draft White House deterrence strategy how the offensive deterrence mission was actually to be accomplished in the absence of clear communication of capabilities. The document states that "signaling can be direct or indirect, private or public." Left on its own, the message seems to be that those past attempts at innuendo, planted stories, and strategic leakage mentioned previously will continue—but it could also just mean that there should continue to be support for such critical tools of diplomatic policy, such as track 1.5 bilateral dialogues between nations. It is impossible to tell based on this statement alone, and again the ambiguity is not welcome. With the primarily Russian-led resurgence of information warfare, and its tools of media manipulation, outright fabrication, and fake news, clarity is absolutely necessary. Otherwise the path may lead directly into what can be considered information warfare, which thrives on deception and ambiguity rather than transparent and truthful official communication.

While the Department of Defense cyber strategy of 2015 was welcome for its readiness to talk about the cyber organization chart, it did not actually say what the organizations are supposed to do, particularly on the offensive side. This is especially significant as far as actual capabilities are concerned, what standard operating procedures are, and even what the overall concept of operations is. Even the most basic terminology is unclear. What, for instance, does Offensive Cyber Effects Operations effectively include or exclude? Everyone by now gets that it can include strikes on the power grid and other critical infrastructure, but does it also include revealing sensitive data of the adversary, like the secret bank accounts of its leaders, to name one example? How about interfering with elections, both national and party specific? Does it include the manipulation of the media? What about the role of foreign NGOs and companies, or citizens for that matter? And what are the roles that American companies play? Is part of the operational preparation of the environment to undermine commercial products used every day by users everywhere, which supposedly has already occurred with the 2012 leak on operation Bullrun, where critical encryption standards, among other things, were intentionally weakened by the NSA? What is the border between what is permissible and what is not in a liberal democracy?

This list of potential questions is extensive. The problem is simply that cyber operations can cover the entire gamut of covert action, and therefore virtually nothing is excludable. One would hope that the law would provide some measure of protection at least for US citizens and companies, but past practice (see the Flame example for one) raises the question whether the interpretation of these laws, be they national or the laws of armed conflict and international law as a whole, has not been remarkably one-sided. More transparency on the legal findings relative to specific types of cyber operations (to say nothing of the classification of the cyber operations themselves) would be an important step in helping to restore transparency and trust as to what these capabilities are really intended to do. The slow release of selected FISA court rulings over the last few years is a good model to follow in providing clarity on how OCEO is scoped. Insight into how these and other activities are defined by the US government would at least provide a baseline from which international security discussions could be better approached.

The lack of transparency measures is particularly unfortunate given the stated intent of the White House document to encourage "whole of nation" cybersecurity. The first uses of the term around 2010 described the ability to leverage all state and non-state resources of a nation in dealing with specific security challenges. Normally, I would have been enthusiastic to see a term that I and others helped coin in 2010 and 2011 find entry into top-level documents. However, the key to achieving whole-of-nation cybersecurity in liberal democracies is for me the "third face" of power of attraction, rather than the Russian or Chinese approach of co-option and coercion. This "soft power" approach requires above all trust—trust from average citizens as well as major corporations so they will cooperate and support the aims of their government. There is little indication that closing this trust deficit is really considered a top priority in buttressing national cybersecurity. This is doubly problematic, for not only does US power abroad (its ability to influence allies and non-allies) rest in its power of conviction, but the very ability to interact positively with one's own national actors (the true whole of national cybersecurity) depends at least partially on an inward-facing soft power. While some countries do engage openly in national propaganda and consciousness-raising to buttress their own national security, most Americans would hardly be comfortable with their government running that type of campaign, which would at best be a return to simple jingoism and crude WW II–style propaganda, and at worst would be a revamped version of McCarthyism. While the US government can try to compel cooperation from its non-state actors with legal instruments or even money, the wide-scale public reaction to much of the post-9/11 bulk intelligence collection programs shows that it may be worthwhile to simply try to raise public trust by making the case for all of these cyber-operations publicly and with transparency. Other countries, such as Sweden, arguably have been able to make decent public cases for these wider-scale intelligence operations. Given the current lack of trust in the US national security establishment by many at home and abroad, it may be well worth a try.

Something like this was very much the apparent intent behind the reforms in intelligence (and cyber) practice that were initiated by Obama's January 2014 speech. There were rather decisive moves toward better national cooperation, the discussion of cyber operations, and even the more open discussion of intelligence resources used in attribution. One senior official told me that he would be happy to have a public version of the 2012 leaked document PPD-20 (which mentions OCEO as well as other relatively new terms) to facilitate a public discussion, but nonetheless this and other important measures have not occurred. The relatively great steps that were taken in Internet governance were being shadowed by only comparatively timid steps in the national security realm—perhaps because in Internet governance there was no national security establishment that needed to be convinced. Sometimes they convince themselves, however.

In February 2016, General Hayden penned a remarkable article for the

Christian Science Monitor's blog *Passcode*. It is titled "The Making of America's Cyberweapons," but it could have been called "Conflicted Contrition of One of the Creators of US Cyber" (this is not, it should be pointed out, a title that General Hayden agrees with). The previously unapologetic cheerleader of many of its most treasured principles, such as "everyone spies," seemed to be having a change of heart. He does not start repentant, writing, in a kind of echo of US policy, that "there is no law in cyberspace." But he admits that he had a slow awakening to the dangers that he had helped create. A turning point for him was a textbook example of the bottom-up problem of placing the tactical before the political that I consider to be an essential part of the US path dependency in cyber operations. Hayden recounts how during his tenure as director of the CIA the United States military took down an al-Qaeda Web site, knowing that this tactical victory would have strategic and political costs—that allies using the same network as al-Qaeda would be furious. When Hayden tried to get the military to stop these attacks, he was effectively ignored: the tactical mission ended up trumping strategic policy making. It clearly shook Hayden, and he "nearly" took the CIA out of the cyber-operations arena as a result. Hayden left government in 2009 and therefore had no qualms indicating his concerns about Stuxnet, a weapon whose purpose he utterly agreed with but that he worried set a dangerous precedent and would no doubt invite a response in the future. He closes his article with a seemingly rueful statement: "I had been a part of it—probably pushed some of it along—and certainly got a chance to be present at some important milestones and decisions. And now I knew that we would all have to live with the consequences of what we had conceptualized, nurtured, and created."

What he and many others had created was the massive edifice of cyber operations and cyber thought, the conjuring of a digital "dragon world" where immense powers over humans were unleashed, and not only in times of warfare, as with the advent of atomic bomb, but in all states of life, even peacetime. None of these creators of cyber operations saw themselves as anything more than honest and decent executors of their most important duty—maintaining the security of the United States. But the father of the atomic bomb, Robert Oppenheimer, had an analogy to describe this adherence to duty. In a 1965 interview on how the first atomic bomb test influenced him and his fellow scientists, he said, "We knew the world would not be the same. A few people laughed. A few people cried. Most people were silent. I remembered the line from the Hindu scripture, the Bhagavad Gita. Vishnu is trying to persuade the prince that he should do his duty and, to impress him, takes on his multiarmed form and says, 'Now I am become Death, the destroyer of worlds.' I suppose we all thought that, one way or another."

PART IV

Chapter 9

RUSSIA'S INVISIBLE WAR

The first sign that an attack was under way was when the mouse cursor started moving across the screen of its own accord.

On the night of December 23, 2015, Ukraine became the first country to suffer a verified large-scale cyberattack on its critical infrastructure. Over 225,000 Ukrainians suddenly lost their light and heating in the middle of winter when a cyberattack disabled part of the country's power grid.

According to an excellent account by Kim Zetter, just before the end of his shift on December 23 a power grid operator saw his terminal suddenly light up, and the mouse cursor started to move across on its own and without responding to the stunned operator's attempts to retake control. With a few clicks, virtual breakers regulating the power supply at an electricity substation were thrown, plunging thousands into darkness. When the operator tried to log back in, he was barred; the attackers had changed his password. He could only watch as more breakers at more substations were thrown and more towns and cities were knocked off the grid. There was nothing he or his colleagues could do.

It would later become clear that the attack was multifaceted and had been planned far in advance: preparations included detailed reconnaissance to understand the power grid system's management software, theft of log-in credentials of workers working from home, writing of specific firmware (that is, hard-coded) updates for the remote-operated breakers that would render them unusable, and a denial-of-service attack that effectively disabled the customer service center and prevented customers from reporting outages and therefore hampered remediation. When the attack was concluded, the computers were completely wiped to render them unusable in the future. While attribution is never 100 percent confirmed, foreign investigators as well as the Ukrainian government itself were nearly certain that the attack had been conducted by the Russian government, or at least with its knowledge.

The attack was not devastating. The power was restored in six hours, and while the remote control software for the breakers was effectively destroyed, the system had a backup that allowed for manual control, something the attackers were surely aware of. Turning off the lights in parts of western Ukraine also played no direct role in the Russian-backed conflict occurring in the East. Despite their sophisticated strike, the attackers could have done more, including damaging the underlying physical infrastructure: In 2007, an American experiment had shown that it took just twenty-one lines of code to physically destroy a power generator, and the Russian attackers could have undertaken something similar if they had wanted to be more efficient and less visible. But they didn't.

According to one of the experts interviewed for the article, the purpose of the attack was pure messaging: the attackers wanted to be seen and identified and didn't really want to inflict catastrophic long-lasting damage. There was no shortage of messaging opportunities to be exploited here: beyond a number of implicit threats being directed at Ukraine, there was a chance to threaten the West as a whole. Only a couple of months earlier,

Russia had agreed to an international norm of state behavior that specifically disavowed attacks against critical infrastructure. Not only did the Russian government immediately violate that norm to show its casual disregard for it, but it used malware called BlackEnergy to do so. BlackEnergy has been found all over the US power grids as well and has long been suspected as being a pre-deployed Russian cyber weapon hiding in place to be used against the United States in case of hostilities. This fact helped generate a large amount of reporting on the Ukrainian blackout in the United States, including a statement from Admiral Michael Rogers, head of the NSA and USCYBERCOM, that an attack on the US power grid was not a "doom and gloom" possibility, but "an eventuality." While the Ukrainian attack was only somewhat successful as a cyberattack, as an act of information warfare it was enormously effective. And information warfare has always been the dominant Russian interest in the cyber domain.

No country has dreamed about cyber longer than Russia. As early as the 1950s, these dreams were connected to notions of state control over information and individuals. While those dreams help explain why the Internet was not born in Russia, they also serve to position the country admirably well for cyber conflict: its military and intelligence strategic thinkers have been reflecting on conflict in the information domain for decades.

Soviet computer systems nearly played a decisive role in world history. Already in the 1940s, Soviet engineers had begun to make significant strides in computer science, and by the early 1970s some parts of Soviet computing were equal to or even better than their US counterparts. Russian programmers have for decades played vital roles in the development of computing in general. Topcoder.com, a community Web site, has consistently ranked Russia the first nation worldwide in terms of providing sophisticated coders (with China second, Ukraine fifth, and the United States only sixth). Indeed, brilliant Russian coders have a reputation of having helped build Silicon Valley. But as good as the individual coders were during the Soviet Union, its technical prowess was always hampered by its political ideology. But the same ideological bent made it keenly interested in considering the wider social implications of networked computing and its application for social control.

The Soviet in-depth consideration of "cyber" was markedly different from the Western approach to network systems. On its surface, the Russian interest in *kibernetika,* or "cybernetics," was heavily informed by the writings of an American mathematician who first coined the term. Norbert Wiener's work was largely ignored in the United States for decades, many having perceived cybernetics as a minor branch of general systems theory. Not so in the Soviet Union, where Wiener was celebrated as a philosopher of renown somewhere between Gramsci and Hegel. As an MIT colleague once put it, "Wiener is the only man I know who conquered Russia, and single-handed at that." The influence that Wiener's cybernetics revolution had on post-Stalinist Russia is simply astonishing.

In 1961, the Twenty-second Congress of the Communist Party remarked in its manifesto that "cybernetics" was one of the crucial factors in achieving true Communism. Cybernetics was described as a side branch of mathematics and network theory that examined optimal organizational and control mechanisms for both machines and humans. Cybernetics would therefore help enable an efficient allocation of resources for totally planned economies. The Soviet press even started referring to computers as "machines of communism." This sparked something akin to a cyber shock in the West. "Based on CIA reports, in October 1962 President Kennedy's top aide wrote in an internal memo that the 'all-out Soviet commitment to cybernetics' would give the Soviets 'a tremendous advantage.' . . . If the American negligence of cybernetics continues, he concluded, 'we are finished.'"

After a shift in attention from cybernetics to the Soviet space program in the 1960s, the Soviet cybernetic dream made a full comeback in the early 1970s. Following reports that the United States was developing the

ARPANET (the ancestor of the global Internet), Soviet scientists attempted to create their own version: OGAS, the "nationwide automated system of accounting and information processing." OGAS was marketed as a tool to unify all existing management systems in an attempt to better allocate resources through central planning—an urgent need, according to the chief scientist Viktor Glushkov, because otherwise "by the mid-1980s nearly the entire adult population of the Soviet Union would be engaged in planning, accounting, and management." OGAS was not simply to be a large enterprise-resource management system. It would also connect to all databases of knowledge and even to automated processes in industry itself—for example, not only would OGAS help produce toilet paper more efficiently, it would also determine fluctuations in need and, at the same time, directly control the means of production. It was effectively the dream of just-in-time production, Communist-style. Some intellectuals began to see in Glushkov's proposal the specter of an omnipresent surveillance system. Others dismissed it as a technological paradise promoting the true Communism of "cybertonia," a somewhat ironic utopian vision shared by some Soviet scientists during this time and manifested in a pulp comic of the same name and lovingly recounted in Benjamin Peters's book *How Not to Network a Nation*. Despite its grand plans, however, OGAS remained stuck in its status as a research project for nearly thirty years—never to be built.

Observers assigned a variety of reasons to the Soviet Union's failure to fully implement OGAS, all tied to the obsession of the Soviet state with security and control. The MIT lecturer Slava Gerovitch points to a culture of security that meant that computers were intended to talk not to each other, or even have generalized tasks: "[The USSR] developed a large variety of small specialized computers with hardwired algorithms. Every type of weaponry was controlled by its own type of computer; over 300 different types of specialized computers were developed by the Soviet defense industry. Their highly specific designs were of no use in a civilian context. The Soviet military-industrial complex functioned as an information 'black hole': everything was coming in, but nothing was coming out." The reason for this was primarily control; no department or ministry wanted to finance a computer that others could profit from. Peters comments memorably that the US Internet was successful where the Soviet Internet was not because "the capitalists behaved like socialists, while the socialists behaved like capitalists": while ARPANET relied as a project on Communist-like cooperation between different US institutions, institutions in the USSR went to great lengths to resist cooperation. Control was everything, not only for the KGB, but for all institutions in the USSR.

Cooperation, let alone trust, was virtually impossible in this environment. ARPANET would not have been able to survive its repeated mutations into the Internet as we know it today without a significant level of trust between its major stakeholders. Trust was such a rare commodity in Soviet Russia that OGAS could not even be born, let alone survive the inevitable evolutionary leaps that would have been necessary to grow into a true internet in an environment obsessed with hierarchy and control. This context was simply the opposite of the trusting network today's Internet heavily relies on. But this has not stopped Russia from putting down deep roots in cyberspace or indulging in its own dark cyber dreams.

As the Soviet tinkering with the embryonic Soviet Internet OGAS showed, Soviet interest in developing an early internet was tilted in one direction: information as the key to control. For the Communist regimes in Eastern Europe, "information" had a decidedly unsettling, and potentially state-upending, aspect to it. From the earliest days of Marxism-Leninism, entire academic courses were dedicated to information control not only at the KGB but also at the party school and, of course, at the military academies. From Lenin's very first orders as the ruler of post-revolution Russia to the collapse of the Soviet Union, Communist strategic thinking has revolved around notions of censorship and propaganda, as well as psychological operations and deception.

The Soviet Red Army was only one of the many outposts of Wiener acolytes in Russia, but it had a decisive impact on how the business of war and conflict was combined with notions of organizational control and information theory. The Military Academy of the General Staff was a key hub for turning out key Soviet military doctrine. It was the home of V. V. Druzhinin and D. S. Kontorov, among the pioneers of controls of systems, a version of organizational theory vaguely related to the systems-of-systems philosophy developed in the United States by the Rand Corporation and promoted by Secretary of Defense Robert McNamara in the 1960s. The strong doctrinal emphasis on the power of information was largely segmented along two different dimensions: controlling the supply chain and movement of troops, and the ability to wage information war against an opponent. Both were intended to strategically defeat the enemy, in the first case very tangibly with the application of physical force on target, in the second case much more subtly, through the manipulation of decision-making processes at every level. For unlike Western military concepts of psychological operations, which viewed psychological warfare as a tactical and operational tool, the Soviets saw it as something that could influence the very theater of operations, as well as the politics. From the Soviet perspective, a war could be waged and won without the other side's knowing that war had been declared.

This concept of strategic PSYOPS is the basis of the concept of reflexive control, which is "a process by which one enemy transmits the reasons or basis for making decisions to another." Reflexive control implies the complete domination of an adversary's decision-making process through various tools, including, for instance, semantics and the choice of terms in public discourse. In every case, the goal is to deliver information to the target to incline it "to voluntarily make the predetermined decision desired by the initiator of the action." Reflexive control, it is important to note, is not considered a fully Russian invention. According to the US Army expert Timothy Thomas, many Russians today are convinced that President Reagan's hyper-expensive "Star Wars" Strategic Defense Initiative was first and foremost an exercise in reflexive control: a fake propaganda research project that forced the Soviet Union to spend huge sums that it did not have and further weakened its national defense. Many leading Russian strategists continue to believe to this day that social media, the Internet, and even the entire concept of cybersecurity are plots that the United States has inflicted on Russia to force it to adapt and submit to its narrative.

Russia's view of the importance of information as a weapon was made clear in 2000, with the publication of the Information Security Doctrine. In this key document, the presumed Kremlin authors clearly outlined two types of "informational" attacks: technical and psychological. Technical attacks include hacking, electronic warfare, and other activities most Westerners would associate with cyber operations. But more important are psychological attacks: the document repeatedly cites "foreign propaganda"—which can also work through inner Russian "agents"—as a threat to the "spiritual renewal of Russia." Other threats to the nation's well-being include "uncontrolled expansion of the foreign media sector in the national information space" as well as the activities of journalists, NGOs, and even missionaries and religious institutions. The word "media" appears in the official translation of the document exactly twenty-three times. It is conceived as a strategic asset in favor of Russian policy—a strategic weapon that should also "[explain] to foreign audiences the goals and major thrust areas in the Russian Federation's state policy and its view of socially significant events in Russian and international life." Time and time again, the document references the threats of disinformation and covert information influence and the consequences that they could have.

While more technical issues appear in the document as well, Russia leaves no doubt that its primary concern is the lack of control over the information consumed within its own borders to this day, and that this "information" is largely what the West would perceive as being simply the media and the functioning of democracy and civil society. An update of the document was drafted in the summer of 2016 but offered little new insight. According to one observer, it showed that the Kremlin still could not break away from its very deep-rooted view of how cyberspace should look and was replete with contradictions. But one thing was clear: Russia still saw itself as being under attack from abroad. The document says, "The special services of certain states provide information and psychological influence, aimed at destabilizing the political and social situation in various regions of the world, resulting in the undermining of the sovereignty and the territorial integrity of other states." This statement is intended as an indication that the pro-democracy uprisings of the last decade were nothing else than CIA plots. While most would consider this an absurd suggestion, the activities described here are exactly what Russia has been accused of doing in the Ukrainian conflict.

The Russian obsession with the foreign media and civil society undermining its information sphere shifted into high gear in the wake of the first wave of pro-democracy color revolutions in Kyrgyzstan, Lebanon, and, most notably, Ukraine. They are, at least from the Chinese and Russian point of view, the direct result of well-funded Western (and in particular American) intelligence operations. Virtually all cases of violent, pro-democracy regime change—including the Arab Spring movements in the summer of 2011 and most recently the revolt against the Ukrainian government in 2014—are seen as nothing more than operations by Western governments.

On the one hand, it is not too hard to see why China and in particular Russia would hold this view. An undoubted supporter of many of these revolutionary activities is the National Endowment for Democracy (NED), an American bipartisan nonprofit organization that was founded in 1983 with the express goal of supporting democratic movements worldwide. Most of its $130 million in funding (in 2013) comes from congressional appropriations and the State Department. In 2012, NED spent more than $3.3 million in support of democracy in Ukraine.

We know this because by its charter NED must publish all its activities and by and large functions much more transparently than any government would. It appears to be a slightly unusual civil society body, beholden to its board, members, and staff—and especially to its core mission. For many used to Western civil society, it would appear most likely that NED is actually what it says it is. Some members of NED will not deny that in the 1980s the organization probably did have links to the CIA but will strenuously state that today the organization operates completely independently, and certainly has an impressively high level of political support in Congress that must provide for a measure of protection. One former employee of NED laconically said that "there were probably easier ways for a CIA official to get fired than get caught trying to utilize NED for a covert operation."

For many in Russia and China, however, the notion that NED would not be intelligence-oriented simply does not compute. The idea of an independent civil society is largely not established in these countries in any meaningful way, a direct reflection on the Marxist-Hegelian view (later taken up by thinkers such as Gramsci) that civil society is simply "the battleground between capitalism and the state." I was once on the receiving end of a harangue by the Soviet-educated former ITU general secretary Hamadoun Touré, who over a small dinner tried to convince me that "civil society did not exist" (which left open the question of exactly why I was invited).

The notion of civil society as a proxy for government is most likely a truly held belief in Russia and not simply political theater. The creation of tame civil society organizations led to the rise of the pro-Putin Nashi youth group in 2007–2008, clearly intended to support the transition of power between Putin and his appointee Dmitry Medvedev, and back again. Nashi greatly declined in importance after this transition phase was completed in 2012. At the same time, the Kremlin moved decisively to limit the influence of foreign NGOs in Russia. The NGO law on foreign agents was enacted in 2012 and was more of a continuation of the sentiments echoed in the Information Security Doctrine of 2000 than an altogether new endeavor. It did, however, represent a considerable reinforcement of the doctrine, or better said, it brought to the public something that had previously been largely handled discreetly. According to Freedom House, "The central, controversial aspect of the amendments was a requirement that organizations engaging in political activity and receiving foreign funding must register as foreign agents, even if the foreign funding they receive does not actually pay for political activities. The state determines whether an organization is engaging in political activity."

Needless to say, the NGO law has had detrimental effects on the existence of an independent civil society in Russia, with raids on the Moscow offices of the rights groups Amnesty International, Human Rights Watch, and Transparency International as well as harassment of individuals affiliated with those organizations. In one case, the director of the Regional Press Institute in St. Petersburg had her iPad confiscated on her way to the United States by Russian border security, only for it to be handed back to her crypto-locked for the next 23,420,874 minutes—forty-five years. In October 2014, a foreign ownership media law went into effect, driving CNN as well as the German media giant Bertelsmann out of Russia. Generally, independent voices in the media have been crushed, driven out, or even killed in the past decade. Particularly in the wake of the Ukrainian conflict, local media is "being bullied by [calls] from Putin's secret services" to pull some articles that do not fit the accepted Kremlin image of the conflict being waged in eastern Ukraine. Some, like a popular online television station called Dozhd but also some regional antigovernment broadcasters (in Siberia, for instance, as well as Russian-occupied Crimea), have even been shut down.

Russian online censorship was for some time virtually undetectable. When something disappeared from the Internet, it happened so totally that the hand of the government was difficult to pin down. But in 2014, it moved into the open with the introduction of a Chinese-inspired "blogger law" requiring that every popular site (defined as anyone with more than three thousand readers) had to "register, disclose personal information and submit to the same regulations as mass media." In one stroke, this put any kind of online political activity—including having Twitter followers—under close scrutiny. In some ways, this law was probably unnecessary, because all larger media platforms have long been considered entirely co-opted by Kremlin-aligned media oligarchs. One holdout—VKontakte, the Russian version of Facebook—succumbed when its young founder, Pavel

Durov, was forced to flee Russia in early 2014 after reportedly refusing to hand over details of Ukrainian users.

According to a study reported in the *Washington Post,* Russian Internet users have become so inured to the Kremlin narrative of the Internet as a tool of Western powers that two out of five Russians distrust foreign media and nearly half of Russians believe that foreign news Web sites need to be censored. These attitudes are driven partly by the fact that 42 percent of Russians believe the Internet is being used by foreign countries against Russia. The study's authors pointedly conclude that "as . . . with Russia, autocratic-leaning governments may use increased Internet regulation and propaganda against dissident voices as a means to close the remaining cracks in the information bubbles surrounding their citizens. Once hardened, these information bubbles allow governments to build further support for their illiberal regimes and to pursue their foreign policy objectives without the democratic accountability that can prevent unprovoked international conflict—as Russia has been doing in Ukraine over the past year." Thus a key objective of Russia's Information Security Doctrine is finally being fulfilled.

But some of the aims, we need to remember, were strictly foreign-policy oriented. The need, in particular, to "communicate a Russian version of events" to audiences abroad was given nearly equal importance. The Ukrainian conflict has certainly cast this effort into a stark light.

One obvious and overt form of propaganda is the Russian TV giant RT (formerly Russia Today). An in-depth report in *Time* magazine painted a striking picture of the organization, which has increasingly become obvious as primarily engaged in what in Russian shorthand is simply called *dez,* or "disinformation." Called "the Kremlin's most sophisticated propaganda machine" and a "propaganda bullhorn" by the US secretary of state John Kerry, RT enjoys a budget ($300 million in 2010) that almost matches that of the world's largest media group—the BBC World Service Group—and is overtly trying to, in the words of Putin himself, break "the Anglo-

Saxon monopoly on global information streams." Of course, RT's practice of abiding by "certain principles expressed by . . . representatives of the Russian state" is presented as no different from the work of independent Western broadcasters. "No one shows objective reality," claims the editor in chief of the network, who joined Putin's election staff in 2012 while retaining her job at RT. RT also has a hyperactive English-language YouTube channel that attracts many visitors outside Russia, especially from right-wing fringes in Europe and the United States.

This attempt at setting international preferences also has subtler incarnations. In 2014, a number of media outlets, including *The Atlantic,* ran reports on the "Kremlin's troll army"—contracted employees who, day in and day out, were paid to post vitriolic comments on Western media, like "Putin makes Obama look weak!" One particular company headquartered in St. Petersburg was documented as employing hundreds of paid commentators and social media posters, each of whom had to make around fifty posts a day, using dozens of different accounts each. Their targets were mainstream English media, like Fox News, Politico, the Blaze, and many others. Some of these memes even reached the mainstream: the idea of comparing supposedly effeminate and "mom jeans"–wearing Obama with the bareback rider Putin fell on very fertile ground in the so-called alt-right fringe in the United States, whose comments were rapidly echoed and reinforced through artificial social media accounts that have at least partially been identified as a component of a wider Russian IW operation.

This attempt to use social media to attack anti-Kremlin voices domestically and abroad is nothing new, and between 2007 and 2009 Nashi regularly employed this strategy. The money available now, however—the St. Petersburg company supposedly spent $10 million on Ukraine-related trolling in 2014 alone—probably puts the efforts of the now-defunct Nashi to shame.

The extreme level of Russian involvement in the 2016 US presidential election was, at the time of finishing this book, just reaching a fever pitch.

One June 2016 article clearly outlines how the Kremlin's troll army was being used to support the candidacy of Donald Trump, with a number of known trolls migrating their accounts to fake conservative personas. It also includes a quotation from a former KGB colonel on how these "active measures"—the Soviet term for covert action, including psychological warfare—were construed during the Cold War:

> It is designed . . . "to drive wedges in the Western community alliances of all sorts, particularly NATO, to sow discord among allies, to weaken the United States in the eyes of the people in Europe, Asia, Africa, Latin America, and thus to prepare ground in case the war really occurs. The most common subcategory of active measures is *dezinformatsiya [dez]*, or disinformation: feverish, if believable lies cooked up by Moscow Centre and planted in friendly media outlets to make democratic nations look sinister."

Preference setting is, however, not only a task conducted in bulk at the media writ large but also one aimed at distinct influential individuals, specifically in the general category of "key opinion formers and influencers" or simply "persons of interest." It relies on the notion that converting "elite" social figures who are able to swing the global debate is at least as important as mass-market propaganda. Some of the efforts undertaken are no different from what pretty much any other government does: large invited junkets for journalists and writers, basically booze cruises with government VIPs in all-inclusive packages. Other measures are somewhat less orthodox: these include attempts to recruit Western researchers and journalists to do pro-Russian pieces (as a particularly amusing anecdote published in *The Atlantic* in 2008 shows) but also more serious attempts to co-opt entire Western civil society organizations and think tanks. Finally, there remains the very real suspicion that former senior statesmen, as well as industry leaders and cultural and civil society personalities in Europe and North America, have been targeted for co-option as well, possibly enticed with lucrative board membership roles and other material benefits. While some of these noted individuals certainly have only spoken to their own personal and deeply held beliefs, it remains depressingly likely that others have simply been bought with material enticements.

Russia has spent decades tinkering with doctrines related to "information warfare." In 1997, a fascinating presentation by Vladimir Markomenko, then deputy director of FAPSI (then the signals intelligence agency and NSA equivalent), helped define what the Russian view of "information war" was, along four dimensions. These four dimensions of information warfare—electronic warfare, intelligence, hacker warfare, and psychological warfare—were all put on display in Russia's conflict in Ukraine nearly twenty years later.

The not-so-mysterious "unknown green men" who started the occupation of the Crimea—Russian naval infantry and special forces, without insignia—were only a small part of Russia's disinformation campaign. Many other assets were employed by the Russian state to confuse and slow the response rate of Western governments, including in cyberspace. These methods started before the conflict began and then expanded during the Russian-backed (and Russian-instigated) insurgency in eastern Ukraine and the resulting civil war.

Some of the capabilities Russia has deployed in Ukraine amount to electronic warfare, also known as "battlefield cyber" (or CEMA, for cyber electromagnetic activities, in the US Army) and concentrated largely on disrupting and misleading the communications and intelligence-gathering signals (such as radar) of your opponent. In previous decades, the Soviet Union's Red Army had been an absolute pioneer in electronic warfare: independent Signal Branch troops with dedicated EW tasks were regularly assigned at all levels of the army, from tactical units up and including strategic and theater-wide EW. These units—and their equipment and doctrine—were carefully observed by NATO.

Today, these units are part of the REB (Russian acronym for Radio Electronic Warfare) service, building on a long tradition of high regard associated with service in this branch. Due to the overall secrecy of these units, we know little about how effective they would be in protecting their command and control infrastructure or attacking those of the enemy. But there is evidence that they have already been practicing for a relatively long time: according to Oleg Ivanov, head of the REB, in the major Russian combined-arms exercise in 2009 REB units were deployed from brigade to presumably company level and assisted in protection and probably attack. There is a clear parallel to the United States' own published CNO JP 3-13 exercises. As with American capabilities, there is a clear chance that these forces are offensive as well as defensive. According to Laurie Buckhout, the former chief of the US Army Electronic Warfare Division, the United States is far behind Russia in terms of electronic warfare. "We have great signals intelligence, and we can listen all day long, but we can't shut them down one-tenth to the degree they can us," she said. "We are very unprotected from their attacks on our network."

As good as the Russian battlefield cyber was, the "strategic cyber" attacks in Ukraine garnered the most attention. A number of cyberattacks hit the Ukrainian government and media service in 2014. The 2015 hack of the Ukrainian power grid described at the beginning of this chapter was the most dramatic, but the actual physical effects of the hack were not as important as the psychological component. For like all Russian cyber operations, the key element is always how it interferes with the decision-making processes of the adversary.

The Russian propaganda warfare offensive around the Ukrainian conflict represents the fourth, and most powerful, aspect of Russian cyber power. A flood of major media reporting orchestrated by the state-funded media giant RT inundated not only Russian speakers but also willing listeners abroad, painting a picture of the Ukrainian conflict that bears little resemblance to reality. Besides slanted reporting and dubious analysis, including the common assertion that the Ukrainian government was fascist, the Russian propaganda included a flood of blatant falsehoods. These included such choice tidbits as maintaining that babies had been crucified by Ukrainian soldiers and faking broadcasts from the front line, as well as the ongoing attempts to attribute the downing of Malaysian Airlines flight MH17, with 298 victims, to the Ukrainian authorities, instead of Russian proxies, as is nearly certain. A former Russia correspondent for the German public broadcaster ARD summarized the tactics used by Russian propagandists: "Russian state television openly speaks about an information war, and Russian propaganda plays a huge role by mixing up the truth. So many theories about flight MH17 were thrown into the mix, for example, that in the end, readers didn't believe anything anymore." This analysis has been verified in detail by a former Kremlin propagandist in the book *Nothing Is True and Everything Is Possible,* which makes *House of Cards* look like kindergarten play. "What they are basically trying to undermine is the idea of a reality-based conversation," the author Peter Pomerantsev wrote of the Kremlin machine, "and to use the idea of a plurality of truths to feed disinformation, which in the end looks to trash the information space." If everything is subjective, after all, where can there be a right and a wrong?

The Ukrainian conflict illustrated many facets of Russian concepts of cyber power that had already been apparent in theory, if not necessarily in practice, before. This is especially apparent in a famous article published one year before the Crimean occupation by none other than the Russian military chief of general staff, Valery Gerasimov. Effectively advancing a theory of "ambiguous warfare," Gerasimov says,

> In the 21st century we have seen a tendency toward blurring the lines between the states of war and peace. Wars are no longer declared and, having begun, proceed according to an unfamiliar template. The experience of military conflicts—including those connected with the so-called colored revolutions in north Africa and the Middle East—confirm

that a perfectly thriving state can, in a matter of months and even days, be transformed into an arena of fierce armed conflict, become a victim of foreign intervention, and sink into a web of chaos, humanitarian catastrophe, and civil war.

The use of the term "colored revolutions" in this context is hard to overemphasize. For authoritarian regimes everywhere, the slow cascade of pro-democracy movements that from 2010 gripped North Africa, the Arab world, and parts of Asia were profoundly frightening occurrences—if they survived these events. Iran's theocrats squashed the 2009 Green Revolution with sheer force, and in 2011 China stifled its latent Jasmine Revolution at birth. But other regimes were not so lucky. Gerasimov's document not only clearly describes the democratic movements in Ukraine, the Arab world, and parts of Asia and Europe as an existential threat but also repeats the narrative that these were the result of a Western information warfare campaign. While there is no public evidence for any of these assertions, and there is much against, it is important for authoritarian states to maintain this fiction: it puts the onus for their failure on foreign enemies and not on their own misrule.

Penned by the most senior soldier in Russia, this document is no mere academic musing. It proved its practicality (and indeed proficiency) as an operational doctrine for Russia's stunning occupation of the Crimea in the spring of 2014: within just a few days, a heavily garrisoned territory the size of the state of Vermont was seized with virtually no bloodshed. And in the ongoing Ukrainian civil war, Russians and Russian proxies have successfully managed to create substantial difficulties for the pro-Western Ukrainian government that tried to break from Russia's orbit after its 2014 Euromaidan revolution. But most significant, the document itself is a message. Written before the Ukrainian conflict, it most likely was intended to provide a signal to the West at large: "covert war," the term used by Gerasimov himself, was here.

Why does Russia seem so keen to phrase things in terms of all-out conflict? A hint was already provided by the then deputy director of the signals intelligence organization in a 1997 presentation titled "Invisible, Drawn-Out War." Quite clearly, there was a very different concept of the term "war" being used than would normally be understood by Western readers. The most instructive of all quotations on war ties back, unsurprisingly, directly to Vladimir Ilyich Lenin. He is most famous for inverting Clausewitz's abridged maxim "war is the continuation of politics by other means" into "politics is the continuation of war by other means." Unlike the Western-Clausewitzian concept of war as a temporary, discontinuous, and abnormal state, Marxism-Leninism defined it as simply permanent and ongoing—a continuous state between hostile nations, not an aberration in their interaction. While the USSR accepted the international legal definition of war, and incorporated this definition in its own legal system, in Marxism-Leninism all the resources of a state were considered a permanent part of a continuing struggle. The state, so the theory goes, ultimately owned every resource in wartime—and the war never ended.

Chapter 10

OF *SILOVIKI* AND CYBER CRIME

T he Soviet Union did end—at least in name. But the theoretical under-pinnings of much of Soviet military thought never went away. Their revival and restoration depended on which parts of the old security state would achieve prominence in the post-Soviet world. By the year 2000, the winners were clear, and their victory was near total.

With the rise to power of Vladimir Putin, a generation of *siloviki,* for-mer members of the security services, have effectively taken over most of the government and even public life. A widely circulated figure is that in 2008 former KGB- or FSB-affiliated officials made up 42 percent of the state elite in Russia. These individuals are bound together not only by com-mon experience but also by a widely shared worldview that puts them, the guardians of the state, at the absolute pinnacle of power. As Putin, himself the former KGB/FSB director, has said, "There is no such thing as a former *Chekist* [KGB operative]." Ten years later, the *siloviki* have not lost any power, but rather have expanded it and still dominate most of Russian pol-itics. Their previous organizations have an iron grip not only on all the political levers of power but also on the Yeltsin-era oligarchs ruling the economy itself.

Today, there are four main intelligence bodies, of which two are by far the most significant. As Putin's power grew in the post-2008 period, he purposely encouraged competition between the various intelligence arms to foster a sense of struggle and prevent challenges to his rule. "This is the same principle of 'competitive intelligence' adopted by the United States," the researcher Mark Galeotti said, "with a strong admixture of bloody-fanged social Darwinism. The blurring of boundaries encourages regular direct and indirect turf wars, and not just over the usual bureaucratic prizes of responsibilities, funding, and access to the leadership but also business opportunities for officers, and sometimes outright survival."

The FSB is the principal successor to the KGB and is widely considered to still dominate but is not all powerful. Despite its internal-security remit, the FSB has been known to consider former Soviet territories its exclusive domain and also ranges far beyond that. The FSB was also the main beneficiary of the wholesale dismemberment of the former FAPSI, the direct equivalent to the US NSA. Today, three former FAPSI departments are responsible for cyber operations. While the FSB probably maintains a wide array of specialized cyber units, none are known publicly by name. Instead, we have only cursory evidence pointing to a number of cyber-espionage groups that are probably associated with the FSB. This includes the group most widely known as APT29 (for "Advanced Persistent Threat").

The second-most significant body for cyber operations is the military-intelligence directorate GRU. The GRU is difficult to compare with its closest equivalent, the US Defense Intelligence Agency, due to its much wider mission, which also includes resources in signals intelligence as well as direct covert action. The GRU maintains its own human spy network as well as large commando and special-operations forces useful for peacetime covert action as well as wartime sabotage missions (the famous *Spetsnaz* troops). Drawing on a long-standing tradition for risk taking, aggression, and covert action, the GRU has made far-ranging forays into what is considered overt expressions of cyber power. According to the company Crowdstrike, they are associated with APT28, also known as "Fancy Bear": one of the longest-lasting and also most overt Russian cyber-espionage groups. "Overt" is, however, a relative term, because Russian units, unlike their Chinese equivalent, are very well hidden and operate at a much higher level of sophistication.

As in all authoritarian states, regime stability is the overriding purpose of all aspects of the government and especially of the *chekists*. The effective inseparability of the state and the personal welfare of its leaders has allowed issues, such as personal criticism, to become matters of state—the modernization of the concept of *lèse-majesté,* where to insult the king was to insult the entire monarchy itself.

Russia's control over its Internet is much subtler than similar efforts in China. For years, many observers would even deny that there was a widespread censorship system active across the Russian Internet. Since 2012, these control mechanisms have started to emerge from the shadows but still provide only an inkling as to what actually happens in Russian cyberspace.

In 2012, the Internet restriction bill was enacted. Its original purpose was to combat child pornography but was rapidly expanded—to combat first political extremism, then product piracy, and later any content subject to a gag order. That content is known to the ISPs that are responsible for blocking the content, but not known to the public. This information helps form an Internet blacklist, often referred to simply as "the register." Blacklisting has hit the regime's political opponents as well as alleged criminal enterprises and many whose crimes are unknown. Data from Rublacklist .net indicates that 97 percent of Web sites on the list committed no offense defined in the attendant legislation. Other acts of censorship are much harder to detect and at best can be considered acts of self-censorship by intimidated content intermediaries. At worst, they are the latest examples of the long-standing tradition of making unwelcome content disappear from the Internet entirely.

This focus on the local information space has long been facilitated by what may amount to one of the most pervasive domestic intelligence-gathering systems in the world: SORM (the Russian acronym for "System of Operational-Investigative Activities"). When the FSB took over most of the signals intelligence agency FAPSI, it also inherited the crown jewels. Described as an "Orwellian network that jeopardizes privacy and the ability to use telecommunications to oppose the government," SORM boasts legislative backing and attendant technology that give the FSB the ability to completely monitor nearly all telecommunications traffic on Russian territory. This includes all Internet traffic within its jurisdiction, with all Internet service providers required to install the necessary technology on their systems.

The increasing ability of the Russian security services to monitor effectively all Internet traffic crossing its territory was always going to bring these services into contact with other actors. For Russian criminal actors had long been a fixture in cyberspace.

Russian organized crime is as singular an institution as the *chekists*: there are no comparable examples within the industrialized world, although the Italian Mafia and the Japanese Yakuza groups in the 1970s and 1980s may come close. It is huge: the largest of the Russian gangs, the Solntsevskaya Brotherhood, was anointed the world's foremost criminal enterprise, with revenues over $8.5 billion, in a 2014 article by *Fortune* magazine. These groups are widely considered less centralized than comparable groups in Italy and Japan, thus more autonomous. This gives them a large amount of flexibility to also work with smaller independent outfits that remain the dominant feature of illicit activity in Russia. As big as Russian organized crime is, Russian *dis*organized crime—the smaller and much more volatile wider ecosystem of small specialized groups—is even larger. In the 1980s, some of the oldest of the groups, such as gangs from Ukrainian Odessa, moved to the United States, where they later competed and cooperated with other groups from Armenia, Georgia, and elsewhere in the Caucasus.

The Ukrainian connection is particularly important because many top coders and cyber-crime gangs of the late 1990s and early years of the twenty-first century associated with Russian cyber crime were actually from (and based in) that country. Today, when we talk of Russian cyber crime, we are often including Azeri, Armenian, Lithuanian, and even Romanian and Bulgarian gangs. What such groups have in common is not only that they are firmly part of the Russian-speaking Internet culture but also that much of their infrastructure is based in Russia. These groups need large, compliant Internet service providers and hosting agencies to not only facilitate their activities but also turn a blind eye to them. They must move large sums of money and merchandise (acquired through credit card theft, and the means to monetize the theft of this data) without too much official scrutiny. And they need to be close to a steady stream of criminal talent that can feed their workforce and provide them with the tools they need. Russia, in the late 1990s and early twenty-first century, provided all of this, in spades.

In a process that is not widely publicly documented, it seems that around the turn of the millennium many of these smaller groups were then co-opted by organized crime. These larger groups muscled in on the enterprise, effectively forcing it under their "roof" (literally *krysha,* or "protection"—a common term for extortion). This pairing of both physical and cyber talent was to help form the complex criminal network known today as Russian cyber crime, sometimes considered the largest single illegal business in the world. In 2012, Russian cyber crime had direct earnings of around $4.5 billion and accounted for more than a third of the entire worldwide income through cyber crime. In 2015, one single Russia-based heist supposedly netted as much as $1 *billion* in the greatest bank theft to date. But all this pales next to what was the ultimate pairing of physical brawn and cyber brain: the Russian Business Network (RBN). At the height of its power, in 2007, the RBN was estimated to be responsible for over 60 percent of worldwide cyber crime. It was also to be the first time that Russian cyber crime clearly took on a role as a proxy for the Russian security services.

Prior to its mysterious disappearance in 2008, the RBN had the dubious distinction of being one of the few crime groups to attract the public disapproval of the Western national security establishment in recent decades. Headed by the mysterious "Flyman" (whom the journalist Brian Krebs has since written about in more depth), the RBN was "one of the most notorious criminal groups on the Internet today," an Internet hosting company of a slightly different kind from Comcast or Verizon: while those companies would probably host your content *as long as* you abide by the law, the whole purpose of the RBN was to host data *because* it was illegal. In fact, if, for instance, as a low-level cyber criminal looking to exchange stolen credit card data on a secure server, you wanted to enter into some kind of contract with the RBN, you had to conduct some kind of theft of consumers' financial and personal data first in order to disprove any suspicion of being associated with law enforcement. *The Economist* described the RBN as having "no legal identity; it is not registered as a company; its senior figures are anonymous, known only by their nicknames. Its web sites are registered at anonymous addresses with dummy e-mails. It does not advertise for customers. Those who want to use its services contact it via Internet messaging services and pay with anonymous electronic cash." Its hosted customers are "cybercriminals, ranging from spammers to phishers, bot-herders and all manner of other fraudsters and wrongdoers from the venal to the vicious." The RBN was the giant of cyber crime, a primarily logistic service that provided the infrastructure for other, lesser criminals, including laundering their cash. It also became one of the main weapons of Russia's government for waging cyberattacks.

While the relationship between the security services (primarily the FSB) and the criminals has taken on various forms over the last decade, the intelligence–cyber crime link remains one of the most enduring aspects of Russian cyber power. One reason for this unholy partnership between criminals and spooks was simply convenience: the cyber criminals are able to invest in significant infrastructure, ranging from malware to physical servers and the like, that is also useful for state cyber operations. Another reason, however, is certainly political: the ability to hide behind the cyber-crime actors and assume no knowledge or control over their activities was always going to be irresistible to the military cyber thinkers in the Russian government. The old Soviet military concept of the *maskirovka,* or "strate-gic deception," could easily be accomplished through the use of proxies and was even a requirement for the deception to succeed. The authors of one piece in the flag-bearing Russian military journal *Reflexive Processes and Control* explained how misdirection could be deployed in cyber con-flict, and specifically how "non-state actors can be used by the state, overtly or covertly, to execute plausibly deniable cyber attacks," writing that

> isolating cyberterrorism and cybercrime from the general context of international information security is, in a sense, artificial and unsupported. . . . [I]t is primarily motivation that distinguishes acts of cyberterrorism, cybercrime, and military cyberattacks. . . . [With-out knowing the motivation one cannot] qualify what is going on as a criminal, terrorist or military-political act. The more so that sources of cyberattacks can be easily given a legend as criminal or terrorist actions.

Effectively, it argued that government actions could easily be camou-flaged as criminal or terrorist activities. The criminal networks needed were easy to identify, but so were the "terrorists": Russia's burgeoning scene of young "hacker patriots" (as opposed to the Chinese "patriot hackers" we will discuss later). Indeed, the highly computer-literate Russian youth is of particular interest in the Russian cyber landscape: the nationalistic-inclined bloggers and script-kiddies who were given the double-positive acclaim of being "hacker patriots" when they engaged in criminal activi-ties. Some of them invested considerable time and effort attacking—both in blogs and in (computer) script—the supposed enemies of Mother Russia.

These activities, in particular attacks on Chechen-friendly Web sites in Sweden and elsewhere, were encouraged by the security services.

How this link actually worked was seldom shown in public, but one of the few examples is the attempted recruitment of the young hacker patriot Anton Moskal by the National Antiterrorism Centre (NAC) in 2009. The NAC caller identified himself as an FSB agent and thought Moskal was connected to the hacking community and, even though "the caller had little technical knowledge . . . , tried to recruit Moskal for future 'patriotic activities.'" He urged Moskal to attack the Swedish Chechen Web site as an indication of good faith. It was a classic example of the Soviet tradition of telephone orders (or telephone direction), where an unknown voice would call up and claim to be from the security services and start handing out orders. The security services controlled all communication links, so the tradition arose: anyone who actually said this on the phone would by definition be authentic. Moskal had never heard of the tradition, however, and therefore, incredulously, posted the whole exchange on a blog on RUNet.

Other recruitment was hardly more subtle. It included posting directly to Web sites frequented by such hacker patriots and inviting them to join direct message groups where they received instructions or malware from unknown parties. In some cases, they were just given the opportunity to join a campaign as a passive participant, simply by providing their computer to be used in a botnet. Taken together, the hacker patriots were to become vital foot soldiers in Russia's experiment with plausibly deniable cyber conflict. The RBN was to be their logistic base and their arsenal. This force was put into action in 2007.

I n the early summer of 2007, Estonia dared challenge the regional supremacy of the Kremlin by announcing that it would move a World War II statue commemorating Soviet soldiers. The Russian Internet erupted with anger, and within days cyberattacks began to mount against Estonia's highly networked society, widely considered at the time to be one of the most "wired" countries in the world, with public services routinely delivered through the Internet and citizens significantly more connected to the Internet than in other similar countries.

During a three-week period starting on April 27, Estonia was the target of a series of escalating DDoS attacks targeting the government, media organizations, and banks, coming from a custom-made botnet of up to eighty-five thousand computers. At the height of the attacks, on May 9, at least six sites were inaccessible, including those of the foreign and justice ministries. Given Estonia's heavy reliance on the Internet, these attacks prompted a reaction by NATO, dispatching cyber experts in Tallinn to aid Estonians in their defense. Estonia had to disable access to its Web sites from overseas users in order to keep them accessible for domestic users. As one Estonian Internet expert said at the time, "We are back to the stone age, telling the world what is going on with phone and fax."

How serious the 2007 Estonian attacks really were has been a matter of heated debate, with assessments of the assault ranging from a "nuisance" to one that "nearly brought the country to its knees." One point not open to debate is that the attack had huge political and media implications, with some declaring that this had been the "first cyberwar." Estonia's prime minister at the time, Andrus Ansip, even asked, "What's the difference between a blockade of harbors or airports of sovereign states and the blockade of government institutions and newspaper websites?"

It was evident that the Russian security services had been, at best, negligent in not helping to stop the attacks. Investigators had a strong interest from the start in Russian "hacker patriots" and the logistical support they had received. Media speculation in the West was supported, initially covertly but later openly, by security specialists' assertion that the attacks had actually been directed by the FSB. But the organization actually executing the attack, pulling the trigger if you will, was also the owner of the cyber infrastructure needed to conduct it: the RBN. After nearly a year of increasing public pressure, one of the then-popular pro-Kremlin youth groups, Nashi, was abruptly identified as the organizer behind the attack (rather than the FSB) by the Duma's parliamentary leader, Sergey Markov, who said in a radio interview, "About the cyberattack on Estonia . . . don't worry, that attack was carried out by my assistant [the Nashi "commissar" Konstantin Goloskokov]. Turns out it was purely a reaction from civil society and, incidentally," he ominously added, "such things will happen more and more." The Kremlin, having been internationally derided for its supposed use of cyber-crime gangs in aggressions directed at other states, had thrown up its hands and pointed at its patriot hackers as the source of the activity, denying its own direct responsibility. The model for cyber war fought by proxy was in place, with the enticing addition of plausible deniability—even if no one considered the Russian denials in any way plausible. Today, the cybersecurity community generally accepts that the FSB not only was guilty of allowing the attacks to happen but also ordered them directly, including using these attacks to mask much more serious penetrations of Estonian government systems: indeed, it seems likely that highly sophisticated hackers used the "noise" of loud RBN attacks to achieve more than what some derided as an act of cyber vandalism. The elegance was profound: one proxy (Nashi) was used to cover another proxy (the RBN), whose activities in turn provided the cover for a more serious cyber intrusion that, to this day, has not been reported in the public media.

In 2008, that elegance started to fray a little. In a sudden escalation with Georgia, which resulted in the physical invasion of the Caucasian republic by over three hundred combat aircraft and nine thousand Russian troops, cyberattacks made another, dual-hatted entry.

A number of researchers found abundant circumstantial evidence pointing to officials within the Russian government directing these attacks, with a prominent role played by the RBN. In this case, the RBN provided the attack infrastructure, while most of the attacks themselves were actually carried out by volunteer Russian hacker patriots who were recruited in the Web comments section of every single major Russian newspaper in the run-up to the attack. There are signs that these attacks were planned before the outbreak of the shooting war: besides the preparation of the botnets themselves for an attack, some of the material that was used in the Web defacements was prepared months in advance.

As in Estonia in 2007, after the overtly loud DDoS attacks on Georgia there were other attacks that were much more sophisticated and very unlikely to be the work of hacker patriots. This included wholesale rerouting of Georgian Internet traffic through Russia, severe disruption of most Georgian communication links out of the country, introduction of fake Georgian Web sites used to infect possible sympathizers, and ultimately a potential military-grade cyberattack on the Baku-Tbilisi-Ceyhan gas pipeline on Turkish soil. The latter attack has attracted a lot of attention, due to alleged video footage that shows two men with laptops entering a pumping station prior to the explosion. The pipeline was certainly subject to a cyberattack of some sort: the pipeline's industrial control system failed, resulting in a spectacular fire that proved difficult to contain.

Following the Georgian war of 2008, there was renewed media interest in the possible Russian use of proxies. By this time, however, RBN seemed to have disappeared—even though some of their net blocks may have been used in the Georgian attacks, as a business they had effectively been shut down by the Russian authorities. After the Estonian attacks and the subsequent fallout (particularly a damning investigatory piece by Brian Krebs), the RBN moved much of its infrastructure to China and Taiwan before disappearing again. Key parts of its (former) infrastructure, however, were used in the Georgian attacks. How was this to be explained? "They were nationalized," explains Jart Armin, one of the founders of RBNExploit, a group dedicated to pursuing the RBN. The world's largest cyber-crime gang—which depending on your estimate made a clear profit of somewhere between $200 million and $2 billion in 2007 alone—had disappeared, leaving its massive logistical web in uncertain hands.

For a few years beginning in 2009, Western information security professionals fighting cyber crime started to observe an interesting phenomenon: Russia seemed increasingly ready to respond to requests for cooperation. The MVD, Russia's Interior Ministry, suddenly started to cooperate not only with official requests from European (and even US) law enforcement but also with requests from the InfoSec community. The head of Europol's European Cybercrime Centre was, for example, repeatedly quoted saying that its collaboration with Russian law enforcers "was improving" or that "Russia had started showing signs of greater cooperation"—that is, before the current standoff with Ukraine started. Concrete examples included in 2013 the arrest of the malware writer "Paunch" as well as the strike against the ringleaders behind a virulent e-banking campaign, using Carberp and RDPdor Trojans.

There are differing theories regarding why the Russian government suddenly seemed to turn on cyber crime. Some voices have speculated that Russian cyber crime was starting to break the unspoken cardinal rule: don't hack other Russians. Others consider the motivations more sinister. By going after minor cyber-crime gangs, who focused on credit card theft and e-banking heists, Russia was effectively protecting the more serious malware writers behind them, along with these coders' own cyber-crime gangs. And there is no doubt that Russian security services still maintain a cozy if not symbiotic relationship with the criminal underground.

In 2015, Dutch-Danish security researchers investigating a particularly virulent piece of eastern European banking malware called Dridex were able to penetrate the core of the criminal operation: a server that functioned as a malware repository, essentially a cyber-weapons arsenal. The repository was interesting due to not only its content—a number of software exploits that were tailored to London-based financial systems—but also its log-in activities. While nearly always masked behind proxies, in one case, probably due to a proxy error, one of the "customers" accessing the server inadvertently revealed himself—pointing straight to a Russian government IP.

This should not be too surprising. One of the most sought-after cyber criminals in the world, nicknamed "Slavik" (real name Evgeniy Bogachev), had been involved in one of the precursors of the Dridex campaign. Originally, Slavik and his GameOver Zeus Network (a popular cyber-crime tool for facilitating online banking theft) concentrated purely on siphoning funds from bank accounts, in particular supporting sophisticated e-banking heists that were global in reach. According to the FBI indictment, Slavik's group stole over $100 million in 2014 and laundered it through Chinese banks. Slavik also seemed to have other goals, however. Hacked logs obtained by the Dutch security firm Fox-IT showed that starting in the late fall of 2013—about the time that the conflict between Ukraine and Russia was heating up—Slavik went behind the back of the rest of the gang and single-handedly retooled a cyber-heist botnet into a dedicated espionage machine. He began scouring infected systems in Ukraine for specific keywords in e-mails and documents that would likely be found only in classified documents. Fox-IT found "all the keywords related to specific classified documents or Ukrainian intelligence agencies [and] in some cases, the actual email addresses of persons that were working at the agencies." Slavik later pulled the same trick in Turkey, penetrating the Turkish Foreign Ministry and police. According to Brian Krebs's Fox-IT interview, Slavik was looking to intercept communications about the conflict in Syria on Turks southern border—one that Russia has supported by reportedly shipping arms into the region. "The keywords are around arms shipments and Russian mercenaries in Syria," the Fox-IT investigator said. "Obviously, this is something Turkey would be interested in, and in this case it's obvious that the Russians wanted to know what the Turks know about these things." Unsurprisingly, Russia has refused to cooperate on this case, and in the fall of 2016 Slavik remained at large.

Slavik and the Dridex gang are just the most recent and high-profile example of the link between cyber crime and cyber espionage. This *siloviki*-cyber-crime symbiosis produces not only infrastructure for crime or espionage but also tailor-made cyber-espionage campaigns. Supporting these campaigns requires significant resources, including, according to the FireEye security researcher Steve Sachs, "entire villages dedicated to malware in Russia—very sophisticated, very organized, very well-funded." It is hard to truly grasp what the notion of "entire villages" means exactly, but be-

sides the top-notch elite coders there is room for grunt work by less sophisticated staff, including functioning as support staff for the cyber-crime
products—for instance, many of these products come with a twenty-four-
hour support hotline, where you can call up for help if your bank heist is
going badly. Some staff are probably engaged in "fuzzing," one of the very
manpower-intensive processes employed to discover zeroday vulnerabilities. In other cases, entire cyber-crime campaigns may be written from
scratch just for espionage use. For some observing the eastern European
malware scene, it sometimes seems that a particular government-backed
espionage campaign will deploy a specific method or zeroday, but later a
strikingly similar campaign will pop up in the more dedicated cyber-crime
underground. While most of the examples of this nature never make the
public news, one finally did, in 2012.

In September 2012, security researchers in Denmark discovered an
e-banking malware campaign that had a previously relatively unknown
wrinkle: the "dropper" for the Trojan (that is, the component that actually
hid in a tampered with PDF file and, upon being activated, downloaded the
rest of the malware) was tiny—only twenty kilobytes. This allowed the
software to remain unnoticed by all existing antivirus systems. The Danish
researchers christened the attack TinBa, for Tiny Banker. Within weeks,
antivirus products adopted the indicator as part of their tool sets. And for
a few months, nothing else seemed to happen.

Then, in February 2013, the Russian security firm Kaspersky Lab announced the discovery of MiniDuke, a cyberattack directed at a wide range
of targets, from government computers in the Czech Republic, Ireland,
Portugal, and Romania to a think tank, research institute, and health-care
provider in the United States—an attack that a secret service spokesman
from Romania said was "pursued by an entity that has the characteristics
of a state actor." A white paper by F-Secure Labs Threat Intelligence on
the family of malware called the Dukes, including the MiniDuke version, detailed "how available evidence supports the conclusion that the

Dukes' primary mission is intelligence gathering to support foreign policy decision-making by the Russian Federation."

The technical similarity to TinBa was apparent: both campaigns depended on similar tiny droppers. The differences, however, were meaningful: first, MiniDuke was clearly an espionage tool, unlike the commercially minded TinBa; second, MiniDuke was much older. Although Kaspersky's initial report was scant on the details, F-Secure stated in 2015 that MiniDuke had probably started as early as 2008 (TinBa had started in 2012) and was part of a family of malware with similar names. Unlike Kaspersky, the Finnish company F-Secure was much happier to point fingers and stated unequivocally that the Duke family of intrusions was linked with the Russian government.

While it is possible that TinBa and MiniDuke had no connections to each other, the timing of the revelations—in particular of MiniDuke—is nonetheless interesting. TinBa was now known in the wild, so it was possible that the writers of MiniDuke knew that their operation would soon be discovered. In that case, the discovery of the virus by Kaspersky was maybe not simply a matter of chance.

Kaspersky is no normal company. Founded in 1997 by Eugene Kaspersky, a former member of FAPSI, the Russian NSA, it can now claim to be one of the largest providers of antivirus and security solutions in the world, with revenues exceeding $700 million in 2014. Together with many of its industry peers, including companies such as FireEye, Crowdstrike, Symantec, Trend Micro, and F-Secure, it has become an important pillar of the InfoSec community. Like these other actors (many of which are American), this firm professes a defense-only agenda and regularly contributes to formal and informal information exchanges that are the lifeblood of InfoSec.

Prior to Kaspersky's rise, the only security organizations publishing research—and quoted in Western media—on suspected cyber-espionage attacks were either North American or European. These companies were playing an increasingly significant role in pointing fingers at Russia and

China. In particular, security professionals had supported the Western narrative of Russia's supposed use of cyber crime to attack Estonia and Georgia, among many other attacks. And there is little doubt that the security researchers such as the (American) Symantec and later Mandiant and FireEye had been setting their research efforts against Chinese and Russian cyber espionage for many years. Since around 2011, reporting from the industry has increasingly supported American government discussions on Chinese and Russian cyberattacks. Many outside (and even some inside) the United States started to think that perhaps this was a little too convenient and that the international InfoSec chorus would benefit from a Russian voice. Kaspersky heard the call and, since 2012, has outed some significant cyber-espionage campaigns, but with a clear slant: most of the campaigns were either Western or, rarely, Chinese, and only one pointed to the Russian government.

Kaspersky's role as an important member of the InfoSec community has often invited suspicion that it may be closely tied to Russian intelligence. An investigative piece by the journalist Noah Shachtman added further juicy rumors to the mill in July 2012, emphasizing Eugene Kaspersky's intelligence background and the alignment of Kaspersky's actions with Russia's interests, and traced the strong personal ties the founder enjoys with the Russian intelligence services. In the summer of 2015, some other members of the InfoSec community accused Kaspersky of actually trying to sabotage the very community it was part of by subtly hampering key community tools used to check malware. According to a Reuters report quoting former Kaspersky employees, the company "tried to damage rivals in the marketplace by tricking their antivirus software programs into classifying benign files as malicious." Some members of the InfoSec community have, however, denied the importance of the episode and tried to protect the company's reputation, stating that even if its investigative reporting was slanted, it wasn't much more so than the reports that US companies had done. This certainly fit the Russian narrative of a "plurality of truths," and it needs to be considered in depth.

For many veteran observers of the scene, there would not be anything particularly surprising or even especially nefarious if Kaspersky was in fact working with the Russian security services. The interesting question is whether the discoveries were simply coincidental and personal, or part of a larger strategy and directed. One argument could be that Russia's use of proxies in a coercive role to exercise cyberattacks (see Nashi and the RBN) had reached certain limits and that a subtler strategy utilizing the public agenda-setting "second face of power" was needed. The ability to reframe the international and media debate in your own terms would simply be one of the most important steps to a final goal: promoting a particular narrative. For instance, helping to underline that cyberspace was "out of control" (mostly due to activities of the United States) would help advance a preference: for example, that only a UN organization should be entrusted to manage the Internet. The ability to set such basic preferences is what Nye called the "third face" of political power. While it was originally intended to be accomplished mostly by attraction and leadership (that is, "leading by example"), there is no reason why preference setting cannot be accomplished by more subtle and more nefarious means. The ability to set the agenda—for instance, by revealing your opponent's cyber operations with the help of an InfoSec company friendly to your goals—would be a significant step to framing the global debate toward a specific set of preferences. This would truly be information warfare at its purest.

The possible connection between the agenda setting and the preference setting seemed sometimes obvious when looking at Kaspersky's strongest institutional partner during its sudden spate of discoveries between 2012 and 2014: the International Telecommunication Union, an organization that featured widely as the source of many of Kaspersky's malware samples and that was referenced in nearly every one of its reports.

This was coincidental with the controversial leadership of the ITU by Hamadoun Touré, during which the ITU had increasingly started making overt moves toward claiming a role in Internet governance, the process of managing the world's Internet resources that at least partially underpin cyberspace. And in this process, it had clear support from Russia. In 2011, the ITU even set up a lavishly endowed technical organization in Malaysia: IMPACT, for International Multilateral Partnership Against Cyber Threats. IMPACT tried very hard to carve out a mandate for itself in Internet governance questions and seemed to be set to challenge ICANN's role. This included a subtle redefinition of what Internet governance should encompass—namely, cyber crime. The fact that ICANN generally refuses to involve itself in cyber-crime matters seemed to leave the field open to a new actor—one that profited enviably from Kaspersky's patronage. From 2012 to 2013, IMPACT was everywhere; you couldn't visit an international conference and not run into its representatives. And during the same period, nearly every Kaspersky press release on a newly discovered attack (of which none were decidedly Russian, except MiniDuke) referenced ITU and/or IMPACT.

There are many less sinister theories than the one I've recounted here, namely that Kaspersky cooperated with the ITU at the strong encouragement of the Russian state and selectively investigated cyberattacks to counter a perceived pro-US bias of the wider industry and media. Personal preferences and ideology alone could have been a sufficiently strong motivator, without any coordination with the Russian government.

Still, that these policy goals aligned perfectly is undeniable. Russia has always seen cyberspace for what it is: a radically new domain of political power, the dominance of which can have drastic consequences on governments, especially those of a more authoritarian bent. It is no surprise therefore that the Russian government would understand very clearly its benefits in promoting a Russian firm at the forefront of the global threat intelligence scene to protect its information sphere. To do so could even be called securing the high ground in information warfare.

PWNAGE DIPLOMACY

The above examples of preference setting all have one thing in common: they are aimed at forming public opinion outside Russia, in particular in the West but also among sympathetic populations in the rest of the world. These include those nations outside the rich-world club that are far more suspicious of the United States as well as fringe groups within the West itself, such as those on the far right of the political spectrum. Unlike these broad-stroke efforts, other signals are directed at a totally different target: a narrow, highly informed group of technical and political policy makers who largely work with government. Compared with the public message, however, the secret message is much more threatening.

Signaling has long been a common practice between governments and took on significantly threatening forms during the Cold War. Today, governments still signal with military maneuvers, for example; Russia is also a leader in this arena, with aircraft (and presumably also submarines) consistently skimming the airspace of a number of NATO (and, in the case of Sweden, non-NATO) nations in activities that only most generously can be called "showing the flag." As aggressive as some of these activities are, they pale in comparison with Russian cyber signaling.

Russian state-sanctioned or state-tolerated hacking has had its ups and downs for the last two decades. Since 2012, however, it is clear that Western political targets have had a much higher level of interest paid to them, with some criminal gangs now more intent on pursuing political and governmental objectives—objectives of interest only to Kremlin clients. According to one American security expert interviewed in October 2015, "Criminal hackers 'that used to hunt banks eight hours a day are now operating two hours a day, turning their guns on NATO and government targets.'" These sanctioned or directed non-state attacks have, since 2014, been matched with a higher risk tolerance of Russian government actors. Whereas previously stealth was a prime objective of their method of operation, loud and obvious efforts, even of the supposed state groups, have clearly risen. Within the InfoSec environment, it has been an article of faith for many years that purported Russian government activities are comparable with suspected American intelligence activities only in terms of sophistication. Dedicated Russian state intrusion sets (cyber groups) remain much more capable than Russian cyber crime, and especially more capable than purported Chinese attempts at the same. Unlike Chinese attempts, however, they are seldom reported in the media.

The sad elegance of the Russian proxy relationship with cyber crime means that some of the signaling is certainly ambiguous—and frightening, on a very personal scale. InfoSec professionals and those investigating Russian cyber-crime and cyber-espionage campaigns have been threatened in particularly shady ways, ranging from dirty tricks on home computers to physical threats and perhaps even kidnapping.

Russian state cyberattacks, like similar ones associated with the US government, are not only many times more sophisticated than even those of good cyber-crime gangs; they also deploy many more resources. Following a particularly brutal Russian-backed cyber-espionage campaign, one European foreign ministry was forced to disconnect from the Internet entirely while it cleaned up its systems. A week after it went back online, the same intrusion set was back, with many hundreds of hours' worth of coding done in between. Few criminal enterprises would show this type of dedication and commitment of resources, even if they were interested in particular Russian political themes—which, according to the analysis of the targeted data, they were. In fact, although the attack wasn't directly attributable to Russia, the indications were overpowering, and the government in question even sent a senior diplomat to Moscow to warn it from doing this again (the warning had little effect). For the technical analyst, it was obvious that the perpetrators were comfortable with the implications and that the attack itself was an exercise in pure signaling of the most aggressive kind, in hacker jargon, "pwnage." The intrusion was a gloating "we own you, totally"—a show of dominance and a very explicit warning to be wary of escalation.

If this case of signaling sounds relatively benign, pretend you are responsible for a company or government department's overall security, and imagine your reaction upon finding a highly sophisticated espionage campaign on the network of your employer. This campaign could get details about the people who work in your company, their Internet usage, and what their e-mails say but also threaten to destroy key parts of your IT infrastructure, such as your very business records. Now imagine you are not just any private company but the power grid company responsible for the electricity distribution for millions of homes. You don't have any juicy intellectual property worth stealing. You just have a highly complicated, supposedly secure load management and distribution system responsible for keeping the lights on in those homes. You are, in fact, a cyber-war target, a possibly valid target in times of declared warfare, for air or cyber strikes. And the espionage "worm" is perhaps not simply an espionage system—there being little to steal at your company—but rather a cyber weapon in waiting. As bad as this discovery in itself already is, now imagine that it is neither by chance nor by skill that you found out about the intrusion. You found out only because the worm started broadcasting and drawing attention to itself in a confident assertion that it is here, in your systems, and that there is nothing you can possibly do about it other than taking yourself off-line for days on end to facilitate the cleanup, to possibly no effect. In other words, "be afraid, because if we can do this, there's no telling what else we can do."

Something similar might have happened repeatedly across the United States. In 2013, a hacker group that Symantec identified as APT28, which had been operating at least since 2011, shifted its focus to American and European energy firms and companies related to industrial control systems. The hackers were targeting grid operators, petroleum pipeline operators, electricity generation firms, and other strategically important energy companies. The attackers were clearly more interested in preparing for cyber war than conducting cyber espionage. At the same time, however, these efforts were obvious enough to indicate that their ostensible purpose—pre-deploying cyber weapons right in the US networks to be ready for conflict or crisis—was not the only goal: indicating loudly that Russia had this capability and intent was probably at least as significant.

If the American power grid intrusions were signaling efforts by the Russian government, they were not necessarily the most aggressive of them. When the French TV channel TV5 was hacked in April 2015, it was reported as one of the first instances of true cyber terrorism: the hackers defaced the network's Web site and Facebook page with ISIS and jihadist propaganda and knocked all twelve TV5 channels off-line. Collaborating with Trend Micro and FireEye, the French investigators first explored the ISIS lead as the media soon reported that the hackers had made clear mentions of the "CyberCaliphate."

Shortly after the attack, however, the French government leaked results of its inquiry, which directly pointed to Russian hackers rather than Syrian online jihadis. Indeed, *L'Express* was soon able to reveal that the investigations had turned toward a group directly associated with Russian intelligence: once again, APT28. It therefore appeared that Russian intelligence willfully tried to impersonate terrorist actors and inflict significant damage in their name. The reasons why Russian actors might have thought it was a clever move to launch a purported cyber terror attack against a French critical infrastructure are twofold. One fairly complicated notion was that the Russian spies behind APT28 wanted to conduct a fake cyber terror attack to help coax other suspected jihadis in Russia out into the open.

A much simpler explanation may be that besides simply threatening the French government with their prowess and aggression, the Russians were quite happy to further the narrative of so-called "cyber terrorism." It is a term often used by Russian leaders and rejected by most Western nations because it is rightfully considered a flimsy pretext to target all types of dissidents, including pro-democracy activists. By pretending to wage what amounted to the first true cyber terrorist attack, the Russians might have hoped to further the narrative in this direction. If that was the case, they succeeded in some small measure, because senior French politicians started to use the term "cyber terrorism" until at last the civil servants were able to convince them otherwise. It helped that it was revealed that instead of a cyber terrorist attack, the attack on one of France's main TV networks was in fact one of the most serious state cyber-sabotage attempts ever carried out.

As serious as the attack on TV5 was, it was not the only case of Russian cyber sabotage carried out in Europe. In 2014, a cyberattack destroyed a multimillion-dollar blast furnace of the steel giant ThyssenKrupp; according to German officials, there were clear links between known Russian surveillance activities and the actual attacks. A specific form of Russian malware known as Havex was discovered in the damaged steel mill, and the facility had previously been under cyber reconnaissance by Russian actors. This may be one of the most significant physical cyberattacks ever carried out, and it is possible that it was not alone and that other attacks were simply not reported.

Linking the French, German, and American cases of cyber sabotage is the largest of all Russian intrusion groups. APT28 has been active since at least 2011 (and perhaps as far back as 2000) and is responsible for a large number of espionage campaigns. These include the deployment of not one but two "Stuxnet type" highly complex cyber weapons that are able to move between "air-gapped systems" (that is, systems not connected to the Internet) and are both espionage and potential cyber-warfare tools. One of the early versions of one of these weapons was the Agent.btz attack discussed previously. APT28 is so prolific and deep rooted that it may in fact be responsible for other Russian cyber campaigns that are presumed to have been coded and launched by other groups. APT28 clearly shares many networks and tools with cyber-crime actors and has a very wide remit, including intelligence of the energy sector, and many different versions of political intelligence gathering. It can target countries worldwide and operate in many different languages; it became clear, for instance, that in March 2016 APT28 developed capabilities in Turkish in a very short amount of time. It may also have a war-fighting role, if indeed it is the group behind the deployment of BlackEnergy used against the US power grid and the Ukrainian blackout in December 2015.

A second Russian APT group is best known as APT29 (or "Cozy Bear"). It is more recent and limited in scope, although it may in fact have been responsible for some espionage such as the Duke operations described previously. It also exhibits in-depth association with Russian cyber-crime networks and malware. What is known for sure is that in 2015 APT29 engaged in a new political espionage campaign that mostly concentrated on Russian and Ukrainian issues and that cunningly hid behind various cloud services and Twitter.

Which government organizations the two intrusion groups can be assigned to is difficult to say with open sources. That they are separate entities was made obvious when both these groups hacked the Democratic National Committee around May 2016, ostensibly both looking for the same information—namely, information that Hillary Clinton's campaign had gathered on Donald Trump but possibly also incriminating e-mails that could embarrass the Democratic candidate. According to the security company Crowdstrike, which investigated the breach, both APT28 and APT29 seemed to launch uncoordinated attacks, indicating that they had no knowledge of each other's activities. According to the article, APT28 was aligned with the GRU, the Russian military intelligence, and APT29 was aligned with the FSB. It needs to be pointed out, however, that exactly the opposite alignment has also been purported, indicating that while a general link between the attacks and the Russian government is clear, parsing exactly who is pulling the strings on the government level is a much taller order.

It is hard to understand exactly why Russia is pursuing such an overt level of aggression. We seldom see the adversary side of the equation; we don't know what cyberattacks Russia has suffered and, at least as important, whether they are real: instead of responding to similar American attacks, for instance, they may be a reaction to the engagement of pro-democracy activists in Ukraine. But it is equally possible that they are simply part of cyber brinkmanship, not too dissimilar to the flying of nuclear bombers at each other during the height of the Cold War, while at the same time diplomatic negotiators sweat it out in Vienna and Geneva. The differences are that in the 1970s and 1980s those discussions centered on deployment of very physical nuclear forces: submarines, bombers, and ultimately missiles. Today, the discussion is not about cyber armament or disarmament, because Russia and China both have denied that they even have such capabilities. Instead, the discussion focuses on how these theoretical capabilities could be used against other states, both in peace and in wartime. But the discussions do have something in common with their Cold War nuclear predecessors: the stakes are high. Any miscalculation significant enough in those signaling activities could lead to potentially dramatic repercussions for millions of civilians.

Russia's philosophy of information conflict is much older than the United States'. In many ways, the rise of cyberspace has breathed new life into former Soviet military strategy, notions that in previous decades were simply interesting academic musings without any technological or political application. No other country seems better prepared to wage information warfare: Sophisticated resources are under relatively tight command and control and can draw upon a wealth of ideas. But like Soviet ideas for cyberspace, these ideas may simply be wrong. Just as the Soviet Union underestimated elements of trust as key issues in creating cyberspace, leading "new Russian" thinkers—such as Vladislav Surkov, widely considered one of the hidden authors of Putinism—have clearly overestimated raw force, simple venality, and outright dishonesty as the prime levers of power. Even though Putin's Russia has had significant success deploying these talents in recent years, in the medium and long term it is much more likely to weaken Russia's economic prosperity and, ultimately, national security. The readiness to use threats and bluster to get its way is reminiscent of North Korea, and like North Korea it promises only long-term isolation and decay. In order to avoid this fate, Putin could well try to latch onto similar strongmen and may even succeed in enchanting more countries into a "Eurasian bloc"—a long-standing dream. But if that fails, the current course of confrontation and increasing economic isolation will only raise the prospect of long-term decay and collapse. This was the outcome for the Soviet Union, and the *chekists* are in no mood for a repeat. Their only logical course of action is therefore not to compete with the United States and the West but somehow to catastrophically weaken them—and therefore raise Russia's own relative power. While presumably any real option would do, the toolbox of information warfare—ranging from the coercive prospect of strategic warfare to the co-optive abilities of deterrence and the capacity to set preferences and convince both key opinion makers and the wider body politic—seems to have prevailed as the best approach available. The threat for everyone is that Russia's leaders and intellectuals will significantly miscalculate in their strategic designs and inflict upon the world and especially their nation a very dark future.

PART V

Chapter 12

THE CHINESE CYBER DREAM

The Great Wall of China is one of the most well-known structures of human civilization. The largest historic man-made edifice on Earth, it stretches over some fifty-five hundred miles. Yet, as the legendary scholar of Chinese history Joseph Needham has pointed out, "it is still a mysterious artifact that we know relatively little about." For it is clear that its obvious purpose—to protect China from foreign armies—was seldom, if ever, successful. While there are many alternative theories as to what function the Great Wall was to perform—from serving as a tool against smuggling to providing a handy road network that made it easier to catch raiding armies when they tried to leave China burdened down with loot—I find one theory particularly attractive: the Great Wall was a massive symbol of imperial power, directly intended to support the ruling claim of the emperor. It was therefore intended primarily not to protect the domestic population—which it repeatedly failed to do—but to awe them: to prove that the emperor was doing something worthy of the mandate to rule. Anyone standing at the massive Ming dynasty edifice in the mountains north of Beijing can hardly fail to consider this theory; the area, heavily wooded and so steep that hiking it is a challenge, was always clearly impenetrable for a horse and rider. Building a wall here clearly had other goals beyond pure military ones. Maybe, as one senior Chinese cyber official once told me, the Great Wall was just the result of officials' trying to impress the capital.

This official's own role in present-day Chinese affairs couldn't have been far from his mind. He was one of the thousands of Chinese cadres directly and indirectly responsible for the modern-day digital equivalent of the Great Wall: the aptly nicknamed Great Firewall of both automated and human censorship tools that guard China's cyberspace from what the nation's leaders deem harmful content. Like its historical antecedent, the Great Firewall is hugely expensive to maintain: in its most expansive definition, more people are employed manning it than currently serve in the People's Liberation Army (PLA), the largest military on Earth. It is of dubious primary utility; that is, it isn't at all clear that it is especially effective in doing its stated job. It is a very visible instrument of political power, however, intended to remind the population of the powers that be.

In the fall of 2015, I attended the grandly named World Internet Conference, held in the heavily restored Ming village of Wuzhen, two hours from Shanghai. An ancient "water village" nestled on canals, Wuzhen is hardwired with broadband Internet access, with the inhabitants supposedly manifesting a social utopia of simple peasant living in a highly structured social system marked by universal harmony. Wuzhen is a beautiful, shrinkwrapped representation of a neo-Confucian Disney World society beloved by the present rulers of China, especially by President Xi Jinping. The one thousand invited attendees, including Russia's prime minister, Medvedev, were shadowed by three thousand security personnel, and an informal game among attendees was trying to name all the various policy, military, and intelligence security forces nervously competing at the dozens of security checkpoints. The highlight of the event was Xi Jinping's opening speech, in which he outlined what amounted to the "China dream" of cyberspace. The watchword was "cyber sovereignty." This speech underlined some of China's stated core objectives in cyberspace: a fundamental shift in the present "unfair" system of Internet governance, a stop to the "unfounded accusations" of cyber espionage (mostly by the United States), and, most important, the plan to expand the already significant controls that the Chinese cyberspace operates under, all the while avoiding foreign interference. The official state news analysis of the speech provided additional prompting if the core message was missed: "After the out [*sic*] of the US National Security Agency's PRISM program, more countries have woken up to the fact that 'absolute Internet freedom' touted by the US will only end up as 'absolute security' in Washington and 'absolute insecurity' for the rest." Under Xi Jinping, China has abandoned its time-honored maxim of "hiding one's strength and biding one's time" and begun to assert cyber power more proactively. This development was a long time coming but, despite a number of seemingly contradictory aspects of external and internal security policy, can be boiled down to one goal above all else: Deng Xiaoping's famous dictum that "social stability overrides everything."

The rise of China as a political and economic power is one of the most defining historical narratives of the current era. Unlike the Soviet Union, whose rise and fall as a superpower occurred within a relatively short period, China has always been a global powerhouse, even if its direct engagement and proactive influence in world affairs have varied greatly over the centuries. In many ways, China is exactly as exceptional as the United States: while the United States is the quintessential modern state, China is the paramount example of a premodern nation, with millennia of social and political traditions that define its interactions both within and beyond its borders. Like the United States, China will likely have a major impact on world affairs for the foreseeable future, though whether that will be the case due to its strengths or its weaknesses only time will tell.

China's development as a cyber powerhouse is marked by a similar sense of inevitability. Since 2008, China has been the world's most dominant presence on the World Wide Web, with spectacular growth from some 22 million users in 2000 to almost 650 million in 2014. By mid-2016, an estimated 720 million Chinese were online, half of the country's current population. Today, more than one in five global Internet users is Chinese, even though half of the Chinese population hasn't joined the global Internet yet. The vast majority of these users, however, interact solely with Chinese Internet content and products; only a tiny percentage visit foreign Web sites. The only truly comparable example of hyper-localization is the United States, where around 90 percent of the content accessed is American-based, although nearly comparable examples do exist in countries such as Japan and South Korea. Ultimately, however, all of these localized Internets are still very much part of the global Internet. In some ways, there are only two large Internets in the world: the US-oriented global patchwork of around forty-two-thousand-odd interconnecting internets with the largely free flow of information over their networks and services, and the Chinese Internet.

There remains only one global cyberspace: the Chinese Internet still depends on hardware and software developed largely outside China and is therefore still rooted in the global cyberspace. The organizing principles of the local Internet are the same as those of the global Internet, and these are set by the global Internet community, not the Chinese Communist Party (CCP). Most significant, China cannot control content outside its borders and, despite its best attempts, cannot completely prevent its own users from accessing this content or engaging in political discussions it opposes.

China's rulers therefore have a deeply ambiguous relationship to cyberspace overall. On the one hand, China's leadership has in recent years increasingly noted the importance of its being connected to the global Internet: leaving it would be too costly for the Chinese economy. China needs the global cyberspace, as much as it needs global trade, for its own economic development. Today, something between 7 and 22 percent of

China's GDP growth depends on the Internet, and over 20 percent of its productivity is derived from it directly, and this share increases every year as China shifts to a more service-oriented economy. The average Chinese Internet user spent about twenty-six hours per week online in 2015 (this number excludes streaming services), and many Chinese Internet products, especially within social media and related economies, are often even more sophisticated than those employed in the West; WeChat and Sina Weibo are widely considered superior to their Western quasi-equivalents, WhatsApp and Twitter, respectively. These companies, unlike virtually all other leading Chinese brands, make nearly all of their money in China itself, and it's a lot of money. Alibaba, the leading Chinese online marketplace, reported $11.6 billion in revenue in 2015, including $5.5 billion of profits. Amazon, in contrast, had a minuscule profit during the same year, despite nearly nine times the revenue.

The driver for much of this online growth is social media. According to a 2012 McKinsey report, China is also the world's most active environment for social media. More than 300 million people used it in 2012, and in 2016 that number is probably closer to 450 million. From blogs to social-networking sites to microblogs (Twitter's Chinese equivalent, Weibo, is more accurately described as a microblogging tool because the amount of information one can put in 140 Chinese characters is widely superior to our 140 Western characters) and other online communities, Chinese users are prolific posters, sometimes using various accounts and identities, often spending as much as two-thirds of their online time on social media—a higher ratio than in the United States or Europe. The McKinsey report explains this with political reasons: "It's harder for the government to censor social media than other information channels."

On the other hand, the relative freedom of Chinese citizens online (or "netizens") may be rapidly deteriorating, a reality that may be connected to an increasingly severe censorship regime. In October 2015, a somewhat breathless article by the American Civil Liberties Union (ACLU) warned of the introduction of a proposed governmental "social-credit score" system.

This system, which would effectively become mandatory by 2020 or so, would basically amount to a tool of social control so vast that it would seem absurd if only it were fiction. Fed by a panoptical deep data mining of virtually all of a citizen's behavior online, it would draw upon a user's blog posts, social media contacts, even purchasing history to penalize or award citizens in a manner indistinguishable from a credit score, but with even more serious ramifications. It amounted to something like this: Watch porn? Lose 50 points. Buy computer games? Lose 30 points. Post something on the Tiananmen massacre? Lose 200 points (at least). Say something nice about party policy? Gain 25 points. Going to recommended events? Gain 30 points. According to the ACLU post, social-credit scores would fall within a range between 350 and 950 points, with bonuses for good behavior such as easy access to Singapore travel permits. The reports on this purported system sparked outrage, including the memorable declaration from the U.K.'s *Independent* newspaper that "with a concept straight out of a cyberpunk dystopia, China has gamified obedience to the State." The article includes rumors that a low score could have additional consequences to those commented on above, including slower Internet speeds and restrictions on what jobs a low-scoring person is allowed to hold.

Subsequently, the online magazine *Tech in Asia* ran a more measured investigation reporting that the social-credit scoring systems being discussed were in fact three separate initiatives: two were private-sector schemes that functioned in a country with no credit-rating system. The third one, the government social-credit scheme, was to be mandatory starting in 2020. According to the only available government directive, its goal was to help foster a "culture of sincerity." The article correctly pointed out that given how similar the private-sector schemes were to the governments, the concerns of the ACLU may in fact be well founded, even if they are not totally factually correct. China could easily develop, in as little as three years from the publication of this book, a fully integrated carrot-and-stick system of rating its citizens' behavior online. If this occurs without being killed at birth due to social reaction, the world will have a model of what the Internet can become when it is fully chained as a tool of population control, and the panopticon of the darkened web, with all its haunting aspects of total social control, will have arrived, at least in embryonic form.

In fact, the principle behind this social-credit system is already well in place. Chinese microlenders who lend money to individuals and small businesses often require their creditors to hand over all access to their social media. An employee of a major Shanghai microlending institution explained to me that such accounts "are used not only for verification of your credit worthiness—do you get drunk often? do you crash cars?—but also as a collection mechanism: default on a debt and we trash your social media presence." The success of this commercial model indicates that there may not be much negative reaction to a government-issued social-credit score after all, even if the consequences of a poor score may be much more serious than a denied loan. And, of course, microlending institutions and the current private-sector schemes remain "opt in" and voluntary. There will be no opting out of the government scoring system, if and when it comes to fruition.

When we reflect on where China's relationship with the Internet may end up in the near future, it is important to remember how it all started. From the development of the first widespread online communities at the turn of the millennium, Chinese citizens have enjoyed significantly more freedom online than off-line. Political discussions have always featured highly in the debates of the netizens (a direct translation of the Chinese word *wangmin*, or "people of the net," and a term that includes anyone who is widely socially active in cyberspace)—much of them critical of the government and officials generally, although also often fiercely nationalistic. Chinese bloggers (although the term is somewhat misleading, given the development of microblogging platforms such as Weibo in recent years) have waged significant campaigns that can be described as political. Many of these campaigns have been targeted at corrupt officials and their family members.

One famous example of such a campaign was led against Yang Dacai, head of the Provincial Bureau of Work Safety in Shaanxi, who in 2013 was photographed grinning broadly at the scene of a deadly traffic accident, sporting a luxury watch. After the incident, netizens conducted a so-called human flesh search, unearthing a number of photographs showing Yang wearing at least eleven different luxury watches and dubbing him "Brother Watch." He would obviously not have been able to afford these on his government salary alone, and he was soon sentenced on corruption charges to fourteen years in prison. So strong was the backlash against Yang that the party secretary of Lushan County in Sichuan Province, Fan Jiyue, took off his watch for photo opportunities with Prime Minister Li Keqiang during earthquake rescue efforts in April 2013. Netizens spotted his watch tan and dubbed him "Brother Watchless." The meme was strong enough that it led to a collapse in the number of Swiss watches sold in China.

Similar movements have targeted a number of other officials and, more often, their family members. In October 2010, Li Qiming, the son of Li Gang, a local deputy chief of the Public Security Bureau, was caught driving drunk after having run over two students on Hebei University campus. Prevented from leaving the scene by university students and security officials, he was alleged to have said, "Sue me if you dare. My father is Li Gang." The phrase "my father is Li Gang" went viral and became a symbol of the perceived impunity of family members of high officials and led to the prosecution of Li Qiming.

Although Chinese officials and reporters like to state that the average Chinese user is completely apolitical, research has shown otherwise. Some of this political focus is directly related to obvious quality-of-life issues, such as the safety of food products, pollution, and public safety writ large. There are numerous other examples of extensive public debate being conducted online, ranging from the mildly to the overtly political. For instance, a large number of netizens have taken to Sina Weibo to express disappointment and lack of faith in the government for its response to national issues, such as the collision of two bullet trains in eastern China in

2011 and its lukewarm efforts to effectively curb pollution and smog. Another well-known example was the heated and very long-running debate that was sparked when the US embassy started to tweet its own measurement data of Beijing air quality in 2009, indicating significantly worse air-quality data than the Chinese monitors. In 2015, a US diplomat even claimed, not implausibly, that this consistent and long-running feud directly helped contribute to rising environmental awareness in China. According to an *Economist* magazine article in 2013, this activism of netizens directly threatens millions of CCP cadres. In a survey conducted in 2010 by a magazine affiliated with the *People's Daily,* the party mouthpiece, more than 70 percent of respondents (presumably party cadres) agreed that local Chinese officials suffered from something called "Internet terror": not only the practice of human flesh searches, but also other activities more difficult to judge but simply classified as "spreading false rumors." In 2015, the government made "spreading false rumors with significant consequences" a crime, punishable with up to seven years' incarceration. This prompted *The Economist* to title its own article on Chinese censorship "This Article Is Guilty of Spreading Panic and Disorder." This law is certainly no paper tiger and was first used within months of being proclaimed. For instance, the devastating 2015 Tianjin blasts (with over 173 fatalities) quickly led to rumors of coup-like activities against Xi Jinping in the blogosphere. The Chinese police cracked down fiercely on these comments and arrested nearly two hundred people (and shut down a number of Web sites) for the crime of "spreading false rumors."

Additionally, Chinese interest in political affairs is by no means limited to domestic matters. Foreign policy issues have had a significant mobilizing effect on Chinese netizens, particularly those with militaristic and nationalistic undertones, from Chinese netizens flooding the Internet with radical anti-American rhetoric after the forced landing of a US EP-3 spy plane on Hainan Island in 2001 to cheering Russia's military support of Syria in 2015 and 2016.

While it may seem that some of these online discourses are particularly problematic for the CCP, almost any discussion on any serious topic is potentially dangerous to the Communist leadership. Nearly any Chinese incident, no matter how mundane, can be linked to a failure of government, be it on the local, provincial, or national level. The same applies for any nationalistic reaction to perceived slights by other nations. If the central government is assessed to have fallen short in its primary duty of standing up for China, then the online community can direct the same criticism at Beijing.

There is no doubt that since the ascendancy of Xi Jinping to China's leadership in 2013 the state has not only steadily expanded its Internet control activities but also shifted its approach to these activities from censorship and punishment to propaganda and reward. Between 2013 and 2015, President Xi undertook wide-ranging reforms of both the external and the internal cyber-power apparatus that clearly align with the primary goal of focusing Chinese cyber power toward maintaining domestic stability. This could be with economic means, large-scale content control directed toward the masses, or even the co-option of the most dangerous parts of society: the elite among the netizens, both hackers and bloggers alike.

The new government body that was to be the focus of these efforts debuted in 2014–15 in spectacular style. In February 2015, China watchers were given a rare treat: the presentation of a new anthem to mark the rise to prominence of the newly installed Cyberspace Administration of China (CAC). Empowered by Xi Jinping (and effectively directly controlled by him), the CAC rapidly consolidated a large amount of cyber power in China and became one of the most powerful of all Chinese government organizations, directly taking over the purview of the domestic security services, industry regulation, and some international briefs. It celebrated this rise with a PLA-opera-style anthem to its new *raison d'être*, "cyberpower":

Devotedly keeping watch over the space every day,
Taking up our mission as the sun rises in the east,

Innovating every day, embracing the clear and bright,
Like warm sunshine moving in our hearts.
Unified with the strength of all living things,
Devoted to turning the global village into the most beautiful scene.
A cyberpower: Where the Internet is, so is the glorious dream.
A cyberpower: From the distant cosmos to the missing home.
A cyberpower: Tell the world that the Chinese Dream is uplifting
  China.
A cyberpower: I represent my nation to the world.
In this world all rivers flow to the sea,
Assuming the measure of Chinese civilization.
Five thousand years of history condensed to illuminate innovation,
Integrity is the clear ripple of a nationality.
We are unified between heaven and earth,
Faith and devotion flow like the Yellow River and Yangtze.
A cyberpower: Where the Internet is, so is the glorious dream.
A cyberpower: Thinking of home from the distant cosmos.
A cyberpower: Tell the world that the Chinese Dream is uplifting
  China.
A cyberpower: I represent my nation to the world.

This text—let alone its opera-style debut—was farcical even by CCP standards, and the text and video disappeared after being roundly mocked in social media at home and abroad. But it was an accurate representation of the new organization's imperial view of its duties: it had assumed formal control of possibly the most advanced and simultaneously the most premodern structure in cyberspace—the interlocking projects known collectively as the Great Firewall.

Chapter 13

MANNING THE GREAT FIREWALL

n 2013, when Professor Fang Binxing tweeted out good wishes for the Chinese New Year via his Weibo microblogging account, tens of thousands of Chinese retweeted the message with variants of "get lost" within hours. The responses were so vitriolic that censors moved to disable most of them within the first day. For Fang is probably the most hated person on the Chinese Internet: he is widely considered the father of the Great Firewall.

When *Wired* magazine coined the term "Great Firewall" (often abbreviated as GFW) in 1997, the firewall itself did not exist outside a rough proposal that Fang delivered that year to what is now the Ministry of Industry and Information Technology (MIIT). Ever since China offered public Internet services in 1995, it has sought to control access to content, both local and foreign. In 1996, the first large-scale blocking of specific foreign Web sites—primarily international news and human rights content—started but was haphazard and easily avoidable. This prompted President Bill Clinton to remark that ambitions to censor Internet activity were akin to "nailing

Jell-O to the wall." This did not discourage Fang, who by 2000 had developed the foundations of his project. By 2003, the most important component had gone active, for a price tag of around $60 million: officially named the National Information Security Management System, and also known as Project 005, this system became instantly known as the Great Firewall by everyone else, including Chinese users.

Today, the GFW is a formidable machine quite unlike its early incarnations; it has become effective at blocking access to content located both in China and abroad. Beginning in 2003, Google became increasingly difficult to use, and today it is largely blocked altogether; Facebook, Twitter, and YouTube suffered similar fates between 2008 and 2009. While there are a number of laws and ordinances in China to determine what content is blocked, they are so wide-ranging that essentially anything can be included if it is determined to be problematic for the CCP. Priority content includes all social media, many foreign news sites, file-sharing sites, overseas Chinese sites; human rights, dissident, and pro-democracy pages; circumvention and encryption offerings; some religious Web sites; and pornography and gambling pages. The most heavily blocked content, however, is that critical of individuals within the Chinese leadership. As part of the wider consolidation of power under Xi Jinping, as well as the greatly increased prioritization on cyberspace control overall, the control of the GFW was moved out of the MIIT around 2012 and into the State Internet Information Office, a subcomponent of the ascendant CAC.

The GFW is often mentioned in the same breath as the Golden Shield Project. This is probably only partially correct: the two systems are related insofar as they share hardware as well as software, but the Golden Shield Project is reportedly run by the Ministry of Public Security and deals only with domestic law enforcement issues, albeit on an epic scale. Essentially, it seems to be a centralized database that has the gargantuan goal of digitizing not only the identities of all Chinese citizens but also their trackable activity and makes this data available to all government ministries that need it. There is no evidence that this mother of all databases could be connected to the Orwellian plan of a social-credit score described previously, but it is likely that it would play a major role if this plan was ever implemented.

But the GFW also uses a number of technical tricks to accomplish its own mammoth task. In its earliest iteration, the GFW relied largely on IP blocking and URL filtering—essentially maintaining a blacklist of blocked Web sites and expanding this list automatically whenever the content migrated to other Web sites. In its latest iterations, the GFW became capable of carrying out deep packet inspection: scanning unencrypted individual data packets, the unit of Internet traffic, for sensitive keywords, such as "Falun Gong." This meant that all Internet traffic, including e-mail communication and even chats within gaming networks, could be more effectively monitored as well. In 2012 and again in 2015, the GFW started to use variants of this approach to block most virtual private networks (VPNs), heretofore the best way to circumvent the GFW because they allowed a user to effectively fool the GFW into believing it was located outside China. The GFW has since expanded that approach to generally (but not universally) interrupting encrypted connections. Today, your chances of getting a successful VPN connection out of China vary greatly: some services work well in some localities, while others appear to be permanently disabled.

One of the GFW's most effective techniques for blocking connections, however, involves the domain name system, often called the telephone book of the Internet itself. To reroute users trying to access banned Web pages, the GFW replaces the associated IP number (for instance, the number corresponding to the *New York Times*' Web site) with another Web site entirely. In a memorable instance during January 2015, a number of Chinese users trying to access banned content were instead directed to a pornographic Web site in Germany (which itself was illegal under Chinese law), supposedly due to a random rerouting of traffic. That Web site promptly collapsed under the weight of new visitors.

Indeed, it is possible, even likely, that this traffic is not redirected randomly but directed on purpose at specific targets. According to the American security company Crowdstrike, the redirection of traffic like this can easily force smaller Web sites off-line. The company's report draws attention to a number of other supposedly random candidates that have been subject to the rerouting of Chinese users, including a government site in South Korea, an American firewall and security company, and a French digital freedom association. It was confirmed on all victims except the South Korean government site that the traffic approximated a DDoS attack as servers not normally prepared to handle that kind of traffic were suddenly pummeled with traffic redirected from China. The report cunningly uses an analogy from the Chinese martial art Wing Chun, in which attack and defense are combined into the same movement. The implication is that the GFW can not only claim to defend Chinese Internet users from harmful content originating abroad but also attack that content by sending a deluge of unsuspected Web traffic to force it off-line.

What used to be a seeming quirk of the GFW has now been officially weaponized. In recent years, a number of Chinese statements and documents seemed to imply that China was developing an "ace weapon" for cyberspace, variously described as a "magic weapon" or an "assassin's mace" in Chinese literature. There are indications that at least one of these "magic weapons" may be the continuation of the idea of the GFW as a massive DDoS tool—potentially the biggest in the world.

In March 2015, GreatFire.org, a Web site that hosts Chinese translations of the US media, and Github, a Web site hosting encryption and VPN tools also of use to Chinese users, came under a sustained DDoS attack from a botnet that had previously been unknown, and were forced off-line. Investigations by the University of Toronto Citizen Lab and others showed that this botnet was composed of thousands of unwitting Internet users worldwide that had little in common with each other, besides the fact that they had visited the servers of Baidu, often called the Chinese Google. Sometime during this visit, malicious code was injected via their browsers, and their machines were used for the DDoS attack. The researchers concluded that while this offensive tool was not actually the GFW itself, it was co-located and used many of the same systems. They christened this new tool the "Great Cannon," although the tool eventually came to be known as the "Great Firehose" in the information security community.

The Great Cannon attack—at the time of writing conducted only once—has attracted considerable interest abroad, for China had indicated that it had the ability to effectively create a botnet out of thin air and launch potentially crippling DDoS attacks with great speed. Based on my conversations in China I think it is likely that this attack was carried out as a very clear warning to the West over Hong Kong. In the run-up to the ten-year anniversary of China's takeover of the former British colony, there were already signs of widespread political protest being organized in the city, and both Github and GreatFire were seen as tools that were directly supporting the work of Hong Kong dissidents. Indeed, just a month after the attack, the so-called Umbrella Revolution broke out, with significant public unrest across the territory. There already had been clear indications months earlier that big trouble was brewing in little Hong Kong, and the Great Cannon could have been a shot across the bows of Western sympathizers: if you interfere in Hong Kong we will unleash the bricks of the GFW at you and knock you off the Internet, no matter where you are hosted.

Even if the GFW has a hidden offensive component, it certainly has an army of its own. If the GFW is the actual wall, then the censors, fake bloggers, and propagandists who man it, combing through the eighty *billion* social media posts executed in China in 2015 alone, are cyber soldiers of a sort. Their mission takes two forms: this aspect of the GFW (which, as said before, is not, strictly speaking, part of the GFW but is often treated as such by Chinese users) is composed of both a negative, "hard" censorship mechanism and a positive, "soft" propaganda element. The harder censorship mechanism is backed by sophisticated analytics that direct tens of thousands of censors, the officially titled "Internet police," to potentially problematic posts. Furthermore, all of the social media and content organizations, such as Sina Weibo, employ thousands of "Internet monitors" legally bound to police their own services using directives issued by the government. It is likely that both the Internet police and the Internet monitors work in lockstep with each other, using the same police directives, even if some regional differences have been observed. These censors directly delete posts, but do not try to change content, and are also limited in what they see by the automated keyword-searching systems that support them. As a result, Chinese netizens have developed a virtual library of terms and sly insinuations to avoid triggering the censors. These codes—largely homonyms to related Chinese words—have achieved legendary status, such as the pictures of a "swamp horse" standing in for a very common curse word that nearly sounds the same in Chinese as the term "swamp horse," to give just one example out of hundreds. Others include nicknames for political figures; in 2012, one politician was widely known as "Teletubby" and another as "Master Kung" (the regular name for Confucius). Trying to keep up with linguistic misdirection and outright code of the bloggers was always going to be a losing proposition for the censors. It was obviously a much better option to distract from and confuse the discussion completely, simply by opening new topics or promoting a new dialogue. The efforts to do so are quite unlike the censorship program and considerably further-reaching.

According to one of the first researchers on the topic, the Hong Kong–based David Bandurski, the present mammoth program originated in 2004 when an article on a major Chinese Web portal alleged that the CIA and the Japanese government had infiltrated Chinese chat rooms with "Web spies" whose chief purpose was to post anti-Chinese content. The allegations were never substantiated (and probably baseless), but they became the catalyst of what was to come. In 2005, Nanjing University, one of the country's most prestigious educational institutions, recruited a team of zealous students to work part time as Web commentators. The team's job was to trawl the university's online forum for undesirable posts and respond to them in defense of the CCP position. In the months that followed, party leaders across Jiangsu Province began recruiting their own teams of Web commentators, often referring to them as the "red vanguard." Rumors traveled quickly across the Internet that these party-backed monitors received five *mao*, half one yuan, for each positive post they made. The term "Fifty Cent Party," or *wumaodang,* was born. They were to become the biggest security organization in the world, and their "enemy" was the average netizen, and especially the burgeoning online civil society.

In 2009, Chinese bloggers seemed to be unstoppable. They were uncovering malfeasance among government officials, rechanneling foreign news, and generally serving as an increasingly critical voice. So confident was the Chinese blogosphere that it even created its own investigation commissions to explore reported incidents of local government's misbehavior. It therefore came as a shock when the respected blogger Zhao Li, who headed one such campaign, was revealed in a *Newsweek* article to be part of a secret network of thirty thousand or so elite bloggers who were on the CCP's list of employees "to be mobilized in times of public-opinion crisis." As high as this number may be, it was dwarfed by the number of citizens who constituted the 50 cent army. While the "50 centers" are only one of a range of different groups of actors espousing political opinions online, they have come to dominate by sheer weight of numbers among other categories.

It is unknown exactly how many people work on Internet policing and Internet propaganda. Lu Wei, the first head of the CAC, claimed in 2014, however, that his sixty thousand full-time government employees were supported by up to two *million* part-time contractors. My interpretation is that the sixty thousand government employees are in fact the Internet police censors, the function of which may have been taken over, at least in part, by the CAC in recent years. The two million–odd part-time contractors are nearly certainly the 50 cent army propagandists. If so, Lu Wei's statement would indicate that more people worked in fake blogging than were actually in the PLA, the largest military on Earth, and that the number of propagandists outnumbered the censors by about thirty to one.

In 2016, Harvard University published quantitative research indicating that this scale was probably right. It determined that in 2015 probably as many as 448 million posts were made by 50 centers, nearly half of which were posted on government Web sites and related discussion forums. This would mean that nearly 1 out of every 178 media posts in China was made by propagandists. On government Web sites, the ratio may be even as high as 1 out of every 2 posts.

Other than the scale of the operation, the primary revelation of the Harvard report was the fact that these 50 centers were not concentrating on arguing with critical posts, or even re-posting base propaganda, as they had in earlier years. Ominously, the Harvard study showed that despite the common association of 50 centers with attacks on foreign countries or arguing with criticism of the government, they now overwhelmingly engage in cheerleading and distraction away from the political argument: making noncontroversial valence statements about prosperity or honoring the war dead, or simply feel-good statements. The comments are something like the New Yorker's favorite "How 'bout them Mets?": inane conversation re-routers that also lead to safe ground. "Think of the last time you had a real good argument," Gary King, one of the authors of the Harvard study, said. "About the single worst way to end it is coming up with the best possible counter argument. A much better way is to say 'Hey, let's go get ice cream' or 'Look at big shiny thing out the window.' Just change the subject; that's the logic the Chinese government follows."

An article in the Voice of America, however, claimed that 50 centers were also employed in an attack role, even if this happens much less often. The example it gives is that during the 2015 election of Tsai Ing-wen as president of Taiwan, Beijing unleashed the 50 centers for offensive purposes, allowing around ten thousand of them to cross the Great Firewall to go online in Taiwan and post on social media, bad-mouthing and vilifying Tsai and democracy. The flood of critical comments did not go unnoticed in Taiwan. In response, Tsai Ing-wen simply posted, "Welcome to the free world."

. . .

The road toward the nightmarish dream of the social-credit score—where the freedom of users to engage in political discourse is tightly directed by both sticks and carrots—has therefore been a long time coming. China has already moved from seeing the Internet as a tolerated evil, an environment in which the only tools of government to guide discourse are suppression and direct censorship, to a much more nuanced practice of soft government control. One of the most disquieting recent developments in China is that social media—in particular but not limited to the Weibo microblogging platform—is clearly being viewed as an asset, not a hindrance, to CCP rule. Social media provides instantaneous feedback on local issues and grievances, effectively functioning as a pervasive and continuous sounding platform for government initiatives as well as an early-warning network for possible criticism and especially civil unrest. This is what King calls a "responsive autocracy," using the feedback from such social media platforms to fine-tune policies and communication to achieve maximum influence with seemingly minimal intervention.

For instance, China has long used its war on pornography as a tool to advance its broader information control agenda, and its ups and downs are a good yardstick by which to judge the current political climate. Some of these campaigns are indeed curious: for instance, in the spring of 2016 the censors sought to ban "erotic banana-eating videos," due to their ostensibly suggestive connotations. But campaigns such as the 2009 "Green Dam Youth Escort" (a supposedly porn-blocking but actually content-monitoring piece of software that the Chinese government wanted to preinstall on all new PCs) were not rolled out due to widespread public resistance that the "responsive autocracy" was able to sense, even at this relatively early period.

The CCP already exerts a significant influence on all online debates. This includes using overt and covert means, both by disappearing unwanted comments and by distracting or disabling potentially troublesome discussions with its gigantic security apparatus. Further, the information gained through extensive real-time mining of social media (and potentially also through actual bulk surveillance of e-mails and even phone calls) can not only provide a continuous assessment of the reception of key government policies but also spot burgeoning concerns of the public at large. As it is already today, its extensive reach and connection with intelligence capabilities make it a much more powerful tool than any Western-style focus group or poll. Essentially, it is well on its way to becoming the perfect propaganda monitoring and planning tool, and if and when it is paired with a "social-credit scoring tool," it will become a nightmarishly effective form of government control. If, that is, the "barbarians" outside the Great Firewall can be kept out.

Chapter 14

HANDLING THE BARBARIANS

n September 2015, Presidents Obama and Xi held a summit specifically to discuss the escalating confrontation over what was simply called "Chinese hacking." To the surprise of virtually everyone in the West, including some seasoned observers of US-China relations, the meeting resulted in a specific agreement that gave the Obama administration nearly everything it asked for. Most important, it, in effect, secured a pledge from Xi to end what to that point had been the backbone of Chinese cyber espionage: the rampant theft of economic data and intellectual property from the private sector. Few if any observers really believed that China was going to end the practice, or even noticeably tone it down—wasn't the whole purpose of Chinese cyber espionage to help gain an economic advantage? many asked. Even President Obama seemed slightly doubtful. "The question now," he said following the summit, "is 'Are words followed by actions?' And we will be watching carefully to make an assessment as to whether progress has been made in this area." Few were prepared to hold their breath.

But something did change—drastically. The first to notice a change in tone were those Westerners who regularly interacted with the "licensed barbarian handlers," the unofficial but nonetheless historically accurate title for those very few Chinese officials who were entrusted to deal directly with foreigners. At the same time, companies operating in the information security business, such as FireEye, watched in real time as once-prolific Chinese spy groups seemed not only to stop attempting new insertions against civilian targets but also to actively curtail existing cyber-espionage campaigns. By the summer of 2016, the reality was undeniable: Chinese cyber-espionage attempts against the US economy had decreased in number. The scale of the retreat was even harder to believe: according to Fire-Eye's tracking of seventy-two specific China-based cyber groups, there was a decrease of around 90 percent in new attacks against the private sector in both the United States and Europe—a stunning, indeed unprecedented number. The decline, although difficult to believe, has subsequently been verified by American government officials. Some observers of the scene privately wondered what they had missed—was the current lull indicative that China was preparing something particularly nefarious elsewhere, perhaps over the South China Sea? Or had the threat of US sanctions, built up over the previous two years, simply forced China to back down? Wasn't there abundant evidence that hundreds of billions of dollars were being reaped, every year, from the Western economy? Was China really walking away from these untold riches? The FireEye report echoed many of these views, soberly stating that the radical decrease included China's reining in the activities of various government and nongovernment hackers: "contractors, patriot hackers, and even criminal elements."

What FireEye's and other such private-sector assessments do not address is the possibility that the intellectual property theft so often reported wasn't all it was made out to be. There is little question that companies were routinely being breached and their data siphoned off, but was it actually used? We may think we know what the damage was to the US economy, but what was the benefit to the Chinese economy? This part of the calculation may have previously been wrong, if China's abandonment of bulk IP theft is to make any sense at all.

The scale and true impact of Chinese IP and economic theft, particularly as far as it relates to the United States, have been hotly debated subjects, especially in recent years. Some of the numbers that have been discussed in public, even by authoritative sources, have obviously been fantastic: in 2012, the first head of USCYBERCOM and former head of the NSA, Keith Alexander, quoted a private-sector study that said $1 *trillion* of damage had been caused to the US economy through Chinese IP theft. He was harshly criticized for the utterance and later retracted the statement. However, in 2015 these claims resurfaced: using numbers produced by the Commission on the Theft of American Intellectual Property, a former federal prosecutor claimed that the actual damage to the American economy was more like $300 billion a year—which was promptly reinterpreted by others to mean that $5 *trillion* in total damage (including opportunity costs and lost income) was inflicted on the US economy every single year. If this was true, over a quarter of the entire US economy would be destroyed, annually, by Chinese spying.

Unsurprisingly, there is little support for such numbers. Although the sheer volume of data that was stolen from US and European companies was certainly dramatic, the ability of those stealing the data to actually act on it varied greatly but was probably limited in nearly all cases. There would seem to be a significant difference between campaigns that target a specific piece of information or set of data and the opportunistic "collect everything" activities by less focused groups. In the worst case, the latter type of theft could indeed devastate entire industries: the renewable energy industry in the United States and Europe was hit hard by IP theft, and there is abundant evidence that stolen IP was eagerly snapped up by their Chinese competitors. But those competitors have seen mixed returns in the marketplace. A *60 Minutes* segment recounts a case in which an American company sued a Chinese company that had clearly profited from stealing its IP. The Chinese company in question not only ended up flooding the market with a glut of products that had no customer but also was banned from selling to the United States and Europe due to IP protection mechanisms—and subsequently folded. The report includes the highly insightful quotation that "what remains perplexing is how the Chinese continue to suffer from self-inflicted wounds brought about by their habitual expropriation of Western technology."

Overall, China seemed to be collecting a huge amount of data that had little or no value and targeting comparatively little data that had great value. Given the marginal costs of cyberattacks, which cost relatively little at low levels of sophistication, this would seem to be a good return on investment. Except, of course, the cost of cyberattacks is measurable not only in manpower hours in coding. For even if very little of what was being stolen was actually converted into new products, the damage on the receiving end was real. Hacked American businesses had to consider that their precious data had been compromised even if it was not, and this had direct opportunity costs, influencing product deployments and market entry plans. It also had direct costs for labor and services that needed to be performed in mitigation and cleanup. This meant that for every couple of billions of dollars of true benefit the Chinese economy might have derived from this activity, hundreds of billions of dollars of damage were inflicted, even if estimates on the numbers in question diverge greatly. It was obvious there would be a robust US response to this, eventually, and indeed the great fortune for the Chinese is that economic sanctions—which would probably have cost the Chinese economy many times more than the benefits extracted from such activities—were avoided. There is no public information as to how significant the US sanctions would have been, but we can guess that for a number of reasons they would not be much smaller than those that targeted Russia for its activities in Ukraine and cost the Russian economy some $100 billion in 2015 alone. But whatever those damages would have been, they clearly outweighed the benefit of IP theft to China. It was therefore no great surprise to see how quickly China acquiesced to US demands at the Xi-Obama meeting.

If the value of IP theft was so out of proportion to its benefits, why did China risk the blowback of sanctions to begin with? The short answer would probably point to the vested interest of some individual actors within the PLA who stood to make a lot of money from these schemes, as well as a large swath of non-state hackers who had grown into an uneasy symbiosis with the governmental security apparatus. By attacking this symbiosis directly, the White House managed to provoke a significant reaction, no doubt facilitated by Xi's plans to restructure the PLA. For the PLA had (once again) become a significant domestic power player, with large commercial interests. One part of those interests was with the disparate components of the PLA cyber force, a huge and sprawling body linked to large state-owned enterprises as well as to grassroots civilian hackers. The PLA cyber force embraced them all and easily outnumbered, outgunned, and simply outplayed the civilian CAC—a main pillar of Xi's new power base. Despite the PLA's mission as the primary organization for conducting cyber operations abroad, it had become a significant domestic political factor as well.

In 2014, the US government took the unique step of bringing federal charges against five named PLA hackers, indicting them for the theft of intellectual property from a number of American companies. The Chinese were furious, raising complaints at virtually every single diplomatic gathering. Then the White House signaled, on the basis of previous discussions including notes circulated within the informal US-Chinese meetings, that the threat of economic sanctions was on the table as a response to Chinese hacking. Just prior to the Xi-Obama summit of October 2015, the United States handed the Chinese a list of Chinese hackers it wanted arrested— possibly the ones mentioned in the indictment—as a show of good faith in the diplomatic process, and also to keep the reality of possible economic sanctions off the table.

The Chinese responded just before the Xi-Obama summit with four arrests of criminal elements, but with a twist: They were accused of being part of the massive hack of the Office of Personnel Management, perhaps one of the most significant breaches of US systems ever, rather than being behind the acts of economic espionage named in the original US indictment. It was a highly interesting development, because while the OPM hack was undoubtedly much more serious, it was also an attack on a government target and therefore unquestionably legal, unlike the theft of private-sector secrets. The Chinese government might have chosen to respond this way for a number of reasons: perhaps it didn't want to respond to the indictment directly, thereby legitimizing it further; or perhaps it wanted to equate national security espionage with economic espionage. In my view, the most plausible theory is that the individuals arrested were perhaps part of a non-state contractor organization and were therefore easier to throw under the bus than the PLA officials mentioned in the US indictment. "It's a face-saving way of saying, 'It wasn't us and we'll put them in jail,'" James Lewis, vice president at the think tank CSIS, said. "Traditional kabuki in espionage is you write off your agents when it's politically useful to do so."

If this theory is correct (and the individuals arrested were in fact responsible for the OPM breach), it simply indicates what a bizarre world Chinese cyber actually was: on the one hand, a classic, state-to-state, and thoroughly legal penetration of a prime US government database collection at OPM was conducted by nongovernment contractors, perhaps operating completely on their own volition or with the loosest of direction by their government. On the other hand, the official PLA cyber spies, perhaps moonlighting as contractors (with or without explicit direction) for a state-owned enterprise, were engaged in what is widely considered nonstandard and even illegal economic espionage against private companies. If this is an accurate picture, it would indicate that the entire Chinese cyber-espionage apparatus was in need of a thorough shake-up, one that Xi was about to initiate for reasons other than just cyber.

Xi started to reform the PLA, the main carrier of government cyber espionage, nearly two years before the landmark Xi-Obama agreement. In the name of a pervasive anticorruption campaign, Xi has taken unprecedented action against the PLA leadership since coming to power. Since

2014 alone, over sixty high-ranking officers, including from the very top of the PLA, have been arrested on charges of corruption. The attempt to weaken the PLA even involved what many analysts considered a stunning public humiliation at the 2015 Beijing National Day military parade, the proudest day of the military, which Xi used to announce that the PLA would undergo a significant cut in manpower. But other changes were already under way.

One was a subtle change in tone. Prior to 2015, China had strenuously denied any suggestions that it maintained official state cyber forces. This was in spite of a mountain of evidence to the contrary that stretched back to the late 1990s. This evidence was seldom completely conclusive to the casual observer, however: while major cyber spying against the United States was already traced back to China in 2002 at least, there was no clear indication available that these attacks were executed by the government. Similarly, although there were prolific writings by Chinese strategists on the concepts of information operations and information warfare, many of these writings could—somewhat plausibly—be considered merely academic musings and not necessarily part of official doctrine, let alone paired with actual official capabilities and resources. In hindsight, however, and in light of the most recent official publications, as well as the increasingly public technical evidence gathered by private Western security firms, it is clear that China has been preparing its official entry into the cyber-war domain for a number of years.

If official documents published in 2013 and 2015 hinted at what was to come, the 2015 military white paper, a key strategic policy document, clearly signaled that China had arrived in cyberspace. Indeed, not only did the paper consider cybersecurity as important as naval, nuclear, or space security, but in fact it seemed to imply that it was the commanding height of all future conflict.

As detailed as the white paper is, a piece in the seminal PLA publication "The Science of Military Strategy" of 2013 gave even more insight, even though there are clear differences between the 2013 and the redrafted 2015 versions. It provides us also with the first-ever official segmentation of China's state-affiliated cyber forces along three tiers: the PLA's own "specialized military network warfare forces"; the "PLA-authorized forces in civilian organizations," such as the foreign-intelligence Ministry of State Security and the domestic Ministry of Public Security (parts of which took their orders from the CAC); and a vague but intensely interesting description of "non-governmental forces." While the three-tiered system would imply that only the first tier (the "specialized forces") was of primary interest, it is the third tier (the non-state actors) that probably told us the most about the focus of Chinese cyber. It connects directly with the long-standing practice of using unofficial forces—a practice that is actually rooted deep in Maoist thought and also has direct connections with the Chinese prime directive of ensuring social stability.

These tier 3 informal forces have long been considered the least sophisticated and easiest to trace and have not featured highly in investigations by security researchers. They have probably been responsible for the bulk of IP theft, however, even if only to help provide for a minimum level of income. I consider it completely plausible that bulk IP theft was simply the cost of maintaining the large tier 3 forces, which obviously needed to be supported somehow: if they weren't, after all, they might have turned to cyber crime against Chinese targets or even antistate activities. Encouraging IP theft might also have been a good way to keep these non-state hackers busy and their efforts resolutely directed outward.

The tier 1 "specialized network forces" were subject to massive reform in 2015–16. These reforms will affect the entire existing PLA cyber structure, which consists of over two dozen division and brigade commands and tens of thousands of personnel. On January 1, 2016, the PLA stood up its first official cyber command intended to unify all of these disparate elements into what is meant to be the direct equivalent to the US Cyber Command, a body unique in the PLA's history. Launched directly by Xi Jinping himself, the new Strategic Support Force (SSF) implies a significant militarization of previously intelligence-driven PLA capacities. There has been speculation that this reorganization will make Chinese cyberattacks more operational—in other words, "real attacks" (as defined in international law) rather than the more mundane cyber espionage and otherwise very common cyberattacks. The establishment of the SSF represents a significant development in China's cyber power, not only because it marked the first time China was willing to talk about its offensive cyber forces, but also because it was effectively part of a massive purge and reorganization of those same forces.

Prior to these watershed reforms, Chinese offensive cyber forces already had a long history—in some cases going back nearly two decades. We know this because, unlike Russia, China has always been remarkably open in its internal discussions on both policy and structures. Much of this openness was inadvertent; the massive size of the country and a tradition of rigorous internal debate (that, it should be said, was never intended for outsiders) have led to a great amount of policy detail being leaked on various forums. Much of this detail has subsequently been confirmed through technical analysis of various cyberattacks, often conducted by a new host of Western private-sector firms specializing in cybersecurity. On the whole, we have a much more complete picture of Chinese cyber today than we had just five or six years ago, and we can now see that much of what we then could consider theory was actually lived in practice.

A number of private studies by think tanks, industry interest groups, security firms, and defense contractors (nearly all American) have been able to paint a remarkably clear picture of the PLA cyber capacity of recent years. Many are so detailed that they are able to name individual heads of specific cyber units, due to the Chinese tradition of inadvertent openness because of either horribly poor operational security or simply a lack of interest in what anyone abroad thinks. The picture that has emerged is consistent, and detailed, especially when compared with that of Russia. There is certainly more information on Chinese military cyber available than there is for any other country, with the possible exception of the United States.

For instance, the PLA cyber capability is overwhelmingly concentrated in departments within the General Staff Directorate (GSD), the commanding organization of the entire PLA and only loosely comparable with the US DoD Joint Chiefs of Staff. While most GSD departments probably have some sort of cyber mission, two departments own the bulk of operational assets: the 4th Department (4PLA), responsible for electronic warfare and "real cyber attack" (that is, in wartime, and not cyberattacks as normal business), and especially the 3rd Department (3PLA), the custodians of the signals intelligence mission. The 3PLA, the direct equivalent to the NSA, is tasked primarily with espionage, while the 4PLA is in charge of operationalizing these espionage capabilities into wartime attack capabilities, quite literally pushing the button on an espionage mission against, say, a critical infrastructure. It also is responsible for ensuring that the conventional field units are able to operate in an environment marked by battlefield cyber capabilities

Although termed "departments," the 3PLA and the 4PLA have more manpower than many countries' entire militaries. One report highlighted that in 2013 the signals intelligence department 3PLA might have had up to 130,000 employees. Although cyber employees would constitute only a fraction of this number, as a counterexample the entire NSA probably has no more than 37,000 employees, of which at best only 6,000 or 7,000 could be said to be directly involved in cyber operations. The 3PLA, in contrast, was reported to have direct control over twelve specialized Technical Reconnaissance Bureaus (TRBs) with specific regional/linguistic or functional focuses (for instance, English speaking or United States oriented), with another twelve to sixteen TRBs working for various combat arms, military regions, and such, and a whole clutch of subordinate research organizations, dedicated listening posts, and the like. Some of the TRBs are massive: according to an in-depth analysis by the Project 2049 Institute's Mark Stokes, the English-oriented TRB headquartered in Shanghai officially known as the Second Bureau is structured similarly to a ground-force division and may have as much staff—maybe as many as 8,000–10,000 individuals. As we will see later, the Second Bureau has been implicated in a number of cyber campaigns against US interests and has therefore been the subject of some intense scrutiny by security professionals.

For its part, the 4PLA also maintains its own TRBs, at least six of which are dedicated to cyber operations. Even more important, it is the principal link to the field army at large, including active, reserve, and militia units, which themselves maintain a large array of cyber units within specific military regions. These also include explicit information warfare militias, groups of badged (but not always uniformed) local militia members, often working out of state-owned enterprises and universities. Some of the units—titled regimental units—are fairly large, and a choice few may also be active in operations abroad. In total, the 4PLA, despite being smaller than the 3PLA, probably has direct interaction with tens of thousands of cyber operators.

Besides the sheer scale of the PLA cyber force, the truly remarkable element is how long it has been in existence. There are indications that the 3PLA Second Bureau, one of the most active attackers against the United States, was already set up in 1995. Although it is unclear whether the Second Bureau already had a specific cyber mission at this time, the sheer longevity of the command probably makes it one of the longest-standing cyber units in the world. Even less high-profile reserve structures can already look back on a long service history. The US Army scholar Timothy Thomas, for instance, wrote as far back as 2004 about the Guangzhou information warfare militia battalion that had specific companies for computer network operations and electronic warfare and was based out of the headquarters of a provincial telecommunications company. This unit was therefore already set up before the US Air National Guard—which today maintains substantial cyber forces—had fully embarked on this mission. Rather than being a newcomer to the field, the PLA probably has a history in cyberspace that is second only to that of the United States.

While the dominant American military narrative has been the over-valuing of the offensive over the defensive, China's has been the need—

both politically and technically—to co-opt non-state structures in support of the prime mission of domestic stability. Prior to Xi's shake-up, this strategy helped create a largely hybrid national cyber force that blurred the lines between not only state and non-state actors but also true government policy and personal economic profiteering. According to this logic, much of the IP theft, especially around 2010 to 2015, might have been in the interest more of individual actors than of the state itself. This would consequently also explain why the dramatic break from rampant IP theft was part of not just the overall PLA purge but also a much-needed cleanup of increasingly chaotic cyber structures that, with the threat of US sanctions looming, were simply not worth the cost.

The plethora of Chinese cyberattacks reported in Western media over the last decade is an adequate representation of the scope of Chinese operations in cyberspace—if not necessarily of their ramifications or relative importance to other attacks. Since 2002, the first year Chinese cyberattacks were reported publicly, incidents associated with China have grown at a steady pace. Today, it is still possible to say that the great majority of obviously politically relevant cyberattacks (that is to say, not related to cybercrime issues such as credit card theft) reported worldwide are Chinese. This is partially due to an observation bias: Russian cyber operations, let alone those of the United States, are much more sophisticated and often escape detection for very prolonged periods. Nonetheless, Chinese actors have traditionally been voracious practitioners of cyber espionage, even if their capabilities have varied greatly.

Two separate leaked NSA documents on Chinese cyber espionage speak to this range of capabilities. One is very basic; in effect, a map of the continental United States with all the victims of Chinese cyber espionage over the last four years mapped with red pins. The result is impressive, with over six hundred pins marking government and private-sector entities that have been hacked. It does not, however, provide any detail, and it seems obvious that some attacks were considerably more serious than others. What is meant by a "serious" attack is detailed in the other NSA document. This one purports that Chinese actors had stolen at least fifty terabytes (or the equivalent of five Libraries of Congress) from American government and defense contractor systems in recent years. The same document makes clear how serious the penetrations at the Department of Defense alone had been: over thirty thousand incidents resulted in more than five hundred successful penetrations of various DoD networks, with over $100 million in damages due to the need to assess and repair the breached systems. And this, it needs to be noted, was due only to the success of a single Chinese intrusion set, a hacking campaign code-named Byzantine Hades, which, we now know, was probably based out of the Shanghai-headquartered Second Bureau of the 3PLA.

Besides the sheer amount of information being acquired, the most striking feature of Chinese cyber is the range of actors that conduct it, many with apparently reckless abandon. The security company FireEye, for instance, stated in 2015 that of two dozen or so major cyber groups it was tracking, all but two were Chinese (the other two were Russian and were much more sophisticated than the Chinese). In its 2016 report, however, the same company stipulated that it was tracking overall seventy-two Chinese "intrusion sets." This would allow an observer without additional information to conclude that of the seventy-two most visible Chinese intrusion sets, no more than twenty were likely associated with the government; the great majority of them were the PLA and especially the 3PLA, with a smattering of other groups such as the foreign-intelligence Ministry of State Security. This would, however, mean that fifty or more of the groups in question would be non-security related (that is, not of the military or intelligence services), and perhaps even nongovernmental.

What is clear is that in the years prior to the 2015 Xi-Obama agreement there was a merging of state and non-state cyber activity. It is possible that going by numbers of individual groups (if not the quality or quantity of cyber campaigns), two-thirds of the active cyber groups were concentrating on lower-skilled opportunistic intrusions, highly automated and therefore able to reap huge amounts of data from poorly protected entities relatively quickly. Sometime after 2011, there seems to have been a merging between the tasks of the various groups; within a couple of years, PLA hackers seemed to be going after private-sector secrets, while private hackers were concentrating on government systems.

This had not always been the case. During the early period of Chinese cyberattacks (from 2002 to 2009), there was a clear split between two levels of activity: a concentrated but fairly skilled range of activity directed largely at governmental enterprises, many of them in the United States, and a much larger swath of mostly primitive "patriotic hacking" (that is, encouraged civilian hacking) directed abroad at political targets of opportunity, such as members of the media. The victim list of organizations that claim to have been hit by Chinese hackers is very impressive indeed: Taiwanese government computers in 2003, Japanese government Web sites and US military installations in 2004, the Naval War College, specific British MPs, and congressional computers in 2006 as well as computers within the US Department of Defense and the German Chancellery in 2007 are just a short extract of a target list that could easily be expanded by dozens more.

The sheer proliferation of various attacking groups, and the rapid harmonization of their capabilities, provided a clear indication for many that government actors were not only hiding in the noise of the non-state actors but actively encouraging the civilian attacks as well. Even within the higher skill-set group, it was by no means sure that these were actually military or intelligence actors at work. Most media reports at the time already pointed out that these attacks were probably nongovernmental in nature, even if they were still officially sponsored. One senior FBI official said in 2002 that "they are Chinese hackers employed by a state-owned industry operating on the state's time."

There is no doubt that the Chinese authorities exercised some degree of control over at least some of these hackers. In May 2002, the US Department of Defense reportedly braced itself for an onslaught of attacks from patriot hackers that never materialized. According to the Pentagon, they were prevented: "The government of China asked them not to do that." This insinuation—namely that there was a clear command chain of sorts between the official and the unofficial hackers—was to be often repeated in the coming years. It was never clear, however, how much of this activity was actually directed, rather than simply encouraged or tolerated. For some observers, many of the attacks were only associated with the government by chance, in a largely ad hoc relationship driven by an unseen demand. According to one FBI expert giving testimony to Congress in 2008, the attackers were largely civilians:

It's the 25-year-olds. Those 25-year-olds or 17-year-olds have 40-year-old fathers who happen to be working within institutions. Very often the opportunistic exploitation of a particular low-tech approach is derived through that chain, completely informally, rather than through somebody sitting in committee and deciding let's build 500 botnets that we're going to use to attack the Tibetan community.

Given the enormous amount of attention that the Chinese government bestows upon the netizens, many of these attacks are probably actively encouraged to distract these hackers from turning their talents to more anti-state activities. The organizing of hacker competitions and the like are attempts not only at finding good talent but at keeping that talent safely occupied. For a period, it seemed clear that the Chinese government was of two minds on how to deal with this burgeoning cyber-crime elite. For instance, in 2006 the Henan Province police arrested members of one such patriot hacker group, the Black Eagle Base, and shut down its Web site. Within only a few months, however, the group's members had reunited, issuing a public statement saying that they had mended their cyber-crime ways and would concentrate their efforts on serving the state and improving information security overall. Even more revealingly, the hackers directly thanked a defense research arm of what is today the Ministry of Industry and Information Technology for the "guidance" they had received. Quite clearly, there was a strong movement to bring the outside hackers into the governmental fold. Within a number of years, many of the formerly legendary Chinese hacker groups commuted themselves into full-fledged entrepreneurs, founding security (even antivirus) companies or entering the online gaming industry.

In hindsight, we can identify a clear trend. In the early period of Chinese hacking, the greatest capabilities were likely concentrated in non-state "patriot hacker" clubs. These groups, with names such as Xfocus, Black Eagle Base, Green Army Alliance, and the Honker Union, were in touch with the state authorities; there are even signs that these authorities competed with each other to exert influence over them. Some of these groups were undeniably large—the Honker Union claimed at its height to have over sixty thousand members—and could launch significant cyberattacks on foreign targets, mostly of the DDoS and Web-defacement variety. As Chinese Internet usage exploded, however, so did the attraction of waging domestic cyberattacks for profit. The period from 2007 to 2010 represented a watershed in Chinese hacking. Whereas previously Chinese hacking groups were nearly exclusively dominated by volunteers—patriotic hackers, often juveniles, who were concentrated on Web-page defacements abroad in line with perceived slights to Chinese national honor—now they officially entered into the hacking-for-hire market.

The question remained what the driving force for this activity really was. Many of the dozens of Chinese intrusions reported on before 2010 had a clear political context—the theft of government information, for example, or even the defacement or blocking of access to Web sites that had somehow attracted the ire of the Chinese authorities. For the many campaigns reported, however, it needs to be highlighted that many more go unreported. This is especially true in the private sector, where revelations of cyber theft of proprietary information could have a significant impact on a company's business prospects. The data on these attacks was therefore relatively slow to collect, even for government, but already by 2009 it was clear that as big as the Chinese desire for classified foreign government information was, a new market suddenly existed: a market for stolen foreign technology and intellectual property.

Until very recently, a virtually unquestioned article of faith among experts was that Chinese cyber espionage had an overall central mission to acquiring foreign technology. China's rate of economic growth, which the CCP itself had often said was one of the most critical factors to maintaining social stability, has been dependent, at least in part, on new technology, and the adoption of foreign technology has for a long time been a cornerstone of Chinese economic policy. Since the late 1980s, for instance, the Chinese government had actively pursued a strategy of building up its own high-tech industry to reduce its dependence on foreigners. The specific project for this "indigenous development" was the so-called 863 Program, but there were many like it. Like many other long-term strategies of the Chinese government, the importance of the 863 Program rose and fell over the years, but sometime in the early to middle years of the first decade of the twenty-first century it took on a new dimension. Although the details are murky, the 863 Program (as well as possibly others like it) was rumored to have directly or indirectly started to encourage the widespread theft of intellectual property for later incorporation into the Chinese economic and defense industries. Basically, anyone with the right skills and a vague access to the right people was in the market. And there was a ready supply of willing labor as well, for by this point—sometime between 2005 and 2010—China had already fostered a virtual army of non-state hackers whose primary target to date had been foreign political targets. Suddenly these non-state hackers stood to make a good deal of money by stealing economic secrets as well.

There is no doubt that some of the targeted acts of cyber theft directly benefited Chinese industry. The most obvious benefits have accrued to the

Chinese defense industrial establishment, whose program for advanced weapons development (the so-called 998 Program) depended to a huge extent on foreign technology. The gains here were probably considerable: China is in the process of fielding a copy of the new F-35 fighter, mostly based on information stolen directly from Lockheed Martin. The scale of this type of theft is hard to quantify, because a huge number of the present Chinese weapon systems and defense products are directly based on cyber theft. One report noted that the entire PLA amounted to a "clone army," with nearly every significant weapon system clearly derived from foreign systems.

According to informed observers writing in 2013, from around 2008, China enacted the National Technology Transfer Promotion Implementation Plan, building up a network of "transfer centers" whose sole purpose was to analyze and distribute the stolen technology; according to the authors, over two hundred of these centers would sprout up across China. It is difficult to ascertain how successful these centers were in actually converting the stolen IP. The Xi-Obama agreement indicates that the benefit would have been outweighed by the potential damage to the Chinese economy through even the mildest of economic sanctions. This points to another key factor in explaining the overall campaign of the IP theft: the ability of a few to gain considerable financial benefit from the task, especially within the PLA.

There is little doubt that members of the PLA have reemerged as powerful economic actors since President Jiang Zemin first tried to cut the ties of the military to public business in the late 1990s. While some of these activities were undoubtedly illegal in any sense, most were at the very least tolerated or sanctioned moneymaking ventures. On a broad scale, these included, for instance, opening the PLA hospitals to fee-paying private patients, who now account for 90 percent of the occupants. On a lower level, they included the moonlighting of PLA specialists in a number of different roles, from drivers to doctors to hackers, earning additional income by engaging in sanctioned side business. There have been repeated hints by knowledgeable sources that this moonlighting includes PLA hackers, who might have targeted foreign companies for additional private pay. Perhaps equally important are the purported financial gains made by heads of the Chinese cyber establishment. It seems likely that at all levels of the PLA there might have been personal benefit derived from supporting IP theft— albeit only "targeted" IP. One individual's story here is relatively well known and may be symptomatic of this national cyber system.

The hacker known as UglyGorilla has many fans in Western government and information security circles. The bespectacled, bald, and hefty Chinese hacker has cast himself as the quintessential recluse. His social media profiles bore the quotation of a Chinese poem referring to himself as the "bored soldier on the battlefield," while at the same time he described himself as a man of "no ambition." As apolitical and quiet as he might have been, his hacking aspirations were widely known in the cyber community for years before his name surfaced in public.

He was first named in a groundbreaking report by the security company Mandiant in 2011 as one of the hackers in a Shanghai-based PLA cyber unit (TRB Unit 61398, the Second Bureau of the 3PLA). This unit was responsible for multiple intrusions and espionage campaigns in the United States, including the *New York Times,* a Mandiant client.

UglyGorilla then had a star mention in what was to be the most significant US government response to Chinese cyber espionage. The 2014 indictment of five employees of the PLA—and in particular the Shanghai TRB unit—mentions him by name. The indictment clearly states that on behalf of an unnamed Chinese state-owned enterprise, UglyGorilla penetrated into the networks of Westinghouse, SolarWorld, US Steel, and four other companies and passed on the information he obtained to the unnamed Chinese state-owned company to give it a competitive edge. In other examples listed in the indictment, the stealing of its IP meant that a solar-energy company, SolarWorld, eventually went bankrupt due to the loss of sales. Some media reports quickly picked up that "UG," as he sometimes called himself, leaving behind little signatures in the malware he authored, was something of a celebrity in the large clandestine world of cybersecurity. "When the indictment came out, my wife asked me if I knew this Ugly-Gorilla guy," said Adam Meyers, who first encountered China's cyber spies as a security specialist at the US State Department. "I told her, 'I've known him longer than I've known you.'" UG's razor-like focus on his own brand and consistency, and his prolific output, made him the poster boy of the "Comments Crew," yet another shorthand for the Shanghai Second Bureau of the 3PLA.

What is interesting in the indictment is that it refers to how UG and others engaged in theft "while they worked for" the PLA unit in question. In other words, the individuals accused were conducting the theft on behalf of the PLA unit, under orders and as part of a larger strategy for the PLA to deliver precious foreign intellectual property to domestic businesses. They could have, however, also been operating as freelancers, paid directly by the companies and attacking US targets on behalf of the state-owned enterprise—in effect, moonlighting on government time, though most likely with a nod and a wink. The US government would consider the distinction between these two versions of events irrelevant: if Chinese PLA-badged hackers were being naughty on their own time, then this would still count as the Chinese government being culpable in a lack of control. There is no information as to UglyGorilla's fate after the abundant publicity he has garnered in recent years. What seems clear, however, is that the old structure of PLA-led espionage, and most important the theft of intellectual property that is associated with it, have been radically brought to heel under the reforms instigated by Xi Jinping.

If previous Chinese military reform is anything to go by, it looks likely that many of the existing PLA cyber institutions will stay in place and may even keep their affiliation with the General Staff Directorate. While it is possible that the TRBs—the mainstay of the government's attack force—will be absorbed into the Strategic Support Force (the new cyber command), it is equally likely that they will effectively remain in place and either be dual hatted (reporting to both commands) or simply be re-tasked to go after more political, and less economic, intelligence. This could mean that China will focus more on building a force that is able to engage in full state-on-state cyber war, rather than on economic espionage. The differences may seem slight, but they are significant: cyber maneuvering intended to prepare the battlefield for confrontation is much quieter and harder to detect due to a lack of traffic. If accurate, this means that Chinese cyber operations may increasingly resemble Russian cyber operations, and their focus is by far not only on kinetic goals.

There are indications that China is seeking to reinforce its long-standing policy of information warfare, as defined in covert propaganda and influencing operations. The so-called Three Warfares doctrine is unique: it is the only official information warfare doctrine that has been published by any government. It is also by far the most famous: references to the Three Warfares can be found in virtually any treatise on Chinese cyber capabilities. The doctrine is remarkable in that it defines at a very abstract level the interstate conflict arena in terms that are unknown in the West: these include legal warfare (often called lawfare, using international law to advance a strategic objective), media warfare (to win public and international opinion), and psychological warfare (to leverage a punishment and award system across national levels of power to coerce an opponent, for instance, by freezing diplomatic relations with governments that meet with prominent dissidents). Since proclaiming the Three Warfares doctrine in 2003, the PLA has heavily operationalized the strategy and incorporated it in the General Political Department/Liaison Department (GPD/LD). The GPD/LD directly works with China's intelligence arms in "identifying select foreign political, business, and military elites and organizations abroad relevant to China's interests or potential 'friendly contacts.'" The GPD/LD investigation and research bureau then analyzes those individuals' positions toward China: career trajectories, motivations, political orientations, factional affiliations, and competencies. The resulting "cognitive maps" (a method of graphically mapping relationships of people and ideas) of these influencers and their respective ways of thinking guide the direction and character of tailored influence operations, including conversion, exploitation, or subversion.

While traditionally focused on Taiwan, the GPD/LD has long turned its sights on many other countries as well. According to the 2014 published annual report of the Czech Republic's counterintelligence service, China's intelligence services put an emphasis on gaining influence over Czech political and state elite in this fashion. The noted China scholar Mark Stokes claims that the GPD/LD as a whole can be described as an instrument of "political warfare," something that is virtually unheard of in democratic societies and has no known equivalent. Given its focus on manipulating both public opinion and elites abroad, however, it is no surprise that it acts as a distant mirror: just as China invests in this aspect of state conflict, it worries that Western nations, primarily the United States, will do the same to it.

China clearly puts great stock in cyber both as a tool of foreign policy and as an instrument of its responsive autocracy, a cyber-enabled rather than a cyber-disabled dictatorship that increasingly leverages the Internet as a tool of social control. But for all their posturing on cyber conflict, their saber rattling with new capabilities, and their previously unchecked theft of foreign intellectual property, China's rulers feel acutely vulnerable from and in cyberspace.

While China continues to modernize its critical infrastructure, government, and armed forces, it increasingly loses the advantage of general technological backwardness that it has enjoyed vis-à-vis its most feared opponent, the United States. Any type of cyberattack that could previously have targeted the United States without fear of equal response can now also target China whether through collapsing power grids or public infrastructure, knocking out government systems, or attacking financial networks.

China has simply grown up—a reality that, ironically, has made it equally vulnerable to the United States and other world powers.

And, in fact, it is much more vulnerable. The CCP's desperate need for control means that its gigantic domestic surveillance apparatus—think Golden Shield—is a juicy target for foreign intelligence operations. While the intelligence-collection aspect would be serious enough, the potential to commit sabotage or indeed undermine the entire rule of the CCP by hijacking or undermining such systems is probably a much greater threat. China, like all open autocracies, is not automatically stable but rather automatically *un*stable; it requires a lot of effort to keep in equilibrium. China is probably not a very resilient political entity overall, and the rule of the CCP depends on strong economic growth as well as the ability to be a responsive autocracy. If either of these two aspects is imperiled—be it through economic sanctions or through poking holes in the Great Firewall—then the consequences for the party, let alone for individuals in the party, could be lethal.

Those protecting the CCP are acutely aware of this vulnerability, and indeed very likely overstate the desire of Western governments to actually "crash" their system. For instance, the Chinese completely share the Russian analysis that the Arab Spring revolts, as well as similar pro-democracy movements, were directly instigated by the US government. Attempts to convince the leading cadres that they simply misunderstand the role and abilities of Western civil society—I tried once with a senior official for two hours—are seldom successful. Indeed, China now considers "civil society" one of its internal buzzwords, a term likely to get an instant response from the censors worrying about collective action. "What are we supposed to think," cried a high-ranking Chinese official in a closed-door meeting between Western and Chinese cyber policy makers, "when Americans say that they should knock down the Great Firewall and that this will bring down the CCP? This is a threat!"

The problem for the Chinese is that while the vast majority of Western policy analysts would have clearly rejected the assertion that Western intelligence services routinely engage in anything approaching information warfare, the constant comments in this direction by both Russia and China are changing the nature of the debate. By constantly restating the fiction while increasing mutual animosity, they are lowering the barriers for those same policies, making it more likely, not less, that the West will start engaging in large-scale propagandist activity and widespread covert influencing. For, as we saw in earlier chapters, there are indications that the West as a whole and the United States in particular may slowly start to embrace the basic precepts of information warfare, even if not consciously.

The Chinese and Russians may therefore inadvertently create that which they most fear: a full-scale IW confrontation with the West. The true tragedy is that Russia and maybe even China may feel that they can win such a confrontation—domestically, if not internationally. But at best such a victory can only be temporary. For as long as there is a free Internet, anywhere, the dissidents in their countries will find support abroad. And in such a world, the supposed nefarious plotting of Western intelligence toward the dreaded "regime change" in Russia and China may become reality.

PART VI

Chapter 15

PARSING CYBER POWER

W hile Russia, China, and the United States have dominated the international cyber landscape, as of 2016 over thirty countries were openly pursuing not only defensive but also offensive capabilities in cyberspace. I would add to that another dozen or so countries that have committed to defensive cyber operations but will undoubtedly go on to develop basic offensive skills to better test their systems as well. In short, almost every single advanced economy and medium-sized country is in the process of setting up capabilities to project state power in cyberspace or has done so already.

While the top three countries discussed in this book are by no means the only advanced cyber powers, there remains a very significant difference between the national cyber capabilities of the top cyber nations and everyone else. Why this is the case is much harder to articulate.

When I was asked to participate in a hearing of the Swiss Ministry of Defense in 2013, I offered my own ranking of national cyber capabilities, based on little more than my own presumed knowledge and the opinions of my peers. I used as my criteria for assessing a country's capabilities its proficiency in the three classic tasks of information operations as defined by the US military: defense, attack, and exploitation (espionage). Using a model developed by the US Department of Defense Science Board as a point of departure, I assigned countries into six classes (or generations) of cyber power.

In an updated version of my report done recently, just over a dozen of the four dozen or so states developing cyber capabilities were categorized as first generation, or Class 1—much less sophisticated than many international companies, with defenses amounting to very basic governmental CERTs and offensive capabilities mostly only implicit (as part of their defensive organization) or dependent on contractors, including mercenaries and cyber-crime gangs. Perhaps a dozen or so countries qualify as second-generation Class 2 cyber powers, with the basic ability to coordinate across government on the issue of cybersecurity and very basic potential offensive capacity limited to penetration testing or the use of non-state actors. This category includes a few of the poorer EU member states, as well as much of Southeast Asia and Latin America. Third-generation Class 3 cyber powers are able to specialize and include a much wider range of actors—some like Pakistan, India, and Brazil with burgeoning offensive programs, or others like Finland that have developed relatively advanced defensive capabilities. Most of the EU member states would fall into this category as well as Japan, but also countries like Iran and North Korea that have taken the opposite direction and have focused heavily on offensive (and not so much on defensive) skills. Class 4 cyber powers strive to achieve operational capabilities in both attack and defense, although they may have different emphases. This is a relatively small group of no more than half a dozen nations, including a few European countries such as the Netherlands and Switzerland, but also South Korea. Fifth-generation Class 5 cyber powers have extensive offensive capabilities and are a very small group— including, besides the U.K. and Israel (which both have roughly similar outlooks to the United States), Russia and China (the latter of which is technically only a Class 4 power but makes up for it in pure bulk). The current top of the pyramid is the sixth-generation cyber power—with the technical skills to not only discover but also create vulnerabilities in the adversary system and then leverage the necessary logistics (like budgets) to make this work. There is only one Class 6 cyber power. The United States, with total annual cyber-related expenditure between $7 billion and around $30 billion, depending on your metric, is far and away in a class of its own.

A senior navy officer once remarked to me that the differences in cyber capability don't seem too dissimilar to how international navy capabilities compare—with the United States far outgunning all other navies combined. At the same time, there are significant differences that make this type of comparison less helpful. Indeed, I am somewhat doubtful about the entire exercise of ranking and comparing national cyber powers. The issue I have with my own lineup was not that it was relatively subjective and inevitably built on imperfect knowledge. Nor was the final country ranking counterintuitive or met with any major disagreement from government professionals in the field whom I consulted.

Instead, the first problem for me is the very premise of comparative evaluation in this arena. Military cyber is not like navies or air forces, where we can simply count the ships or planes deployed: more is not necessarily better in measuring cyber power, and ranking skill is always going to be as arbitrary as comparing countries' special force units or intelligence agencies. As we saw in previous chapters, military offensive cyber in the West can be categorized according to two broad segments, what I refer to as "battlefield cyber" and true "strategic cyber," which concentrates on what most people traditionally associate with cyber warfare: disrupting the adversary's ICT networks and associated systems, most likely with a kinetic effect (be it a large-scale power blackout, financial crash, or the disabling of a military logistic system). The former is partially measurable—where known—through similar programs that track national armament capabilities. We therefore can say that it is highly likely that the United States, Russia, and Israel have some of the best

304 | THE DARKENING WEB

"battlefield cyber" capabilities simply due to the known activities of their defensive industrial base. For instance, in Operation Orchard in 2007, Israel most likely used a derivative of a US offensive cyber weapon to hack and mislead the Syrian integrated air-defense network and allow its bombers to destroy a suspected nuclear installation unimpeded.

Whatever counts as a nation's "strategic cyber" capability is much harder to grasp. In the United States, the original model for the cyber teams were the Tailored Access Operations teams of the NSA, small elite teams that were similar to US Special Forces teams in size and originally amounted to no more than a dozen individuals each, while the new US Cyber Mission Teams might have grown to units of between thirty-nine and sixty-four persons (but included non-cyber-operator support personnel). Each of the operators will have a specific skill set, some of it related to programming and such, but also including intelligence or language specialists. Truly proficient teams will be supported by a wide logistic base that is a critical difference between advanced-generation cyber powers and those less advanced. That logistic base can include "weapon components" (repositories, or arsenals, of ready-made malware, or modular bits of malware that can be rapidly pieced together depending on the situation), "targeting aids" (ranging from passive intelligence assets to implants already pre-positioned in the target system), and "transport and forward operating bases" that help facilitate the operation, ranging from rented botnets to totally subverted larger private networks that can be used as staging grounds). Essentially, this support base can range from a collection of yet-undiscovered zerodays, stocked like laser-guided bombs in an arsenal and ready to be plugged into custom tools, to the ability to access highly integrated intelligence networks based perhaps on hardware-level penetration, to sophisticated large-scale cyber weapons that require thousands of man-hours to code. Advanced cyber powers will also inadvertently have access to a number of different "cyber foundries" where new weapon components are developed and tested and vulnerabilities developed or integrated.

The logistic side of the cyber-power equation is by far the most variable component and is perhaps even the most important. Crucially, it is by no means necessary to have the logistic base in-house, and as previous chapters have shown, cyber-crime actors can sometimes be a vital part of this equation, developing cyber capabilities for their state sponsors that are first used by their state actors but are later released back to the cyber-crime ecosystem when they are not considered state of the art anymore. Although sometimes military cyber teams do compete with each other in international hacking competitions, this is probably not an accurate view of who has the best "strategic cyber" teams. For instance, the most recent winners of the NATO Cooperative Cyber Defence Centre of Excellence Locked Shields network defense competition have been Austria (2014) and Slovakia (2015), both countries that most likely do not play in the top class of cyber actors. The size and sophistication of the all-critical logistic base, in contrast, are even harder to assess.

The defense category is equally difficult to evaluate, but for different reasons. Are we talking about the ability of the military to defend its own systems from intrusion? In that case, the least sophisticated nations are among those that are most secure: they simply cannot be targeted, because there is nothing to target. Or are we talking about the national cybersecurity capability, the integrated defense of not only governmental systems but also the civilian critical infrastructure? In all cases, the concept of attack surface is key: the larger and more complex your systems, the greater the challenge to your defense. In his May 2010 essay entitled *Cyber Power,* Joseph Nye encapsulates the challenge as being fundamentally one of "asymmetric vulnerability"—larger actors depend on "easily disrupted complex systems," and the larger the actor the greater the complexity and the burden of defense. In this case, smaller is undeniably better: countries such as Israel, the Netherlands, and Switzerland are able to field highly effective national cybersecurity programs due to their smaller size and thus much smaller attack surface. Further, the United States is nearly unique in the restrictions that it places on federal power—not even hyper-federal Switzerland has such a weak central government, at least in cyber terms—

and the heavy limits it places on using military means (including intelligence) within its own borders, even for cyber defense. All of these smaller countries are probably better positioned than the United States in helping to protect their critical infrastructure and may even have an edge in a state-on-state serious cyber confrontation (read: cyber war). In fact, a number of small nations have already exploited this comparative advantage in defense to push other aspects of cyber power.

Israel is widely considered a fully established cyber power whose tiny size belies a highly sophisticated defense industrial base that has increasingly merged with both a burgeoning tech industry and a deeply rooted intelligence community. Israel not only cooperated with the United States as part of the Stuxnet "strategic cyber" attack on the Iranian uranium enrichment facilities but also might have been the first country to have used a "battlefield cyber" weapon in actual conditions, during the 2007 attack on Syria described previously. Other alleged Israeli campaigns have included Duqu (which is very similar to Stuxnet in design, although with an unknown purpose) and potentially even Flame (although the latter is largely considered a US-only operation), both directed at Iranian interests. Israeli companies have long been at the forefront of developing network surveillance equipment and are a serious force in the cybersecurity marketplace, with exports totaling $6 billion in 2014, surpassing even conventional arms exports. Israeli Intelligence Unit 8200, the home of most of the country's cyber-combat troops, received an investment of $515 million in 2012 to help expand its cyber program.

Although Israel's rise to the top tiers of cyber power is unique, other small countries have been very successful in positioning themselves in the international cyber-diplomacy agenda and therefore exert at least some soft power. Estonia, officially touted as the first victim of serious state-backed cyber aggression due to a massive Russian DDoS attack in 2007, has been remarkably proficient at asserting its presence in the international dialogue. Switzerland and the Netherlands have also suffered significant cyber incidents that helped to concentrate the minds of policy makers and leveraged this political interest to strong effect. Both countries now field increasingly advanced national cybersecurity programs that not only are among the best in class in defense but also include overt offensive programs. Singapore, long a technology leader, has also invested considerable resources in its national cybersecurity program.

Other countries have been less vocal about their recently developed capacities, which means that they are largely ignored in conversations about relative national cyber power. These countries could include Sweden, an early thought leader in information warfare with excellent technical proficiency; France, whose technical skills are buttressed by deep attention to methodological details; and Spain, which has built up a surprisingly advanced critical infrastructure protection program that often gets missed by non-Spanish speakers.

Another reason cyber powers are so hard to rank is that states that are highly vocal about their alleged capabilities—or have used them aggressively—feature much larger in public than those capabilities alone would necessarily warrant. Two good examples of this are Iran and North Korea, countries whose ambitions are much larger than their capabilities but whose acts of cyber aggression have granted them an oversized importance in the public media narrative. Iran and North Korea are, at best, third-generation cyber actors that are able only to "exploit preexisting vulnerabilities," according to the classification scheme of the Defense Science Board, and whose capabilities are quite far behind most Western countries, let alone the United States. This lack of relative ability, however, has not stopped these states from garnering a lot of attention and even, at times, inflicting real damage.

Iran has been especially ambitious in cyberspace and has become one of the most worrying cyber actors in the eyes of many national governments, sometimes even ranked on threat assessments third after Russia and China. In March 2016, the United States announced its second-ever legal indictment of foreign state–affiliated hackers (following the indictment of the five PLA contractors in 2015), filing against a number of Iranian hackers and claiming that they were part of a campaign conducted at the behest of the Iranian Revolutionary Guard Corps (IRGC).

This campaign occurred as part of a flood of Iranian cyberattacks that were supposedly launched in retaliation for purported American cyberattacks, in particular the Stuxnet attacks against the Iranian nuclear program. Most notably, these included the corruption of tens of thousands of computers of Saudi Arabia's national oil company Saudi Aramco in 2012 and consistent attempts to disrupt the US banking sector through prolonged DDoS attacks of various sophistication from 2011 to 2013. In both cases, significant damage resulted, although the exact numbers are very much under debate: the US 2016 indictment reports that the attack on the American financial system involved forty-six US banks over 176 days, costing victims tens of millions of dollars in remediation costs. As part of a related campaign, Iranian hackers even managed to infiltrate and take over the operational controls of a small dam in upstate New York and attacked a Las Vegas casino. Iranian cyber actors were also accused of the 2011 subversion of DigiNotar, an important Dutch-based certificate issuer needed to secure Internet communication, including with Google Gmail (Gmail accounts of Iranian dissidents were probably one of the main targets, rather than the Netherlands per se). This triggered a full-scale cyber crisis management response in the Netherlands. In addition to a number of other operations, mostly intelligence related to or directed against its own dissidents, Iran has been behind the formation of other cyber programs, including that of the Syrian Electronic Army (supporting the Assad regime) and the Yemen Cyber Army (supporting the Shiite insurgents in that country's civil war).

The Iranian Revolutionary Guard Corps boasted in 2013 that it fields the "fourth biggest cyber power among the world's cyber armies." This boast, like virtually all other Iranian defense-related claims, needs to be taken with a big pinch of salt. At least until 2015, it was obvious to many civilian security professionals that the majority of Iranian cyberattacks were actually carried out by a small group of equally small contractor companies based in Tehran, companies that despite their private nature were clearly enjoying at the very least the permission of the government for their activities, or working directly on its behalf.

The 2016 indictment of the four Iranian hackers is even more specific, naming the companies in question and asserting a direct link to the IRGC. This does not mean that Iran has not yet developed the ability to conduct these operations in-house, but it does show that despite years of investment their capabilities were probably not good enough to compete with non-state contractors. This can and probably will change in time. Iranian operations will probably seek to invest more in defense (the next step to become a fourth-generation actor) but could also change their attack methods—moving away from loud, messy, and primitive destruction attacks—as the government ability improves.

North Korea is another country that, despite relatively primitive technical abilities, has consistently managed to launch highly aggressive and often damaging attacks that have generated significant responses in the public media. The hermit dictatorship has been involved in a spate of cyberattacks, mostly against South Korea. In fact, for South Korea there seems to be no question that its northern neighbor is engaged in full-scale cyber war. In 2009, North Korea attacked both South Korea and the United States with a number of limited DDoS attacks that caused some disruption to the White House's and the Pentagon's public Web sites, as well as a number of South Korean targets. In 2013, a number of South Korean media organizations as well as banks suffered much more serious cyberattacks, causing disruption that was widespread if ultimately limited in consequences. In March 2016, a gigantic dormant botnet was discovered in South Korea, where hundreds of thousands of machines were compromised but not activated, perhaps in preparation for a very large-scale attack that was disrupted due to this discovery. North Korea has even managed to hack the company responsible for nuclear energy, Korea Hydro and Nuclear Power; although the hackers were unable to take over operational control of the reactors themselves, they published details of individual workers as well as working documents to prove that they had gained access and presumably to imply that they could cause greater damage if they wished.

For the American public, however, North Korean cyber really only leaped onto the scene when in November 2014 Sony Pictures Entertainment was hacked and subsequently blackmailed to prevent the release of a slapstick comedy that painted a thoroughly unflattering picture of North Korea's ruler, Kim Jong-un. When it looked as if Sony Pictures were going to acquiesce to the demands and pull the film from general release, the public firestorm gathered into a very long-reaching media event, demanding repeated statements from the US government and culminating in the first-ever positive attribution from an American president of the cyber operations of another country. Following questions as to the accuracy of American attribution, the US government took the equally unheard-of step of releasing the source of its intelligence.

The reality that cyberattacks can have both data-related and psychological effects means that an offensive operation can be its own reward and that even unsuccessful attempts can be successful on a political level. The focus of both Iran and North Korea on executing flashy and sometimes even clumsy destructive attacks is an attempt to exert deterrence or develop political leverage where otherwise none would exist. The political deterrence of inflating themselves as an overall security threat, through cyber but also missile and nuclear technology, is of considerable gain to both rogue states and increases their negotiation potential. This focus is shared by not only North Korea and Iran but also many other authoritarian regimes: information is the weapon, and cyber is just one of many tools to deploy it. Of course, that weapon threatens authoritarian regimes not only from the outside but also from the inside: the more authoritarian a state, the more likely it is to view information as a weapon per se.

The NGO Freedom House regularly assesses how "free" a country's Internet is, a contentious exercise that has to depend on publicly available documentation on a country's censorship regime. Using the classifications

"free," "partially free," and "not free," it put a total of twenty-three countries in the "not free" category in its most recent assessment in 2015, including Russia, China, and a number of Arab nations. The "partially free"
is itself a fairly large group that includes nearly two dozen countries, among
them India and Turkey, at least one of which can safely be called a fully
functioning democracy. Of significant concern among Western nations is
the reality that a number of more or less settled democracies have shown a
disquieting interest in the ability to limit the content that is consumed by
their citizens. A colleague from a Malaysian think tank once pointed out
that the foremost cyber threat for many South Asian and Southeast Asian
democracies is that of social media and how to control its "destabilizing"
effect. Turkey, a democracy and NATO ally, has clearly become more
authoritarian-minded in recent years, repeatedly blocking Twitter, Facebook, and YouTube and expanding laws on "protecting Turkishness from
denigration" to include all types of political criticism. On the other hand,
India has seen its supreme court repeal some of the more contentious
legislation aimed at controlling social media activity, and Brazil, despite
sometimes high-handed behavior by the legislative branch, has produced
the *Marco Civil da Internet,* a document that seeks to protect civil rights
online.

The developments in these other states are far from being merely of cursory interest. Together, these countries form the vaguely defined group of
"swing states" between those seeking to protect the libertarian basis of the
Internet and limit the control of governments (the Free Internet faction)
and the more authoritarian-minded that want governments to exert more
control over the crucial information space overall (the Cyber-sovereignty
faction). Many of these swing states also have a somewhat conflicted approach to viewing information as a weapon: while they are willing to listen
to the Free Internet point of view (and would probably rather belong to its
club, with its prestigious "first world" aura), their instincts pull them toward the argument of the Cyber-sovereignty advocates.

Unfortunately, the Free Internet faction is often not able to respond well to the concerns of these swing states. Many of the government representatives in this space hail from a traditional arms control background, with sometimes decades of experience negotiating strategic arms issues. They are the most likely to pivot toward traditional major power actors, which does not often correspond with the actual balance of power in cyberspace, therefore overvaluing some underperforming major powers and demoting other upstart nations in the process. The Free Internet faction won't by necessity prioritize nations like Finland that have oversized reputations in the InfoSec community or comparatively underpowered Romania, a nation that has a good counter-cyber-crime reputation earned battling its legendary cyber–crime scene (one town in Romania, Râmnicu Vâlcea, is known as Hackerville and is home to a hundred-odd cyber-crime gangs). The same could be said about Nigeria or even some Latin American nations. Other nations with comparatively low-profile cyber power (like Japan and Norway) are important overseas development actors, whose interest and activities in cyber capacity building (CCB) mean they have other roles to play than simply being recipients of norms and rules drafted by a club that, not by surprise, suspiciously resembles the P5 of major nuclear powers—often with little regard for small "upstart" nations, let alone the vital non-state actors that effectively define cyberspace.

This is my greatest problem with the notion of segmenting cyber powers in the fashion that I and quite a few others are often asked to do. It does provide part of the answer—namely, indications of some parts of nations' "hard power" in cyberspace. But it is a dangerous simplification if a wider definition of relevance is needed. I believe cyber to be the epitome of a soft-power problem: one that depends on highly intangible issues such as legitimacy, cooperation, and trust—not only among governments, but also between governments and the crucial non-state actors that build and maintain the Internet. Parsing cyber power requires seeing beyond the traditional hallmarks of brute force encapsulated in national security structures and understanding that there are many ways for nations to play crucial roles in this domain. This is a significant challenge in particular for the diplomats working in this area, many of whom come from a hard-power (political-military) background and are used to seeing the issues at hand in relatively straightforward terms. But lateral thinking is needed if a true assessment of an actor's cyber power is to be attempted. The toolbox of those dealing with arms control issues is relatively straightforward, but it may also be somewhat limiting. For as the old saying goes, if all you have is a hammer, then every problem looks like a nail.

Chapter 16

THE GREAT CYBER GAME

The science fiction writer William Gibson is often credited with the popularization of the term "cyberspace" in his 1984 book, *Neuromancer*. In it he describes a postapocalyptic world where megacorporations have largely replaced states as the world's dominant powers, and "cyberspace" is the term used to refer to the global information grid known as "the Matrix," an artificial space populated with physical representations of data that form entire cities and mountains and where criminals, states, and corporations battle each other using viruses and other cyber weaponry. The users, the common people, are just cogs in the system, at best.

Neuromancer spawned an entire genre of so-called cyberpunk literature in which cyberspace often has a distinctly ominous feel to it, dominating the lives of average people who are virtual slaves to the complete information control of the powerful: states, corporations, and hackers. In these worlds, the Internet has morphed into something all encompassing, intimate, and rather sinister: the Matrix. The idea of the Matrix went on to have a long cultural life, most prominently in the hit 1999 movie of the same name, starring Keanu Reeves. It often represents the pure dystopia made digital, a panopticon-like system that willfully employs data for one purpose only: the subjugation of the individual. The Matrix and its cultural descendants represent today's light, joyful, and somewhat anarchic Internet distorted into a darkened web of digital control.

For any technophile of my generation and younger, this vision of the conversion of the Internet from an instrument of freedom to one of domination is profoundly frightening. It is my generation's nuclear winter, the quintessential vehicle to convey existential angst of a society's possible dystopian future. But unlike nuclear winter, there is no single visible apocalypse to mark a clear delineation, no cyber mushroom cloud big enough to finally indicate that we as a civilization face a real danger. It is a slow-onset threat, much more akin to climate change than nuclear war. Except that we can stop this climate change event cold.

As with climate change, it is easy for doubters to claim that the threat is overstated—given that the technology of the Internet differs completely from that of the fictional Matrix and its various other dark web analogies in fiction, for instance. This is true. But the dream of states exercising power in and through cyberspace shows that there are powerful incentives to push the Internet into becoming something akin to the dark web Matrix. While Western societies have defined national security as it relates to cyberspace mostly as a matter of "kinetic effects"—that is, physical damage to or destruction of physical infrastructure—authoritarian states have long since viewed the principal security threat as arising from "informational effects," that is, the infiltration of problematic political messages. The danger is that Western governments may slowly, inadvertently, adopt this line of thinking themselves. This could happen not only through a number of small, apparently innocuous steps but also relatively suddenly: if, for instance, a major cyber terrorist attack is launched in, say, the next ten years or so, Western governments could radically switch their present position in supporting the multistakeholder approach to Internet governance and push to facilitate the development of a new type of Internet architecture—one quite different from what we have today.

There is no shortage of special interests that would leap at the chance to redefine the Internet. Some corporations and states would love to set up so-called walled gardens, highly regulated smaller internets not too dissimilar to the old America Online model, where commercial services are tightly regulated and user behavior effectively highly constrained and where all activities are reduced to pay for play. Others would strive for much stronger government oversight over their own particular "national" Internets, with an even more dramatic outcome: citizens with social-credit scores working within a fully contained information bubble that allows nothing disruptive or troublesome to get through. In both cases, the key would be to vanish the comparative anonymity of much of Internet user behavior, making it easier to target the individual, either for political or for commercial purposes. Effort in this direction would bring us at least half a step closer to the dark web by seeking to bring "order" into where something akin to "managed chaos" was the previous organizational paradigm. These structural changes may seem remote but could potentially happen relatively quickly, if the political environment is conducive enough—say, after a massive attack on the Internet itself facilitated by state or non-state actors. The only protection against this development would be vigilance, not only by the InfoSec guardians, but by all of us. If we fail, we may indeed get our very own version of the postapocalyptic vision that Gibson bestowed on us.

If you think that the dark web is a far-fetched or rather singular notion, you may be surprised to know that among those who spend their days thinking about the future of cyber conflict, this prediction is fairly conservative. Some of the greatest technophiles share visions of cyber doom that are much more sinister and free from direct human agency entirely. In 2015, a group of prominent individuals, including Bill Gates, Elon Musk, Steve Wozniak, and Stephen Hawking, signed a letter with hundreds of others to warn of one danger: the rise of artificial intelligence (AI). According to these leading lights, AI could produce virtual demigods of pure logic that would make their own decisions on human life and the universe and everything, and this may not be a good thing for mankind. The assembled great minds followed Hawking's 2014 newspaper editorial in which he stated, quite plainly, that the potential rise of AI could be an existential threat on the level of nuclear weapons.

I certainly do not disagree with their assessment. The potential power of AI, running off the yet-to-be-deployed but immensely powerful quantum computing infrastructure meshed with unimaginable data storage capacity, could even be a more immediate threat than that of the Internet turning into the dark web. To use another climate change comparison, those concerned with the rise of malignant AI are more like those interested in a sudden collapse of the oceanic currents and resulting sudden-onset ice age, an event that is unlikely to occur—but still might—in the next hundred or even fifty years. My vision of a slow but inexorable shift to a dark web of informational control has a longer road, dominated by the rise of perpetual information warfare between states, and is more like the rise of oceanic sea levels over the next two hundred years or so. It is coming, one way or another, even if we don't know exactly how long it will take for it to present a significant threat to the human population. And no one really knows what a hundred years in geological time is equivalent to in cyber time. It could be thirty, twenty, or even just ten years ahead.

Like climate change, our cyber crisis requires a number of steps from a number of actors. The global climate is one of the ultimate physical global commons, beyond that of the oceans, and presents a means of both sustenance and destruction. For cyberspace to remain a positive domain, for the Internet to continue to be a driver of economic prosperity but also simply universal human freedoms, no matter how defined, we need to tackle the burgeoning pollution of this environment. This pollution is information warfare—both technical and psychological—and it will have a final and endlessly tragic cost on human civilization if it is allowed to get out of hand. The body of cyber is a wonderful human achievement, something that can actively be perceived as an unadulterated good on the level of the invention of movable print, or maybe even the wheel or the seafaring canoe. Maybe it will forever face possible perversion by man's Hobbesian side, like most inventions, and be made into a tool of violence and domination while also being a tool for civilizational growth. As a former US secretary of the navy, Richard Danzig, pointed out, the way we came to technology defines how we think of it, and the West came to cyberspace through computers and hacking. Other cultures, however, approached cyber differently, primarily from its basic theoretical premise of providing a tool for control of populations. All inventions can shift their utility depending on the cultural needs, and sometimes the first utility is not the most impactful. For instance, one of the most defining inventions of human civilization, the wheel, was not originally used for transportation at all. Instead, for nearly a thousand years its only use was as a tool to produce clay pottery. Probably around 3500 B.C.E. someone discovered that the wheel could be used as a tool to facilitate transport, and a great leap in warfare occurred (along with, of course, tremendous advances in the efficiency of daily life and commerce).

But humanity has come together to deal with existential challenges before, both of the rapid-onset nuclear Armageddon variety and of the slow-burn climate change variety. We need to have a similar global consensus that cyberspace presents a unique challenge and thus requires a unique approach to manage.

The distinctive challenge of cyber governance is that it simply touches on so many different actors, single institutions, and collections of institutions working together on specific parts of the wider body of cyberspace. This requires a unique approach of cooperation fairly unusual for governments. The likelihood of governments legislating themselves out of the present conundrum of achieving technical security and stability while at the same time guaranteeing basic freedoms is slim. Not only are the ideological differences between states too large to achieve agreement, but also the normative capacity of the private sector is virtually impossible to fully move in a specific direction; the development of products and services will continue to disrupt all attempts by governments to control it. And the civil society that was critical in the Internet's early rise will continue to play a dominant role in cyberspace. If somehow the key Internet governance institution were subverted, these engineers would just start a new Internet; as long as there are hobbyists ready to sacrifice their time to code as they like, and as long as there is a community to share their dreams and promote their code and connect it to the wider public, there will be an internet. The question is how free and how widely available that internet will be—whether it will be bounded by loyalty to a brand, ideology, or country or be the global Internet we know today.

States and their abiding interest in conflict both physical and otherwise constitute the single most significant threat to the stability of cyberspace. For the same reason, they are certainly a major part of the solution, and governmental institutions worldwide are showing an increasing interest in how cyberspace affects them and their countries. Cyber, whatever exactly that means, is therefore very much in the geopolitical mainstream as a topic, especially where it touches on the international peace and security dimension of diplomacy, but also as it relates to economic growth, social and cultural affairs, and law enforcement.

The first major UN resolution related to cybersecurity was proposed in 1998 (by Russia), and since then the UN has played a key role in the evolving international peace and security discussion on cyber conflict. In 2003, the UN helped to initiate the WSIS process, an important and ongoing state contribution to the Internet governance debate. The WSIS process gave birth to the Internet Governance Forum, a large yearly jamboree of the Internet governance community and one of the few areas where state and non-state actors are able to freely interact. In October 2001, with 9/11 still very much dominating all political thought, the Council of Europe concluded negotiations on the so-called Budapest Convention on Cyber-crime, the only binding treaty that specifically regulates cyberspace behavior. The diplomatic arena of states is increasingly accommodating of dialogue on cybersecurity and is steadily discovering new facets to the issue that demand state attention. And there are a lot of them.

There are different ways to envision what has been called the "cyberspace ecosystem" of various organizations, agencies, government alliances, civil society processes, and industrial groupings that somehow play a role in the stability of cyberspace. Although the ecosystem model of cyberspace has a certain popularity in various discussions, it also has its limits, such as the problem of defining classes like predators, let alone apex predators. Ecosystems are largely organized in a hierarchical fashion, and with notable technical exemptions (such as the domain name system) the Internet is resolutely nonhierarchical and defies attempts to easily categorize much of its work this way. It is much easier to approach the subject through the discipline of international relations, whose brightest minds have spent some time grappling with the problem of mapping the power dynamics of these types of actors. In this parlance, these actors or groups of actors are called "regimes."

The Stanford University professor Stephen D. Krasner coined the most common definition of a regime: "an institution possessing norms, decision rules, and procedures which facilitate a convergence of expectations." An institution, it is important to note, does not have to be a physical entity: any kind of agreed-upon behavior can be categorized as an institution, and it doesn't even require a contract to be instituted; a tradition of practice is enough.

Later, Robert Keohane and David Victor applied the regime-theoretical framework. One of the most exciting developments in international policy of the late 1990s and early 2000s was the rise of environmental diplomacy. Keohane and Victor used this approach to plot a model of all the relevant actors in environmental diplomacy in a visual manner, a "regime complex for climate change" that graphically showed how many different actors were engaged in this space. In 2014, Joseph Nye adopted this work and applied it to cyberspace. This became the first in a number of visualizations of what we now call the cyber regime complex: an attempt to physically plot the various relevant actors in this space.

When I map my version of the cyber regime complex—for instance, at a meeting hosted by the UN's Office of Disarmament Affairs in June 2016—it looks indeed like a miniature galaxy: there are over two dozen larger regimes competing for attention. These range from military alliances (NATO, the Shanghai Cooperation Organization, and so on) and intelligence alliances (the Five Eyes alliance) to international law conventions, network alliances (such as the North American Network Operators Group), and civil society groups (such as those responsible for the technical standards like the Internet Engineering Task Force). I use a three-circle overlapping Venn diagram to represent the three major stakeholder communities—government, private sector, and civil society—and position the regime with respect to how much it can be assigned to one of these stakeholders (security alliances, such as NATO, are, for instance, very heavily oriented toward government).

The first thing to notice about this representation is how many of the regimes involved in the overall cyberspace galaxy are actually, to at least some significant extent, multistakeholder based. These include many of the regimes most critical to cyberspace stability—what Nye called the "core regimes"—such as the technical "incident responders" (the cybersecurity "firefighters," such as the CERTs), the ICANN and so-called "names community," and the UN-initiated WSIS process.

The second meaningful conclusion to draw from this model is that the various regimes that work on similar topics often share some commonalities in the stakeholder composition and alignment. These regimes form groups called regime clusters and respect each other's positions. For instance, one of the largest groups is the international cybersecurity regime cluster (also known as the international peace and security regime cluster), a group whose members are all concerned primarily with state conduct in cyber-conflict situations. These include very different institutions and processes, from economic groupings such as the G20 and the OECD to the UN First Committee to human rights NGOs. These very different institutions, however, recognize each other and accept each other's resolutions and documents, citing their decisions as part of the process of mutual reinforcement that is part and parcel of all international diplomacy.

There are a number of such regime clusters, or major topic groups, related to cyberspace, and of course the individual institutions/regimes can potentially belong to many different ones at the same time. While there are many topics (and therefore many regime clusters) relevant to international cyberspace stability, three regime clusters are particularly important. These are effectively the three dimensions of policy on which any hope for a lasting stability of cyberspace must rest.

The first is the aforementioned political-military or international cybersecurity dimension, which deals largely with the conduct of states during hostilities—be they warfare or activity below the threshold for war—and how to prevent war from occurring in the first place. The second is the economic and justice dimension, which concerns itself predominantly with aspects of crime and law enforcement, as well as trade, economic growth, and development. The third dimension is Internet governance, which relates to the actual management of the world's Internet resources.

These three dimensions—political-military, economics and law enforcement, and Internet governance—are, for the most part, addressed in highly different diplomatic settings. The political-military dimension has a strong anchor in the United Nations, but much of its day-to-day work is conducted in regional and security organizations, such as the Organization for Security and Co-operation in Europe or the ASEAN Regional Forum, or increasingly in bilateral agreements. Each of the economic, development, and law enforcement components is connected to different international organizations and agreements, from the World Trade Organization

(WTO) to the UN, Interpol, and international treaties. The subject of Internet governance—arguably not even a subject for diplomacy per se—has a tenuous link with the United Nations (through the WSIS process) but much stronger rooting in its own web of related non-state regimes. On the face of it, these three topics therefore have little in common. Together, however, they represent the different campaigns on which the international struggle of states to exert cyber power is fought, even though states remain only one of the major stakeholders that can exert power in and through cyberspace.

The noted scholar Laura DeNardis once asserted that the question of who should control the Internet, whether the United Nations or some other organization, makes no sense whatsoever. The more appropriate question involves determining the most effective form of governance in each specific context. While DeNardis is undoubtedly correct, it is important to understand that states do view it as possible to treat the Internet (and cyberspace overall) as part of a digital Great Game—a chessboard on which their respective interests can be advanced, and key points captured, all toward the notion of occupying the commanding heights of what will be the dominant domain of the future: cyberspace. And while cyberspace cannot be wholly owned more than any physical domain such as air, sea, or space, it can be dominated, at least temporarily, as can all other domains, real and abstract. And there are many reasons why, for some states at least, cyberspace may be the ultimate domain—the one that matters more than any other.

If, as liberal democrats in the classical sense, we agree that the basic objective is to prevent the final subversion of cyberspace by those who wish to control or inflict harm on human beings, we need to rapidly address a number of significant contradictions. These contradictions have made up the mainstay of the global Great Cyber Game between the Free Internet forces and those pushing for cyber sovereignty. The latter, with their standard-bearer, Russia, leading the way, have been able to rub the West's collective noses in their occasional hypocrisies and slowly erode the logical foundation of much of their arguments. Their narrative is beguilingly simple: How can countries like Germany and France insist that "bad content"—for instance, Nazi propaganda, which these countries have outlawed—is not a topic for discussion, given that they have their own methods to curtail free speech? How can the United States campaign against the evils of widespread surveillance and cyber espionage while maintaining the largest and apparently most indiscriminate intelligence-gathering operation on Earth? How can the Internet truly be seen as an instrument for creating economic wealth, when most of the private businesses profiting from it are American? And how can NGOs, whose leaders have never been elected to their jobs, not only claim to speak on behalf of any constituents but exert actual technical power over the Internet?

This book has tried to provide some nuance to these questions, many of which address the core issue of legitimacy of action. Nonetheless, we are often forced to return to the same themes again and again. The consistent fuzzy overlap of topics in various discussion forums—be they at the UN or elsewhere—is a sign that we need clarity on which topic belongs where. We need to finally fulfill the urgent need that decision makers across the board have insisted upon and simplify the landscape to better enable the discussion.

Simplification has long been perceived as a term of the enemy of those supporting the multistakeholder approach, but in fact complexity is increasingly a greater danger, leading to confusion on basic facts even at the highest levels of diplomatic decision making. This confusion is often exploited by those who think they can get away with misrepresenting the facts. I have personally witnessed respectable senior officials spread total untruths, facilitated by the fact that the necessary details would simply disappear in yawning cracks of ignorance that are perhaps unavoidable with a landscape so complex.

Whereas at one time the complexity of the cyber regime complex meant that some regimes could hide in plain sight, and would therefore be spared overbearing public attention, those times are gone. While many in the Info-

Sec community would prefer not having their practices made public—for rather sensible reasons, like not being sued—it is clearly time to explain to others how they do their jobs. Today, it is more likely that the obscurity of some regimes—like the detailed practices of the Internet governance community—are simply going to be broadly misunderstood by others. Diplomatic delegations happily set up rhetorical straw men using completely incorrect interpretations of how Internet governance functions and then try to use this wrong interpretation to push an unrelated agenda; all the while, the other diplomats, nonexperts themselves, are simply forced to react and take these interpretations for granted. I once stood by in awe while one major nation told another in a diplomatic gathering that because it already had a hotline communication dedicated to cyber, no other hotlines were needed. I then pointed out that in case of a serious cyber incident, that hotline would probably be useful only for the two nations to assure each other that they were innocent, while the technical community would be using its own hotline to clean up the mess.

propose an overall policy of reinforcing the distinctions among the three most important policy dimensions relevant to cyberspace: the international peace and security component; the economic, development, and crime component; and the Internet governance component. These also translate to three different focus areas—data security, cybersecurity, and Internet governance.

The basic organization of the United Nations can facilitate this division, albeit at very different levels of intensity. Therefore, cyber-related developments in the international peace and security arena—that is, those that directly address interstate conflict—can fall squarely into the remit of the UN General Assembly First Committee (Disarmament and International Security), which is responsible for exactly this topic and which most experts would also understand to be a resolutely state-to-state affair, where non-state actors would play only a secondary role. The opposite would be true for the Internet governance component, which would continue to be resolutely steered according to the multistakeholder approach and thus largely outside the UN system, tenuously connected to the UN only via the UNGA Third Committee (Social, Humanitarian, and Cultural) and the WSIS process. In between would be the related twins of economic development and law enforcement. The UNGA Second Committee (Economic and Financial) would emphasize the critical capacity development discussion— the importance of ICT for economic and political development in the world's poorer nations—and could potentially see a stronger link established to the UN Office on Drugs and Crime, which is not tied to any committee. Most of the work in this dimension, however, would likely continue to be done outside the UN system, similar to that of the Internet governance communities.

The importance of keeping these dimensions separate is immense; for me, it is valid to compare it with the importance of the well-rooted separation of powers among the executive, legislative, and judicial branches of government. That said, each of these dimensions interlocks with the others, and those working within each one must be aware of developments occurring in the others to avoid colliding on key topics of mutual interest, a regretfully common event today. This does not mean, however, that there has to be a convergence of policy; in fact, this would violate the crucial injunction of keeping the domains separate. But just as executive action must be rooted in law and subject to political approval, the three domains in cyberspace need to be able to work together, if not to do the same thing.

The political-military arena requires some of the most urgent changes. The need to address the rapid militarization of cyberspace, as well as the increasing level of hostilities between states, means that we need to refocus the conversation not only semantically but also institutionally. The changes I propose come in the form of both seemingly subtle and hugely meaningful modifications to the way we discuss sensitive topics in cyberspace, as well as institutional shifts that will distribute responsibility for key decisions and oversight more appropriately.

The term "cybersecurity" has been the cause of much confusion and needs to be clarified or retired, at least in the diplomatic context. For in common usage and increasingly legal definitions, "cybersecurity" is inherently linked to "bad online behavior," and that is only a small step from the most difficult and controversial concept of all, "bad content." The definition of this can range from the seemingly obvious (child pornography) to the contentious (hate speech and Nazi revisionism, but also radical Islamist "online jihadi" content) to the outright antiliberal (when pro-democracy and human rights activism is branded as such). The framing of supposed information warfare attacks on Western social media as "bad content" would equally be a very dangerous move, because it would advance the narrative of information as a weapon and of the media as its carrier. While important, these issues could be dealt with as the cyber crimes that they either are or aren't, as the case may be. But introducing the notion of propaganda and covert influencing into the international peace and security arena would be dangerous. Given the danger of linking questions of free expression and censorship to those of national security, the term "cybersecurity" needs to be either finally defined within an international context or kept as far away from international security discussions as possible.

This should not be terribly difficult, for two reasons. First, the term "cybersecurity" is not an officially acknowledged or defined term within the UN. The commonly used term, "ICT security," is itself a compromise. From its first draft resolutions in 1998, Russia has consistently advanced "information security" as the operative term, a term also used by China and many others in the Cyber-sovereignty bloc. This was a rather cunning gambit: as we have seen, "information security" is indeed the technical term for much of what is today commonly included under cybersecurity, but it also has consistently been misrepresented in a policy context. The policy use term by Russia, China, and others clearly goes beyond the international standards organization's definition of securing the confidentiality, integrity, and availability of information to also include its *use*. It clearly implies that the use of information to wage "psychological attacks" against a nation—which explicitly includes "foreign propaganda," terrorism, and indeed anything that bothers the ruling elite—is a matter of information security and national security. Therefore, the common-use political term advanced by Russia and China has nothing to do with the original technical term "information security."

Because Russia, among other Cyber-sovereignty advocates, has managed to steer the common use term "information security" away from its technical origins, the term probably cannot be recaptured. The term "cybersecurity" would be acceptable to these countries only if the barrier to "bad content" remained weak or indeed fell completely—an excellent reason for Free Internet governments to not push for its adoption. Instead, these governments should consider advancing another term in this context that has an equally specific meaning to the technical concept of information security but is as of now uncontaminated by political use: "data security."

Data security is commonly dealt with as a subset of information security. The differences between the two terms are difficult to pin down, because data security does deal exactly with the same questions of confidentiality, integrity, and availability of data. At best, it can accurately be said that information security is further reaching and includes protecting information irrespective of its medium; information security applies as much to protecting secrets on paper as it does to protecting them on a computer network system. This ambiguity between the two definitions is a good thing, because it may leave room for much-needed compromise.

In 2015 and 2016, there were the clear beginnings of a reinterpretation of the term "data security" to include it in a wider setting. An interview on Federal News Radio featured a number of American government information security professionals specifically debating the difference between "cybersecurity" and "data security." While many of them agreed that a great deal of overlap existed between the terms, only the former head of

US-CERT, Ann Barron-DiCamillo, actually addressed the question directly. For her, data security was clearly a subcategory of cybersecurity and was intended to provide guidance for those who were struggling to secure all of their information, when only some of it was truly critical and needed highest-level protection. Data security, according to this interpretation, was intended to identify and protect only the most critical of all data and keep it, as needed, confidential, available, and safe from unwarranted changes. The focus on data security is also very much in line with some of the most important norms of state behavior agreed on within the UN GGE. The norms against interfering with critical infrastructure or hindering the work of CERTs are much better applied within a data security, rather than a cybersecurity, context. The data security approach counters the consistent attempts of the Cyber-sovereignty advocates to push toward an arms control agreement for cyberspace. As mentioned before, the idea of a cyber-weapons treaty is probably a hopeless and misguided venture. Besides the problem of enforcement, it could easily be extended to include non-kinetic effects without too much difficulty—meaning that in some not-too-distant future social media platforms like Reddit and Facebook or even the *New York Times* could be classifiable as weapons. The focus on data security allows, however, the prospect of a treaty to be reexamined, and two options are possible.

First, the concept of "digital weapons" is possible (if still not necessarily desirable), because the reconceptualization of the topic around the C-I-A triad tightly constrains what "malicious use" can mean. This would open the door to proper international peace and security negotiations in the vein of the Non-proliferation Treaty, the Helsinki Accords, or even the bilateral US-Soviet strategic arms reduction talks. Even a digital weapons convention (analogous to the Biological Weapons Conventions) is possible, as long as the topic is constrained to data security. The ability to properly describe a "digital weapon" would be crucial for this domain as well and would effectively close the door on any attempt to define "bad content" as a weapon.

Second and even more interesting, it allows the international law and in particular the law of armed conflict specialist to more explicitly investigate C-I-A breaches against data and their implications, allowing certain inter-operations to be pushed forward and others to be safely buried. For instance, the current interpretation of *jus ad bellum* favored by the West can very well be tied to the overall notion of data security. The fact that other *jus in bello* issues, such as the status of proxies or irregular forces, cannot be easily addressed is actually no loss; I personally believe a literal interpretation of the present guidelines is the best defense against abuse.

Data security also adds another much-needed perspective to the debate: the role of data protection, or the regulations and standards needed to shield the data of individual human beings from unlawful use. Data protection does not play a major role in the political-military environment, first because national security concerns usually override it, and second because the objects of foreign espionage (although not domestic) are usually completely without any data protection rights. The legal requirement of the NSA to refrain from collecting the data of Americans (unless specifically mandated to do so) is tied to the legal fact that foreigners (outside the United States) have effectively no protection whatsoever. While this is certainly correct from a purely legal standpoint, different interpretations of human rights documents notwithstanding, it is politically and arguably morally misguided. The intent of the Obama administration, announced in January 2014, to limit the information collected on non-US persons (meaning that there will be limits, not that these limits are particularly stringent) is a clear reflection of this urgent political need.

Finally, data security helps address several interesting institutional ideas that have been mentioned in the context of political-military cybersecurity. For a number of years, there has been discussion among cyber pundits that has sometimes approached farcical levels: What kind of international organization do we need for cyber? While the standard non-state response has been "none," this has not stopped the deliberations, and they are not uninteresting. The most popular models have included looking at a potential FATF (Financial Action Task Force) for cyber, or a WHO (World Health

Organization) for cyber, or even an ICAO (International Civil Aviation Organization) for cyber. Exactly what these organizations would do was never clear until recently.

One of the more interesting proposals in this space is an "attribution and adjudication council" for cyberattacks. While it was at least partially a Chinese proposal, it has been picked up by some private-sector entities (including Microsoft) and does have some support in Western Europe and elsewhere. The different sides have supported such a proposal for different reasons: Western supporters hope it will provide more naming and shaming of Cyber-sovereignty campaigns, while those countries may be hoping that more Western cyber spying will be revealed. One of the largest problems with this approach to date was the danger that cybersecurity attacks could be slowly reinterpreted to include the "bad content" that is such a significant concern for the Cyber-sovereignty advocates.

Focusing on violations of data security alone will limit this threat. A new data security investigation council could be directly formed from the private sector—maybe even largely funded by it—and could either include its own in-house team of technical specialists or be completely dependent on outside investigators from major companies, or, perhaps most promising, a hybrid of the two. Countries that would wish to secure their attribution efforts could directly task this council with investigations into alleged state-supported cyber activity and would have the ability to provide them with classified intelligence as well, although there would have to be some fancy legal footwork to make sure that private companies would not derive an unfair commercial advantage from these briefings. The deliberations of such a council could then be used as evidence within international adjudication efforts; for instance, a finding could play a crucial role when trying to impose punishment sanctions within the WTO framework. Such a council could also be the home of legal experts who would investigate issues of surveillance/bulk collection and data protection, given the urgent need for clarity on how bulk collection can be performed in a manner that is in accordance with human rights. If this attribution council manages to deliver authoritative work in both technical and legal contexts, then a future version could even see such a council be commuted into something akin to a multistakeholder version of the International Atomic Energy Agency (IAEA), a body that today also is entrusted with its own research and monitoring missions. It is equally possible, however, that instead of a cyber IAEA we would benefit from something like an Amnesty International or Human Rights Watch for cyber. Either path—or even both—could be promising.

The second dimension of supporting cyber stability includes cyber crime, economic affairs (including trade), and cyber capacity building. While it may seem counterintuitive to include issues of law enforcement and development (that is, international aid) under the same thematic umbrella, this pairing reflects existing practice: one of the main duties of cybersecurity capacity building is assisting developing countries in building up their own defensive structures, such as computer emergency response teams, but also widening access to the Internet to those who currently have little or none. Economic affairs is also the context for discussions on protecting critical infrastructure, a wide-ranging effort that also involves non-UN bodies, such as the OECD. Finally, large content providers and intermediaries, including social media companies like Facebook and Twitter, play a significant role in trade conversations as well as law enforcement ones, the majority of which also do not occur under a direct UN mandate.

The Budapest Convention on Cybercrime is currently the only wider international agreement focusing on law enforcement cooperation regarding cyber crime. It has faced significant resistance from countries outside Europe, but there are hopes that an additional adjustment to the convention may persuade at least some of these countries to eventually sign it, or at least implement it. This is to be welcomed, because one of its key advantages—that it resolutely concentrates on facilitating law enforcement cooperation and does not try to define cyber crime in any way—will remain the only workable approach to any future cyber-crime agreement. This also allows not only governments but also private enterprise to find ways of interacting on subjects where there is no "double illegal" status, in which something that is a crime in one country is not illegal in another. This will also have to address issues related to social media use as well as "bad content" in all its variations—from pornography to incitements to terrorism—two issues of paramount importance for not only Cyber-sovereignty governments but also many of the crucial "swing states."

The "bad content" issue is, as noted earlier, one of the most persistent challenges for Western governments, which face continual accusations by Cyber-sovereignty nations that not only do they ignore their concerns regarding specific types of content, such as "terrorist incitement," but they host it as well. The only way around these issues has been to concentrate on the instrument of law enforcement cooperation and highlight that such cooperation should be necessary only where there is a "double bad" violation in both jurisdictions. This would certainly apply to issues of standard cyber crime, such as fraud, and the underlying creation of botnet infrastructures. While botnets have a clear relevance for the political-military environment, because much of cyber crime can sometimes be employed by state actors as a tool, it is vital to effectively firewall the cyber-crime discussions from those related to political-military issues so as to avoid the inclusion of any kind of "bad content" discussion. As was described earlier in this book, "cyber terrorism" as a concept is likely to remain a highly contentious point: the Western view is that it effectively describes acts of terror (with kinetic effect—that is, death and destruction) carried out with cyber means, while the Cyber-sovereignty governments want a much wider interpretation. The proper place for this discussion is within the counter-cyber-crime environment. It will not be possible to ignore this topic completely, because the interests of many of the "swing states" are very much toward issues of bad content and the terrorist use of the Internet, and need to be taken seriously by Western governments, if they are not to lose these votes in the future.

The issue of "bad content" has already largely been dealt with on a new bilateral and corporate level—that is to say, in interactions between governments and "intermediation platforms," like Facebook. The French scholar Frédérick Douzet argues that the easiest way for government and law enforcement to interact with these companies is through—or in conjunction with—civil society organizations. She says in an interview that "these companies are much more comfortable dealing with the civil society groups in establishing rules on hate speech and dealing with radicalization than with government," especially on problematic issues such as incitement to violence. Over the next couple of years, it may be possible to provide wider guidance for governments wishing to expand this type of public-private collaboration. The expansion of the Budapest Convention could, for instance, include recommendations on standard practices for how these interactions with such critical companies can be managed. Also, governments could encourage civil society organizations to work together with social media outlets in addressing the burgeoning use of fake news and outright propaganda.

New legal instruments may also provide the best way to deal with issues surrounding encryption. Currently, the American debate is largely stuck between the demands of some law enforcement supporters to provide legal back doors to encryption products to ensure acceptable access and the concerns of business and civil rights campaigners in protecting privacy at all costs. The argument of those in law enforcement is that there is no physical feature that counts as a legal-free zone, where the writ of government has no meaning and where it is not expected to be able to gain access. They therefore demand that the same must be possible for cyberspace-related data, which they often equate with a safe or vault. The counterargument of those in favor of encryption is that encryption is the glue of the new economy and that undermining it in any way not only creates a full-fledged security risk that cyber criminals may gain illegitimate access but also will lower the trust in the technology (and therefore the benefit) across the board.

For me, a better argument would equate encryption not with a safe that law enforcement must have access to if needed but rather with the human brain. As a general rule, the information that is stored in the brain cannot be extracted against that person's will using, for instance, drugs or torture. Instead, what it is possible to criminalize is a person's resistance to providing that information. Today, it is already possible to jail someone in the United States for failing to provide his password, although the law is still a bit nebulous. As draconian an approach as this may seem, mandatory decryption orders may be the best and safest way to deal with the conundrum of encryption and legal access.

Another key issue pertaining specifically to developing economies is the rising field of cyber capacity building. Often termed "cyber*security* capacity building" in the context of security issues, it recognizes two critical elements simultaneously: first, that ICT is critical for developing economies' growth, and that growth can be endangered through cyber crime, and, second, that combating global cyber crime requires strong local law enforcement partners with the skills needed to cooperate in international investigations. As I have argued in a report prepared for the Norwegian government, even though CCB is only a small part of overall overseas development assistance (that is, international aid), this is likely to increase drastically in the coming years. A key way in which aid organizations can assist governments in the developing world is by supplying budgetary support instruments that would allow local cybersecurity experts to be not only trained but also paid by foreign donors—and according to a different pay scale than if they were funded by local government. Establishing a functioning CERT, or even police forensic unit, in African countries can often meet the challenge that as soon as the professionals are trained up, they leave for jobs in the private sector where they can earn not slightly more but up to twenty or thirty times as much as in the public sector. A short-term solution may simply be for donor nations to pay the salaries of these experts at levels more comparable to their private-sector peers. There are a number of government-oriented frameworks that already deal with

CCB. One of the most prominent is the 2015 Global Forum on Cyber Expertise, a large fund that is effectively intended to help cover the expenses for cybersecurity training, besides other tasks.

The CCB component is often considered a subcomponent of the larger question of ICT development for economic growth, and in part this is already well established in pure technical terms. For instance, the World Bank actively finances broadband development—often considered directly relevant to economic growth—all across Africa, with three projects alone accounting for many hundreds of millions of dollars of World Bank funding. These sums are truly astronomical and show that ICT is a top priority for development. Safeguarding this development, however, requires CCB, and it can be hoped that at least 10 percent of the sums dedicated to ICT and broadband development could be raised to deal with cybersecurity issues.

The development of connectivity is certainly a task not only for governments. Both the private sector and civil society are active as well, although in very different ways. Google has often stated its interest in developing high-flying balloons that would deliver wireless connectivity to broad reaches of the planet where there is not even standard electricity. Facebook offered to help provide low-scale connectivity for free in India but was widely criticized given that this connectivity would largely force the users to use Facebook-approved products. The work of civil society is very often much less spectacular but at least as important. Packet Clearing House, which bills itself as a nonprofit research institution, also directly supports countries in setting up new Internet exchange points, key access points to the Internet. In 2013, it announced that it had helped set up and run around one-third of the world's 350 IXPs and therefore provides an essential service to development, albeit a much less flashy one.

The significance of cyber capacity building is not only a matter of financing the growth of the Internet and Internet-related business, or even providing a measurable impact on the GNP of these countries. Over a billion humans will be joining the Internet in the next five to ten years, and the type of experience that they have will largely depend on their ability to feel secure in this ecosystem.

The third dimension toward supporting the stability of cyberspace is Internet governance. As has been pointed out at length in this book, Internet governance regimes and their related processes are the true custodians of the core of the Internet. These actors are not states, and states, which have acted as the ultimate free riders in cyberspace, have the least to offer in this discussion. A principal fallacy of many Cyber-sovereignty advocates but also representatives of swing states is that the Internet governance system as a whole can somehow be subordinated to governments. Even if this outcome were desirable, it would be impractical: the efforts of those individuals volunteering their time to build the Internet cannot simply be decided by fiat. The delicate multistakeholder balance is already under threat, however, not only by government encroachment and attempts to push ICANN and other organizations toward security but by simple "crowding out": both governments and large private-sector corporations have greatly increased their participation in this domain and, by raising the bar for participation, are slowly squeezing out the voluntary civil society members. Thankfully, however, this is largely a matter of funding: civil society can most likely continue to perform its stated role if liberal democracies and like-minded corporations, as well as ICANN itself, can be persuaded to invest substantially in their weakest but most vital sibling. A thriving civil society remains the best insurance policy against a subversion of the Internet by those forces wishing to recast it as a tool of control. As of the writing of this book, Internet governance may be set to embark on a new hopeful era. It needs to be reinforced nonetheless if this path is to be ultimately successful.

"Internet governance is over as a topic," a senior European diplomat claimed at a meeting in the spring of 2016. "There is nothing more to discuss." This assessment, while not something I or many others would agree with on its own, was nonetheless understandable. In the last few years, the wider ICANN community has undertaken a mammoth review process and in the summer of 2016 was about to enter a new era, if the US Congress did not try to block the transition of the IANA contract (which authorizes changes to the root zone file, the basic telephone book of the Internet) to the new, reformed ICANN body, which the Department of Commerce agreed to do in the summer of 2016. Many of the fixes are already under way due to the reform of ICANN and its hoped-for assumption of full responsibilities for the IANA contract.

"Cybersecurity" has never been a very popular term in Internet governance circles. Both interpretations of it—international security and cyber crime—invoke negative connotations of government's exercising its ultimate right over force to dominate these discussions. Nonetheless, Internet governance has been dragged into these debates. Following the Snowden revelations, the policy side of the Internet governance community came under enormous pressure from its grass roots to take a stronger stance on data security given the US bulk intelligence collection programs. This had little to do with ICANN's remit or indeed its capabilities, but the pressure was immense—even if it abated somewhat following the US government's announcement to give up IANA in March 2014.

ICANN has long resisted pressure to become more involved in combating cyber crime. Not all of the pressure to cooperate came from the Cyber-sovereignty states; Western police forces also clamored for a more open ear to their concerns. In 2009, ICANN itself seemed to be encouraging this process by joining a discussion on "cyber safety," a term that is usually identified with protecting minors online. From this small start for a supposedly clearly positive cause, ICANN has been invited with greater frequency to participate in a number of causes: combating child pornography, protecting intellectual property, and working to prevent illegal drug sales. While it has largely succeeded in halting its slide down this slippery slope, ICANN has sometimes stumbled in resisting such entreaties.

In my mind, there is little question that registries (those organizations that assume responsibility for names in a slice of the Internet, like .org, .com, and country codes) have some role to play in law enforcement, and especially the registrars (those entities that are licensed by registries to re-sell domain space, like the company GoDaddy, which resells .com space). I do not think that ICANN's role, however—with perhaps the very small exception of helping to draft the specifications surrounding the registra-tion of Internet addresses—should be based on extensive cooperation with law enforcement, for no other reason than that it does not have this man-date from its stakeholders. In a separation-of-powers context, it should be free to set the laws of the Internet freely, subject to the restrictions imposed on it by its stakeholders.

ICANN does have a security role to play, a very important one that is tightly framed—namely, as it says as part of its core mission statement, "Internet security, stability and resiliency." ICANN and the assorted orga-nizations that are tasked with this critical project of "Internet security"—of literally keeping the domain name system running and contributing to the other key protocols that form the nervous system of the Internet—already have a mammoth responsibility. As has already been described in this book, this responsibility is far-reaching, and ICANN should not be spread any more thinly; indeed, distractions may make a potential cyber catastro-phe, such as the widespread failing of the DNS and therefore all routing on the Internet, more likely.

Keeping ICANN independent of law enforcement issues is only part of the challenge. With the introduction of generic domain names, like .white, .wisconsin, and .wine, a huge amount of trouble descended on ICANN—as well as a lot of cash. The ability of some entities to claim restrictions—for instance, for country or city names—was limited. This was a good thing, but it also left a lot out. Brush fires emerged everywhere there was a con-flict of interest. When, for instance, the online retailer Amazon purchased the domain .amazon, the response from South American interests was in-tense: How could an American company own the name of one of their most significant geographic features? France even went so far as to make the battle for .wine an issue of EU diplomacy.

These interventions had little effect but did illustrate the need that ICANN has to avoid a content-judging role. While ICANN made a great deal of money from the sale of the new domains, as a nonprofit operation it finds its options on how to spend the money fairly limited.

The abundance of cash that ICANN collected in recent years initiated a large-scale discussion of what to do with that money. In 2013, I commented at length in an Internet governance publication that the best use of this money was also one of its most urgent: investing and funding the civil society that underpinned it.

The greatest challenge to Internet governance as it stands now—and its test for the future—is to uphold a true balance of power between the three stakeholder groups of government, private sector, and civil society. While on the face of it civil society is still responsible for most of the critical functions in Internet governance, the pressures from both states and corporations are immense due to one simple matter: resources. Since 2010, the proliferation of various Internet governance meetings worldwide means that only the most well-endowed civil society bodies can truly continue to play active roles in this space. Corporations and governments, on the other hand, are happy to invest a rising number of personal resources in contributing to this space. Still, while both Western governments and the private sector are often vocally committed to civil society and the multistakeholder approach, their increased engagement bears the real risk of smothering civil society completely. The key allies of the multistakeholder approach are at risk of crowding out their weakest member.

This challenge is all the more acute given that civil society is by no means geographically diverse: it overwhelmingly includes members from the West and Free Internet countries, the richer, developed world. While they previously accounted for over 90 percent of Internet users, the rapid growth of Internet access in the emerging world means that this balance is shifting, and these voices are increasingly underrepresented. At least as important, the narrative of an unrepresentative ICANN community has long been the standard of those wishing to reap support from the "swing voters," and it is not completely wrong. The developing world, critical voices in the future of Internet governance, is often not able to leverage the human capital to participate in both policy and technical Internet governance.

It is critical that sums dedicated to civil society participation be massively increased, across the board in both political and technical domains. Much of these funds could probably come from ICANN directly, if its stakeholders decide that this is a critical mission. But sponsorship by both government and the private sector could also easily be encouraged—for instance, by making such donations tax deductible where national laws on philanthropic giving allow for this. It is not just a question of more travel money being made available to those who know where to apply for it. It requires a much more ambitious program of providing educational scholarships, institutional support, long-term advocacy position, and, yes, travel money to allow individuals to build up meaningful careers in this space; indeed, some of the more established individuals in this space call themselves "Internet public servants," a term that I believe is worthy of support in every way. Due to the "crowding out" by greatly increased government and private-sector participation in Internet governance, there is an urgent need for proactive efforts by the very same stakeholders—the government, the private sector, and the established parts of civil society—to reenergize the professionals of the global civil society and help them maintain their role as both figurative and literal key holders of the Internet. The noted expert (and former ICANN board member) Wolfgang Kleinwaechter has also recommended that a fourth category—that of the academic and technical research community—be added as distinct from civil society. This approach has benefits as well as dangers—while it neatly sidesteps the issue of defining what a "civil society actor" includes, it also, in my mind, potentially undermines the very concept of self-legitimization that is so important to the entire Internet, including the concept of civil society itself.

Securing the multistakeholder approach as the future of Internet governance may be one of the most significant aspects in ensuring that we never reach a dark web future. It is the only way to ensure that governments or private corporations cannot reform cyberspace to their liking, but also that the Internet as we know it today remains the most attractive of all possible networked cyberspace worlds—and not dark, illegal, and positively criminal nets that may replace it if the encroachment becomes too great.

In order for these different dimensions to properly do their job, they need to be held independent from each other, both as an insurance policy against co-option and to be effective in their day-to-day work. This does not mean being ignorant of each other's concerns, agendas, or even epistemic language. In fact, this mutual knowledge is critical: it not only prevents them from developing contradictory norms of practice that work against each other but also interferes with attempts of some actors to effectively exploit this ignorance and spread disinformation.

The problem of competing norms being developed by different parts of the wide cyberspace ecosystem was addressed previously. A snapshot illustrates the problem: while all major regimes will address the need for crisis communication networks, they will implement them differently, and consequently a number of crisis communication networks exist side by side. The question can easily arise in a major incident of which of these networks to use: the US-Russia cyber hotline? The OSCE communication network? The Meridian contact list? Or the INOC-DBA system (the first real voice-over-IP network, which connects those managing the major autonomous networks of the global Internet), which was built and maintained by the technical community exactly for this purpose? While some may think that this abundance is actually redundancy—and therefore a positive—I think there exists an equally likely threat of confusion at a critical time. The solution is not to pare down these and other networks, because this would remove the benefit of redundancy. Instead, the best path is to make sure that these various instruments are aware of each other during all stages of their planning and implementation processes.

The watchword here is norm coherence, not norm convergence. The disparate parts of the cyberspace ecosystem, which often have only the dimmest awareness of the existence of the other norms, let alone their plans or intent, need to greatly increase their mutual awareness to better facilitate their work. There are different options for how to best accomplish this in the short run. The easiest way to implement it is the blue-ribbon approach, the inception of high-level commissions staffed by authoritative and knowledgeable people with legitimacy in their respective fields. These commissions are key to the urgent mission of mutual awareness. But because they are commissions and their duration and membership are usually limited to a span of some years, a larger, more long-term solution will be needed.

It's useful to return to the example of environmental diplomacy, the origin of much of the modern Internet governance interpretation of the multistakeholder approach. Both spheres require scientific and authoritative advice from experts to political decision makers on how to best avert possible disaster.

One of the best examples for this standing body may be the Intergovernmental Panel on Climate Change (IPCC), established in 1988 by a group of national governments led by the United States. Despite having the word "intergovernmental" in its title, and even if its greatest weakness may be the ability of governments to edit its scientific decisions, the IPCC is a scientific body. In fact, many perceive the IPCC as a failure in light of the need of its scientists to accept government edits to their scientific conclusions. Still, the IPCC has played a very important role in outlining the threats of climate change and its likely consequences and bringing these concerns to a much wider audience. It may be worthwhile, then, to examine the idea of setting up an IPCC for cyberspace stability, with one critical difference: it would have to be a multistakeholder body. This entity could adopt many of the IPCC's structures, such as multiple working groups and chairs on various topics. Experts from across the multistakeholder spectrum—governments, businesses, and academics and researchers of civil society—could take a longer and closer look at the aspects of global cyberspace that most contribute to cyber instability. These experts could not only provide final and authoritative judgment on a number of technical and legal issues that are still far from being resolved but also provide, through their own epistemic communities, the basis for keeping their own constituents and stakeholders aware of the workings in other parts of the cyberspace ecosystem, or regime complex. Constituted as a multistakeholder rather than as an intergovernmental entity, it would also help concentrate the minds of both policy and business leaders on what decisions they will need to make in the future. Otherwise, the complexity of the challenge of achieving a stable cyberspace may well overburden everyone: the single-issue expert, the generalist political or business leader, and especially the average global Internet user.

Chapter 17

AN END-TO-END WORLD

F or many of my generation, the "end-to-end principle" is more than simply a significant network science standard with core relevance to the Internet. It is something close to magical in its application outside the realm of computer networks as well.

The simplest explanation of the e2e principle is that the critical work in a network should occur at the margins rather than in the center, to maximize efficiency. This means that the entire growth of the Internet has been determined by actions at its end points: the rise in the Internet-using population in a certain locality, the types of services they access, and the products and services they themselves develop to be used on the Internet. In all cases, the end user is more important than the network nodes in between. The network does not determine how it grows; the users do. And that means that the Internet does not really change behaviors, but that the end nodes change the Internet—and those end nodes are not only the academics and hobbyists of yesteryear but, increasingly, big business and government as well.

The e2e principle thus assumes the most democratic, most perfect type of network possible. In such a system, users determine which features in the network are priorities—security? reliability? privacy?—and their preferences would force changes to the shared components of the Internet.

The e2e principle is still alive and well. Besides playing a major role in securing some form of "net neutrality" in the United States and Europe (which limits the ability of the telecom companies to dictate which content users can view), the e2e principles have proved a vehicle to address security concerns. Increased hand-wringing about surveillance has led to increased development of encryption products and privacy services at every level. Worries about cyber crime and cyber espionage have already had a notable effect on the behavior of both consumers and governments.

The very definition of the network in the e2e context outlines what most today consider obvious: the Internet is a public good, a resource that is available to all. Public goods do suffer one particular danger, however: that of the free rider who wishes to reap the benefits of a network without investing in it.

The free riders on the Internet are governments. No matter what their ideological orientation, governments worldwide have benefited from the Internet, socially and economically, without having to contribute much in return. Even worse, they are often happy to exploit this domain to the largest extent possible, often for internal and external security purposes that actually serve to undermine the Internet.

Areas where governments can do their part to protect this public good certainly exist. In 2015, the notion of a state-led defense of the "public core" of the Internet started to gain traction. I fully support the idea that the core protocols of the Internet deserve special protection. There are different ways to accomplish this, but overall governments would need to not only refrain from harming or hijacking these services but also invest in their continued development.

The second part of the "public core of the Internet" notion goes further, and the original Dutch proposal specifically mentions "infrastructure." I find this very intriguing. Does this mean the root zone file? Or all the root zone operators? Or perhaps even the large IXPs themselves? The clear implication here is that we are actually stepping beyond the boundaries of a "public good" and entering the wider discussion of the "global commons"—for as soon as we say "infrastructure," we also say "rivalrous" (in that access may be blocked and not available to all).

In historic terms, a commons refers to land that was communally held (in England, for instance, by the local parish) and endowed with certain communal using rights such as mowing hay or grazing livestock. While it is a term closely connected to English common law, in fact many preindustrial societies in Europe as well as Asia had similar arrangements, even if there were substantial differences in actual execution. In modern-day usage, the idea of a commons manifests itself in the notion of a "common-pool resource," as defined by Elinor Ostrom as something that all have access to and the use of which is difficult to limit—a "rivalrous but nonexcludable good" in economic terms. The challenge is of course that a resource that belongs to all is accordingly exploited by all—until it is irreversibly gone. In modern-day terms, the most obvious example for this would be overfishing—say, within the North Atlantic—but historical contexts can be even bleaker than the collapse of present-day fishery stocks. As Jared Diamond shows in his book *Collapse*, rampant exploitation of common resources (in particular wood) has repeatedly led to the collapse of entire premodern societies. This trend, first noted in nineteenth-century Britain and later picked up and expanded on by the ecologist Garrett Hardin, has been called "the tragedy of the commons."

The discussion of this so-called tragedy of the commons has always been highly politicized. Some on the political left have suggested that it has been appropriated as a tool of neoliberal economists keen on prioritizing private ownership over communal ownership and who to this end have greatly exaggerated the historic propensity of communal ownership to fail. Interestingly, some on the political right have claimed the opposite, saying that the narrative of a "tragedy of the commons" is a warning that government will seek to impose some sort of regulation on otherwise free enter-prise. Hardin himself has tried to walk the discussion back a bit: the tragedy was not the commons per se but the "unmanaged" commons. It is therefore important to note that the famous "tragedy of the commons" argument may be historically inaccurate as to its specific example but that its crucial distinction—whether the common-pool resource is managed or not, by ei-ther religious or cultural injunction or international treaty—is nonetheless meaningful.

The late 1950s saw many attempts to introduce various components of a "global commons" into international treaties. These included the Antarctic Treaty as well as the first negotiations on the UN Convention on the Law of the Sea (UNCLOS), which itself was based on the seventeenth-century legal concept of the freedom of the seas. This trend accelerated after the scare of the Cuban Missile Crisis. The Outer Space Treaty (1967), whose goal was to limit the militarization of space, became the first treaty to di-rectly invoke a new formulation for the commons principle, which became known as the "common heritage of mankind." The adoption of this princi-ple, with slight variations, continued into subsequent agreements (such as the Moon Treaty) well into the 1980s.

Considerable debate exists as to whether or not any kind of legal con-cept of a global commons will prove effective in practice. Some argue that once a state—presumably, one big enough to be able to shrug off interna-tional opprobrium—actually sees a clear benefit in the exploitation of a common resource, it will pursue it. According to this logic, the idea of the global commons may be doomed.

On the other hand, the ability of governments to recognize common binding resolutions to face commonly accepted dangers has been proven. Examples range from the worldwide banning of substances toxic to the global ozone layer by treaty in 1985 to the global Kyoto Protocol on emis-sion reductions and indeed the COP21 Paris agreement on combating cli-mate change.

The most meaningful model for a global commons for cyberspace is the

UN Convention on the Law of the Sea. Its effectiveness is arguably tied to its inclusion of gradients of state sovereignty—such as "territorial waters" or "exclusive economic zone"—that satisfy the urgent needs of states to claim some slice of the territory, be it the sea or the Internet, as their own. There are also a raft of rules regarding safeguarding the freedom of navigation, prevention of pollution, environmental protection, and many other issues that, in their design, could be transposed to cyberspace as well. For instance, the UNCLOS component dealing with environmental protection would seem to be a good approximation of data protection, and the components dealing with piracy on the high seas could be useful in defining international cyber-crime acts. In fact, UNCLOS seems to offer so many hints for an overarching yet not excessively stringent framework for regulating at least state behavior in cyberspace that it is worth asking why it has failed to attract the attention of policy makers. It may simply be that many of the international law specialists who have previously had the most to say on cyber conflict dislike treaty law per se. Or perhaps there is an awareness of the risks of seeking to set up an international convention for what may be working well on its own.

The Industrial Revolution gave birth to concrete ideologies that soon came to play a key role in the most recent chapters of the perpetual struggle between states. It led to a polarization of much of the world between two competing power blocs, blocs that at their height were led by superpowers that each alone had the ability to effectively end human civilization and that were able to find a balance of terror most aptly defined as mutual assured destruction.

The information revolution, it is often said, has not yet reached this stage. Today, there is no ideology close to the equivalent of Marxism-Leninism, there is no long-suffering industrial proletariat that can function as an agent of mass political change, and there are no governments that have wholly subscribed to a system of subversive world revolution that directly threatens to undermine the national sovereignty of individual governments. And, of course, there are no superpowers to promote this ideology.

This is certainly not the view of all governments in the world. Some would argue that in fact the Internet has given rise to an implicit ideology—one that clearly diminishes the role of states and raises that of the private sector and civil society, threatens the political stability of many governments by insisting on the free flow of information, and therefore limits governments' ability to control the information consumed by their citizens. Finally, it leaves not only the economic and social welfare but also the very national security of many countries dependent on infrastructure and services that they do not control. And one nation, in particular, seems set to benefit more than others from this ideology and its very practical repercussions.

The argument I've just outlined is not only one that authoritarian governments articulate publicly but also one that some civil servants of the allied group among Western nations have raised in private. Some of these government officials, who valiantly fight for the multistakeholder approach in public and turn down every coy suggestion made by the Cyber-sovereignty bloc and others, are often disagreeing with their own instincts. How is it possible, a European diplomat and apparent stalwart member of the Internet Freedom bloc said to me privately, that governments are supposed to effectively accept the primacy of individual companies such as Facebook and Google, surrender their ability to control their part of the Internet to a small NGO resident in California, and on top of all this accept that a bunch of unelected engineers tinkering in their spare time can literally just hum and change the future of this ultracritical infrastructure on a whim? These civil servants are simply obeying the orders of their political leaders, who have internalized the notion of a Free Internet, rather than always believing it themselves. At a cyber conference held in 2016 at MIT, one of those engineers, sitting on a panel, somewhat smugly suggested that everyone else simply had to accept various strange civil society rules of the Internet as inherent to the reality of its creation. As he said, "We built it;

therefore, it's ours." This led one attendee to shout angrily, "You are not above the law!"

F. Scott Fitzgerald is credited with the line "the test of a first-rate intelligence is the ability to hold two opposed ideas in the mind at the same time, and still retain the ability to function." The sentence could have been written about Western cyber diplomacy, which is seemingly beset with contradictions. On the other hand, first-rate diplomats are also supposed to live up to Fitzgerald's dictum, and in any case it is possible that these apparent contradictions are not as meaningful as they are often made out to be. It is also important to avoid the recency bias and not make too much of our most immediate observations, rather than looking at long-term developments.

It is perhaps a good idea to take a couple of steps back and take a historic view on the rise of cyberspace as a key factor in international affairs. From one perspective, we may simply be witnessing a continuation of the last great ideological battle of the twentieth century carried over to the twenty-first, where the Internet today is nothing more than the physical manifestation of an ideology often referred to as neoliberalism, a space in which government has been marginalized for the sake of ideology. Seen through this lens, everything we are experiencing today is merely the result of the 1990s deregulation and privatization wave in the United States that included the Internet.

Besides not completely agreeing with this analysis, or its implied outcome, I think we need to go further. If we are truly to understand where the Internet fits within a larger narrative, I think we should take a bigger step back. The challenge is to resolve how exactly the current Internet governance method, with its strong emphasis on a multistakeholder approach, can best be explained in broader historical terms. I find two narratives somewhat helpful in thinking through this issue.

The first is that the Internet arose in a relative power vacuum left by states. For whatever reason—be it intentional or through carelessness—governments' lack of interest in the Internet in its formative years allowed it to stumble through childhood and awkward adolescence to explode onto the wider economic scene in the beginning of the 1990s, dressed as the World Wide Web and ready for a rock-star career. While the Web turned out to be the career path of the Internet, its core attributes—such as a lack of security and a consistent emphasis on trust—were not really conducive to its role as a tool of global power. Nonetheless, despite—or perhaps because of—this utopian DNA, the Internet shot to fame with new users, products, and services. As it enters middle age, however, the Internet's preferences and circumstances are changing.

What is certainly true is that the Internet was never intended to be a critical infrastructure, let alone carry *other* critical infrastructures. A decade or more ago, it was not unreasonable to say that if you, an average user or even a government, wanted to engage in this space, you needed to adhere to the rules of the club, be it the dominance of the non-state sector, the end-to-end principle, or other hallowed precepts. Because the Internet and cyberspace were an "opt-in" and voluntary construct, it was your choice to join and then accept the inevitable restrictions of the domain without much right to demand that your views be considered. Today, it is different: the Internet is a basic utility and an essential component of everyday life. You could try to opt out—to do without the Internet entirely—but that is an extreme position; it would be virtually impossible to remove yourself from cyberspace entirely (that is, to ensure that there is no data on you held anywhere).

Because the Internet is now a basic need for modern populations, the hobbyist engineers who invented and built the Internet cannot, in all good conscience, continue to insist that they serve as its only rule-making constituency. In this narrative, long-absent governments are the legitimate representation of those interests, and their increased involvement in the multistakeholder approach is therefore not only warranted but welcome. For the fun-loving Internet has grown older and acquired dependents— quite a lot of them—and to do this job well requires the support of other institutions that it might have previously scorned.

The second narrative is a little different. From this perspective, the Internet did not simply manage to exploit a temporary crack within the edifice of state power—due to disinterest or ideology—and grow as a result of this historic accident. Instead, the Internet itself is part of a large-scale transformation of political power away from established hierarchies to— well, it depends on whom you ask. According to Joseph Nye in his 2004 book, *Soft Power,* the process of power diffusion means that it is a question not of whether, for instance, the West is in decline and the rest on the rise but of which actors—be they corporations, civil society, or international organizations—are gaining power instead and under what circumstances. Thomas Friedman echoes this perspective in his Globalization 3.0 theory in his 2005 book, *The World Is Flat.*

I largely agree with both Friedman's and Nye's assessments on the diffusion of power—with one exception. In cyberspace, it seems apparent that it is possible for governments to lose and gain power simultaneously, even over the same subject (such as an individual citizen). In fact, another notion of Friedman's, the super-empowered individual, describes this new reality, though in my view this super-empowerment can be shared by any organization that is able to fully reap the benefits of cyberspace for its purposes. It seems that everyone—states, corporations, and non-state actors— has been emboldened by cyberspace and that at the moment there is no clear loser, at least in a relative sense and at least not yet.

The respected cryptologist and security thinker Bruce Schneier once postulated a future of a "feudal Internet." In it, the average user would be forced to take refuge from the predations of state and non-state attackers alike and would seek the protection of the new feudal cyber lords: states or companies (or other entities) that were best equipped to protect the poor user from attackers. Schneier postulates that the only ones who could possibly remain "free" in this near-dystopian future would be the digital Robin Hoods, experts whose cyber field craft would enable them to survive where less knowledgeable users would immediately be victimized.

Schneier points in an intriguing direction. It would seem to be primitive historical determinism to argue that there is an overall trend toward the flattening of hierarchies that makes it inevitable that flat power structures will prevail. Inevitable, after all, can take a while to unfold. A lot can happen in the meantime.

If the multistakeholder system is to truly be an advancement of democratic society, we need to be aware that this advancement is by no means inevitable. The dark web of matrix lore is inevitably one dominated by evil megacorporations, but an Orwellian *1984* scenario is also possible if authoritarian governments have their way. Even if they are only able to inflict this fate only on their own populations and not on the global Internet, this would be a tragedy for the world.

To keep the Internet free, we need to keep Internet governance free, and doing this is not an easy task. As the ability of states to attack each other in and through cyberspace using both kinetic information operations and, even more worryingly, concepts of information warfare increases, so will their implicit or explicit claim to be the final arbiter of the information domain in all its forms. This is a trap liberal democracies must not fall into, and it will require some effort and resources. But the costs in terms of compromise and expense are worth it. For the multistakeholder system may indeed be the worst system by which to govern the Internet—except for all the rest.

CONCLUSION

n a speech to industry and policy leaders in February 2015, President Obama described cyberspace as being like the Wild West. The analogy seems straightforward: in both the settling of the Old West and the colonization of cyberspace, internecine conflict and lawlessness are mirrored by the hopes of prosperity and freedom and above all the conquering of great distances and the nearly visceral sensation of endless space and new horizons. President Obama also immediately showed how limited that comparison was, however, and how much more cyberspace is than simply the occupation of some uncultivated pasture. For while the settling of the Old West was a risk-free proposition for the United States as a whole (if not for the settlers themselves), the growing dependency on cyberspace poses significant dangers not only for individuals and corporations but for any modern connected nation. "It's one of the great paradoxes of our time," Obama said, "that the very technologies that empower us to do great good can also be used to undermine us and inflict great harm."

Unlike the physical reaches of the western United States, cyberspace is still being settled. Although already four billion human beings are now online, that is only half of the population of the world, and what's more, those who are connected spend only about, on average, thirty hours per week actively interacting with the Internet—less than a third of our waking moments. The rise of always-on interactions, presently epitomized in the smart phone, means that in the not-too-distant future this metric will become meaningless: we will effectively always be on the Internet and interacting with cyberspace. In less than a decade from now, cyberspace will be such a dominant domain that the idea of being "online" or "connected" will be meaningless, and cyberspace will be consistent and all pervading.

Further, cyberspace is still growing, and changing, in a way no physical realm can. There are no natural grand canyons or high plains in cyberspace; everything that happens there is a result of code and human intentions. Cyberspace is fully artificial, and its landscape, its basic geographic features, its laws, can be altered by man. As a result, we are able to transform the very space we seek to occupy: imagine a Wild West where the cowboys and the Indians and the bandits and the cavalry can raise mountains and divert rivers nearly at will, and even use them against each other. And while government has until the recent decade or so had only a cursory interest in the magically terra-forming nature of cyberspace, those days are over: the cavalry has arrived to the cyber Wild West, but it is far from certain that it is welcome or beneficial.

The danger is that the spotlight of the global discussion has consistently managed to drift toward security topics. Liberal democratic governments are under real pressure to "do something" in cyberspace, and this is a conversation authoritarian governments are eager to have. For by engaging in the discussion, governments have, justifiably but perilously, ventured onto a slippery slope. The increased focus on international security issues as being an issue for governments alone explicitly threatens the primacy of the multistakeholder of governance, and therefore also the best hope that the Internet as a whole does not succumb to the baser wishes to surveil and control. If there is a catastrophic cyber incident in the near future—with substantial damage to lives and property—then we can expect that governments' inclination to take on a more prominent role in the Internet will become very difficult to resist. A collapse or fundamental dissolution of the multistakeholder approach would amount to something similar to the three branches of a country's government suddenly all being dissolved into one branch. As much as this would be a crisis in a modern democracy, this would be at least as serious a development for the Internet itself.

The suggestions outlined in the last two chapters account for the wishes, and the real need, of states to have their say in cyberspace as it relates to international security. We may need to set up new bodies associated with the United Nations to accommodate these wishes very soon. But the implicit as well as explicit function of these bodies is crucial: they need to support, and not undermine, the wider principle of the multistakeholder management of the Internet resources that clearly puts the non-state actors—the private sector and civil society—in a position of leadership. The glue that binds these actors together is trust.

Trust is a tangible resource in cyberspace. It is hard coded into its most basic protocol development and has therefore clearly played a role in the extremely successful growth of the global Internet to date. It may even be the most decisive factor in the Internet itself. The power of individual actors on the Internet, not only states, but also single corporations and even individual people, is so extensive that there is a basic need to trust in each other's good intentions. For instance, the ability to reroute a small segment of global Internet traffic, to put yourself in the middle of a massive amount of data and hence spy on or manipulate it at will, is not only within the realm of states; thousands of individuals outside government have this power as well. More encouragingly, tens of thousands of individuals outside government play an important and non-malicious role in supporting cybersecurity in its truest sense: protecting networks and data from all offensive action, be it on the part of criminals or even their own governments. And hundreds of individuals are truly essential to the security of cyberspace, finding and sharing the most significant vulnerabilities and trying to form policies and processes to ensure that the leviathan of government does not succeed in suppressing individual freedoms online.

Trust-based networks are sometimes dismissed by government officials who think that the civilian version of trust is limited to looking someone deep in the eye and giving a firm handshake. But it goes much deeper than that. The norms among InfoSec professionals have given birth to extremely complicated and balanced processes for handling data and engaging in sensitive tasks, like renewing the keys of the Internet. Anyone who has any doubts as to how serious these non-state professionals take their task needs to only look at the specifications and elaborate ceremony for root signing (needed to authenticate identities and secure Internet connections) hosted by this very community.

But trust has long been an intangible feature of cyberspace as well. Prior to the Snowden revelations on American intelligence gathering, civil society and the cyber industry felt an implicit amount of trust in the workings of their liberal democratic governments. It was commonly accepted that as bad as the Russians, the Chinese, and others might have been in the casual violation of confidentiality or the conduct of true cyberattacks, the democratic governments of the United States and Europe would not play by these rules, would show a higher level of restraint. Civil society researchers and private-sector product managers shared the basic expectation that the Western powers, including their intelligence agencies, fundamentally wanted or understood the need for all-around improvement in defense, for everyone. NSA coders were invited to provide their input on key encryption protocols and the like in the belief that they would naturally help improve defenses and not actually weaken Internet security itself.

The flood of spontaneously declassified PowerPoint documents, often nearly indecipherable to even more experienced eyes, showed that this was simply not the case. Following the disclosures by Snowden and many other unexplained leaks, the trust in government of the InfoSec community, both civil society and business, was undeniably weakened. Silicon Valley has taken a much more combative stance versus US national security interests, and the global civil society has practically fallen over itself in its rush to re-move Internet governance functions from the possible influence of the US government. Western governments—which on the whole try to encourage the cooperation of their non-state actors instead of coercing it, often bru-tally, as the Russians and Chinese do—cannot do without the support of these actors. Obama's attempts to address this sudden and extreme trust gap in various public speeches and policy pronouncements in the final years of his presidency were notable and sometimes brilliant. After years of ago-nizing, the White House—unlike Congress and the FBI, but with the back-ing of the Department of Defense—came out in favor of strong personal encryption in 2016. Obama went so far as to announce reforms on "cyber-spying" and new guarantees regarding how personal identifiable informa-tion of both foreigners and US persons would be treated. There was even a large step taken to limit the growing marketplace for zeroday vulnerabili-ties and to order the NSA to share these newly discovered attack roots with the wider InfoSec community wherever possible. All of these steps were more than most members of that community could have hoped for. And yet it has still not been enough, and the trust between key parts of the multi-stakeholder coalition is still nearly as shaky as it was when the NSA leaks first received widespread attention. This lack of trust is in the interest only of those who wish to dissolve the multistakeholder model completely.

Though many may question Secretary of Defense Ashton Carter's com-parison of the Snowden leaks to 9/11, there shouldn't be any doubt that the momentous disclosures by Snowden and others massively undermined the trust that Western governments—in particular the United States—need to be able to interact with their international and domestic partners. The gen-eral response to these disclosures has been highly negative, even though a remarkably large portion of the American population did not find them particularly troubling. Some observers (and many of my colleagues) have claimed that besides being completely naive, the general media assess-ment of US wrongdoing was entirely inaccurate. The disclosures actually showed—to those who could understand them—how much conscientious care the US government had put into a globe-spanning spy network and how essential legal and even human rights issues are to it. The leaks even included information on the extent to which the NSA prosecuted its own analysts when they exploited their spy toys for personal use. Just as the leaked US State Department cables on WikiLeaks revealed little scandal but actually a well-functioning bureaucracy, some have maintained that the NSA leaks have shown the same for American intelligence collection. The challenge is simply that unlike the plain English used by American diplomats writing classified cables, the NSA documents are virtually impenetrable to even experts in related fields. And even if one understands the documents themselves, one hardly grasps the context of these capabilities.

Much confusion exists as to what these vaunted cyber capabilities are, what they are intended for, and how they can impact our daily lives. This is why large sections of this book are concerned with explaining how the dreams of states—most notably the United States, but also its often-perceived adversaries in Russia and China—are lived in practice. We cannot understand what is necessary to safeguard cyberspace stability if we do not understand those very actions that seek to undermine it—and, most important, the differences that they represent in underlying ideologies. There are significant differences in how and why states operate in cyberspace.

The struggle for the free Internet—more or less what it is now—and the hypothetical dark web of government domination that the Cyber-sovereignty faction favors is very real and very tangible. Neither the Free Internet nor the Cyber-sovereignty faction treats the prospect of war lightly, whether that means traditional war or cyber war. Nonetheless, a significant cyber confrontation—with full kinetic-equivalent effects—is very possible, especially if they are close rather than clearly over the threshold of armed attacks, and therefore acts of war according to international law. Already state adversaries are inching up to an imaginary line in the sand, and already the consequences of some espionage attacks are so significant as to incur hundreds of millions of dollars in US government spending and to cost billions to the economy as a whole. If this is cyber peace, anyone can imagine that a real cyber war would be significantly worse.

In theory, the cybergeddon scenario of country-crashing cyber conflict should be a common nightmare for all. As unlikely as it may seem, such a real cyber war is certainly no less probable than a nuclear exchange was during the Cold War, and my guess is that the threat is many orders of magnitude larger. This estimation is shared by many in the policy-making community. For instance, in 2014 the Pew Research Center polled around sixteen hundred experts worldwide as to the chance that by 2025 there would be "a major cyberattack that will cause widespread harm to a nation's security and capacity to defend itself and its people" and ranging in the tens of billions of dollars in damage to life and property. Sixty-one percent of the respondents stated that this was likely to occur—an alarming measure of confidence in such an outcome.

There is a substantial movement in disarmament departments of the major cyber powers to somehow initiate a strategic discussion about significant cyber conflict to deter a full-blown cyber clash. The hope is that, like the deterrence brought on by the mutual assured destruction of the nuclear standoff, each side is equally afraid of such an exchange. Achieving the Cold War nuclear balance of terror, as it was known for many decades, required much fine-tuning of American and Soviet Union strategic forces and agreed-upon protocols to limit the threat of inadvertent escalation. Generations of diplomats, engineers, and military and intelligence officers toiled away through much of the twentieth century in Geneva, Vienna, and elsewhere to maintain this fine balance of threats and ensure that neither side had an incentive to seek a first strike. All were joined in the common belief that we shared one nightmare: the nuclear doomsday. The present discussion within the UN and bilateral frameworks is not too dissimilar and holds a common core element to it: like nuclear winter, the cyber winter would be equally threatening to all. No matter how different the positive hopes and dreams of cyberspace may be, all nations would equally share the nightmare of a total cyber confrontation. Thus the basic assumption. And I believe the basic assumption is wrong.

The lack of symmetry is not simply due to the combined desire to avoid a full-scale cyber conflict, but is also because the entire discussion of security in cyberspace inadvertently favors the government mandate, sometimes even to the exclusion of the other stakeholders. It therefore already implicitly diminishes the multistakeholder model, simply because many of the other actors are excluded from the wider discussions of state cyber power. If there is a catastrophic cyber incident in the next few years—even if not the full cyber mushroom cloud of a true "Cyber 9/11" or "Cyber Pearl Harbor"—then the urge even of Western democracies to fully co-opt this space will be intense. As I hope I have illustrated in this book, the prospect of a *1984*-type dystopian outcome is already quite tangible in some countries, and this trend will only increase.

The best worst case may not sound too bad. If the Free Internet and the Cyber-sovereignty factions cannot find a workable détente, then the best we can hope for is the splitting of the global Internet into wholly national Internets, potentially even complete with their own routing and address structure. In truth, we are already halfway there: as research by the Internet pioneer (and senior Google executive) Vint Cerf and others shows, the global Internet is already largely split into different identifiable segments. But in a more extreme version, the World Wide Web would simply cease to be, and individual communications between the various internets would probably be slow and unreliable. While you might think, "Well, I don't send e-mail to China anyway," that is not the only significant interference there may be. Global trade and manufacturing have adapted to a fully functioning global Internet, and a serious reconfiguration of data traffic that a truly divided Internet would require would have significant implications here as well. It would also likely make the Internet a lot more expensive and decrease bandwidth for everyone despite the creation of new broadband infrastructure.

Worse than this, however, is the implication of what this split Internet world would mean. What about the people on the other side of these newly lowered cyber curtains? They would be effectively trapped in a total information bubble unlike anything we have ever seen in modern history, and probably explored only within the context of dystopian fiction. Imagine a North Korean–style population-wide truth distortion bubble, apply that to the modern Internet, and multiply that by the hundreds of millions of lives it affects, and the outlines of the danger become clear. If a major state does break away from the Internet entirely and forms a hermit cyber world, we will be faced as democracies with the essential question of whether this is morally acceptable. No matter what our decision, the outcome will certainly be a further danger to world peace and a rise in the prospect of all-out war between feuding states.

And this is only the best worst outcome. The worst of the bad outcomes is that liberal democracies somehow fumble on the slippery slope of discussing international cybersecurity and Internet governance and through a series of tiny but nonetheless momentous decisions undermine the present delicate balance of Internet governance and shift it to states. There will be no thunderclap if this happens, nor rising mushroom cloud of doom, and the effects will not be instantly visible. But within a relatively short period of time after these events, less than a decade perhaps, Western democracies will have finally succumbed to the narrative of information conflict and in the name of security will accept measures and restrictions that will directly convert the Internet that we know to an object of control. It is equally possible that Western governments may seek to compromise and, in desperation, turn to the private sector to save them from this terrible choice and simply risk another dystopian nightmare, with the Internet reduced to tiny highly controlled walled gardens at best or indentured workhouses at worst. In neither dark future, the panopticon society or the corporate matrix environment, will liberal democracy as we know it have much of a chance. How can it, when all the magical power that cyberspace has bestowed on so many becomes concentrated in the hands of a few? How will elections proceed fairly if a true civil discourse accessible to all no longer exists, if the companies or political parties can influence even the individual voter with exceeding precision, from the news that is consumed to the results that are displayed in Internet searches to the censoring of comments shared on social media? If fake news and covert influencing is able to advance the conceit of fake relativism, a plurality of truths of equal validity, then how can there be trust in any larger societal contract? Can democracy in any conceivable form really continue under such circumstances at all?

This slow-moving collapse of democracies and all that it entails is hopefully not likely to happen. But it is undeniably possible. While it is by no means certain that the response of democratic governments to a cyber calamity will be to abandon the multistakeholder model and succumb in the name of security to a state-led system, I think the stakes are simply too high to ignore or dismiss these possibilities as morbid fantasies.

There is a virtual cyber veil of esoteric detail and complexity that has traditionally made this topic difficult even for experienced policy makers to grasp. Such a broad spectrum of essential topics and themes exists within the realm of cyberspace studies that it is not surprising that even the most knowledgeable individuals in their particular segment of cyberspace can be completely ignorant of developments occurring within a closely related field. The old cyber hippies of Internet governance don't often meet the spies and soldiers who play the game of states online—and vice versa. Even among the good guys—those in theory fighting on the same side for similar values—there is little common understanding of each other's dreams and each other's nightmares.

The only way that we will get trust back into the wider issue of cybersecurity or data security is if these different communities at least try to understand each other's wishes and fears. We don't need to have the same dreams of cyberspace. But those of us who share the vision of the Internet as an agent for civilizational change need to understand what the sum of our fears is and what we can do about it.

EPILOGUE

History, the statesman and thinker John Gardner once said, never looks like history when you are living through it. And history can unravel very quickly in cyberspace.

This book started many years ago, written largely in 2015 and early 2016, and was conceived of many years before that. It was always threatening to be overrun by events, but I did not think that its core message—the dangers to liberal democracies of the rise of an Internet increasingly marked by state informational conflict—would lose any of its relevance. What I did not expect was the rapid escalation not only in the cyber domain, but in the larger information warfare space as well—a development that I have routinely described as being more threatening than the more overt danger of kinetic-equivalent cyber warfare. While the deployment and use of some governments' information warfare tactics has been apparent to researchers and practitioners in the field for many years, it had remained, as a political concept, resolutely outside wider public discourse. With the deluge of public reporting in 2016 on the purported Russian attempts to influence and delegitimize the US presidential elections, few of the educated public can be left in any doubt as to the reality of this practice as a tool of statecraft. While I do not think the US election was effectively turned around by these actions alone, public sentiment was significantly influenced, and remains so after the election.

The specific tools of Russian information warfare included the attempts at influencing public opinion through "strategic leakage" of hacked e-mails of the Democratic Party. This avenue of attack was able to take root only due to a simultaneous and I think even more pernicious weakening of the overall trust in the broader and mainstream media. Some of this weakening was clearly intentional—the deployment of paid-for trolls and support for Russian allies in the American (and European) far right. But at least some (or even most) of the purported "fake news" and similarly harmful memes that seemed to ricochet through social media, and which have been given significant weight by journalists and commentators, were most likely not directed by any foreign information warfare campaign. Many of the crazier rumors and stories, items that even put the so-called "birther" lie to shame, were not produced by Russian info war spooks. According to some truly excellent journalistic work by a number of outlets, they were at least partially fabricated by a couple of dozen well-educated and hyper-fluent teenagers in a small town in Macedonia. These kids—often younger than eighteen—had been trying to make money feeding Facebook and other social media outlets for years, creating over 150 "news sites," whose only job was to function as "click bait" that easily attracted readers, even if only for some moments—moments that meant advertising income of many thousands of dollars a month when it went well. And there was a clear market to be fed in the "red" (read: Republican-leaning) Facebook bubble, where the company's algorithms reliably delivered up a menu of content it thought would appeal to its readers. While I can't discount that even these Macedonian teens were somehow co-opted by a foreign nation's information warriors, who undeniably pulled as many different levers of covert strategic influence in the US election as they could grab, I think it is most likely that the general truth about the fake newscasters in the Balkans is simply what it seems to be. It would essentially be a rerun of a familiar story: a bunch of teens had hacked cyberspace, only that this cyberspace was social media and the hack was pure social engineering.

Cyber, as I said in the beginning of this book, used to mean sex. Now it means war, and increasingly, it means information war. However, the success of this new breed of state or non-state hackers—for that is essentially what many of these producers of fake news are—is possible only due to the susceptibility of their target population. While a small proportion of the US public was always ready to believe that the black helicopters of the new world order were just waiting to seize them, the ability of tens of millions of the electorate to be so thoroughly confused and subtly discouraged by these often totally fake news items, be it for profit or politics, says at least as much as the state of American public awareness as anything else. Other social media–addicted populations, especially in northern Europe, have been the target of specific information warfare campaigns, laced with fake news, fake commentators, and even very real intimidation. But the national resilience of some of these populations and their systems seems to have at least partially helped inoculate them, at least so far. Why, then, has the same failed to occur in the United States?

For me, the same question has a simple counterquestion: why are so many Americans ready to think the worst of their political and civil society institutions? A running Gallup poll on the trust in government shows a continual decline in the United States, and, depending on the exact numbers you prefer, trust in all aspects of the US body politic is pretty dismal. In June 2016, only 36 percent of respondents had confidence in the general office of the presidency. As low as that is compared with polls in much of Europe, the number of respondents who thought that Congress was doing a good job was simply staggering: only 6 percent had confidence in it as an institution. It is hard to imagine that any political system can be left unchallenged when only 6 percent of an electorate thinks of its representatives in positive terms. Whatever the cause for this, it is clear that it is home-grown. No foreign cyber giant has somehow crossed the Atlantic (or the Pacific) and induced this weakness of trust in the US body politic, although foreign powers could well be enticed to exploit it. That exploitation wasn't hard, for the level of trust in the wider media was equally shocking: only about 20 percent polled had confidence in newspaper and media news.

However, the positive surprise for me is how rapidly the public awareness has developed in regard to the crash-course introduction to this new dimension of human conflict. The ability of the civil society and news media in democratic societies everywhere to respond to the so-called "fake news phenomenon" leaves me very hopeful that the technical vulnerabilities in the wider information ecosystem can be patched. Some of the potential topics are already being discussed, dealing for instance with algorithmic informational bubbles and the general workings of large social media organizations, and tempered with the need to preserve human rights and above all the freedom of speech. As a result, many thousands or even tens of thousands of new individuals will earnestly engage in this issue in the future and involve themselves directly and indirectly in the governance of this new domain of human behavior. Many more than that will have been warned by this seeming small detonation of info war, and will tacitly support the efforts of the civil society, industry, and government actors that have taken up the fight on their behalf. They will reinforce the battle taking place for the future of cyberspace and the free web, which is nothing less than the struggle for the heart of modern democratic society. It will not be a struggle that passes quickly—but just as singular individuals in previous decades made a crucial difference, we can all do so today.

Cambridge, Massachusetts, December 2016

ACKNOWLEDGMENTS

This book owes much to many people. I am grateful to my publishers at Penguin Press for taking on *The Darkening Web,* for no amount of academic writing prepares you for a trade book, especially one that is done in the margins of a somewhat normal working life. They showed admirable patience. And my warm thanks to my editor, Emily Cunningham, for shepherding me around the process, and for being very generous in time—and indeed page count. All of this wouldn't have been possible without my agent, Markus, whose insights into the market were invaluable. Both Hugo and Louk are to be thanked for the invaluable support in the arduous and labor-intensive process of cleaning up the research notes and my own memory.

But the book really owes everything to the wider communities that I have had the great fortune to know and interact with over the last few years, and I am indebted to them all: the wider InfoSec community has truly remarkable individuals, who like all real hackers have an innate sense of responsibility and ethics that could not be explained well in this book. I am also indebted to my many friends and colleagues in this space. To the government officials and security communities, for their service and dedication, and for providing glimpses into their dragon world, and whose belief in a shared mission leads them to support even that which they cannot completely trust. The Internet governance community, whose great size and massive depth often speaks to the wisdom of crowds, and yet produces true believers of great intelligence and dedication. And, in particular, many of my esteemed colleagues working on international cybersecurity issues, who have provided more input than could be covered in citations and acknowledgments alone. The wide activity of this relatively small research community belies the vital normative policy-forming work done by experts in the government, the private sector, and that crucial civil society. The "traveling circus" of these experts at talks and conferences worldwide provides much more than academic exchanges, and it is a great privilege to be able to work alongside them. Many of these individuals, with storied careers in government service, academia, or simply being uniquely themselves, are my senior in every way, and deserve to have been able to write this book instead of me. I am especially indebted to Joe Nye—working with him at Harvard and receiving his guidance and support has been one of the most rewarding experiences of my life. My deepest thanks to Nigel Inkster, Jeff Moss, Sean Kanuck, Jack Whitsitt, Wolfgang Kleinwaechter, and Joe Nye for taking the time to review at least parts of the first draft at great speed, for even a hundred pages takes usually more than a few days. For that reason, any grievous errors of judgment or fact in the book are very simply mine and mine alone.

I am profoundly grateful to Nina for the endless support, and for enduring the equally endless suffering that a new author inflicts upon their significant other. Behind every such completed book is surely a greatly relieved spouse.

Most of all, however, I thank my mother, whose unceasing belief and endless support were at the very beginnings of this book. It therefore belongs to her.

NOTES

INTRODUCTION

4 the philosopher Marshall McLuhan: Marshall McLuhan is credited with the most prescient quotation of information warfare: "World War III is a guerrilla information war with no division between military and civilian participation," Marshall McLuhan, *Culture Is Our Business* (New York: McGraw-Hill, 1970), 66.

4 "an infowar arms race": Douglas Waller Washington, "Onward Cyber Soldiers," *Time,* Aug. 21, 1995.

6 the Cray-1 supercomputer: B. N. Malinovsky, *Computer Pioneers of CIS Countries* (International Charitable Foundation for the History and Development of Computer Science and Technology, 1995).

6 *The Dead Hand*: David Hoffman, *The Dead Hand: The Untold Story of the Cold War Arms Race and Its Dangerous Legacy* (New York: Doubleday, 2009).

8 The message triggered emergency survivability measures: *The 3 A.M. Phone Call: False Warnings of Soviet Missile Attacks During 1979–80 Led to Alert Actions for U.S. Strategic Forces,* National Security Archive Electronic Briefing Book No. 371 (2012).

9 for more than fifteen years: Bruce G. Blair, "Keeping Presidents in the Nuclear Dark (Episode 1: The Case of the Missing 'Permissive Action Links')," *Bruce Blair's Nuclear Column,* Center for Defense Information, Feb. 11, 2004.

9 "I came to appreciate the truth": Memorandum for the Chairman, Joint Chiefs of Staff, from General George L. Butler, Commander in Chief, US Strategic Command, Subject: Renaming the Single Integrated Operational Plan (SIOP), Sept. 2, 1992 (CONFIDENTIAL/declassified). This document was obtained through the Freedom of Information Act by Hans M. Kristensen, director of the Nuclear Information Project at the Federation of American Scientists, www.nonproliferation.org/wp-content/uploads /npr/142kristensen.pdf.

11 the effect of a large-scale electromagnetic pulse attack: When a thermonuclear device is detonated in outer space, its energy is converted into free electrons that, upon impact with the atmosphere, can literally fry unprotected electronics, from power grids to computers to cars. The effect is similar to—if profoundly worse than—what a bad solar storm could cause. There are increasingly alternate methods for creating a strong electromagnetic pulse blast. *Report of the Commission to Assess the Threat to the United States from Electromagnetic Pulse (EMP) Attack, Volume 1: Executive Report, 2004* (EMP Commission, 2008), accessed Oct. 26, 2016, www.empcommission.org/docs /empc_exec_rpt.pdf.

11 $6 billion in economic damages: J. R. Minkel, "The 2003 Northeast Blackout—Five Years Later," *Scientific American,* Aug. 13, 2008.

12 Google searches, for instance, have long: Eli Pariser, "Beware Online 'Filter Bubbles,'" TED, March 2011, accessed Oct. 19, 2016, www.ted.com/talks/eli_pariser_beware _online_filter_bubbles.

14 *"Governments . . . I come from Cyberspace":* John Perry Barlow, "A Declaration of the Independence of Cyberspace" (1996), accessed Oct. 26, 2016, www.eff.org/cyberspace -independence.

16 I have often talked about "cyber power": Alexander Klimburg, "Mobilising Cyber Power," *Survival* 53, no. 1 (2011).

CHAPTER 1: THE BODY OF CYBER

23 "cybersecurity" was introduced: Annalee Newitz, "The Bizarre Evolution of the Word 'Cyber,'" *Gizmodo,* Sept. 16, 2013.

24 "data is the new money": See, for instance, the reporter Kim Nash's comment on the purchasing of a social club by a large manufacturer, whose sole intent was to get hold of the precious membership data: twitter.com/knash99/status/755774237722443776.

24 "data is even more important": See, for instance, Chris Skinner, "The Future Is All About the Data," *European Financial Review,* June 28, 2014.

25 over three billion humans: *Global Internet Report 2015. Mobile Evolution and Development of the Internet* (ISOC, 2015), accessed Oct. 26, 2016, www.internetsociety .org/globalinternetreport/assets/download/IS_web.pdf.

25 the Internet economy itself accounts for: Matthieu Pélissié du Rausas et al., *Internet Matters: The Net's Sweeping Impact on Growth, Jobs, and Prosperity* (McKinsey, 2011), accessed Oct. 26, 2016, www.mckinsey.com/~/media/McKinsey/Industries/High%20 Tech/Our%20Insights/Internet%20matters/MGI_internet_matters_full_report.ashx; Mark Knickrehm, Bruno Berthon, and Paul Daugherty, *Digital Disruption: The Growth Multiplier* (Accenture, 2016), accessed Oct. 26, 2016, www.accenture.com/_acnmedia /PDF-4/Accenture-Strategy-Digital-Disruption-Growth-Multiplier.pdf.

25 An exabyte is one billion: Stephanie Pappas, "How Big Is the Internet, Really?," *Live Science,* March 18, 2016.

26 four thousand to five thousand times larger: Technically, the term "deep web" is a definite misnomer, because the Web is defined by the ability to access it using http, and a great amount of data is not reachable through http—let alone accessible to the average user.

26 the White House published one of the earliest: Presidential Decision Directive/NSC-

63, "Critical Infrastructure Protection," White House, May 22, 1998, accessed Oct. 26, 2016, http://fas.org/irp/offdocs/pdd/pdd-63.htm.

27 **"Cyberspace means the interdependent network":** National Security Presidential Directive/NSPD-54, Homeland Security Presidential Directive/HSPD-23, White House, Jan. 8, 2008, accessed Oct. 26, 2016, www.fas.org/irp/offdocs/nspd/nspd-54.pdf.

27 **"world behind your screen":** John Naughton, *A Brief History of the Future: The Origins of the Internet* (London: Phoenix, 1999), 311.

27 **"Cyberspace includes all forms":** *Cyber Security Strategy of the United Kingdom: Safety, Security, and Resilience in Cyber Space* (U.K. Office of Cyber Security and U.K. Cyber Security Operations Centre, 2009), accessed Oct. 26, 2016, http://webarchive .nationalarchives.gov.uk/+/http:/www.cabinetoffice.gov.uk/media/216620/css0906.pdf.

28 **famously described it as a "consensual hallucination":** William Gibson, *Neuromancer* (New York: Ace Books, 1984), 51.

31 **By 2018, all those data centers:** Yevgeniy Sverdlik, "IDC: Amount of World's Data Centers to Start Declining in 2017," *Data Center Knowledge,* Nov. 11, 2014.

31 **the total use of electricity:** James Glanz, "Power, Pollution, and the Internet," *New York Times,* Sept. 23, 2012.

31 **Official numbers for the Internet giants':** Jeff Paschke, "The Mega-datacenter Battle Update: Internet Giants Increased Capex in 2014," 451 Research, March 24, 2015.

31 **Google ran dedicated data centers:** "Data Center Locations" (Google, 2016), accessed Oct. 19, 2016, www.google.com/about/datacenters/inside/locations/index.html.

31 **Microsoft has reported:** "Microsoft's Cloud Infrastructure: Datacenters and Network Fact Sheet" (Microsoft, 2015), accessed Oct. 26, 2016, http://download.microsoft.com /download/8/2/9/8297F7C7-AE81-4E99-B1DB-D65A01F7A8EF/Microsoft_Cloud _Infrastructure_Datacenter_and_Network_Fact_Sheet.pdf.

31 **Amazon Web Services:** Timothy P. Morgan, "A Rare Peek into the Massive Scale of AWS," *EnterpriseTech,* Nov. 14, 2014.

31 **Facebook has three huge data centers:** Ingrid Burrington, "A Journey into the Heart of Facebook: How the 'Sharing' Company's Data Centers Reveal Its Values," *The Atlantic,* Dec. 2015.

34 **an interview in Andrew Blum's *Tubes*:** Andrew Blum, *Tubes: A Journey to the Center of the Internet* (New York: Ecco, 2012), 139.

34 **data that can be lost forever:** There is not much technical difference between an IXP and a data center; the only difference is that IXPs tend to be more carrier neutral: whereas Internet giants increasingly build data centers to manage their own infrastructure instead of renting racks and racks of servers, IXPs are carrier neutral and allow different providers to interconnect.

35 **computer standards that are relevant:** For a deeper look, consider the seven-layer OSI model; for an introduction, see http://computer.howstuffworks.com/osi1.htm.

36 **it was "trusting":** Jean Camp, *Trust and Risk in Internet Commerce* (Cambridge, Mass.: MIT Press, 2001).

37 **There are thirteen DNS root servers:** James Ball, "Meet the Seven People Who Hold the Keys to Worldwide Internet Security," *Guardian,* Feb. 28, 2014.

39 **The implementation of the e2e principle:** Marjory S. Blumenthal and David D. Clark, "Rethinking the Design of the Internet: The End-to-End Arguments vs. the Brave New World," *ACM Transactions on Internet Technology* 1, no. 1 (Aug. 2001).

39 This seemingly innocuous shift: In Europe, the debate took a slightly different form because, beyond no blocking or throttling rules, the European approach has historically been more lenient toward "specialized services." On June 30, 2015, the European Commission issued a fact sheet expressing an agreement that "all traffic will be treated equally," hence banning paid prioritization while at the same time allowing for "reasonable day-to-day traffic management according to justified technical requirements . . . which must be independent of the origin or destination of the traffic." See "Roaming Charges and Open Internet: Questions and Answers" (European Commission, 2015), accessed Oct. 19, 2016, http://europa.eu/rapid/press-release _MEMO-15-5275_en.htm.

39 there were reports that Verizon: Jon Brodkin, "Netflix Performance on Verizon and Comcast Has Been Dropping for Months," *Ars Technica,* Feb. 10, 2014.

40 This was the final chapter: The entire existence and rise of the present-day Internet greatly exceeded the expectations of the early Internet pioneers. Every growth spurt came as a surprise, at least to those engineers building it. The development of e-mail was one of those accidental leaps. The hypertext transfer protocol and the Web browser were constructed as afterthoughts, without anticipation of what could come next. Very seldom were iron laws set up with the intention that they define the future of the network: this was precisely a network that wasn't built with any particular purpose in mind other than routing packets. Code was drafted not on the basis of principles but on the basis of what made sense. For instance, one of the most important protocols on the Internet, the Border Gateway Protocol (BGP) used by IXPs to route traffic, was first thought of in 1989 as a short-term fix. Twenty-five years later, the BGP, despite its many security problems, has uninterruptedly been at the core of how we route our data, exceeding by far the expectations of Kirk Lougheed and Yakov Rekhter when they first drafted the protocol on cafeteria napkins over lunch. See Craig Timberg, "The Long Life of a Quick 'Fix,'" *Washington Post,* May 31, 2015.

40 "Data is the new oil": Perry Rotella, "Is Data the New Oil?" *Forbes,* April 2, 2012.

40 the world's Internet traffic: According to a 2016 report: *The Zettabyte Era—Trends and Analysis* (Cisco, 2016).

41 65 percent to 85 percent of all traffic: Jillian D'Onfro, "More Than 70% of Internet Traffic During Peak Hours Now Comes from Video and Music Streaming," *Business Insider,* July 12, 2015.

41 "network of networks which enables": Pierre-Jean Benghozi et al., *The Internet of Things: What Challenges for Europe?* (Paris: Maison des Sciences de l'Homme, 2012).

41 This number will grow to fifty billion devices: *Internet of Things: Privacy & Security in a Connected World* (FTC Staff Report, 2015).

42 invented by a Netscape engineer: Dominique Cardon, *A quoi rêvent les algorithmes: Nos vies à l'heure du Big Data* (Paris: Seuil, 2015).

43 Internet marketing already accounts: Ingrid Lunden, "Internet Ad Spend to Reach $121B in 2014, 23% of $573B Total Ad Spend, Ad Tech Boosts Display," *TechCrunch,* April 7, 2014.

43 "There's not a sharp distinction": Spencer Ackerman, "NSA Review Panel Casts Doubt on Bulk Data Collection Claims," *Guardian,* Jan. 14, 2014.

43 "are enough to uniquely re-identify": Yves-Alexandre de Montjoye et al., "Unique in the Shopping Mall: On the Reidentifiability of Credit Card Metadata," *Science* 347 (Jan. 30, 2015), 536–39.

44 **"Privacy is necessary"**: Eric Hughes, "A Cypherpunk's Manifesto," March 9, 1993, accessed March 1, 2016, www.activism.net/cypherpunk/manifesto.html.

45 **Bitcoin, which was invented in 2008**: Satoshi Nakamoto, "Bitcoin: A Peer-to-Peer Electronic Cash System," 2008, accessed Sept. 1, 2006, http://bitcoin.org/bitcoin.pdf.

47 **"Strong encryption is the cornerstone"**: Ellen Nakashima, "Tech Giants Don't Want Obama to Give Police Access to Encrypted Phone Data," *Washington Post,* May 19, 2015.

47 **the case of a murdered boy**: Devlin Barrett, Danny Yadron, and Daisuke Wakabayashi, "Apple and Others Encrypt Phones, Fueling Government Standoff," *Wall Street Journal,* Nov. 18, 2014.

47 **arguments that anticipated a 2016 standoff**: "Breaking Down Apple's iPhone Fight with the U.S. Government," *New York Times,* March 21, 2016.

47 **there have been repeated claims**: Tom Simonite, "Statistical Tricks Extract Sensitive Data from Encrypted Communications," *MIT Technology Review,* June 19, 2014.

48 **the self-named Dread Pirate Roberts**: "Undercover agent reveals how he helped the FBI trap Silk Road's Ross Ulbricht," *Wired,* Jan. 14, 2015.

49 **"All data leaks"**: Rick Falkvinge, "Collected Personal Data Will Always Be Used Against the Citizens," *Falkvinge & Co.,* 2012, accessed Oct. 19, 2016, http://falkvinge .net/2012/03/17/collected-personal-data-will-always-be-used-against-the-citizens.

49 **concept of digital labor**: Trebor Scholz, *Digital Labor: The Internet as Playground and Factory* (New York: Routledge, 2012).

49 **"Facebook isn't a charity"**: Evgeny Morozov, "Facebook Isn't a Charity: The Poor Will Pay by Surrendering Their Data," *Guardian,* April 25, 2015.

51 **"the physical network layer"**: Brett T. Williams, *Cyberspace Operations* (US Cyber Command, 2013).

CHAPTER 2: MIND OVER MATTER

55 **including the bus network**: John Christensen, "The Trials of Kevin Mitnick," CNN, March 18, 1999.

55 **Phishing comes in many forms**: Kim Zetter, "Hacker Lexicon: What Are Phishing and Spear Phishing?," *Wired,* April 7, 2015.

56 **large encryption company RSA**: Christopher Drew and John Markoff, "Data Breach at Security Firm Linked to Attack on Lockheed," *New York Times,* May 27, 2011.

56 **multinational gangs of hackers**: Brian Krebs, "Gang Hacked ATMs from Inside Banks," *Krebs on Security,* Dec. 22, 2014.

56 **stealing over $300 million**: David E. Sanger and Nicole Perlroth, "Bank Hackers Steal Millions via Malware," *New York Times,* Feb. 14, 2015.

57 **"massive insider trading ring"**: Matthew Goldstein and Alexandra Stevenson, "Nine Charged in Insider Trading Case Tied to Hackers," *New York Times,* Aug. 11, 2015.

57 **a large botnet can have hundreds**: According to the security firm Trend Micro, in August 2015 there were about 7.5 million computers active in botnets, which were controlled by an estimated fifty-five hundred "command and control" (C&C) servers. This number is probably much too low, because it depends on the reach of Trend Micro's own products (sensors) and does not include some geographies at all. Depending on the complexity and size of a botnet, each botnet can have between one and twenty C&C servers on average—meaning ten is a good number to work with,

indicating that there were probably around five hundred distinct botnets operating at this time, with an average size of 15,000 computers each. In fact, averages are only slightly helpful, because there are great differences in the visibility, sophistication, and function of a botnet that are often more important than its size. Some of the most advanced botnets use peer-to-peer technology, which means that there is no C&C server (although there is something called a super peer).

57 **The largest botnet:** John Leyden, "Conficker Zombie Botnet Drops to 3.5 Million," *Register,* April 3, 2009.

57 **As large as Conficker was:** See Karl Thomas, "Nine Bad Botnets and the Damage They Did," *We Live Security,* Feb. 25, 2015.

57 **Swiss army knives of cyberattacks:** A segmentation was conducted by the Honeynet Project (a "honeypot" is a computer that is intentionally allowed to become infected so as to infiltrate the network). It concluded that there are ten major uses for botnets. Drupal, "Uses of Botnets," Honeynet Project, Oct. 8, 2008, accessed Oct. 19, 2016, www .honeynet.org/node/52.

57 **links between spam operators and Russian organized crime:** Brian Taylor, "Spam Nation: Cybercrime and Spam Are Far Bigger Security Threats Than You Think," *TechRepublic,* Nov. 18, 2014.

57 **Spam remains remarkably profitable:** Back in 2011, a team of researchers at UC San Diego took control of a spamming botnet to estimate the money that it made, coming up with a first estimate of $2 million per year. Extrapolating, they concluded that spam could be worth up to $1 billion every year, even though these figures really are speculative.

58 **$38 an hour to execute:** James Griffiths, "Price of Website Disabling DDoS Attacks Falls to US$38 per Hour as Botnets Proliferate in China, Vietnam," *South China Morning Post,* June 12, 2015.

58 **$40,000 per hour to the defender:** Eduard Kovacs, "DDoS Attacks Cost $40,000 per Hour: Incapsula," *Security Week,* Nov. 12, 2014.

58 **Sophisticated DDoS attacks:** Nicole Perlroth and Quentin Hardy, "Bank Hacking Was the Work of Iranians, Officials Say," *New York Times,* Jan. 8, 2013.

58 **Indeed, the list of possible victims:** The Anonymous collective conducted attacks on Visa, Mastercard, and PayPal during Operation Payback in 2011 in retaliation for these companies withdrawing their services from WikiLeaks. See Sean Gallagher, "Anonymous Takes Down DoJ, UMG Websites—Attack on Whitehouse.gov Underway," *Ars Technica,* Jan. 19, 2012, and Jason Fekete and Ian Macleod, "Hacker Group 'Anonymous' Claims Credit for Federal Cyber Attacks," *Ottawa Citizen,* June 17, 2015, among others. In retaliation for the takedown of Megaupload.com in 2012, attacks were allegedly conducted on the NSA Web site in 2013, on the Canadian federal government's computer servers in 2015. Targets also included Nasdaq's Web site in 2012 (Edward Krudy, "Websites of Exchanges Nasdaq, BATS Hit in Online Attack," *Reuters,* Feb. 14, 2012) and a series of major US bank institutions, including Bank of America, Citigroup, Wells Fargo, and JPMorgan Chase, in 2013 (Perlroth and Hardy, "Bank Hacking Was the Work of Iranians, Officials Say").

59 **the world's "Cyber War I":** It is difficult to overestimate: Kertu Ruus, "Cyber War I: Estonia Attacked from Russia," *European Affairs* (Winter/Spring 2008).

60 **utilize some publicly available tools:** For instance, an attacker could use the XSS or SQLI method to gain access to the Web-facing part of the network and grab the MD5

hash of the user accounts. Using modern rainbow tables, one can decrypt by brute
force most five-character passwords in a couple of days.

60 **"guidance system of a cyberweapon"**: Pierluigi Paganini, "Zero-day Market, the
Governments Are the Main Buyers," *Security Affairs,* May 21, 2013.

61 **"the bullets of cyberwar"**: Ryan Gallagher, "Cyberwar's Gray Market: Should the
Secretive Hacker Zero-day Exploit Market Be Regulated?," *Slate,* Jan. 16, 2013.

61 **in Microsoft Word, Windows, and Firefox**: A groundbreaking article: Andy
Greenberg, "Shopping for Zero-Days: A Price List for Hackers' Secret Software
Exploits," *Forbes,* March 23, 2012.

61 **those vulnerabilities often remain unpatched**: Stefan Frei, *The Known Unknowns:
Empirical Analysis of Publicly Unknown Security Vulnerabilities* (NSS Labs, 2013).

61 **the French company Vupen**: Andy Greenberg, "Meet the Hackers Who Sell Spies the
Tools to Crack Your PC (and Get Paid Six-Figure Fees)," *Forbes,* March 21, 2012.

61 **US defense contractor Endgame**: Pratap Chatterjee, "How Hackers and Software
Companies Are Beefing Up NSA Surveillance," *Mother Jones,* Feb. 7, 2014.

62 **"the digital arms trade"**: "The Digital Arms Trade: The Market for Software That
Helps Hackers Penetrate Computer Systems," *The Economist,* March 30, 2013.

62 **That effort culminated in May 2015**: Industry and Security Bureau, *Wassenaar
Arrangement 2013 Plenary Agreement Implementation: Intrusion and Surveillance Items*
(Industry and Security Bureau, 2015).

62 **drain the market for zerodays**: Sean Gallagher, "CIA's Venture Firm Security Chief:
US Should Buy Zero-days, Reveal Them," *Ars Technica,* Aug. 6, 2014.

62 **US government disclosed parts of its VEP**: Andrew Crocker, "EFF Shines a Light on
the NSA's Plans for Disclosing (or Not) Software Weaknesses" (Electronic Frontier
Foundation, 2015).

63 **"It's not that we didn't think about security"**: Craig Timberg, "Net of Insecurity: A
Flaw in the Design: The Internet's Founders Saw Its Promise but Didn't Foresee Users
Attacking One Another," *Washington Post,* May 30, 2015.

64 **Cisco routers received an implant**: Dan Goodin, "Malicious Cisco Router Backdoor
Found on 79 More Devices, 25 in the US," *Ars Technica,* Sept. 16, 2015.

65 **programs to develop trust**: This includes industry programs such as the Trusted
Foundry program managed by the Trusted Access Program Office of the NSA.
"Programs for Business: Trusted Access Program Office (TAPO)." "NSA Offers a Wide
Variety of Programs and Opportunities Designed to Allow Companies to Partner with
NSA" (National Security Agency, 2016), accessed Oct. 20, 2016, www.nsa.gov/business
/programs/tapo.shtml.

CHAPTER 3: EVERYONE CAN BE A GOD

69 **the international standards body ISO:** "ISO/IEC 27033:2010+ Information
technology—Security techniques—Network security," accessed Oct. 20, 2016, www
.iso27001security.com/html/27033.html.

70 **a dozen definitions across different governments**: Alexander Klimburg, ed., *National
Cyber Security Framework Manual* (Tallinn, Estonia: NATO Cooperative Cyber
Defense Center of Excellence, 2012).

70 **"'cybersecurity' as a synonym"**: Joe Franscella, "Cybersecurity vs. Cyber Security:
When, Why, and How to Use the Term," *Infosec Island,* July 17, 2013.

71 **if we were to score cyber:** Dan Geer, "Driven by Data" (paper delivered at The Language-Theoretic Security (LangSec) IEEE Security & Privacy Workshop, May 21, 2015).

71 **"In some hacking circles":** Misha Glenny, "Tap Into the Gifted Young Hackers," *New York Times,* March 8, 2012.

72 **some of the most dramatic breaches:** These include the 2011 attack on the major defense contractor Lockheed Martin and BAE Systems (which lost secrets related to the 1.5. trillion-dollar F-35 stealth fighter jet program, and details on nearly two dozen other critical weapon systems), and even the Australian foreign intelligence agency had the blueprints of its new headquarters stolen—before it even moved in. See "Lockheed Martin Customer, Program, and Employee Data Secure" (Lockheed Martin, 2011), accessed Oct. 20, 2016, www.lockheedmartin.com/us/news/press-releases/2011/may/LockheedMartinCustomerPro.html; Sydney Freedberg, "Top Official Admits F-35 Stealth Fighter Secrets Stolen," *Breaking Defense,* June 20, 2013; and "China Blamed After ASIO Blueprints Stolen in Major Cyber Attack on Canberra HQ," ABC, May 27, 2013.

74 **CERTs are an omnipresent feature:** Some companies will maintain a SOC (Security Operations Center) or a NOC (Network Operations Center), depending on their focus and assets. Both of these commonly have the same role as CERTs.

74 **according to Gartner research:** Eduard Kovacs, "Global Cybersecurity Spending to Reach $76.9 Billion in 2015: Gartner," *Security Week,* Aug. 25, 2014.

75 **The legendary story of how Dan Kaminsky:** Joshua Davis, "Secret Geek A-Team Hacks Back, Defends Worldwide Web," *Wired,* Nov. 24, 2008.

77 **When, in 2011, Spamhaus blacklisted:** Brian Krebs, "Dutchman Arrested in Spamhaus DDoS," *Krebs on Security,* April 26, 2013.

79 **group of experts known as NSP-SEC:** Estonia suffered a debilitating cyberattack that some have proclaimed the first case of "cyberwar": John Arquilla, "Cyberwar Is Already upon Us, but Can It Be Controlled?," *Foreign Policy,* Feb. 27, 2012.

79 **"zero involvement, zero activity":** Peter W. Singer and Allan Friedman, *Cybersecurity and Cyberwar: What Everyone Needs to Know* (Oxford: Oxford University Press, 2014), 196.

80 **The line between offense and defense:** Joseph Nye, "Is Cybersecurity Like Arms Control?," *World Post,* May 17, 2016.

83 **a large plastic ball started to inflate:** "The Meaning of 'Hack,'" Appendix A: Hacker Folklore, Eric S. Raymond's Home Page, http://catb.org/jargon/html/meaning-of-hack.html.

83 **especially its system of tone dialing:** The movement started in the late 1960s with a young boy called Joe Engressia who had a perfect pitch and discovered that whistling a certain tone would either stop a phone call or allow him to make long-distance calls at no cost—all the more interesting because long-distance calls were pretty expensive then. Engressia is considered the father of the "phreakers," a group of people who started trying to reverse engineer the system of tone dials, exploiting any flaws they could discover to make their way in. One of the most famous phreakers, John Draper, was better known by his nickname "Cap'n Crunch": he discovered that a toy whistle in the Cap'n Crunch cereals generated the exact frequency unlocking AT&T's long-distance switching system, then started building "blue boxes" so that phreakers would be able to make free calls. Among notable phreakers were also Steve Wozniak and Steve Jobs, who made and sold those blue boxes long before they founded Apple

Computer together. Ron Rosenbaum, "Steve Jobs and Me: He Said My 1971 Article Inspired Him. His iBook Obsessed Me," *Slate,* Oct. 7, 2011.

83 **"love bug" caused anywhere:** There are a wide range of estimates for this virus, but Symantec estimates the worm's damage at over $10 billion. Sebastian Z, *Security 1: 1—Part 1—Viruses and Worms* (Symantec, 2013), www.symantec.com/connect/articles /security-11-part-1-viruses-and-worms.

85 **the FBI used a version of Metasploit:** Kevin Poulsen, "The FBI Used the Web's Favorite Hacking Tool to Unmask Tor Users," *Wired,* Dec. 16, 2014.

CHAPTER 4: RULING THE DOMAIN

87 **"If the Net does have a god":** The full quote reads: "GOD, at least in the West, is often represented as a man with a flowing beard and sandals. Users of the Internet may be forgiven for feeling that nature is imitating art—for if the Net does have a god he is probably Jon Postel." *The Economist,* Feb. 8, 1997, quoted in Andrew D. Murray, *The Regulation of Cyberspace: Control in the Online Environment* (Abingdon, U.K.: Routledge, 2007), 97.

88 **Postel ended what he described as a "test":** Jack Goldsmith and Tim Wu, *Who Controls the Internet? Illusions of a Borderless World* (New York: Oxford University Press, 2006), 45.

89 **The term "Internet governance":** Internet governance is explicitly defined as "the development and application by governments, the private sector and civil society, in their respective roles, of shared principles, norms, rules, decision-making procedures, and programmes that shape the evolution and use of the Internet." This is also the commonly used definition of the multistakeholder approach, making the two fundamentally inseparable. Internet Society, "History of Internet Governance," accessed Oct. 25, 2016, www.internetsociety.org/history-internet-governance.

90 **What initially started as a simple project:** The Web site of the world's first-ever Web server is available at "World Wide Web," CERN, 2008, accessed Oct. 25, 2016, http:// info.cern.ch/hypertext/WWW/TheProject.html.

90 **over 900 million hosts:** Matthew Gray, "Internet Growth: Raw Data" (MIT, 1996), accessed Oct. 25, 2016, www.mit.edu/people/mkgray/net/internet-growth-raw-data .html; "December 2015 Web Server Survey" (Netcraft, 2015), accessed Oct. 25, 2016, https://news.netcraft.com/archives/2015/12/31/december-2015-web-server-survey .html.

92 *Internet* **(with an uppercase *I*):** This differentiation first appeared in a 1989 IBM handbook, which summarized a number of preceding RFCs. It states: "The words internetwork and internet are simply a contraction of the term interconnected network. However, when written with a capital 'I,' the Internet refers to the worldwide set of interconnected networks. Therefore, the Internet is an internet, but the reverse does not apply." See Lydia Parziale et. al., *TCP/IP Tutorial and Technical Overview,* 8th ed., (International Business Machines Corporation, December 2006).

93 **Each AS is a set of routers:** Kirk Lougheed and Yakov Rekhter, *RFC 1267: A Border Gateway Protocol 3 (BGP-3)* (IETF, 1991).

93 **the collection of these forty-two thousand or so ASs:** Paul Krzyzanowski, "Understanding Autonomous Systems" (CS Rutgers—Internet Technology, 2016).

93 **From the start, the Internet was pushed:** For the most complete short history, see Barry Leiner et al., *Brief History of the Internet,* ISOC, accessed Oct. 25, 2016, www .internetsociety.org/internet/what-internet/history-internet/brief-history-internet.

95 **Internet Engineering Task Force:** Ibid.

96 **This quickly became the style:** Stephen D. Crocker, "How the Internet Got Its Rules," *New York Times,* April 7, 2009.

97 **An RFC in the year 2014:** Pete Resnick, *RFC 7282: On Consensus and Humming in the IETF* (IETF, 2014).

99 **"We reject: kings, presidents and voting":** David D. Clark, "A Cloudy Crystal Ball— Visions of the Future" (MIT CSAIL, 1992).

101 **the Clinton administration announced its intention:** Milton Mueller, "Dancing the Quango: ICANN and the Privatization of International Governance" (paper presented at the Conference on New Technologies and International Governance, Paul H. Nitze School of Advanced International Relations, Johns Hopkins University, Feb. 11 and 12, 2002).

102 **"coordinate, at the overall level":** "Bylaws for Internet Corporation For Assigned Names And Numbers | A California Nonprofit Public-Benefit Corporation" (ICANN, 2011), accessed Oct. 25, 2016, www.icann.org/resources/pages/bylaws-2012-02-25-en.

104 **"let the US give up control":** The Web site PolitiFact did an excellent job in summarizing both Ted Cruz's statement and lack of veracity. See W. Gardner Selby, "Ted Cruz Incorrect About Obama Giving Control of Internet to UN-Like Body," PolitiFact, Sept. 14, 2016, www.politifact.com/texas/statements/2016/sep/14/ted-cruz /ted-cruz-incorrect-about-obama-giving-control-inte.

104 **memorandum of understanding:** "Memorandum of Understanding Between the U.S. Department of Commerce and the Internet Corporation for Assigned Names and Numbers" (US Department of Commerce National Telecommunications & Information Administration, 1998), accessed Oct. 25, 2016, www.ntia.doc.gov /page/1998/memorandum-understanding-between-us-department-commerce-and -internet-corporation-assigned-.

104 **Affirmation of Commitments:** "Affirmation of Commitments by the United States Department of Commerce and the Internet Corporation for Assigned Names and Numbers" (ICANN, 2009), accessed Oct. 25, 2016, www.icann.org/resources/pages /affirmation-of-commitments-2009-09-30-en.

105 **Internet was a "CIA project":** Ewen MacAskill, "Putin Calls Internet a 'CIA Project' Renewing Fears of Web Breakup," *Guardian,* April 24, 2014.

105 **intergovernmental supporters, the multilateralists, or the Cyber-sovereignty:** William Drake, Vinton Cerf, and Wolfgang Kleinwächter, *Internet Fragmentation: An Overview* (Future of the Internet Initiative White Paper, World Economic Forum, 2016).

106 **Aligned against the Cyber-sovereignty nations:** "UK Contribution to NETmundial" (U.K. Department for Culture, Media & Sport, 2014), accessed Oct. 25, 2016, www.gov .uk/government/uploads/system/uploads/attachment_data/file/330739/UK _contribution_to_NETmundial.docx.

108 **called an "Internet Yalta":** Alexander Klimburg, "The Internet Yalta" (Center for a New American Security, 2013).

108 **"an Internet policy landscape":** Milton Mueller, "Are We in a Digital Cold War?" (paper presented at the GigaNet workshop "The Global Governance of the Internet," Graduate Institute, Geneva, Switzerland, May 17, 2013).

110 **"the information released by Snowden"**: Milton Mueller, "Do the NSA Revelations Have Anything to Do with Internet Governance?," Internet Governance Project, Feb. 19, 2014.

110 **"the big consequence of Edward Snowden's NSA leaks"**: "The Snowden Effect," *The Economist*, Jan. 24, 2014.

111 **keys to the Internet**: Charles C. W. Cooke, "Handing Over the Keys to the Internet," *National Review*, March 18, 2014.

114 **Code of Conduct for Information Security**: General Assembly letter 69/723, "Letter Dated 9 January 2015 from the Permanent Representatives of China, Kazakhstan, Kyrgyzstan, the Russian Federation, Tajikistan, and Uzbekistan to the United Nations Addressed to the Secretary-General" (UN General Assembly, 2015).

115 **highlight is the actual authorization of the HSM**: "DNSSEC Signing Service" (Packet Clearing House, 2015), accessed Oct. 25, 2016, www.pch.net/services/dns.

CHAPTER 5: PIN-STRIPED CYBER

121 **The fourth GGE report**: UN General Assembly A/70/174, United Nations Group of Governmental Experts on Developments in the Field of Information and Telecommunications in the Context of International Security (UNGA A/70/174, 2015).

121 **the United States managed to get consensus**: Ibid.

122 **The ability to define information**: For an excellent analysis of how the Shanghai Cooperation Organization Code of Conduct has changed in different drafts, see Sarah McKune, "An Analysis of the International Code of Conduct for Information Security," Citizen Lab, Sept. 28, 2015.

122 **inflicting simple "mental harm"**: Thomas Rid, *Cyber War Will Not Take Place* (Oxford: Oxford University Press, 2013).

123 **called "battlefield cyber"**: This is known under many different terms in the West overall, none of which are standard. In the United States, the official term for this, at least in the US Army, is "CEMA," or "cyber electromagnetic activities." Unfortunately, this term is not highly known even within the US government, let alone outside it, so I stick with the term "battlefield cyber" for clarity purposes.

123 **call "strategic cyber"**: This is captured in a number of different acronyms, although they are as always somewhat different in connotation. For instance, in the United States the common term is "Offensive Cyber Effects Operations" (OCEO), which may also have some overlap with the traditional battlefield cyber mission.

123 **simply as "covert action"**: In the U.K., the term "online covert action" was revealed in leaked documents to be popular within the intelligence community, most particularly the signals intelligence agency GCHQ. The training document makes highly recommended reading, with a title page of a hidden figure handing over a piece of paper saying, "I'm not trying to impress you, but I'm Batman." See "The Art of Deception: Training for a New Generation of Online Covert Operations," *Intercept*, Feb. 24, 2014, accessed Oct. 25, 2016, https://theintercept.com/document/2014/02/24 /art-deception-training-new-generation-online-covert-operations.

123 **British Operation Cupcake**: Duncan Gardham, "MI6 Attacks al-Qaeda in 'Operation Cupcake,'" *Telegraph*, June 2, 2011. The JTIG training document was released on NBC, "Exclusive: Snowden docs showed British spies used honey pots and dirty tricks." *NBC*, Feb. 7, 2014.

125 **does not include the theft of data:** Katharina Ziolkowski, "*Ius ad bellum* in Cyberspace—Some Thoughts on the 'Schmitt Criteria' for the Use of Force" (NATO Cooperative Cyber Defense Center of Excellence, 2012).

125 **any action that disables the functioning:** Terry Gill et al., *ILA Study Group Interim Report: The Conduct of Hostilities and International Humanitarian Law* (International Law Association, 2014), accessed Oct. 25, 2016, www.ila-hq.org/download.cfm /docid/806C2DED-87FF-4744-8CC8EDAF47787AE6.

126 **Governments are forced to evaluate:** For instance, an abiding account is that President Bush turned down a planned 2003 cyberattack on the Iraqi financial system, because it could have had significant effects on other (civilian) banks, including one in France.

CHAPTER 6: NO ONE BUT US

134 **"The pipeline software that was to run the pumps":** Thomas Reed, *At the Abyss: An Insider's History of the Cold War* (Novato, Calif.: Presidio Press, 2005), 269.

134 **A former KGB officer:** Anatoly Medetsky, "KGB Veteran Denies CIA Caused '82 Blast," *Moscow Times,* March 18, 2004.

134 **"according to an informed source":** Jeffrey Carr, "The Myth of the CIA and the Trans-Siberian Pipeline Explosion," *Digital Dao,* June 7, 2012.

135 **version that validates much of Reed's account:** The passage in question reads, "Contrived computer chips found their way into Soviet military equipment, flawed turbines were installed on a gas pipeline, and defective plans disrupted the output of chemical plants and a tractor factory. The Pentagon introduced misleading information pertinent to stealth aircraft, space defense, and tactical aircraft. The Soviet Space Shuttle was a rejected NASA design." Note that Weiss refers to "flawed turbines" rather than tampered software. Other sources have decried that the Soviet Space Shuttle design was based on a stolen US design that was, however, crucially altered—the heat shield would have failed on re-entry. Gus W. Weiss, "The Farewell Dossier: Duping the Soviets" (Central Intelligence Agency, 2007).

135 **Independent of whether that attack happened or not:** The question of whether the attack actually happened or whether it is pure fiction has not been completely answered. A Canadian TV documentary in 2012, however, provided many additional details on the US efforts to slow down the construction of a Siberian pipeline and featured a whole cast of seemingly credible witnesses. According to them, the massive explosion described in Reed's book happened not in 1982 but in 1983, near Nadym in western Siberia. The incident was kept secret by Soviet authorities at the time, but a former Soviet deputy minister confirmed the explosion and said it caused "dozens" of casualties—if true, the first fatalities of cyber conflict. The documentary also links the development of the software not only to the CIA but to Canadian and French intelligence as well. Vincent Frigon and Yves Bernard, *Bon baiser du Canada* [From Canada with love], 2011.

135 **As questionable as this tactic:** There is, however, at least one example of "pwnage" (that is, domination-submission) with traditional security policy. For instance, in antisubmarine warfare (ASW) a Cold War practice was that a submarine that was being hunted by ASW assets in territorial waters would be "hounded," once the pursuers had effective firing solutions, sometimes even including dropping miniature depth bombs. The submarine in question showed its "submission" by coming to the surface and

leaving the engagement area by cruising on the surface. The tactical "standard operating procedures" perhaps don't carry over well to strategic and political levels, however.

136 "guerrilla information war with no division": McLuhan, *Culture Is Our Business,* 99.

136 military cyber budget alone is $7 billion: Cheryl Pellerin, "Carter Previews FY2017 Defense Budget Request" (US Department of Defense, 2016). Also see Lloyd McCoy Jr. and Stephanie Meloni, "Cyber, Cloud Lead DOD Budget Priorities," *Washington Technology,* Feb. 10, 2016.

136 DoD IT budget: "Information Technology," White House FY 2017 Budget (White House, 2016), accessed Oct. 25, 2016, www.whitehouse.gov/sites/default/files/omb /budget/fy2017/assets/ap_17_it.pdf.

136 fiscal year 2017 federal budget: Dustin Volz, "Obama Budget Proposal Includes $19 Billion for Cybersecurity," *Fortune,* Feb. 9, 2016.

137 Joseph Nye identifies "three faces": Joseph S. Nye Jr., *The Future of Power* (New York: Public Affairs, 2011), 10–14.

139 cyberattacks against the private sector: *Cost of Cybercrime* (Ponemon Institute, 2015).

139 and sheer volume: "Global State of Information Security Survey" (PwC, 2016), accessed Oct. 25, 2016, www.pwc.com/gx/en/consulting-services/information-security -survey/assets/pwc-gsiss-2016-retail-consumer.pdf.

139 A survey of top business and security leaders: "US State of Cybercrime Survey" (PwC, 2015), accessed Oct. 25, 2016, www.pwc.com/us/en/increasing-it-effectiveness /publications/assets/2015-us-cybercrime-survey.pdf.

139 the energy sector and the power grid: Rene Marsh, "Congressman: National Power Grid Frequently Attacked," CNN, Oct. 21, 2015.

139 to the financial sector: Kara Scannell and Gina Chon, "Cyber Insecurity: When 95% Is Not Enough," *Financial Times,* July 28, 2015.

139 the nuclear sector, and: Sam Jones, "Nuclear Power Plants in 'Culture of Denial' over Hacking Risk," *Financial Times,* Oct. 4, 2015.

139 even the health sector: Shannon Pettypiece, "Rising Cyber Attacks Costing Health System $6 Billion Annually," *Bloomberg,* May 7, 2015.

140 The data stolen includes: Andy Greenberg, "OPM Now Admits 5.6M Feds' Fingerprints Were Stolen by Hackers," *Wired,* Sept. 23, 2015.

140 "They got everyone's": David Larter and Andrew Tilghman, "Military Clearance OPM Data Breach 'Absolute Calamity,'" *Military Times,* June 17, 2015.

141 A 2012 McAfee-paid poll: For a summary, see "Cyber Defense Report: Country Defense Ranking," *Street,* Jan. 30, 2012.

141 The United States probably spends: As an example, the government of the Netherlands, a world leader in national cybersecurity, decided in 2015 to increase the overall cyber budget by around $110 million. In comparison, in 2016 President Obama requested an increase of $5 billion a year to an already much larger cyber budget. Overall, the United States probably outspends the Netherlands around sixty or even a hundred to one on cyber (depending on how you count it), while the US economy is around twenty times the size of the Dutch economy. At the same time, the Dutch are consistently ranked higher by industry groups in getting "national cybersecurity" right. The Netherlands has the highest per capita spending related to cybersecurity in the EU; other countries, especially in the former Eastern bloc, do not even spend one-tenth of the annual Dutch budget increase alone.

142 Private-sector cybersecurity spending: *Europe Cyber Security Market* (MicroMarketMonitor, 2016), accessed Oct. 26, 2016, www.micromarketmonitor.com /market/europe-cyber-security-4129808188.html. For the United States, see Steve Morgan, "Cybersecurity Market Reaches $75 Billion in 2015; Expected to Reach $170 Billion by 2020," *Forbes,* Dec. 20, 2015.

142 the private sector in North America: "Fortinet Issues 7 Stage Cyber Defence for CIOs" (CSO Forum, 2016), accessed Oct. 26, 2016, www.cioandleader.com /article/2016/07/08/fortinet-issues-7-stage-cyber-defence-cios.

144 cyber budget of at least $1.25 billion: "Fact Sheet: Department of Homeland Security Fiscal Year 2016 Budget (US Department of Homeland Security, 2015), accessed Oct. 26, 2016, www.dhs.gov/news/2015/02/02/fact-sheet-dhs-fy-2016-budget, and Stephanie Sanok Kostro and Garrett Riba, "Major Takeaways from the President's FY 2015 Budget Request for DHS," Center for Strategic and International Studies, March 13, 2014.

146 Under President Obama: "Improving Critical Infrastructure Cybersecurity," White House, Feb. 12, 2013, accessed October 26, 2016, www.whitehouse.gov/the-press -office/2013/02/12/executive-order-improving-critical-infrastructure-cybersecurity.

146 technical cyber-defense program EINSTEIN: "FACTSHEET: Administration Cybersecurity Efforts 2015," White House, July 9, 2015, accessed Oct. 26, 2016, www .whitehouse.gov/the-press-office/2015/07/09/fact-sheet-administration-cybersecurity -efforts-2015.

147 in a 2014 meeting at Harvard: For a video record of the talk, given by Joseph Nye and myself, as well as the statement of Ash Carter toward the end, see: www.youtube.com /watch?v=Z8KMytNsMlM.

148 "building up a huge stockpile": Michael Daniel, "Heartbleed: Understanding When We Disclose Cyber Vulnerabilities," White House, April 28, 2014.

149 This announcement has unleashed: One voice in favor of such an open policy comes from Ari Schwartz and Rob Knake, *Government's Role in Vulnerability Disclosure: Creating a Permanent and Accountable Vulnerability Equities Process* (Harvard Kennedy School Belfer Center for Science and International Affairs, 2016). For an opposite view, see Dave Aitel and Matt Tait, "Everything You Know About the Vulnerability Equities Process Is Wrong," *Lawfare,* Aug. 18, 2016.

149 In August 2016, it became clear: Jason Healey calculated that the NSA could only afford to purchase around fifty zerodays a year on the open market, although this provided no indicator of how many zerodays it could have discovered internally. The release of some "attack code" attributed to the NSA around 2012 indicated that it used a number of zerodays that have never been disclosed and that were arguably of particular interest to protecting civilians.

150 At that time, no formal doctrine: Paul R. Henning, *Air Force Information Warfare Doctrine: Valuable or Valueless?* (Montgomery, Ala.: Research Department Air Command and Staff College, 1997).

151 "most of what US forces can usefully do": Martin Libicki, *What Is Information Warfare?* (National Defense University, 1995), 85.

152 uniformed soldier and a civilian spy to switch chairs: A common account that I cannot confirm in detail is that at least until recently within the NSA/CSS framework if an operation fell under US Code Title 10 (national defense) rather than Title 50 (which includes espionage), it had to be "carried out" by a uniformed member of the armed forces. This would literally involve the uniform sitting down and pressing "return" to switch a spy operation to a military operation. The rest of the operation would fall under Title 50.

153 **But claiming that CNE is a defensive task:** The new keystone document for cyber, JP 3-12, was published in 2012 and is still largely classified. What is known about it in public, however, indicates that it has simply doubled down on some of the core issues within the wider concept of CNO. For instance, CNE is now subdivided into two intelligence tasks—OPE (for the operational preparation of the environment) and ISR (intelligence, surveillance, and reconnaissance). Even more worrying, CNA has been redefined as Offensive Cyber Effects Operations, a definition that may well be more conducive to including psychological operations and the like than CNA was.

153 **This assertion was called into question:** Jaikumar Vijayan, "Federal Cybersecurity Director Quits, Complains of NSA Role," *Computerworld,* March 8, 2009.

153 **a category that includes defensive:** "Presidential Policy Directive/PPD-20: US Cyber Operations Policy" (published by FAS, 2013), accessed Oct. 26, 2016, https://fas.org/irp /offdocs/ppd/ppd-20.pdf.

154 **Cyber Mission Force:** Colin Wood, "U.S. Cyber Commands Launches 13 New Cyber Protection Teams," *GovTech,* Dec. 16, 2015.

154 **Combat Mission Teams:** The Combat Mission Teams are the only openly offensive component of the new structure. Situated with the relevant commands—most likely meaning "combat commands" such as PACCOM (Pacific)—they appear to function as geographic and sectorial specialized units that will engage in offensive cyber operations within their area of responsibility. This could have virtually unlimited range, meaning supporting the penetration of an air-defense network but also potential attacks on the enemies' critical infrastructure. It would appear that for this to work, each CMT will have to draw on a collection of resources and capabilities that are provided centrally, while the CMTs themselves are responsible for the individual planning components— that is, knowing the best time and best place to activate individual implants or "cyber bombs" or the like. The CMTs are particularly interesting because they are highly localized to specific commands, provided by the different branches (such as the marines and the air force), and clearly subordinate to the combat commands. It would thus appear that the previous discussions of pooling all CMT resources within Strategic Command (STRATCOM), the command previously responsible for most cyber operations (as well as nuclear weapons), failed—but not totally. In a 2015 talk, the head of STRATCOM, Admiral Cecil Haney, revealed that he would have two CMTs, both of which can be expected to have a somewhat different focus from those assigned to, for instance, African Command.

154 **Combat Protection Teams:** The Combat Protection Teams are supposedly dedicated to the most important DoD cyber task—protecting the DoD network and the Joint Information Environment that connects virtually all aspects of DoD with each other— as well as working with the computer network defense service providers to make sure that relevant civilian infrastructure is also protected. According to other reports, however, they will also play a major role in supporting civilian national defense. One article says that the Air National Guard will deploy ten of its thirteen teams in specific FEMA (civil defense) regions. The same article also states that each "team" will have about five hundred personnel, the equivalent of a regular battalion or squadron.

154 **"to help defend the nation's critical infrastructure":** Mark Pomerleau, "What Will the Cyber Mission Force Look Like?," *Defense Systems,* Oct. 13, 2015. Also see "The

Department of Defense Cyber Strategy" (US Department of Defense, April 2015), accessed Oct. 26, 2016, www.defense.gov/Portals/1/features/2015/0415_cyber-strategy /Final_2015_DoD_CYBER_STRATEGY_for_web.pdf.

154 **NMF is charged with waging:** "Statement of Admiral Michael S. Rogers, Commander of the US Cyber Command, before the Senate Armed Services Committee, 5 April 2016," accessed Oct. 26, 2016, www.armed-services.senate.gov/imo/media/doc /Rogers_04-05-16.pdf.

155 **"Offensive Cyber Effects Operations":** "Presidential Policy Directive/PPD-20: US Cyber Operations Policy," (published by FAS), accessed Oct. 26, 2016, https://fas.org /irp/offdocs/ppd/ppd-20.pdf.

155 **it is impossible to judge:** A key leaked document was the 2012 PPD-20 document of the Obama administration which mentions OCEO as well as a host of other abbreviations, but does not define them in depth. See ibid.

157 **"devised to disable Iran's air defenses":** David E. Sanger and Mark Mazzetti, "U.S. Had Cyberattack Plan if Iran Nuclear Dispute Led to Conflict," *New York Times,* Feb. 16, 2016.

CHAPTER 7: ATTACK TO EXCESS

159 **the eerie similarity of much of present-day US cyber thought:** Peter W. Singer and Allan Friedman, "Cult of the Cyber Offensive: Why Belief in First-Strike Is as Misguided Today as It Was In 1914," *Foreign Policy,* Jan. 15, 2014.

160 **An episode with a freelancing German hacker:** Jessica Ramirez, "The History of Computer Hacking," *Newsweek,* March 8, 2010.

161 **This German computer hacker:** Stanley H. Kremen, "Apprehending the Computer Hacker: The Collection and Use of Evidence," *Computer Forensics Online* 2, no. 1 (Nov. 1998), accessed Oct. 26, 2016, www.shk-dplc.com/cfo/articles/hack.htm.

161 **"the split between defensive and offensive":** Jason Healey, ed., *A Fierce Domain: Conflict in Cyberspace, 1986 to 2012* (Vienna, Va.: Cyber Conflict Studies Association, 2013).

162 **"The United States possesses":** "Presidential Decision Directive/NSC-63: Critical Infrastructure Protection," White House, May 22, 1998, accessed Oct. 26, 2016, http:// fas.org/irp/offdocs/pdd/pdd-63.htm.

163 **"a Pentagon ghost story":** Justin Joque, "Cyber-Catastrophe: A Pedagogy of Entropy," in *Pedagogies of Disaster,* ed. W. J. Vincent et al. (Brooklyn: Punctum Books, 2013).

164 **A series of attacks on the DoD networks:** "Solar Sunrise" (Global Security, 2011), accessed Oct. 26, 2016, www.globalsecurity.org/military/ops/solar-sunrise.htm.

164 **"one of the most potentially damaging breaches":** *Newsweek* staff, "'We're in the Middle of a Cyberwar,'" *Newsweek,* Sept. 19, 1999.

164 **another outlet reported that the Defense Department:** "Cyberwar! The Warnings?," *Frontline,* PBS, April 24, 2003, accessed Oct. 26, 2016, www.pbs.org/wgbh/pages /frontline/shows/cyberwar/warnings.

165 **Some commentators doubted:** As, for instance, elucidated by Adam Elkus in his in-depth review of Moonlight Maze in Healey, *Fierce Domain: Conflict in Cyberspace, 1986 to 2012* (Vienna, Va.: Cyber Conflict Studies Association, 2013).

165 **an internal power play of the rising FSB:** This theory makes particular sense because only a few years later the former signals intelligence agency FAPSI was largely subsumed by the FSB as part of the latter's rise to the predominant security

organization in Russia under the new leader, Vladimir Putin. All of my interview partners have clearly stated that the attack was carried out by the FSB, not FAPSI—indicating that perhaps it was part of the FSB making a claim that it would be the best organization to take over FAPSI only two years later.

169 **The Section 215 metadata:** Michael Price, "The Legal Legacy of the NSA's Section 215 Bulk Collection Program," Brennan Center for Justice, New York University School of Law, Nov. 16, 2015.

169 **"possible 'tangible things'":** "Section 215 of the USA PATRIOT ACT," Electronic Frontier Foundation, Oct. 25, 2011, accessed March 1, 2016, www.eff.org/de/foia /section-215-usa-patriot-act.

171 **"What if your job":** "The ROC: NSA's Epicenter for Computer Network Operations" (Remote Operations Center, leaked in 2015), accessed Oct. 26, 2016, www.eff.org /files/2015/01/23/20150117-speigel-document_explaining_the_role_of_the_remote _operations_center_roc.pdf.

171 **Tailored Access Operations group:** TAO (S32) is subordinate to signals intelligence (s3) division and included includes S321: Remote Operations Center, S323: Data Network Technologies, S324: Telecommunication Network Technologies, S325: Mission Infrastructure Technologies, S327: Requirements & Targeting, and S328: Access Technologies Operations.

171 **TAO played a crucial part:** Craig Whitlock and Barton Gellman, "To Hunt Osama bin Laden, Satellites Watched over Abbottabad, Pakistan, and Navy SEALs," *Washington Post,* Aug. 29, 2013.

171 **Section 215 Patriot Act powers:** Maggie Ybarra, "FBI Admits No Major Cases Cracked with Patriot Act Snooping Powers," *Washington Times,* May 21, 2015.

172 **Section 702 powers exercised by the NSA:** Michael Isikoff, "NSA Program Stopped No Terror Attacks, Says White House Panel Member," NBC News, Dec. 20, 2013.

172 **"50 terrorist plots":** John Parkinson, "NSA: 'Over 50' Terror Plots Foiled by Data Dragnets," ABC News, June 18, 2013.

172 **joint CIA-NSA Special Collection Service:** The Special Collection Service (SCS) is a joint NSA-CIA covert action unit that has been said to be its "mission impossible" force, specializing in "close surveillance, burglary, wiretapping, breaking and entering." In other words, it specializes in getting physical access to hardware that is then compromised. It has been rumored to accomplish this "close access" mission in some very imaginative ways; in the Cold War, the SCS supposedly tried to plant bugs on pigeons that frequented the Soviet embassy. Today, the SCS also supports the US-embassy-wide "collection" missions, including the embassy-based surveillance of mobile networks.

174 **upstream collection can cover around 75 percent:** Siobhan Gorman and Jennifer Valentino-DeVries, "New Details Show Broader NSA Surveillance Reach: Programs Cover 75% of Nation's Traffic, Can Snare Emails," *Wall Street Journal,* Aug. 20, 2013.

174 **the NSA sidestepped this:** "Snowden Leaks: Google 'Outraged' at Alleged NSA Hacking," BBC, Oct. 31, 2013, accessed Oct. 26, 2016, www.bbc.com/news/world-us -canada-24751821.

174 **this data included e-mail, voice, chat, and video:** "PRISM/US-984XN Overview" (Special Source Operations, 2013), accessed Oct. 26, 2016, www.eff.org/files/2013 /11/21/20131022-monde-prism_april_2013.pdf.

175 inject malware directly into the target's computer: Lennart Haagsma, "Deep Dive into QUANTUM INSERT," *Fox-IT,* April 20, 2015, accessed Oct. 26, 2016, https://blog .fox-it.com/2015/04/20/deep-dive-into-quantum-insert.

177 In 2013, it was reported: Lucian Constantin, "NSA Infected 50,000 Networks with Specialized Malware," *PCWorld,* Nov. 25, 2013.

177 the US government had conducted: David E. Sanger and Martin Fackler, "N.S.A. Breached North Korean Networks Before Sony Attack, Officials Say," *New York Times,* Jan. 18, 2015.

178 A more in-depth analysis: Lucian Constantin, "The NSA Not Only Creates, but Also Hijacks, Malware with Quantumbot," *Computerworld,* Jan. 19, 2015.

178 "the NSA spied on a foreign intelligence agency": Ibid.

178 "I have a word of advice": Michael Martinez, "Allies Spy on Allies Because a Friend Today May Not Be One Tomorrow," CNN, Oct. 31, 2013.

179 arrested trying to sell the same data: Philip Oltermann, "Germany Arrests BND Member on Suspicion of Spying for US," *Guardian,* July 4, 2014.

181 the number of known Iranian centrifuges decreased: David Albright, Paul Brannan, and Christina Walrond, "Did Stuxnet Take Out 1,000 Centrifuges at the Natanz Enrichment Plant?," Institute for Science and International Security, Dec. 22, 2010.

181 Stuxnet "broke out": David E. Sanger, "Obama Order Sped Up Wave of Cyberattacks Against Iran," *New York Times,* June 1, 2012.

181 "We think there was a modification": Ibid.

183 objective of remaining undiscovered: Sanger and Mazzetti, "U.S. Had Cyberattack Plan if Iran Nuclear Dispute Led to Conflict."

183 Forging a Microsoft code: "Spy virus Flame got help from doctored Microsoft certificates," *SC Magazine,* June 4, 2012.

CHAPTER 8: STRATEGIC INNUENDO

186 how information operations would be deployed: *Information Operations: Doctrine, Tactics, Techniques, and Procedures (FM 3-13)* (Washington, D.C.: Department of the Army Headquarters, 2003), accessed Oct. 26, 2016, http://fas.org/irp/doddir/army/fm3 -13-2003.pdf.

186 the use of loud rock music: For an overview of the "music playlist," see "The Noriega Playlist," *No Fear of the Future,* Dec. 26, 2006, accessed Oct. 26, 2016, http:// nofearofthefuture.blogspot.co.at/2006/12/noriega-playlist.html.

187 "Milosevic's phone ring incessantly": Michael V. Hayden, "The Making of America's Cyberweapons," *Christian Science Monitor,* Feb. 24, 2016. See also William M. Arkin, "The Cyber Bomb in Yugoslavia," *Washington Post,* Oct. 25, 1999.

187 The Smith-Mundt Act expressly forbids: The Smith-Mundt Act and the limits of propaganda were recently back in the news, due to legislative changes in 2013 that would allow the State Department "greater leeway" on how to engage in foreign strategic communications. John Hudson, "U.S. Repeals Propaganda Ban, Spreads Government-Made News to Americans," *Foreign Policy,* July 14, 2013.

188 the act's modernization: Weston R. Sager, "Apple Pie Propaganda? The Smith-Mundt Act Before and After the Repeal of the Domestic Dissemination Ban," *Northwestern University Law Review* 109, no. 2 (2015).

188 acceptable in strategic communication: The term "strategic communication" is applied differently at different levels of the decision-making pyramid. For instance, there are guidelines for military commanders on how to engage in strategic communication. See *Commander's Handbook for Strategic Communication and Communication Strategy (Version 3.0)* (US Joint Forces Command, Joint Warfighting Center, 2010). These clearly overlap with information operations, which include psychological operations. While "honesty" is mentioned as the best way to counter enemy disinformation, it is not mentioned otherwise as a key ingredient in building reliability and credibility.

190 **"how often we could provide high confidence attribution":** This particular message has been referred to in a transcript of a cyber strategy talk in Japan in 2011 by an unnamed individual at CSIS, in the following: "A senior American intelligence official recently told me that attribution is not a problem because he can use espionage techniques to identify the attacker. Attribution is hard, but is it [*sic*] not impossible and it is getting easier." "Rethinking Cybersecurity—a Comprehensive Approach" (Sasakawa Peace Foundation, Tokyo, Sept. 12, 2011), accessed Oct. 26, 2016, https://csis-prod.s3.amazonaws.com/s3fs-public/legacy_files/files/publication/110920_Japan_speech_2011.pdf.

190 **a more nuanced vision of attribution:** House Permanent Select Committee on Intelligence, Statement for the Record, Worldwide Cyber Threats by James R. Clapper, Director of National Intelligence, House Permanent Select Committee on Intelligence, 2015, accessed Oct. 26, 2016, www.dni.gov/index.php/newsroom/testimonies/209-congressional-testimonies-2015/1251-dni-clapper-statement-for-the-record,-worldwide-cyber-threats-before-the-house-permanent-select-committee-on-intelligence.

191 **"high confidence" cyber attribution:** There are no public numbers on what level of certitude the dual phenomenology approach can provide, but we know the history of it. It was introduced after the 1979 missile scare, when a computer error led to NORAD screens suddenly showing a massive strike under way. The error was caused by computer tapes of an exercise not being swapped out. Since then, dual phenomenology requires at least two different sensor groups from the four (IMAGINT, SIGINT, MASINT, RADINT) to independently confirm a strike before that strike is even registered as such.

191 **the Suter system was employed:** David A. Fulghum, "Why Syria's Air Defenses Failed to Detect Israelis," *Aviation Week & Space Technology,* Oct. 3, 2007.

192 **ABC interview with Woodward:** "Bob Woodward Talks to ABC's Diane Sawyer About 'Obama's Wars,'" ABC News, Sept. 27, 2010.

194 **The book was so influential:** For an obituary of the author of *The Terror Network,* see Wolfgang Achtner, "Obituary: Claire Sterling," *Independent,* June 25, 1995.

194 **framed by a seminal work:** Franklin Kramer, *Cyberpower and National Security* (Washington, D.C.: National Defense University Press, 2009).

195 **National Security Space Strategy:** In the case of the National Security Space Strategy, this proceeds smoothly through establishing norms of behavior, to seeking alliance and common interest (that is, "entanglement," in traditional speak), to resiliency and redundancy of systems (that is, "denying the adversary success"), and finally possibilities for offensive action (that is, "punishment").

196 **"Dr. Strangelove taught us":** Scott Maucione, "White House Finally Acquiesces to Congress on Cyber Deterrence Policy," Federal News Radio, Dec. 29, 2015.

198 **"whole of nation" cybersecurity:** "Foreign Policy: Cybersecurity," White House,

Feb. 12, 2013, accessed Oct. 26, 2016, www.whitehouse.gov/issues/foreign-policy
/cybersecurity; Klimburg, "Mobilising Cyber Power."

199 **General Hayden penned:** Hayden, "Making of America's Cyberweapons."

CHAPTER 9: RUSSIA'S INVISIBLE WAR

205 **account by Kim Zetter:** Kim Zetter, "Inside the Cunning, Unprecedented Hack of
Ukraine's Power Grid," *Wired,* March 3, 2016.

207 **BlackEnergy has been found:** Paul Roberts, "If Cyberwar Erupts, America's Electric
Grid Is a Prime Target," *Christian Science Monitor,* Dec. 23, 2014.

207 **an attack on the US power grid:** Susan Duclos, "NSA Chief Warns Black Energy
Attack on U.S. Power Grid a 'Matter of When, Not If'—Lights Out Scenario Not a Myth
but a Coming Reality," *All News Pipeline,* March 8, 2016.

207 **Soviet engineers had begun to make:** According to one source, during the planning
of the 1975 joint Apollo-Soyuz space mission, the Soviets claimed to have completed
the necessary calculations in one minute, while NASA needed around thirty minutes.
See Boris Nikolaevich Malinovsky, *Pioneers of Soviet Computing* (n.p.: SigCis, 2010).

208 **"Wiener is the only man":** Quoted from "'Machines of Communism': The USSR,
Cybernetics (and the CIA)," appendix to *Wiener World,* accessed Oct. 26, 2016, http://
larroucheplanet.info/pmwiki/pmwiki.php?n=Library.MachinesOfCommunism.

208 **"all-out Soviet commitment'":** Slava Gerovitch, "InterNyet: Why the Soviet Union
Did Not Build a Nationwide Computer Network," *History and Technology* 24, no. 4
(Dec. 2008).

209 **"by the mid-1980s nearly the entire adult population":** Ibid.

209 **a somewhat ironic utopian vision:** Benjamin Peters, *How Not to Network a Nation:
The Uneasy History of the Soviet Internet* (Cambridge, Mass.: MIT Press, 2016).

209 **"[The USSR] developed a large variety":** Gerovitch, "InterNyet."

210 **Trust was such a rare commodity:** For more background on a Russia-specific
network-versus-hierarchy tale, see Irina Borogan and Andrei Soldatov, "Putin Can't
Stop the Internet," *Slate,* Oct. 14, 2015.

211 **The Military Academy of the General Staff:** Thierry Gongora and Harald Von
Riekhoff, eds., *Toward a Revolution in Military Affairs?* (Westport, Conn.: Praeger,
2000), 96.

211 **"a process by which one enemy":** As quoted from Vladimir E. Lepsky in Timothy L.
Thomas, "Russia's Reflexive Control Theory and the Military," *Journal of Slavic
Military Studies* 17 (2004): 237–56.

211 **a fake propaganda research project:** Ibid.

212 **Information Security Doctrine:** Approved by the president of the Russian Federation,
Vladimir Putin, on Sept. 9, 2000, accessed Oct. 26, 2016, http://archive.mid.ru//bdomp
/ns-osndoc.nsf/1e5f0de28fe77fdcc32575d900298676/2deaa9ee15ddd24bc32575d
9002c442b!OpenDocument.

213 **"The special services of certain states":** Vadim Shtepa, "Russia's Draft Information
Security Doctrine at Odds with Realities of Modern Information Environment,"
Eurasia Daily Monitor, July 15, 2016.

214 **"The central, controversial aspect":** Katherin Machalek, "Factsheet: Russia's NGO
Laws," Freedom House, accessed Oct. 31, 2016, https://freedomhouse.org/sites/default
/files/Fact%20Sheet_0.pdf.

215 **NGO law has had detrimental effects:** Miriam Elder, "Russia Raids Human Rights Groups in Crackdown on 'Foreign Agents,'" *Guardian,* May 27, 2013.

215 **harassment of individuals:** Kate Lyons and Mark Rice-Oxley, "Harassed and Shunned, the Russians Labelled Foreign Agents by Kremlin," *Guardian,* April 26, 2015.

215 **"being bullied by":** Benjamin Bidder and Matthias Schepp, "Defying the Kremlin Crackdown on Press Freedom," *Spiegel,* July 2, 2015.

215 **online television station called Dozhd:** "Russia Sees Harsh Crackdown on Independent Media," *Moscow Times,* December 21, 2014.

215 **in Siberia, for instance:** Robert Coalson, "Independent Siberian TV Channel Faces Shutdown," Radio Free Europe/Radio Liberty, Dec. 9, 2016.

215 **Russian-occupied Crimea:** "Russian Watchdog Shuts Down Country's Only Crimean Tatar TV Channel," *Moscow Times,* April 1, 2015.

215 **"register, disclose personal information":** Michael Birnbaum, "Russian Blogger Law Puts New Restrictions on Internet Freedoms," *Washington Post,* July 31, 2014.

216 **42 percent of Russians believe:** Erik C. Nisbet and Sarah Mikati, "Russians Don't Trust the Internet—and It's Making the Country Worse," *Washington Post,* Feb. 18, 2015.

216 **"as . . . with Russia, autocratic-leaning governments":** Ibid.

216 **Russian TV giant RT:** Simon Shuster, "Inside Putin's On-Air Machine," *Time,* March 5, 2015.

217 **on the "Kremlin's troll army":** Daisy Sindelar, "The Kremlin's Troll Army," *The Atlantic,* Aug. 12, 2014.

218 **"It is designed . . . 'to drive wedges'":** Natasha Bertrand, "It Looks Like Russia Hired Internet Trolls to Pose as Pro-Trump Americans," *Business Insider,* July 27, 2016.

218 **recruit Western researchers:** Joshua Kucera, "Spooked: The Spies Who Loved Me," *The Atlantic,* Dec. 2008.

218 **more serious attempts to:** Giles Keir, "Russia's 'New' Tools for Confronting the West: Continuity and Innovation in Moscow's Exercise of Power," Chatham House, March 2016.

219 **In 1997, a fascinating presentation:** "Cyber Wars," Agentura.ru, accessed Sept. 20, 2016, accessed Oct. 31, 2016, www.agentura.ru/english/equipment.

220 **according to Oleg Ivanov:** "Electronic Warfare Chief Interviewed," *Russian Defense Policy,* April 22, 2010, accessed Oct. 31, 2016, https://russiandefpolicy.wordpress .com/2010/04/22/electronic-warfare-chief-interviewed.

220 **"We have great signals intelligence":** Joe Gould, "Electronic Warfare: What US Army Can Learn from Ukraine," *Defense News,* Aug. 2, 2015.

221 **"Russian propaganda plays a huge role":** Janina Semenova, "Behind Russia's TV Propaganda Machine," *DW,* Sept. 2, 2015.

221 **verified in detail by a former Kremlin propagandist:** Stephen Castle, "A Russian TV Insider Describes a Modern Propaganda Machine," *New York Times,* Feb. 14, 2015.

221 **"What they are basically trying to undermine":** Ibid.

221 **"In the 21st century we have seen a tendency":** The article was published under Gerasimov's name in the Russian newspaper *Voenno-Promyshlenni Kurier* in early 2013 and laid down the contours of what came to be known as the Gerasimov doctrine. For a translation of the article, see Mark Galeotti, "The 'Gerasimov Doctrine' and Russian Non-linear War," *In Moscow's Shadow* (2013), accessed Oct. 31, 2016, https:// inmoscowsshadows.wordpress.com/2014/07/06/the-gerasimov-doctrine-and-russian -non-linear-war.

222 **so keen to phrase things in terms:** Vladimir Markomenko, "Invisible, Drawn-Out War," *Nezavisimoye Voyennoye Obozreniye,* Aug. 16–21, 1997.

223 **"war is the continuation":** The exact quotation is "war is not merely a political act, but also a real political instrument, a continuation of political commerce, a carrying out of the same by other means." Carl von Clausewitz, *On War* (1832).

223 **"politics is the continuation":** The exact quotation is "war is the core of politics, its violent continuation by other means," cited in José C. D'Odrico, "The Ideological Underpinnings of Soviet Military Thought," *Air University Review,* March–April 1982.

CHAPTER 10: OF *SILOVIKI* AND CYBER CRIME

225 **former KGB- or FSB-affiliated officials made up 42 percent:** Mark Galeotti, "Putin's Hydra: Inside Russia's Intelligence Services," European Council on Foreign Relations, May 11, 2016.

225 **"There is no such thing as a former *Chekist*":** "The Making of a Neo-KGB State," *The Economist,* Aug. 23, 2007.

225 **Ten years later, the *siloviki* have not lost:** Yekaterina Sinelschikova, "The Spying Game: The Former KGB Officers Who Run Russia Today," *Russia Beyond the Headlines,* June 28, 2016.

226 **"principle of 'competitive intelligence'":** Galeotti, "Putin's Hydra."

226 **dismemberment of the former FAPSI:** According to a briefing ("Russian Cyber Espionage to Become More Aggressive," *Oxford Analytica Daily Brief,* Dec. 16, 2014), cyber operations include four main elements: the Centre for Radio-electronic Communications Intelligence (TsRRSS) runs both electronic eavesdropping and cyber-espionage operations and is effectively GURRS in original form. The Information Security Directorate has a similar role to TsRRSS, although it focuses on defensive operations. The Institute of Cryptography, Telecommunications, and Computer Science, part of the FSB Academy in Moscow, trains computer security and intrusion specialists. The Centre for the Security of Information and Special Communications also provides security against foreign cyber intrusions. The FSB also inherited all the SIGINT hardware that went with the former FAPSI, including signals intelligence gathering locations in Vietnam and Cuba.

227 **Russian units, unlike their Chinese equivalent:** The two remaining major intelligence agencies are bit players in comparison, especially as far as cyber is concerned. The foreign-intelligence SVR has seen a string of humiliations, in particular in regard to its penchant for deep-cover agents, many of whom were revealed in recent years in the United States and elsewhere and who were notable primarily for their stunning uselessness as intelligence assets. The Russian equivalent of the US Secret Service, the FSO, is responsible for directly guarding the Kremlin elite. According to Galeotti, it also increasingly plays a role in supervising the other intelligence agencies and is therefore a vital extension of Putin's personal power. The FSO includes the signals intelligence unit SSSI, which, although largely defensive, is perfectly capable of directing cyber-intelligence operations and, in one instance I am aware of, has at least had contact with a cyber-crime gang (see note below for "the greatest bank theft to date"). According to one report, SSSI also has a lot of influence over the local Russian networks—including over GAS Vybory, the official system that logs and transmits election results. Mark Galeotti, "'Siloviks & Scoundrels': My New Column in the

Moscow News," *In Moscow's Shadow,* July 18, 2011. The original article is no longer available because the *Moscow News* Web site is no longer online.

227 97 percent of Web sites on the list: Alexey Eremenko, "Anonymous Browser Mass Hit as Russians Seek to Escape Internet Censorship," *Moscow Times,* June 18, 2014.

228 "System of Operational-Investigative Activities": In fact, according to the World Policy Institute, SORM includes three different pieces of legislation with different targets: the first level, SORM-1, targets all communications from phones; the second level, SORM-2, extracts Internet traffic through direct underground cables connecting ISPs with the local FSB headquarters; and the third level, SORM-3, targets all other forms of communications while retaining personal data on a long-term basis. Andrei Soldatov and Irina Borogan, "Russia's Surveillance State," *World Policy Journal* 30, no. 3, Sept. 2013.

228 SORM boasts legislative backing: Alexander Klimburg and Heli Tiirmaa-Klaar, *Cybersecurity and Cyberpower: Concepts, Conditions, and Capabilities for Cooperation for Action Within the EU* (European Parliament, 2011).

228 the world's foremost criminal enterprise: Chris Matthews, "Fortune 5: The Biggest Organized Crime Groups in the World," *Fortune,* Sept. 14, 2014.

229 the greatest bank theft to date: Kaspersky Lab indeed found out that a criminal gang, dubbed "Carbanak," had been targeting banks in Japan, the Netherlands, Switzerland, the United States, and other countries (report available here: www.securityweek.com /hackers-hit-100-banks-unprecedented-1-billion-cyberattack-kaspersky-lab). It accessed internal networks and administrators' computers and conducted its activities through two main strategies: either by artificially inflating the accounts of individuals before transferring the difference to one of the gang's accounts or by instructing ATMs to dispense cash at specific times when a gang member was waiting in front of the ATM. At the time of reporting (February 2015), there was no sign that the attacks were fading, and there had already been three hundred IP addresses targeted in some hundred financial institutions pertaining to almost thirty countries worldwide.

229 in 2007, the RBN was estimated to be responsible: Peter Warren, "Hunt for Russia's Web Criminals," *Guardian,* Nov. 15, 2007.

230 the mysterious "Flyman": Brian Krebs, *Spam Nation: The Inside Story of Organized Cybercrime—from Global Epidemic to Your Front Door* (Naperville, Ill.: Sourcebooks, 2014).

230 "one of the most notorious criminal groups": Marcus Sachs, "MPack Analysis," *Internet Storm Center,* June 20, 2007, accessed Oct. 31, 2016, https://isc.sans.edu/diary /MPack+Analysis/3015.

230 enter into some kind of contract with the RBN: Brian Krebs, "Shadowy Russian Firm Seen as Conduit for Cybercrime," *Washington Post,* Oct. 13, 2007.

230 *The Economist* described the RBN: "A Walk on the Dark Side," *The Economist,* Aug. 30, 2007.

231 "non-state actors can be used": Klimburg, "Mobilising Cyber Power."

231 "isolating cyberterrorism and cybercrime": Quoted in ibid.

232 attacks on Chechen-friendly Web sites: Paul Goble, "Russia: Analysis from Washington—a Real Battle on the Virtual Front," Radio Free Europe/Radio Liberty, Oct. 11, 1999.

232 young hacker patriot Anton Moskal: See Roland Oliphant, "Patriot Hackers," *Moscow News,* Aug. 18, 2008.

232 **"the caller had little technical knowledge"**: Klimburg, "Mobilising Cyber Power." An interesting aside of this anecdote was its consequences. The researcher and blogger Jeff Carr shared with me a copy of the original post on RUNet—a text that he had received as soon as it had gone up and was subsequently quoted in the *Novaya Gazeta*. He asked for help in translation and analysis, and we subsequently posted a full translation of the text on his blog, *Intelfusion*, with an accompanying commentary. Within a couple of weeks, the *Intelfusion* blog suffered a catastrophic failure significant enough that, according to Carr, "it was not even possible to recover it from backup." Of course, the original RBN post had disappeared within days of the posting, but even weirder was the fact that even Internet archive services such as the Wayback Machine had failed to index either of those Web sites. The post, and any reference to it, had been totally erased from the face of the Internet, as if they had never existed and the whole thing had been a figment of our imagination.

233 **Estonia was the target**: Thomas Rid, "Cyber War Will Not Take Place," *Journal of Strategic Studies* 35, no. 1 (2012): 5–32.

233 **on May 9, at least six sites**: "A Cyber-riot," *The Economist*, May 10, 2007.

233 **assessments of the assault ranging**: Steve Mansfield-Devin, "Estonia: What Doesn't Kill You Makes You Stronger," *Network Security* 2012, no. 7 (July 2012): 12–20.

234 **In a sudden escalation with Georgia**: Roy Allison, "Russia Resurgent? Moscow's Campaign to 'Coerce Georgia to Peace,'" *International Affairs* 84, no. 6 (2008): 1145–71.

234 **cyberattacks made another, dual-hatted entry**: The physical attacks started after the shooting of an unmanned drone over Abkhazia on April 20, later found to have been struck by a missile from a Russian fighter jet. After a sudden escalation, Russia sent unarmed troops into the province of Abkhazia, allegedly needed for railway repairs, on May 30, and separatists in South Ossetia began attacking Georgian troops in the beginning of August; a September 2009 EU fact-finding mission later established that this escalation had been provoked by Georgia's illegal attack on Tskhinvali on August 7. At the time, though, the attacks prompted a response from Georgia's president, Mikheil Saakashvili, to send more troops into the region. Russia then flew aircraft over Georgia and began air strikes in South Ossetia, advancing tanks and soldiers in a proper invasion on Georgian territory on August 10 before halting and negotiating a cease-fire brokered by France's president, Nicolas Sarkozy, on August 15.

235 **cyberattack on the Baku-Tbilisi-Ceyhan gas pipeline**: Jordan Robertson and Michael Riley, "Mysterious '08 Turkey Pipeline Blast Opened New Cyberwar," *Bloomberg*, Dec. 10, 2014.

235 **damning investigatory piece**: Krebs, "Shadowy Russian Firm Seen as Conduit for Cybercrime."

235 **"They were nationalized"**: "RBN—Georgia CyberWarfare," *RBN Exploit*, Aug. 9, 2008, accessed Oct. 31, 2016, http://rbnexploit.blogspot.com/2008/08/rbn-georgia -cyberwarfare.html.

236 **collaboration with Russian law enforcers "was improving"**: Warwick Ashford, "Cybercrime Fighters to Target Kingpins, Says Top EU Cyber Cop," *Computer Weekly*, Oct. 13, 2014.

236 **"Russia had started showing signs"**: Tom Brewster, "Trouble with Russia, Trouble with the Law: Inside Europe's Digital Crime Unit," *Guardian*, April 15, 2014.

236 **arrest of the malware writer "Paunch"**: Brian Krebs, "A Busy Week for Cybercrime Justice," *Krebs on Security*, March 26, 2012.

236 **unspoken cardinal rule:** The other unspoken rules can be said to be "when Russian intelligence asks for help, provide it" and "watch where you spend your vacation" (most Russian cyber criminals are apprehended on holiday abroad). Mathew J. Schwartz, "Russian Cybercrime Rule No. 1: Don't Hack Russians," *Bank Info Security*, Sept. 14, 2015.

237 **Hacked logs obtained by the Dutch security firm:** Brian Krebs, "Inside the $100M 'Business Club' Crime Gang," *Krebs on Security*, Aug. 5, 2015.

237 **Russia has refused to cooperate:** "US Offers Highest-Ever Cybercrime Reward for Arrest of Russian Hacker," *Guardian*, Feb. 24, 2015.

237 **"entire villages dedicated to malware in Russia":** Roger LeRoy Miller, *Business Law: Text & Cases—an Accelerated Course* (Stamford, Conn.: Cengage Learning, 2015).

238 **"pursued by an entity":** Ioana Patran, "Romania Believes Rival Nation Behind 'MiniDuke' Cyber Attack," Reuters, March 1, 2013.

238 **"how available evidence":** *The Dukes: 7 Years of Russian Cyberespionage* (F-Secure, 2015), accessed Oct. 31, 2016, www.f-secure.com/documents/996508/1030745/dukes _whitepaper.pdf.

239 **F-Secure stated in 2015 that MiniDuke:** Sara Peters, "MiniDuke, CosmicDuke APT Group Likely Sponsored by Russia," *Dark Reading*, Sept. 17, 2015.

240 **outed some significant cyber-espionage campaigns:** Campaigns outed by Kaspersky include Flame, targeting Middle Eastern countries and especially Iran and presumed to be American or Israeli; the Red October campaign, which has been attributed to Russian-coded but Chinese-directed "diplomatic and government agencies"; Duqu, which is supposedly related to Stuxnet, and most important the work of the Equation Group, which Kaspersky bills (with some justification) as being one of the most advanced macro-campaigns in the world and which is hinted as being the NSA.

240 **An investigative piece:** Noah Shachtman, "Russia's Top Cyber Sleuth Foils US Spies, Helps Kremlin Pals," *Wired*, July 23, 2012.

240 **"tried to damage rivals in the marketplace":** Joseph Menn, "Exclusive: Russian Antivirus Firm Faked Malware to Harm Rivals—Ex-employees," Reuters, Aug. 14, 2015. It is, however, important to note that not only does Kaspersky deny this, and has made at least plausible explanations to the contrary, but many in the InfoSec community also refuse to give this much credence. Kaspersky published a statement saying that he had "never conducted any secret campaign to trick competitors into generating false positives to damage their market standing." He admitted, however, to a "one-time experiment uploading only 20 samples of non-malicious files" in 2010 in order to "draw the security community's attention" to certain problems and shortcomings of the system of data sharing.

242 **IMPACT was everywhere:** IMPACT claimed 152 countries as its members, which was disingenuous; member countries of the ITU were automatically members of this organization unless they tried to opt out. As I personally witnessed a number of times, many of the Western government "members" of IMPACT had no idea that they were members; the communication from IMPACT ran to the old-style infrastructure groups within government and was not to those entrusted with cybersecurity.

242 **none were decidedly Russian:** Besides MinDuke, Kaspersky has hardly ever identified a purported Russian cyber attack. There has been substantial confusion as to whom the Red October espionage campaign can be attributed. Kaspersky never took a position, and the implication was that it was Chinese, with perhaps support by (non-state)

Russian actors. The distribution of the attacks—none of which were in China, many of which were in Russia and the former USSR—implied that it was Chinese, perhaps even non-state and affiliated with the oil and gas sector.

CHAPTER 11: PWNAGE DIPLOMACY

244 **"Criminal hackers 'that used to hunt banks'":** Cory Bennett, "Kremlin's Ties to Russian Cyber Gangs Sow US Concerns," *Hill*, Oct. 11, 2015.

244 **threatened in particularly shady ways:** For instance, in one case recounted by the cyber-crime hunter Jart Armin, the daughter of one investigator disappeared for years, only to reappear after her father swore off the investigation. See the interview in Philip Banse, *Bier mit den Bösen* (2011), accessed Oct. 31, 2016, www.dctp.tv/filme/bier-mit-den-boesen-jart-armin.

246 **identified as APT28:** *Dragonfly: Cyberespionage Attacks Against Energy Suppliers* (Symantec, 2014), accessed Oct. 31, 2016, www.symantec.com/content/en/us/enterprise/media/security_response/whitepapers/Dragonfly_Threat_Against_Western_Energy_Suppliers.pdf.

246 **pre-deploying cyber weapons right in the US networks:** Amy Thomson and Cornelius Rahn, "Russian Hackers Threaten Power Companies, Researchers Say," *Bloomberg*, July 1, 2014.

246 **French TV channel TV5 was hacked:** Rik Ferguson, "TV5 Monde, Russia, and the Cyber Caliphate," Trend Micro, June 10, 2015.

246 **Collaborating with Trend Micro and FireEye:** Pierluigi Paganini, "FireEye Claims Russian APT28 Hacked France's TV5 Monde Channel," *Security Affairs*, June 10, 2015.

246 **mentions of the "CyberCaliphate":** Aurelien Breeden and Alissa Rubin, "French Broadcaster TV5 Monde Recovers After Hacking," *New York Times*, April 9, 2015.

246 **L'Express was soon able to reveal:** Emmanuel Paquette, "Piratage de TV5 Monde: L'enquête s'oriente vers la piste russe," *L'Express*, June 9, 2015.

247 **APT28 wanted to conduct a fake cyber terror attack:** Joseph Menn and Thomas Leigh, "France Probes Russian Lead in TV5Monde Hacking: Sources," Reuters, June 10, 2015.

247 **not the only case of Russian cyber sabotage:** Michael Riley and Jordan Robertson, "Cyberspace Becomes Second Front in Russia's Clash with NATO," *Bloomberg Technology*, Oct. 14, 2015.

247 **the largest of all Russian intrusion groups:** For a good overview of Russian malware families as well as probable associations, see James Scott and Drew Spaniel, "Know Your Enemies: A Primer on Advanced Persistent Threat Groups" (Institute for Critical Infrastructure Technology, 2015).

248 **highly complex cyber weapons:** "Two other families of supposed Russian government malware include Havex and Uroburos (or Snake). The latter shows clear relations to the Agent.btz family of malware.

248 **APT28 developed capabilities in Turkish:** "Cyber Politics: Why Did Putin Unleash APT28 on Turkey?," Ninjadmin, March 13, 2016, http://0x90.ninja/apt28-in-turkey.

248 **APT29 engaged in a new political espionage campaign:** Kelly Jackson Higgins, "Can't Touch This: 'Hammertoss' Russian Cyberspies Hide in Plain Sight," *Dark Reading*, July 29, 2015.

249 **APT28 was aligned with the GRU:** Catalin Cimpanu, "Russian Hackers Breached

Democratic Party to Gather Info on Rival Donald Trump," Softpedia, June 14, 2016.

250 leading "new Russian" thinkers: Peter Pomerantsev, "The Hidden Author of Putinism: How Vladislav Surkov Invented the New Russia," *The Atlantic*, Nov. 7, 2014.

CHAPTER 12: THE CHINESE CYBER DREAM

253 "it is still a mysterious artifact": Joseph Needham, *Science and Civilization in China* (Cambridge, U.K.: Cambridge University Press, 1971).

253 there are many alternative theories: Arthur Waldron, *From History to Myth* (Cambridge, U.K.: Cambridge University Press, 1990).

254–55 "China dream" of cyberspace: While Xi did not actually use the term "Chinese cyber dream," one of his most famous speeches is regarding the "China Dream." The Chinese "Internet dream," however, makes a common reappearance in other texts and can be seen as being subsidiary to the Chinese dream: one of national greatness, marked by an extensive interpretation of the term "sovereignty." For Xi Jinping's full speech, see Xi Jinping, "Remarks by H.E. Xi Jinping President of the People's Republic of China at the Opening Ceremony of the Second World Internet Conference" (Ministry of Foreign Affairs of the People's Republic of China, 2016), accessed Oct. 31, 2016, www.fmprc.gov.cn/mfa_eng/wjdt_665385/zyjh_665391/t1327570.shtml.

255 "'absolute security' in Washington": "China Voice: Why Does Cyber-sovereignty Matter?," Xinhua, Dec. 16, 2015.

256 the world's most dominant presence: "China Internet Users," Internet Live Stats, accessed Oct. 31, 2016, www.internetlivestats.com/internet-users/china.

256 China needs the global cyberspace: Jonathan Woetzel et al., *China's Digital Transformation: The Internet's Impact on Productivity and Growth* (McKinsey Global Institute, 2014), accessed Oct. 31, 2016, www.mckinsey.com/~/media/McKinsey /Industries/High%20Tech/Our%20Insights/Chinas%20digital%20transformation /MGI%20China%20digital%20Full%20report.ashx.

257 The average Chinese Internet user spent: "Average Online Time of Internet Users in China per Week in 2011 and 2015 (in Hours)" (Statista, 2016), accessed Oct. 31, 2016, www.statista.com/statistics/265176/average-online-time-of-users-in-china.

257 "It's harder for the government": Cindy Chiu, Chris Ip, and Ari Silverman, "Understanding Social Media in China," *McKinsey Quarterly*, April 2012.

257 proposed governmental "social-credit score" system: Jay Stanley, "China's Nightmarish Citizen Scores Are a Warning for Americans," ACLU *Free Future* (blog), Oct. 5, 2015.

258 "China has gamified obedience to the State": Samuel Osborne, "China Has Made Obedience to the State a Game," *Independent*, Dec. 22, 2015.

258 a more measured investigation: Charlie Custer, "China's 'Citizen Scores' Credit System Isn't as Orwellian as the ACLU Thinks . . . Yet," *Tech in Asia*, Oct. 7, 2015.

258 the only available government directive: Rogier Creemers, "Planning Outline for the Construction of a Social Credit System (2014–2020)," *China Copyright and Media*, April 25, 2015.

260 Similar movements have targeted: David Tormsen, "10 Stories of China's Human Flesh Search Engines," *ListVerse*, April 22, 2015.

260 research has shown otherwise: Daniel C. Lynch, *After the Propaganda State: Media,*

Politics, and "Thought Work" in Reformed China (Stanford, Calif.: Stanford University Press, 1999).

260 **collision of two bullet trains:** Josh Chin, "Weibo Watershed? Train Collision Anger Explodes Online," *Wall Street Journal,* July 26, 2011.

261 **lukewarm efforts to effectively curb:** "Chinese Netizens React to Beijing's Red Smog Alert," *GB Times,* Dec. 8, 2015.

261 **US embassy started to tweet:** Jeremy Page, "Microbloggers Pressure Beijing to Improve Air Pollution Monitoring," *Wall Street Journal,* Nov. 8, 2011.

261 **a US diplomat even claimed:** David Roberts, "Opinion: How the US Embassy Tweeted to Clear Beijing's Air," *Wired,* March 6, 2015.

261 **In a survey conducted in 2010:** "A Giant Cage," *The Economist,* April 6, 2013.

261 **This prompted** *The Economist*: "This Article Is Guilty of Spreading Panic and Disorder," *The Economist,* Dec. 5, 2015.

261 **the crime of "spreading false rumors":** Chun Han Wong, "China 'Punishes' Nearly 200 for Spreading Rumors," *Wall Street Journal,* Aug. 31, 2015.

261 **radical anti-American rhetoric:** "Chinese Netizens React to South China Sea Dispute," *GBTimes Beijing,* May 19, 2016.

261 **cheering Russia's military support of Syria:** Bethany Allen-Ebrahimian, "Chinese Netizens Are Cheering Putin's Syria Campaign," *Foreign Policy,* Oct. 16, 2015.

262 **anthem to its new** *raison d'être*: Paul Mozur, "China's Internet Censorship Anthem Is Revealed, Then Deleted," *Sinosphere* (blog), *New York Times,* Feb. 12, 2015. The original translation uses the term "Internet power" instead of "cyber power." There is an endlessly boring discussion on the correct translation of "Internet," "network," and "cyberspace," especially in conjunction with the adjunct "power." For me, it is clear that original Chinese refers to "cyber" rather than "the net." For all the deliberations of a few Western analysts, this really is the Chinese's own conclusion as well, which uses the term 网络—given as "Internet" in many translations, as "cyberspace" in its own publications. Hence "cyber power," rather than "Internet power." We could all be wrong, however: an Oxford academic published his own translation of the song and instead of "Internet" or "cyber power" actually read the key term of the refrain to be "cybercountry"; the vagaries in Chinese are clearly extensive. See Rogier Creemers, "China's Cyberstrategy Celebrated in Song," *China Copyright and Media,* Feb. 12, 2015.

CHAPTER 13: MANNING THE GREAT FIREWALL

266 **anything can be included:** Fei Shen, "The Great Firewall of China," in *Encyclopedia of Social Media and Politics,* ed. Kerric Harvey (Los Angeles: Sage, 2014).

267–68 **According to the American security company:** Adam Kozy, "Cyber Kung-Fu: The Great Firewall Art of DNS Poisoning," *Crowdstrike* (blog), Feb. 23, 2015.

270 **one politician was widely known as "Teletubby":** Tania Branigan, "China's Microbloggers Turn to Teletubbies to Discuss Politics," *Guardian,* March 22, 2012.

270 **the present mammoth program:** David Bandurski, "China's Guerrilla War for the Web," *Far Eastern Economic Review,* July 2008.

271 **"Fifty Cent Party":** Ibid.

271 **"to be mobilized in times":** Melinda Liu, "Chinese Bloggers Uncover the Truth," *Newsweek,* Feb. 27, 2009.

271 **"50 centers" are only one of a range:** Gary King, Jennifer Pan, and Margaret E.
Roberts, "How the Chinese Government Fabricates Social Media Posts for Strategic
Distraction, Not Engaged Argument" (Harvard University, 2016). The Harvard study
by Gary King also correctly points out that there are a number of segmentable groups
among the Chinese blogosphere. As it says, "Thus, 50c party members are distinct from
'volunteer 50c members' (literally 'self do 50c' also translated as 'bring your own
grain'), who express pro-regime or anti-western sentiment online without being paid
by the government, the 'little red flowers,' an unpaid red guard who also attack
opponents of the regime online, the 'American Cent Party' who express western
democratic values and criticize the Chinese communist regime online [and are
sometimes considered to be in the pay of the US government], and the 'internet water
army,' which refers to for-hire astroturfers working for and advancing the interests of
companies and other actors willing to pay their fees. None are known to be organized
groups."

271 **up to two *million* part-time contractors:** Christopher Cairns, "Seizing *Weibo*'s
'Commanding Heights' Through Bureaucratic Re-centralization" (2015), accessed
Oct. 31, 2016, www.chrismcairns.com/uploads/3/0/2/2/30226899/chapter_3_-_seizing
_weibos_commanding_heights_through_bureaucratic_re-centralization
_-_final_7.30.15.pdf.

272 **448 million posts were made by 50 centers:** King, Pan, and Roberts, "How the
Chinese Government Fabricates Social Media Posts for Strategic Distraction, Not
Engaged Argument."

272 **"Think of the last time":** Doug Bernard, "China's 50 Cent Party: The Other Side of
Censorship," *VOA News,* May 31, 2016.

272 **article in the Voice of America:** Ibid. Personally, I think it is more likely that these
were not specifically 50 centers but members of the "Little Red Flowers," the Red Guard
volunteers who are probably civil servants and low-ranking party members and who do
regularly engage in coordinated attacks on dissenters and especially Taiwanese
politicians.

273 **a "responsive autocracy":** Jason Koebler, "Researchers Made a Fake Social Network to
Infiltrate China's Internet Censors," *Motherboard,* Aug. 21, 2014.

273 **war on pornography:** "Historically in China . . . the technology used to censor porn
has ended up being used more vigorously to censor political content than smut," said
Rebecca MacKinnon, who has written extensively on the Chinese Internet. The
Chinese blogger Zhang Jialong said in a *Foreign Policy* blog that "at its core, this is
about going after rumors—party parlance for destabilizing falsehoods—in the name of
going after porn." According to him, the government cares more about showing that it
has the ability to control content than about controlling the content per se. On China's
long-standing war on pornography, see Lily Kuo, "China's Latest Crackdown on Porn
Has Little to Do with Porn," *Quartz,* April 14, 2014. Also see Anthony Tao, "The Real
Reason China Blocks Porn," *Daily Dot,* Jan. 27, 2015.

273 **"erotic banana-eating videos":** "China Bans 'Erotic' Banana-Eating Live Streams,"
BBC, May 6, 2016.

273 **"Green Dam Youth Escort":** While Green Dam was ultimately not rolled out due to
large-scale public derision (it supposedly does see spotty use within Internet cafés), one
of the more interesting features was that it used pixel-identification technology to
gauge whether a large number of flesh-colored pixels—that is, nudity—were in a

picture. This led to the interesting result that while a photograph of a pig was banned as pornographic, pictures of naked black women were not recognized. As an aside, similar to elsewhere, porn trading is a staple component of some parts of hacker culture in China. "One way you recruit good [cyber-crime] sources in China is by hanging out on hacker forums," a specialist in Chinese threat intelligence shared with me. "This means engaging in porn trading. Besides some really sick shit, the interesting thing is how much black porn is easily available in China—and which correspondingly does not make a good trading item."

274 **the information gained through extensive real-time mining:** A businessman in China once sought to convince me that purchasing telephone recordings of your business partners through corrupt security officials was relatively easy with the right contacts. The kicker was that these recordings were not ordered in advance but brought up from the archive, and this archive went back at least three months. While the notion that all Chinese mobile phone conversations may be recorded and stored automatically may seem fanciful, this is probably not far from current practice in Russia, as well as some Arab states: hardware memory has become so cheap that storage is not the issue anymore.

CHAPTER 14: HANDLING THE BARBARIANS

275 **agreement that gave the Obama administration:** Julie Hirschfeld Davis and David E. Sanger, "Obama and Xi Jinping of China Agree to Steps on Cybertheft," *New York Times,* Sept. 26, 2015.

276 **decrease of around 90 percent:** "Red Line Drawn: China Recalculates Its Use of Cyber Espionage," *Threat Research* (blog), FireEye, June 20, 2016, accessed Oct. 31, 2016, www.fireeye.com/blog/threat-research/2016/06/red-line-drawn-china-espionage.html.

276 **the radical decrease included:** *Redline Drawn: China Recalculates Its Use of Cyber Espionage.* FireEye, 2016.

277 **Some of the numbers that have been discussed:** Peter Maass and Megha Rajagopalan, "Does Cybercrime Really Cost $1 Trillion?" ProPublica, Aug. 1, 2012.

278 **"what remains perplexing":** Jennifer Runyon, "60 Minutes Investigates Chinese Cyber-espionage in Wind Industry," *Renewable Energy World,* Jan. 18, 2016.

279 **Then the White House signaled:** James Lewis, head of such a US-Chinese contact group, specifically draws attention to a non-paper circulated within the informal US-Chinese meeting as the start of this rapprochement. This non-paper specifically mentions the threat of economic sanctions as a response to Chinese hacking. David E. Sanger, "U.S. Decides to Retaliate Against China's Hacking," *New York Times,* July 31, 2015.

279 **the United States handed the Chinese a list:** Andrew Blake, "China Arrests Hackers Following Request from U.S.—Report," *Washington Times,* Oct. 12, 2015.

280 **"It's a face-saving way of saying":** Paul Carsten and Mark Hosenball, "China's Xinhua Says U.S. OPM Hack Was Not State-Sponsored," Reuters, Dec. 2, 2015.

281 **2015 military white paper:** Steven Aftergood, "China's Science of Military Strategy (2013)," Federation of American Scientists, Aug. 3, 2015, accessed March 1, 2016, http://fas.org/blogs/secrecy/2015/08/china-sms.

281 **"The Science of Military Strategy":** There are clear differences between the original December 2013 "Science of Military Strategy" publication and the 2015 sanctioned translation into English. The differences have been the subject of vigorous debate

among Western scholars, but the essential categorization remains the same. See, for instance, Joe McReynolds, "China's Evolving Perspectives on Network Warfare: Lessons from the Science of Military Strategy," *China Brief* 15, no. 8 (2015), and Steven Aftergood, "China's Science of Military Strategy (2013)," Federation of American Studies, Aug. 3, 2015.

282 **the new Strategic Support Force:** John Costello, "The Strategic Support Force: China's Information Warfare Service," *China Brief* 16, no. 3 (2016).

284 **3PLA might have had up to 130,000 employees:** Quoted from Mark A. Stokes, Jenny Lin, and Russell Hsiao, *The Chinese People's Liberation Army Signals Intelligence and Cyber Reconnaissance Infrastructure,* Project 2049 Institute, Nov. 11, 2011, accessed Oct. 31, 2016, https://project2049.net/documents/pla_third_department_sigint_cyber_stokes_lin_hsiao.pdf.

284 **the TRBs are massive:** Ibid.

285 **the Guangzhou information warfare militia battalion:** Timothy Thomas, "Comparing US, Russian, and Chinese Information Operations Concepts" (Foreign Military Studies Office, 2004), accessed Oct. 31, 2016, www.dodccrp.org/events/2004 _CCRTS/CD/papers/064.pdf.

286 **The plethora of Chinese cyberattacks:** Laura Saporito and James A. Lewis, "Cyber Incidents Attributed to China," Center for Strategic and International Studies, March 11, 2013.

287 **over thirty thousand incidents:** Robert Windrem, "Exclusive: Secret NSA Map Shows China Cyber Attacks on U.S. Targets," NBC News, July 30, 2015.

288 **The victim list of organizations:** Bill Hagestad, "People's Republic of Cyber Warfare," Academia.edu, 2014.

288 **"they are Chinese hackers":** Doug Nairne, "State Hackers Spying on Us, Say Chinese Dissidents," *South China Morning Post,* Sept. 18, 2002.

289 **"The government of China":** Pamela Hess, "China Prevented Repeat Cyber Attack on US," UPI, Oct. 29, 2002.

289 **"It's the 25-year-olds":** *China's Propaganda and Influence Operations* (US-China Economic Security Review Commission, 2008), accessed Oct. 31, 2016, www.au.af.mil /au/awc/awcgate/china/09_04_30_infl_ops.pdf.

290 **thanked a defense research arm:** *Capability of the People's Republic of China (PRC) to Conduct Cyber Warfare and Computer Network Exploitation* (US-China Economic Security Review Commission, 2009) accessed Oct. 31, 2016, http://nsarchive.gwu.edu /NSAEBB/NSAEBB424/docs/Cyber-030.pdf.

290 **Chinese hacking groups:** Wun Nan, "From Hackers to Entrepreneurs: The Sino-US Cyberwar Veterans Going Straight," *South China Morning Post,* Aug. 21, 2013.

292 **China is in the process of fielding a copy:** Franz-Stefan Gady, "New Snowden Documents Reveal Chinese Behind F-35 Hack," *Diplomat,* Jan. 27, 2015.

292 **a "clone army":** "China's Military Built with Cloned Weapons," *USNI News,* Oct. 27, 2015, accessed Oct. 31, 2016, https://news.usni.org/2015/10/27/chinas-military-built -with-cloned-weapons.

292 **According to informed observers:** William C. Hannas, James Mulvenon, and Anna B. Puglisi, *China's Industrial Espionage* (New York: Routledge, 2013).

292 **National Technology Transfer Promotion Implementation Plan:** Joshua Philipp, "Exclusive: How Hacking and Espionage Fuel China's Growth," *Epoch Times,* Sept. 10, 2015.

292 tolerated or sanctioned moneymaking ventures: Minnie Chan and Liu Zhen, "China's President Xi Jinping Wants 'PLA Inc' to Stop Its Song and Dance, Plans End for Profit-Making Activities," *South China Morning Post,* Nov. 27, 2015.

294 "When the indictment came out": Michael Riley and Dune Lawrence, "UglyGorilla Hacker Left Tracks, U.S. Cyber-hunters Say," *Bloomberg Technology,* May 22, 2014.

294 the poster boy of the "Comments Crew": Brian Grow and Mark Hosenball, "Special Report: In Cyberspy vs. Cyberspy, China Has the Edge," Reuters, April 14, 2011.

295 so-called Three Warfares doctrine: Timothy Walton, *China's Three Warfares* (Delex Consulting, Studies, and Analysis, 2012).

295 "identifying select foreign political": Michael Raska, "China and the 'Three Warfares,'" *Diplomat,* Dec. 18, 2015.

296 China's intelligence services: Jakub Janda, "Czech Intelligence Alarmed by Russian 'Threat,'" *EU Observer,* Sept. 2, 2015.

296 an instrument of "political warfare": Mark Stokes and Russell Hsiao, *The People's Liberation Army General Political Department: Political Warfare with Chinese Characteristics,* Project 2049 Institute, Oct. 14, 2013, accessed Oct. 31, 2016, www .project2049.net/documents/PLA_General_Political_Department_Liaison_Stokes _Hsiao.pdf.

CHAPTER 15: PARSING CYBER POWER

301 over thirty countries were openly pursuing: James Lewis, "The Rationale for Offensive Cyber Capabilities," Center for Strategic and International Studies, June 8, 2016.

302 Using a model developed: Department of Defense Science Board, *Resilient Military Systems and the Advanced Cyber Threat* (2013), accessed Oct. 31, 2016, www.acq.osd .mil/dsb/reports/ResilientMilitarySystems.CyberThreat.pdf.

304 in Operation Orchard: Kim Zetter, "Mossad Hacked Syrian Official's Computer Before Bombing Mysterious Facility," *Wired,* Nov. 3, 2009.

306 exports totaling $6 billion: Barbara Opall-Rome, "Israeli Cyber Exports Double in a Year," *Defense News,* June 3, 2015.

307 Iran has been especially ambitious: The Netherlands intelligence agency AIVD, for instance, has classified Iran as being third in the list of the most worrying cyber actors, behind Russia and China, despite its being in no way of comparable technical standard. For more information, see the AIVD 2015 Annual Report, accessed Oct. 31, 2016, https://english.aivd.nl/binaries/aivd-en/documents/annual-report/2016/05/26/annual -report-2015-aivd/annual-report-2015-aivd.pdf.

308 the US 2016 indictment reports: "Seven Iranians Working for Islamic Revolutionary Guard Corps–Affiliated Entities Charged for Conducting Coordinated Campaign of Cyber Attacks Against U.S. Financial Sector," Department of Justice, Office of Public Affairs, March 24, 2016, accessed Oct. 31, 2016, www.justice.gov/opa/pr/seven-iranians -working-islamic-revolutionary-guard-corps-affiliated-entities-charged.

308 2011 subversion of DigiNotar: As was explained elsewhere in this book, certificates are critical elements of Internet security, because they validate Web sites and are necessary to establish encrypted links. If these are falsified, then a hacker can pretend to be any Web site that uses this particular certificate, from a bank to Facebook to government. The DigiNotar hack suddenly opened up large parts of government Web sites and many banks to attack and even managed to directly target the port of Rotterdam—the largest in the world—because the certificates ended up being used in "the most unlikely of places," such as heavy crane machinery.

308 **"fourth biggest cyber power":** For this quotation and more summary of the present purposed condition of the Iranian cyber forces, see Jordan Brunner, "Iran Has Built an Army of Cyber Proxies," *Tower,* Aug. 2015.

309 **The 2016 indictment of the four Iranian hackers:** In the indictment, these companies are called "ITSec" and "Mersad." US District Court Southern District of New York, *United States of America v. Ahmad Fathi, Hamid Firoozi, and Others,* www.justice.gov/opa/file/834996/download. Other companies are known, according to Jeff Bardin in his testimony to the US Senate, as "Ashiyane, Arad Group, FullSecurity," accessed Oct. 31, 2016, www.justice.gov/opa/file/834996/download. Jeff Bardin, "What It's Like to Be a Hacker in Iran," *Business Insider,* Feb. 23, 2016.

309 **a gigantic dormant botnet:** Sanger and Fackler, "N.S.A. Breached North Korean Networks Before Sony Attack."

310 **NGO Freedom House regularly assesses:** Sanja Kelly et al., *Freedom on the Net 2015: Privatizing Censorship, Eroding Privacy* (Freedom House, 2015), accessed Oct. 31, 2016, https://freedomhouse.org/sites/default/files/FOTN%202015%20Full%20Report.pdf.

311 **"protecting Turkishness from denigration":** Article 301 of the Turkish Criminal Code was first passed in 2005 and replaced the previous ninety-year-old Article 159, which had been amended often to soften its impact on civil society. In contrast, in 2008 Article 301 was expanded in its definition and is now used regularly to prosecute those simply engaging in criticism of the government.

311 **India has seen its supreme court repeal:** In particular, this applies to the 2015 repeal of the highly contentious Article 66A of the Indian Information Technology Act of 2000.

CHAPTER 16: THE GREAT CYBER GAME

317 **Some of the greatest technophiles:** "Autonomous Weapons: An Open Letter from AI & Robotics Researchers" (Future of Life Institute, 2015). In an op-ed, Stephen Hawking wrote that "success in creating AI would be the biggest event in human history. Unfortunately, it might also be the last, unless we learn how to avoid the risks." Accessed Oct. 31, 2016, http://futureoflife.org/open-letter-autonomous-weapons. A major concern is the development of autonomous-weapon systems, which has already begun in several forms, such as Boston Dynamics' six-foot-tall, 320-pound humanoid robot named Atlas. The company, which was bought by Google in 2013 and receives grant money from the Department of Defense, is working on developing an even more agile version. Michael Sainato, "Stephen Hawking, Elon Musk, and Bill Gates Warn About Artificial Intelligence," *Observer,* Aug. 19, 2015.

318 **AI could be an existential threat:** Stephen Hawking et al., "Stephen Hawking: 'Transcendence Looks at the Implications of Artificial Intelligence—but Are We Taking AI Seriously Enough?,'" *Independent,* May 1, 2014.

318 **a sudden collapse of the oceanic currents:** Stefan Rahmstorf et al., "Exceptional Twentieth-Century Slowdown in Atlantic Ocean Overturning Circulation," *Nature Climate Change,* March 23, 2015, www.pik-potsdam.de/news/press-releases/atlantic-ocean-overturning-found-to-slow-down-already-today.

319 **the way we came to technology:** Richard Danzig, "The Technology Tsunami and the

US National Security Establishment: An Irresistible Force Meets a Movable Object," unpublished draft manuscript, 2017.

321 most common definition of a regime: Stephen D. Krasner, ed., *International Regimes* (Ithaca, N.Y.: Cornell University Press, 1983).

321 the rise of environmental diplomacy: R. O. Keohane and D. G. Victor, "The Regime Complex for Climate Change," *Perspectives on Politics,* 9(1) (2011), 7–23.

322 call the cyber regime complex: Joseph S. Nye Jr., "The Regime Complex for Managing Global Cyber Activities," Global Commission Internet Governance, May 2014.

322 When I map my version: *Cyber Stability Seminar 2016: Taking Security Forward—Building on the 2015 Report of the GGE* (UNIDIR, 2016), www.unidir.org/programmes /emerging-security-threats/cyber-stability-conference-series/cyber-stability-seminar -2016-taking-security-forward-building-on-the-2015-report-of-the-gge.

324 most effective form of governance: DeNardis writes, "A question such as 'who should control the Internet, the United Nations or some other organization' makes no sense whatsoever. The appropriate question involves determining what is the most effective form of governance in each specific context." Laura DeNardis, *The Global War for Internet Governance* (New Haven, Conn.: Yale University Press, 2014), 266.

325 respectable senior officials: The number of cyber myths that have circulated seems to grow with each year, and they surely get more brazen. I was told by the head of an important international agency, for instance, that "the US has disconnected countries from the Internet at will, and could do it again" (untrue), while in a UN setting in 2016 one country's delegate promptly declared that Regional Internet Registries obviously had a crisis management function, and this should be reflected in the UN text (also untrue). This phenomenon of creative reinterpretation is not restricted to cyber. In an OSCE negotiation I was party to, a government representative quoted from Article 4 of the International Covenant on Civil and Political Rights (a key human rights document) that allows the most important Article 19 rights to be suspended due to national security concerns "at any time." This is incorrect, because these so-called emergency derogations (temporary suspensions) are allowed only in extremis and with proper notification. The wording of the government representative, however, was nearly included in a draft resolution and would have completely called into question the meaning of Article 4 after having received official sanction—if it had not been spotted in time.

329 An interview on Federal News Radio: Jason Fornicola, "Cybersecurity vs. Data Security: Government's Two-Pronged Challenge," Federal News Radio, Oct. 7, 2015.

331 investigate C-I-A breaches against data: In particular, there are disquieting voices within the international law community that have indicated that as part of *jus ad bellum* we should reassess both what "essential national security" interests and what "domestic affairs" (*domaine réservée*) mean. I consider this the quintessential slippery slope and have advised against a too-wide interpretation of international law in this context.

332 "attribution and adjudication council": Jason Healey et al., *Confidence-Building Measures in Cyberspace: A Multistakeholder Approach for Stability and Security,* Atlantic Council, Nov. 5, 2014.

332 evidence within international adjudication efforts: For instance, if a government wanted to claim that a violation of TRIPS (the Trade-Related Aspects of Intellectual

Property Rights) should trigger sanctions within the WTO, then it needs to provide a level of evidence that is far beneath that required within a US criminal court but still considerable as "evidence." DSIC could help assess whether this evidence was indeed sufficient or be tasked to provide its own investigations.

336 jail someone in the United States: For instance, in 2016 a US court ordered a man jailed indefinitely who refused to provide passwords for two encrypted devices that were thought to hide child pornography. The legal basis for this is complex; for a discussion on it, see Tim Cushing, "So Much for the Fifth Amendment: Man Jailed for Seven Months for Not Turning Over Password," *Techdirt,* April 28, 2016.

336 CCB is only a small part: Alexander Klimburg and Hugo Zylberberg, *Cyber Security Capacity Building: Developing Access* (Norwegian Institute of International Affairs, 2015).

337 World Bank funding: "Key African Broadband Projects Supported by the World Bank," *OAfrica,* Oct. 23, 2013, accessed Oct. 31, 2016, www.oafrica.com/broadband /key-african-broadband-projects-supported-by-the-world-bank.

340 registration of Internet addresses: Signing up for an Internet address is invariably connected to a registration process known as WHOIS. The amount of information collected under WHOIS, however, depends on the rules of the registry responsible. For instance, Verisign, the company that runs .com, requests relatively little information from individuals purchasing a domain. If, however, you want to buy a domain for .fn, the Finnish domain run by the office FICORA, you have to provide a lot of personal information, and registration is even partially limited to Finnish citizens. Overall, a stronger WHOIS provides less chance for cyber crime but also presents a greater possibility to control content and activity in a specific domain or "Internet segment."

341 investing and funding the civil society: Alexander Klimburg, "Watering the Grass Roots," *Multistakeholder Internet Dialog (MIND): #6 Internet and Security* (2013).

CHAPTER 17: AN END-TO-END WORLD

348 the "public core" of the Internet: Dennis Broeders, *The Public Core of the Internet: An International Agenda for Internet Governance* (Amsterdam: Amsterdam University Press, 2015).

350 the "unmanaged" commons: See Garrett Hardin, "The Tragedy of the 'Unmanaged' Commons," in *Commons Without Tragedy,* ed. Robert V. Andelson (London: Shepheard-Walwyn, 1991), and, on governance mechanisms, Ostrom, *Governing the Commons.*

350 "common-pool resource": Elinor Ostrom, *Governing the Commons: The Evolution of Institutions for Collective Action* (Cambridge, U.K.: Cambridge University Press, 1990).

350 a "global commons": For one view on this, see Scott J. Shackelford, "The Tragedy of the Common Heritage of Mankind," *Stanford Environmental Law Journal* 27 (2009).

350 common binding resolutions: The Vienna Convention for the Protection of the Ozone Layer (1987) led to the worldwide ban on chemicals known as CFCs and HCFCs, also known as Freon, from overall use. Freon was most commonly used in refrigeration equipment and hair spray.

352 a bunch of unelected engineers: Resnick, *RFC 7282.*

355 a "feudal Internet": Bruce Schneier, "When It Comes to Security, We're Back to Feudalism," *Wired,* Nov. 26, 2012.

CONCLUSION

357 President Obama described cyberspace: Bill Chappell, "Obama: Cyberspace Is the New 'Wild West,'" NPR, Feb. 13, 2015.

360 elaborate ceremony for root signing: "DNSSEC Signing Service."

363 in 2014 the Pew Research Center polled: Rainie Lee, Janna Anderson, and Jennifer Connolly, "Cyber Attacks Likely to Increase," Pew Research Center, Oct. 29, 2014.

364 different identifiable segments: Drake, Cerf, and Kleinwächter, *Internet Fragmentation,* accessed Oct 31, 2016, www3.weforum.org/docs/WEF_FII_Internet _Fragmentation_An_Overview_2016.pdf.

INDEX